Financial Instruments

Martin Friedhoff · Jens Berger

Financial Instruments

IAS 32 und IAS 39

 Springer Gabler

Martin Friedhoff
London, United Kingdom

Jens Berger
Frankfurt am Main, Deutschland

ISBN 978-3-658-00606-8
DOI 10.1007/978-3-658-00607-5

ISBN 978-3-658-00607-5 (eBook)

Die Deutsche Nationalbibliothek verzeichnet diese Publikation in der Deutschen Nationalbibliografie; detaillierte bibliografische Daten sind im Internet über http://dnb.d-nb.de abrufbar.

Springer Gabler
© Gabler Verlag | Springer Fachmedien Wiesbaden 2013

Lektorat: Elnas Nazem

Gedruckt auf säurefreiem und chlorfrei gebleichtem Papier

Springer Gabler ist eine Marke von Springer DE. Springer DE ist Teil der Fachverlagsgruppe Springer Science+Business Media
www.springer-gabler.de

Vorwort

Die Bilanzierung von Finanzinstrumenten ist eines der komplexesten Bilanzierungsgebiete der *International Financial Reporting Standards* (IFRSs) und stellt alle Konstituenten, v.a. die Ersteller und Abschlussprüfer immer wieder vor Herausforderungen. Viele Finanzinstrumente sind einfache Vermögenswerte oder Verbindlichkeiten, wie z.B. Forderungen oder Verbindlichkeiten aus Lieferungen und Leistungen, deren Bilanzierung regelmäßig keine Schwierigkeiten bereiten dürfte. Finanzinstrumente bieten jedoch auch die Möglichkeit, mittels vertraglicher Gestaltung wirtschaftlich sehr ähnliche Ergebnisse zu erzielen, diese aber rechtlich verschieden aussehen zu lassen (oder umgekehrt). Dies betrifft z.B. die Verbriefung von Finanzinstrumenten (*Securitisation*), eingebettete Derivate (*Structured Finance*) oder Sicherungsgeschäfte (*Hedging*). Daneben hat die Finanzmathematik Einzug in die Bilanzierung von Finanzinstrumenten gehalten. Diese Entwicklung spiegelt wider, dass viele Finanzinstrumente auf der Basis von finanzmathematischen Methoden strukturiert werden. Dies hat zur Folge, dass die Bewertung von Finanzinstrumenten diese Methoden aufgreift, wie z.B. bei der Effektivzinsmethode, bei der Bewertung zum beizulegenden Zeitwert, wenn diese auf Bewertungsmodelle zurückgreift, sowie bei der Bilanzierung von Sicherungsgeschäften.

Diese Gestaltungsmöglichkeiten haben dazu geführt, dass sich die Finanzinstrumente zu einem Bereich mit hoher Regelungsintensität und -komplexität entwickelt haben. Das gilt nicht nur für die Bilanzierung.

Seit 2008 kam die Finanzmarktkrise als weiterer Einflussfaktor auf die Bilanzierung von Finanzinstrumenten hinzu. Der *International Accounting Standards Board* (IASB) ist seitdem mit einer umfangreichen, grundlegenden Überarbeitung der Vorschriften zur Bilanzierung von Finanzinstrumenten beschäftigt. Aufgrund der Komplexität dieses Themengebiets, sowie der politischen Einflussnahme auf den IASB (die u.a. dazu führte, dass einige Projektabschnitte in Zusammenarbeit mit dem U.S.-amerikanischen *Financial Accounting Standards Board* (FASB) durchgeführt werden), hat sich dieser Reformprozess als langwierig herausgestellt. Immer wieder muss der IASB seinen Arbeitsplan überarbeiten und die Fertigstellungszeitpunkte einzelner Phasen zeitlich nach hinten verschieben. Daraus ergeben sich – fast schon zwangsläufig – Auswirkungen auf den verpflichtenden Erstanwendungszeitpunkt. Im Dezember 2011 hat der IASB den verpflichtenden Erstanwendungszeitpunkt für den neuen Standard zur Bilanzierung von Finanzinstrumenten (**IFRS 9 Finanzinstrumente**) vom 1. Januar 2013 auf den 1. Januar 2015 verschoben. Ob an diesem Erstanwendungszeitpunkt festgehalten wird, hängt v.a. davon ab, wie schnell der Fortschritt bei der Abarbeitung der offenen Themenbereiche ist, sowie von der Komplexität der Lösungen. Derzeit arbeitet der IASB noch an der Fertigstellung neuer Regelungen zur Bilanzierung von Sicherungsgeschäften, wobei er die Vorschriften zur Bilanzierung von Makro-Sicherungsbeziehungen aus IFRS 9 ausgeklammert hat. Außerdem sind Standardentwürfe für ein neues Modell zur Bilanzierung von Wertminderungen sowie einige Anpassungen der bereits verabschiedeten Vorschriften zur Klassifizierung von Finanzinstrumenten geplant. In der Europäischen Union ist der Übernahmeprozess für IFRS 9 seit 2009 nicht vorangekommen, so dass der neue Standard noch nicht in EU-Recht übernommen worden ist. Dies liegt auch daran, dass die Europäische Kommission den Übernahmeprozess erst dann anstoßen will, wenn alle Phasen von IFRS 9 veröffentlicht worden sind und sich somit ein zusammenhängendes Bild über die künftige Bilanzierung von Finanzinstrumenten ergibt. Somit bleibt Unternehmen, die aufgrund der IAS-Verordnung der EU nach IFRS bilanzieren, die Möglichkeit einer vorzeitigen Übernahme von IFRS 9 vorerst verwehrt.

Daher konzentriert sich dieser Kommentar auf die Anwendung der derzeit in Kraft befindlichen Standards **IAS 32 Finanzinstrumente: Ausweis** sowie **IAS 39 Finanzinstrumente: Ansatz und Bewertung**. Die vom IASB bereits 2009 verabschiedeten Vorschriften zur Klassifizierung und Bewertung von finanziellen Vermögenswerten werden ebenfalls im Kommentar behandelt. Es handelt sich hierbei um die unserem Kommentar zur internationalen Rechnungslegung entnommene ausführliche deutsche Kommentierung. Der Kommentar erläutert die wesentlichen Aspekte der Bilanzierung von Finanzinstrumenten:

- Anwendungsbereich
- Bilanzierungseinheit einschließlich eingebetteter Derivate,
- Ansatz und Ausbuchung,
- die Kategorisierung einschließlich Umgliederungen,
- Zugangs- und Folgebewertung – einschließlich der Bilanzierung von Wertminderungen,
- die Bilanzierung von Sicherungsgeschäften (*Hedge Accounting*),
- Anhangangaben.

Die übrigen Neuregelungen (für die Bewertung finanzieller Verbindlichkeiten sowie die weiteren noch geplanten Änderungen) werden dagegen nicht behandelt. Nachfolgend geben wir jedoch einen tabellarischen Überblick über den Status Quo der einzelnen Projektabschnitte und sonstigen relevanten Neuregelungen. Der Stand dieser Ausführungen ist August 2012.

Die Herausgeber

London und Frankfurt im August 2012

Geänderter Standard/ Phase	Erstanwendung	Wesentliche Inhalte/Änderungen	Nächstes „Due Process"- Dokument
IFRS 7 – Angaben bei Übertragungen von finanziellen Vermögenswerten	1. Juli 2011 – keine Anpassung der Vergleichszahlen notwendig	▪ Erweiterte Offenlegungspflichten für übertragene, aber nicht ausgebuchte finanzielle Vermögenswerte ▪ Ausweitung der Angaben zum anhaltenden Engagement (Begriff nicht deckungsgleich mit dem *continuing involvement* iSd. Ausbuchungsvorschriften)	Keines, da endgültiger Standard
IFRS 7 – Saldierung von Finanzinstrumenten	1. Januar 2013 – Anpassung der Vergleichszahlen erforderlich	▪ Ausweitung der Offenlegungsvorschriften zu saldiert ausgewiesenen Finanzinstrumenten sowie zu Aufrechnungvereinbarungen ohne Saldierung ▪ Ein Ziel ist die Vergleichbarkeit bei Globalaufrechnungsvereinbarungen zwischen IFRS und US GAAP herzustellen	Keines, da endgültiger Standard
IAS 32 – Saldierung von Finanzinstrumenten	1. Januar 2014 – retrospektive Anwendung	▪ Klarstellungen terminologischer Natur ▪ Klarstellung, dass sich Aufrechnungssysteme auf Bruttobasis unter Umständen für eine Saldierung eignen, sofern keine signifikanten Ausfall- und Liquiditätsrisiken entstehen und die Verrechnung in einem einzigen Abrechnungsprozess abgewickelt wird	Keines, da endgültiger Standard
IFRS 9 – Bilanzierung von finanziellen Verbindlichkeiten	Nach aktuellem Stand 1. Januar 2015 – retrospektive Anwendung – keine Anpassung der Vergleichszahlen notwendig	▪ Grundsätzlich Beibehaltung des Klassifizierungsmodells für Finanzpassiva aus IAS 39 ▪ D.h. finanzielle Verbindlichkeiten werden zu fortgeführten Anschaffungskosten bewertet außer sie erfüllen die Definition von „zu Handelszwecken gehalten" (dies schließt alle Derivate ein) oder es wurde die Fair-Value-Option ausgeübt – dann hat eine Bewertung erfolgswirksam zum beizulegenden Zeitwert zu erfolgen ▪ Die Regelungen für die Nutzung der Fair-Value-Option sowie zur Abtrennung eingebetteter Derivate bleiben erhalten ▪ Für Finanzpassiva in der Fair-Value-Option sind jedoch im Gegensatz zu IAS 39 die Fair-Value-Änderungen aus Veränderungen im eigenen Ausfallrisiko nicht mehr in der GuV, sondern im sonstigen Ergebnis zu zeigen ▪ Dies gilt nicht, wenn die Erfassung im sonstigen Ergebnis zu einer Bilanzierungsinkongruenz führen oder eine solche vergrößern würde	Keines, da endgültiger Standard

Geänderter Standard/ Phase	Erstanwendung	Wesentliche Inhalte/Änderungen	Nächstes „Due Process"- Dokument
		▪ Die Berechnung des Effekts aus Veränderungen des eigenen Ausfallrisikos kann auf Basis der Residualmethode gemäß IFRS 7.10 erfolgen oder aber auf einer anderen Berechnungsgrundlage, sofern diese relevantere Informationen liefert	
IFRS 9 – Begrenzte Änderungen	Nach aktuellem Stand 1. Januar 2015 – retrospektive Anwendung mit Erleichterungen – keine Anpassung der Vergleichszahlen notwendig	▪ Klarstellungen hinsichtlich der Geschäftsmodellbedingung für eine Folgebewertung zu fortgeführten Anschaffungskosten ▪ Einführung einer dritten Bewertungskategorie für Schuldinstrumente, wo zwar eine Fair-Value-Bewertung erfolgt, Wertänderungen jedoch im sonstigen Ergebnis (*other comprehensive income*) erfasst werden (Ausnahme: Effektivzins und Wertminderungen) ▪ Bei Auseinanderlaufen der Beziehung zwischen Zins und Tilgung kann eine Bewertung zu fortgeführten Anschaffungskosten dennoch statthaft sein, sofern der Unterschied nur zu insignifikanten Änderungen in den Zahlungsströmen im Vergleich zum „perfekten" Instrument führt	Standardentwurf
IFRS 9 – allgemeines Hedge Accounting	Nach aktuellem Stand 1. Januar 2015 – grundsätzlich prospektiv mit Möglichkeit der Fortführung von bestimmten existierenden Sicherungsbeziehungen	▪ Stärkere Verknüpfung von Risikomanagement und bilanzieller Abbildung ▪ Ausweitung von zulässigen Sicherungsbeziehungen für Bilanzierungszwecke (bspw. Risikokomponenten von nicht-finanziellen gesicherten Grundgeschäften, Kombinationen aus Kassageschäften und Derivaten als in toto designiertes Grundgeschäft, bestimmte Netto-Risikopositionen) ▪ Wegfall der starren 80%-125%-Grenzen für die Effektivitätsfestellung (jedoch weiterhin Erfassung jeglicher Ineffektivität in der GuV) ▪ Rekalibrierung von Sicherungsbeziehungen im Hinblick auf Änderungen der wirtschaftlichen Beziehung zwischen Sicherungsgeschäft und gesichertem Grundgeschäft ohne Auflösung der Selbigen möglich/erforderlich ▪ Grundsätzlich keine freiwillige Dedesignation möglich (dies steht jedoch der Beendigung von Sicherungsbeziehungen bei bestimmten dynamischen Sicherungsstrategien nicht entgegen)	Review Draft (kein „Due Process" Dokument im engeren Sinne)

Geänderter Standard/ Phase	Erstanwen- dung	Wesentliche Inhalte/Änderungen	Nächstes „Due Process"- Do- kument
		<ul><li>Geänderte Bilanzierung von Sicherungen mit erworbenen Optionen auf Grundlage eines Versicherungsprämienansatzes</li><li>Ausweitung der Offenlegungsvorschriften mit dem Ziel die Auswirkungen des Risikomanagements auf die primären Rechenwerke besser darzustellen</li></ul>	

Inhaltsübersicht

	Seite
Vorwort	5
Englischer Originaltext IAS 32	13
IAS 32 – Financial Instruments: Presentation	37
Englischer Originaltext IAS 39	55
IAS 39 – FI: Recognition/Measurement	117

International Accounting Standard 32
Financial Instruments: Presentation

Objective

1   [Deleted]

2   The objective of this Standard is to establish principles for presenting financial instruments as liabilities or equity and for offsetting financial assets and financial liabilities. It applies to the classification of financial instruments, from the perspective of the issuer, into financial assets, financial liabilities and equity instruments; the classification of related interest, dividends, losses and gains; and the circumstances in which financial assets and financial liabilities should be offset.

3   The principles in this Standard complement the principles for recognising and measuring financial assets and financial liabilities in IAS 39 *Financial Instruments: Recognition and Measurement*, and for disclosing information about them in IFRS 7 *Financial Instruments: Disclosures*.

Scope

4   **This Standard shall be applied by all entities to all types of financial instruments except:**

(a)   **those interests in subsidiaries, associates and joint ventures that are accounted for in accordance with IAS 27** *Consolidated and Separate Financial Statements*, **IAS 28** *Investments in Associates* **or IAS 31** *Interests in Joint Ventures*. **However, in some cases, IAS 27, IAS 28 or IAS 31 permits an entity to account for an interest in a subsidiary, associate or joint venture using IAS 39; in those cases, entities shall apply the requirements of this Standard. Entities shall also apply this Standard to all derivatives linked to interests in subsidiaries, associates or joint ventures.**

(b)   **employers' rights and obligations under employee benefit plans, to which IAS 19** *Employee Benefits* **applies.**

(c)   **[deleted]**

(d)   **insurance contracts as defined in IFRS 4** *Insurance Contracts*. **However, this Standard applies to derivatives that are embedded in insurance contracts if IAS 39 requires the entity to account for them separately. Moreover, an issuer shall apply this Standard to financial guarantee contracts if the issuer applies IAS 39 in recognising and measuring the contracts, but shall apply IFRS 4 if the issuer elects, in accordance with paragraph 4(d) of IFRS 4, to apply IFRS 4 in recognising and measuring them.**

(e)   **financial instruments that are within the scope of IFRS 4 because they contain a discretionary participation feature. The issuer of these instruments is exempt from applying to these features paragraphs 15–32 and AG25–AG35 of this Standard regarding the distinction between financial liabilities and equity instruments. However, these instruments are subject to all other requirements of this Standard. Furthermore, this Standard applies to derivatives that are embedded in these instruments (see IAS 39).**

(f)   **financial instruments, contracts and obligations under share-based payment transactions to which IFRS 2** *Share-based Payment* **applies, except for**

(i)   **contracts within the scope of paragraphs 8–10 of this Standard, to which this Standard applies,**

(ii)   **paragraphs 33 and 34 of this Standard, which shall be applied to treasury shares purchased, sold, issued or cancelled in connection with employee share option plans, employee share purchase plans, and all other share-based payment arrangements.**

5-7   [Deleted]

8   **This Standard shall be applied to those contracts to buy or sell a non-financial item that can be settled net in cash or another financial instrument, or by exchanging financial instruments, as if the contracts were financial instruments, with the exception of contracts that were entered into and continue to be held for the purpose of the receipt or delivery of a non-financial item in accordance with the entity's expected purchase, sale or usage requirements.**

9   There are various ways in which a contract to buy or sell a non-financial item can be settled net in cash or another financial instrument or by exchanging financial instruments. These include:

     (a)   when the terms of the contract permit either party to settle it net in cash or another financial instrument or by exchanging financial instruments;

     (b)   when the ability to settle net in cash or another financial instrument, or by exchanging financial instruments, is not explicit in the terms of the contract, but the entity has a practice of settling similar contracts net in cash or another financial instrument, or by exchanging financial instruments (whether with the counterparty, by entering into offsetting contracts or by selling the contract before its exercise or lapse);

     (c)   when, for similar contracts, the entity has a practice of taking delivery of the underlying and selling it within a short period after delivery for the purpose of generating a profit from short-term fluctuations in price or dealer's margin; and

     (d)   when the non-financial item that is the subject of the contract is readily convertible to cash.

A contract to which (b) or (c) applies is not entered into for the purpose of the receipt or delivery of the non-financial item in accordance with the entity's expected purchase, sale or usage requirements, and, accordingly, is within the scope of this Standard. Other contracts to which paragraph 8 applies are evaluated to determine whether they were entered into and continue to be held for the purpose of the receipt or delivery of the non-financial item in accordance with the entity's expected purchase, sale or usage requirement, and accordingly, whether they are within the scope of this Standard.

10   A written option to buy or sell a non-financial item that can be settled net in cash or another financial instrument, or by exchanging financial instruments, in accordance with paragraph 9(a) or (d) is within the scope of this Standard. Such a contract cannot be entered into for the purpose of the receipt or delivery of the non-financial item in accordance with the entity's expected purchase, sale or usage requirements.

Definitions (see also paragraphs AG3–AG23)

11   **The following terms are used in this Standard with the meanings specified:**

A *financial instrument* is any contract that gives rise to a financial asset of one entity and a financial liability or equity instrument of another entity.

A *financial asset* is any asset that is:

     (a)   **cash;**

     (b)   **an equity instrument of another entity;**

     (c)   **a contractual right:**

         (i)   **to receive cash or another financial asset from another entity; or**

         (ii)   **to exchange financial assets or financial liabilities with another entity under conditions that are potentially favourable to the entity; or**

     (d)   **a contract that will or may be settled in the entity's own equity instruments and is:**

    (i)   a non-derivative for which the entity is or may be obliged to receive a variable number of the entity's own equity instruments; or

    (ii)   a derivative that will or may be settled other than by the exchange of a fixed amount of cash or another financial asset for a fixed number of the entity's own equity instruments. For this purpose the entity's own equity instruments do not include puttable financial instruments classified as equity instruments in accordance with paragraphs 16A and 16B, instruments that impose on the entity an obligation to deliver to another party a pro rata share of the net assets of the entity only on liquidation and are classified as equity instruments in accordance with paragraphs 16C and 16D, or instruments that are contracts for the future receipt or delivery of the entity's own equity instruments.

A *financial liability* is any liability that is:

(a)   a contractual obligation:

    (i)   to deliver cash or another financial asset to another entity; or

    (ii)   to exchange financial assets or financial liabilities with another entity under conditions that are potentially unfavourable to the entity; or

(b)   a contract that will or may be settled in the entity's own equity instruments and is:

    (i)   a non-derivative for which the entity is or may be obliged to deliver a variable number of the entity's own equity instruments; or

    (ii)   a derivative that will or may be settled other than by the exchange of a fixed amount of cash or another financial asset for a fixed number of the entity's own equity instruments. For this purpose, rights, options or warrants to acquire a fixed number of the entity's own equity instruments for a fixed amount of any currency are equity instruments if the entity offers the rights, options or warrants pro rata to all of its existing owners of the same class of its own non-derivative equity instruments. Also for these purposes the entity's own equity instruments do not include puttable financial instruments that are classified as equity instruments in accordance with paragraphs 16A and 16B, instruments that impose on the entity an obligation to deliver to another party a pro rata share of the net assets of the entity only on liquidation and are classified as equity instruments in accordance with paragraphs 16C and 16D, or instruments that are contracts for the future receipt or delivery of the entity's own equity instruments.

As an exception, an instrument that meets the definition of a financial liability is classified as an equity instrument if it has all the features and meets the conditions in paragraphs 16A and 16B or paragraphs 16C and 16D.

An *equity instrument* is any contract that evidences a residual interest in the assets of an entity after deducting all of its liabilities.

Fair value is the amount for which an asset could be exchanged, or a liability settled, between knowledgeable, willing parties in an arm's length transaction.

A *puttable instrument* is a financial instrument that gives the holder the right to put the instrument back to the issuer for cash or another financial asset or is automatically put back to the issuer on the occurrence of an uncertain future event or the death or retirement of the instrument holder.

12   The following terms are defined in paragraph 9 of IAS 39 and are used in this Standard with the meaning specified in IAS 39.

•   amortised cost of a financial asset or financial liability

•   available-for-sale financial assets

•   derecognition

•   derivative

- effective interest method

- financial asset or financial liability at fair value through profit or loss

- financial guarantee contract

- firm commitment

- forecast transaction

- hedge effectiveness

- hedged item

- hedging instrument

- held-to-maturity investments

- loans and receivables

- regular way purchase or sale

- transaction costs.

13   In this Standard, 'contract' and 'contractual' refer to an agreement between two or more parties that has clear economic consequences that the parties have little, if any, discretion to avoid, usually because the agreement is enforceable by law. Contracts, and thus financial instruments, may take a variety of forms and need not be in writing.

14   In this Standard, 'entity' includes individuals, partnerships, incorporated bodies, trusts and government agencies.

Presentation

Liabilities and equity (see also paragraphs AG25–AG29A)

15   **The issuer of a financial instrument shall classify the instrument, or its component parts, on initial recognition as a financial liability, a financial asset or an equity instrument in accordance with the substance of the contractual arrangement and the definitions of a financial liability, a financial asset and an equity instrument.**

16   When an issuer applies the definitions in paragraph 11 to determine whether a financial instrument is an equity instrument rather than a financial liability, the instrument is an equity instrument if, and only if, both conditions (a) and (b) below are met.

(a)   The instrument includes no contractual obligation:

(i)   to deliver cash or another financial asset to another entity; or

(ii)   to exchange financial assets or financial liabilities with another entity under conditions that are potentially unfavourable to the issuer.

(b)   If the instrument will or may be settled in the issuer's own equity instruments, it is:

(i)   a non-derivative that includes no contractual obligation for the issuer to deliver a variable number of its own equity instruments; or

(ii)   a derivative that will be settled only by the issuer exchanging a fixed amount of cash or another financial asset for a fixed number of its own equity instruments. For this purpose, rights, options or warrants to acquire a fixed number of the entity's own equity instruments for a fixed amount of any currency are equity instruments if the entity offers the rights, options or warrants pro rata to all of its existing owners of the same class of its own non-derivative equity instruments. Also, for these purposes the issuer's own equity instruments do not include instruments that have all the features and meet the conditions described in paragraphs 16A and 16B or paragraphs 16C and 16D, or instruments that are contracts for the future receipt or delivery of the issuer's own equity instruments.

A contractual obligation, including one arising from a derivative financial instrument, that will or may result in the future receipt or delivery of the issuer's own equity instruments, but does not meet conditions (a) and (b) above, is not an equity instrument. As an exception, an instrument that meets the definition of a financial liability is classified as an equity instrument if it has all the features and meets the conditions in paragraphs 16A and 16B or paragraphs 16C and 16D.

Puttable instruments

16A   A puttable financial instrument includes a contractual obligation for the issuer to repurchase or redeem that instrument for cash or another financial asset on exercise of the put. As an exception to the definition of a financial liability, an instrument that includes such an obligation is classified as an equity instrument if it has all the following features:

(a)   It entitles the holder to a pro rata share of the entity's net assets in the event of the entity's liquidation. The entity's net assets are those assets that remain after deducting all other claims on its assets. A pro rata share is determined by:

     (i)   dividing the entity's net assets on liquidation into units of equal amount; and

     (ii)   multiplying that amount by the number of the units held by the financial instrument holder.

(b)   The instrument is in the class of instruments that is subordinate to all other classes of instruments. To be in such a class the instrument:

     (i)   has no priority over other claims to the assets of the entity on liquidation, and

     (ii)   does not need to be converted into another instrument before it is in the class of instruments that is subordinate to all other classes of instruments.

(c)   All financial instruments in the class of instruments that is subordinate to all other classes of instruments have identical features. For example, they must all be puttable, and the formula or other method used to calculate the repurchase or redemption price is the same for all instruments in that class.

(d)   Apart from the contractual obligation for the issuer to repurchase or redeem the instrument for cash or another financial asset, the instrument does not include any contractual obligation to deliver cash or another financial asset to another entity, or to exchange financial assets or financial liabilities with another entity under conditions that are potentially unfavourable to the entity, and it is not a contract that will or may be settled in the entity's own equity instruments as set out in subparagraph (b) of the definition of a financial liability.

(e)   The total expected cash flows attributable to the instrument over the life of the instrument are based substantially on the profit or loss, the change in the recognised net assets or the change in the fair value of the recognised and unrecognised net assets of the entity over the life of the instrument (excluding any effects of the instrument).

16B   For an instrument to be classified as an equity instrument, in addition to the instrument having all the above features, the issuer must have no other financial instrument or contract that has:

(a)   total cash flows based substantially on the profit or loss, the change in the recognised net assets or the change in the fair value of the recognised and unrecognised net assets of the entity (excluding any effects of such instrument or contract) and

(b)   the effect of substantially restricting or fixing the residual return to the puttable instrument holders.

For the purposes of applying this condition, the entity shall not consider non-financial contracts with a holder of an instrument described in paragraph 16A that have contractual terms and conditions that are similar to the contractual terms and conditions of an equivalent contract that might occur between a non-instrument holder and the issuing entity. If the entity cannot determine that this condition is met, it shall not classify the puttable instrument as an equity instrument.

Instruments, or components of instruments, that impose on the entity an obligation to deliver to another party a pro rata share of the net assets of the entity only on liquidation

16C   Some financial instruments include a contractual obligation for the issuing entity to deliver to another entity a pro rata share of its net assets only on liquidation. The obligation arises because liquidation either is certain to occur and outside the control of the entity (for example, a limited life entity) or is uncertain to occur but is at the option of the instrument holder. As an exception to the definition of a financial liability, an instrument that includes such an obligation is classified as an equity instrument if it has all the following features:

(a)   It entitles the holder to a pro rata share of the entity's net assets in the event of the entity's liquidation. The entity's net assets are those assets that remain after deducting all other claims on its assets. A pro rata share is determined by:

(i)   dividing the net assets of the entity on liquidation into units of equal amount; and

(ii)   multiplying that amount by the number of the units held by the financial instrument holder.

(b)   The instrument is in the class of instruments that is subordinate to all other classes of instruments. To be in such a class the instrument:

(i)   has no priority over other claims to the assets of the entity on liquidation, and

(ii)   does not need to be converted into another instrument before it is in the class of instruments that is subordinate to all other classes of instruments.

(c)   All financial instruments in the class of instruments that is subordinate to all other classes of instruments must have an identical contractual obligation for the issuing entity to deliver a pro rata share of its net assets on liquidation.

16D   For an instrument to be classified as an equity instrument, in addition to the instrument having all the above features, the issuer must have no other financial instrument or contract that has:

(a)   total cash flows based substantially on the profit or loss, the change in the recognised net assets or the change in the fair value of the recognised and unrecognised net assets of the entity (excluding any effects of such instrument or contract) and

(b)   the effect of substantially restricting or fixing the residual return to the instrument holders.

For the purposes of applying this condition, the entity shall not consider non-financial contracts with a holder of an instrument described in paragraph 16C that have contractual terms and conditions that are similar to the contractual terms and conditions of an equivalent contract that might occur between a non-instrument holder and the issuing entity. If the entity cannot determine that this condition is met, it shall not classify the instrument as an equity instrument.

Reclassification of puttable instruments and instruments that impose on the entity an obligation to deliver to another party a pro rata share of the net assets of the entity only on liquidation

16E   An entity shall classify a financial instrument as an equity instrument in accordance with paragraphs 16A and 16B or paragraphs 16C and 16D from the date when the instrument has all the features and meets the conditions set out in those paragraphs. An entity shall reclassify a financial instrument from the date when the instrument ceases to have all the features or meet all the conditions set out in those paragraphs. For example, if an entity redeems all its issued non-puttable instruments and any puttable instruments that remain outstanding have all the features and meet all the conditions in paragraphs 16A and 16B, the entity shall reclassify the puttable instruments as equity instruments from the date when it redeems the non-puttable instruments.

16F   An entity shall account as follows for the reclassification of an instrument in accordance with paragraph 16E:

(a)   It shall reclassify an equity instrument as a financial liability from the date when the instrument ceases to have all the features or meet the conditions in paragraphs 16A and 16B or paragraphs 16C and 16D. The financial liability shall be measured at the instrument's fair value at the date of reclassification. The entity shall recognise in equity any difference between the carrying value of the equity instrument and the fair value of the financial liability at the date of reclassification.

(b)   It shall reclassify a financial liability as equity from the date when the instrument has all the features and meets the conditions set out in paragraphs 16A and 16B or paragraphs 16C and 16D. An equity instrument shall be measured at the carrying value of the financial liability at the date of reclassification.

No contractual obligation to deliver cash or another financial asset (paragraph 16(a))

17   With the exception of the circumstances described in paragraphs 16A and 16B or paragraphs 16C and 16D,a critical feature in differentiating a financial liability from an equity instrument is the existence of a contractual obligation of one party to the financial instrument (the issuer) either to deliver cash or another financial asset to the other party (the holder) or to exchange financial assets or financial liabilities with the holder under conditions that are potentially unfavourable to the issuer.. Although the holder of an equity instrument may be entitled to receive a pro rata share of any dividends or other distributions of equity, the issuer does not have a contractual obligation to make such distributions because it cannot be required to deliver cash or another financial asset to another party.

18   The substance of a financial instrument, rather than its legal form, governs its classification in the entity's statement of financial position. Substance and legal form are commonly consistent, but not always. Some financial instruments take the legal form of equity but are liabilities in substance and others may combine features associated with equity instruments and features associated with financial liabilities. For example:

(a)   a preference share that provides for mandatory redemption by the issuer for a fixed or determinable amount at a fixed or determinable future date, or gives the holder the right to require the issuer to redeem the instrument at or after a particular date for a fixed or determinable amount, is a financial liability.

(b)   a financial instrument that gives the holder the right to put it back to the issuer for cash or another financial asset (a 'puttable instrument') is a financial liability, except for those instruments classified as equity instruments in accordance with paragraphs 16A and 16B or paragraphs 16C and 16D. The financial instrument is a financial liability even when the amount of cash or other financial assets is determined on the basis of an index or other item that has the potential to increase or decrease. The existence of an option for the holder to put the instrument back to the issuer for cash or another financial asset means that the puttable instrument meets the definition of a financial liability, except for those instruments classified as equity instruments in accordance with paragraphs 16A and 16B or paragraphs 16C and 16D. For example, open-ended mutual funds, unit trusts, partnerships and some co-operative entities may provide their unitholders or members with a right to redeem their interests in the issuer at any time for cash, which results in the unitholders' or members' interests being classified as financial liabilities, except for those instruments classified as equity instruments in accordance with paragraphs 16A and 16B or paragraphs 16C and 16D. However, classification as a financial liability does not preclude the use of descriptors such as 'net asset value attributable to unitholders' and 'change in net asset value attributable to unitholders' in the financial statements of an entity that has no contributed equity (such as some mutual funds and unit trusts, see Illustrative Example 7) or the use of additional disclosure to show that total members' interests comprise items such as reserves that meet the definition of equity and puttable instruments that do not (see Illustrative Example 8).

19   If an entity does not have an unconditional right to avoid delivering cash or another financial asset to settle a contractual obligation, the obligation meets the definition of a financial liability, except for those instruments

classified as equity instruments in accordance with paragraphs 16A and 16B or paragraphs 16C and 16D. For example:

(a)   a restriction on the ability of an entity to satisfy a contractual obligation, such as lack of access to foreign currency or the need to obtain approval for payment from a regulatory authority, does not negate the entity's contractual obligation or the holder's contractual right under the instrument.

(b)   a contractual obligation that is conditional on a counterparty exercising its right to redeem is a financial liability because the entity does not have the unconditional right to avoid delivering cash or another financial asset.

20   A financial instrument that does not explicitly establish a contractual obligation to deliver cash or another financial asset may establish an obligation indirectly through its terms and conditions. For example:

(a)   a financial instrument may contain a non-financial obligation that must be settled if, and only if, the entity fails to make distributions or to redeem the instrument. If the entity can avoid a transfer of cash or another financial asset only by settling the non-financial obligation, the financial instrument is a financial liability.

(b)   a financial instrument is a financial liability if it provides that on settlement the entity will deliver either:

(i)   cash or another financial asset; or

(ii)   its own shares whose value is determined to exceed substantially the value of the cash or other financial asset.

Although the entity does not have an explicit contractual obligation to deliver cash or another financial asset, the value of the share settlement alternative is such that the entity will settle in cash. In any event, the holder has in substance been guaranteed receipt of an amount that is at least equal to the cash settlement option (see paragraph 21).

Settlement in the entity's own equity instruments (paragraph 16(b))

21   A contract is not an equity instrument solely because it may result in the receipt or delivery of the entity's own equity instruments. An entity may have a contractual right or obligation to receive or deliver a number of its own shares or other equity instruments that varies so that the fair value of the entity's own equity instruments to be received or delivered equals the amount of the contractual right or obligation. Such a contractual right or obligation may be for a fixed amount or an amount that fluctuates in part or in full in response to changes in a variable other than the market price of the entity's own equity instruments (eg an interest rate, a commodity price or a financial instrument price). Two examples are (a) a contract to deliver as many of the entity's own equity instruments as are equal in value to CU100,[*] and (b) a contract to deliver as many of the entity's own equity instruments as are equal in value to the value of 100 ounces of gold. Such a contract is a financial liability of the entity even though the entity must or can settle it by delivering its own equity instruments. It is not an equity instrument because the entity uses a variable number of its own equity instruments as a means to settle the contract. Accordingly, the contract does not evidence a residual interest in the entity's assets after deducting all of its liabilities.

22   Except as stated in paragraph 22A, a contract that will be settled by the entity (receiving or) delivering a fixed number of its own equity instruments in exchange for a fixed amount of cash or another financial asset is an equity instrument. For example, an issued share option that gives the counterparty a right to buy a fixed number of the entity's shares for a fixed price or for a fixed stated principal amount of a bond is an equity instrument. Changes in the fair value of a contract arising from variations in market interest rates that do not affect the amount of cash or other financial assets to be paid or received, or the number of equity instruments to be received or delivered, on settlement of the contract do not preclude the contract from being an equity instrument. Any consideration received (such as the premium received for a written option or warrant on the entity's own shares) is added directly to equity. Any consideration paid (such as the premium paid for a purchased option) is deducted directly from equity. Changes in the fair value of an equity instrument are not recognised in the financial statements.

---

[*]   In this Standard, monetary amounts are denominated in 'currency units' (CU).

22A   If the entity's own equity instruments to be received, or delivered, by the entity upon settlement of a contract are puttable financial instruments with all the features and meeting the conditions described in paragraphs 16A and 16B, or instruments that impose on the entity an obligation to deliver to another party a pro rata share of the net assets of the entity only on liquidation with all of the features and meeting the conditions described in paragraphs 16C and 16D, the contract is a financial asset or a financial liability. This includes a contract that will be settled by the entity receiving or delivering a fixed number of such instruments in exchange for a fixed amount of cash or another financial asset.

23   With the exception of the circumstances described in paragraphs 16A and 16B or paragraphs 16C and 16D, a contract that contains an obligation for an entity to purchase its own equity instruments for cash or another financial asset gives rise to a financial liability for the present value of the redemption amount (for example, for the present value of the forward repurchase price, option exercise price or other redemption amount). This is the case even if the contract itself is an equity instrument. One example is an entity's obligation under a forward contract to purchase its own equity instruments for cash. When the financial liability is recognised initially under IAS 39, its fair value (the present value of the redemption amount) is reclassified from equity. Subsequently, the financial liability is measured in accordance with IAS 39. If the contract expires without delivery, the carrying amount of the financial liability is reclassified to equity. An entity's contractual obligation to purchase its own equity instruments gives rise to a financial liability for the present value of the redemption amount even if the obligation to purchase is conditional on the counterparty exercising a right to redeem (eg a written put option that gives the counterparty the right to sell an entity's own equity instruments to the entity for a fixed price).

24   A contract that will be settled by the entity delivering or receiving a fixed number of its own equity instruments in exchange for a variable amount of cash or another financial asset is a financial asset or financial liability. An example is a contract for the entity to deliver 100 of its own equity instruments in return for an amount of cash calculated to equal the value of 100 ounces of gold.

Contingent settlement provisions

25   A financial instrument may require the entity to deliver cash or another financial asset, or otherwise to settle it in such a way that it would be a financial liability, in the event of the occurrence or non-occurrence of uncertain future events (or on the outcome of uncertain circumstances) that are beyond the control of both the issuer and the holder of the instrument, such as a change in a stock market index, consumer price index, interest rate or taxation requirements, or the issuer's future revenues, net income or debt-to-equity ratio. The issuer of such an instrument does not have the unconditional right to avoid delivering cash or another financial asset (or otherwise to settle it in such a way that it would be a financial liability). Therefore, it is a financial liability of the issuer unless:

(a)   the part of the contingent settlement provision that could require settlement in cash or another financial asset (or otherwise in such a way that it would be a financial liability) is not genuine;

(b)   the issuer can be required to settle the obligation in cash or another financial asset (or otherwise to settle it in such a way that it would be a financial liability) only in the event of liquidation of the issuer; or

(c)   the instrument has all the features and meets the conditions in paragraphs 16A and 16B.

Settlement options

26   **When a derivative financial instrument gives one party a choice over how it is settled (eg the issuer or the holder can choose settlement net in cash or by exchanging shares for cash), it is a financial asset or a financial liability unless all of the settlement alternatives would result in it being an equity instrument.**

27   An example of a derivative financial instrument with a settlement option that is a financial liability is a share option that the issuer can decide to settle net in cash or by exchanging its own shares for cash. Similarly, some contracts to buy or sell a non-financial item in exchange for the entity's own equity instruments are within the scope of this Standard because they can be settled either by delivery of the non-financial item or net in cash or another financial instrument (see paragraphs 8–10). Such contracts are financial assets or financial liabilities and not equity instruments.

Compound financial instruments (see also paragraphs AG30–AG35 and Illustrative Examples 9–12)

28   The issuer of a non-derivative financial instrument shall evaluate the terms of the financial instrument to determine whether it contains both a liability and an equity component. Such components shall be classified separately as financial liabilities, financial assets or equity instruments in accordance with paragraph 15.

29   An entity recognises separately the components of a financial instrument that (a) creates a financial liability of the entity and (b) grants an option to the holder of the instrument to convert it into an equity instrument of the entity. For example, a bond or similar instrument convertible by the holder into a fixed number of ordinary shares of the entity is a compound financial instrument. From the perspective of the entity, such an instrument comprises two components: a financial liability (a contractual arrangement to deliver cash or another financial asset) and an equity instrument (a call option granting the holder the right, for a specified period of time, to convert it into a fixed number of ordinary shares of the entity). The economic effect of issuing such an instrument is substantially the same as issuing simultaneously a debt instrument with an early settlement provision and warrants to purchase ordinary shares, or issuing a debt instrument with detachable share purchase warrants. Accordingly, in all cases, the entity presents the liability and equity components separately in its statement of financial position.

30   Classification of the liability and equity components of a convertible instrument is not revised as a result of a change in the likelihood that a conversion option will be exercised, even when exercise of the option may appear to have become economically advantageous to some holders. Holders may not always act in the way that might be expected because, for example, the tax consequences resulting from conversion may differ among holders. Furthermore, the likelihood of conversion will change from time to time. The entity's contractual obligation to make future payments remains outstanding until it is extinguished through conversion, maturity of the instrument or some other transaction.

31   IAS 39 deals with the measurement of financial assets and financial liabilities. Equity instruments are instruments that evidence a residual interest in the assets of an entity after deducting all of its liabilities. Therefore, when the initial carrying amount of a compound financial instrument is allocated to its equity and liability components, the equity component is assigned the residual amount after deducting from the fair value of the instrument as a whole the amount separately determined for the liability component. The value of any derivative features (such as a call option) embedded in the compound financial instrument other than the equity component (such as an equity conversion option) is included in the liability component. The sum of the carrying amounts assigned to the liability and equity components on initial recognition is always equal to the fair value that would be ascribed to the instrument as a whole. No gain or loss arises from initially recognising the components of the instrument separately.

32   Under the approach described in paragraph 31, the issuer of a bond convertible into ordinary shares first determines the carrying amount of the liability component by measuring the fair value of a similar liability (including any embedded non-equity derivative features) that does not have an associated equity component. The carrying amount of the equity instrument represented by the option to convert the instrument into ordinary shares is then determined by deducting the fair value of the financial liability from the fair value of the compound financial instrument as a whole.

Treasury shares (see also paragraph AG36)

33   If an entity reacquires its own equity instruments, those instruments ('treasury shares') shall be deducted from equity. No gain or loss shall be recognised in profit or loss on the purchase, sale, issue or cancellation of an entity's own equity instruments. Such treasury shares may be acquired and held by the entity or by other members of the consolidated group. Consideration paid or received shall be recognised directly in equity.

34   The amount of treasury shares held is disclosed separately either in the statement of financial position or in the notes, in accordance with IAS 1 *Presentation of Financial Statements*. An entity provides disclosure in accordance with IAS 24 *Related Party Disclosures* if the entity reacquires its own equity instruments from related parties.

Interest, dividends, losses and gains
(see also paragraph AG37)

35 **Interest, dividends, losses and gains relating to a financial instrument or a component that is a financial liability shall be recognised as income or expense in profit or loss. Distributions to holders of an equity instrument shall be debited by the entity directly to equity, net of any related income tax benefit. Transaction costs of an equity transaction shall be accounted for as a deduction from equity, net of any related income tax benefit.**

36 The classification of a financial instrument as a financial liability or an equity instrument determines whether interest, dividends, losses and gains relating to that instrument are recognised as income or expense in profit or loss. Thus, dividend payments on shares wholly recognised as liabilities are recognised as expenses in the same way as interest on a bond. Similarly, gains and losses associated with redemptions or refinancings of financial liabilities are recognised in profit or loss, whereas redemptions or refinancings of equity instruments are recognised as changes in equity. Changes in the fair value of an equity instrument are not recognised in the financial statements.

37 An entity typically incurs various costs in issuing or acquiring its own equity instruments. Those costs might include registration and other regulatory fees, amounts paid to legal, accounting and other professional advisers, printing costs and stamp duties. The transaction costs of an equity transaction are accounted for as a deduction from equity (net of any related income tax benefit) to the extent they are incremental costs directly attributable to the equity transaction that otherwise would have been avoided. The costs of an equity transaction that is abandoned are recognised as an expense.

38 Transaction costs that relate to the issue of a compound financial instrument are allocated to the liability and equity components of the instrument in proportion to the allocation of proceeds. Transaction costs that relate jointly to more than one transaction (for example, costs of a concurrent offering of some shares and a stock exchange listing of other shares) are allocated to those transactions using a basis of allocation that is rational and consistent with similar transactions.

39 The amount of transaction costs accounted for as a deduction from equity in the period is disclosed separately under IAS 1. The related amount of income taxes recognised directly in equity is included in the aggregate amount of current and deferred income tax credited or charged to equity that is disclosed under IAS 12 *Income Taxes*.

40 Dividends classified as an expense may be presented in the statement(s) of profit or loss and other comprehensive income either with interest on other liabilities or as a separate item. In addition to the requirements of this Standard, disclosure of interest and dividends is subject to the requirements of IAS 1 and IFRS 7. In some circumstances, because of the differences between interest and dividends with respect to matters such as tax deductibility, it is desirable to disclose them separately in the statement(s) of profit or loss and other comprehensive income. Disclosures of the tax effects are made in accordance with IAS 12.

41 Gains and losses related to changes in the carrying amount of a financial liability are recognised as income or expense in profit or loss even when they relate to an instrument that includes a right to the residual interest in the assets of the entity in exchange for cash or another financial asset (see paragraph 18(b)). Under IAS 1 the entity presents any gain or loss arising from remeasurement of such an instrument separately in the statement of comprehensive income when it is relevant in explaining the entity's performance.

Offsetting a financial asset and a financial liability
(see also paragraphs AG38 and AG39)

42 **A financial asset and a financial liability shall be offset and the net amount presented in the statement of financial position when, and only when, an entity:**

(a) **currently has a legally enforceable right to set off the recognised amounts; and**

(b) **intends either to settle on a net basis, or to realise the asset and settle the liability simultaneously.**

In accounting for a transfer of a financial asset that does not qualify for derecognition, the entity shall not offset the transferred asset and the associated liability (see IAS 39, paragraph 36).

43   This Standard requires the presentation of financial assets and financial liabilities on a net basis when doing so reflects an entity's expected future cash flows from settling two or more separate financial instruments. When an entity has the right to receive or pay a single net amount and intends to do so, it has, in effect, only a single financial asset or financial liability. In other circumstances, financial assets and financial liabilities are presented separately from each other consistently with their characteristics as resources or obligations of the entity.

44   Offsetting a recognised financial asset and a recognised financial liability and presenting the net amount differs from the derecognition of a financial asset or a financial liability. Although offsetting does not give rise to recognition of a gain or loss, the derecognition of a financial instrument not only results in the removal of the previously recognised item from the statement of financial position but also may result in recognition of a gain or loss.

45   A right of set-off is a debtor's legal right, by contract or otherwise, to settle or otherwise eliminate all or a portion of an amount due to a creditor by applying against that amount an amount due from the creditor. In unusual circumstances, a debtor may have a legal right to apply an amount due from a third party against the amount due to a creditor provided that there is an agreement between the three parties that clearly establishes the debtor's right of set-off. Because the right of set-off is a legal right, the conditions supporting the right may vary from one legal jurisdiction to another and the laws applicable to the relationships between the parties need to be considered.

46   The existence of an enforceable right to set off a financial asset and a financial liability affects the rights and obligations associated with a financial asset and a financial liability and may affect an entity's exposure to credit and liquidity risk. However, the existence of the right, by itself, is not a sufficient basis for offsetting. In the absence of an intention to exercise the right or to settle simultaneously, the amount and timing of an entity's future cash flows are not affected. When an entity intends to exercise the right or to settle simultaneously, presentation of the asset and liability on a net basis reflects more appropriately the amounts and timing of the expected future cash flows, as well as the risks to which those cash flows are exposed. An intention by one or both parties to settle on a net basis without the legal right to do so is not sufficient to justify offsetting because the rights and obligations associated with the individual financial asset and financial liability remain unaltered.

47   An entity's intentions with respect to settlement of particular assets and liabilities may be influenced by its normal business practices, the requirements of the financial markets and other circumstances that may limit the ability to settle net or to settle simultaneously. When an entity has a right of set-off, but does not intend to settle net or to realise the asset and settle the liability simultaneously, the effect of the right on the entity's credit risk exposure is disclosed in accordance with paragraph 36 of IFRS 7.

48   Simultaneous settlement of two financial instruments may occur through, for example, the operation of a clearing house in an organised financial market or a face-to-face exchange. In these circumstances the cash flows are, in effect, equivalent to a single net amount and there is no exposure to credit or liquidity risk. In other circumstances, an entity may settle two instruments by receiving and paying separate amounts, becoming exposed to credit risk for the full amount of the asset or liquidity risk for the full amount of the liability. Such risk exposures may be significant even though relatively brief. Accordingly, realisation of a financial asset and settlement of a financial liability are treated as simultaneous only when the transactions occur at the same moment.

49   The conditions set out in paragraph 42 are generally not satisfied and offsetting is usually inappropriate when:

(a)   several different financial instruments are used to emulate the features of a single financial instrument (a 'synthetic instrument');

(b)   financial assets and financial liabilities arise from financial instruments having the same primary risk exposure (for example, assets and liabilities within a portfolio of forward contracts or other derivative instruments) but involve different counterparties;

(c)   financial or other assets are pledged as collateral for non-recourse financial liabilities;

(d)   financial assets are set aside in trust by a debtor for the purpose of discharging an obligation without those assets having been accepted by the creditor in settlement of the obligation (for example, a sinking fund arrangement); or

(e)   obligations incurred as a result of events giving rise to losses are expected to be recovered from a third party by virtue of a claim made under an insurance contract.

50   An entity that undertakes a number of financial instrument transactions with a single counterparty may enter into a 'master netting arrangement' with that counterparty. Such an agreement provides for a single net settlement of all financial instruments covered by the agreement in the event of default on, or termination of, any one contract. These arrangements are commonly used by financial institutions to provide protection against loss in the event of bankruptcy or other circumstances that result in a counterparty being unable to meet its obligations. A master netting arrangement commonly creates a right of set-off that becomes enforceable and affects the realisation or settlement of individual financial assets and financial liabilities only following a specified event of default or in other circumstances not expected to arise in the normal course of business. A master netting arrangement does not provide a basis for offsetting unless both of the criteria in paragraph 42 are satisfied. When financial assets and financial liabilities subject to a master netting arrangement are not offset, the effect of the arrangement on an entity's exposure to credit risk is disclosed in accordance with paragraph 36 of IFRS 7.

Disclosure

51-95   [Deleted]

Effective date and transition

96   **An entity shall apply this Standard for annual periods beginning on or after 1 January 2005. Earlier application is permitted. An entity shall not apply this Standard for annual periods beginning before 1 January 2005 unless it also applies IAS 39 (issued December 2003), including the amendments issued in March 2004. If an entity applies this Standard for a period beginning before 1 January 2005, it shall disclose that fact.**

96A   *Puttable Financial Instruments and Obligations Arising on Liquidation* (Amendments to IAS 32 and IAS 1), issued in February 2008, required financial instruments that contain all the features and meet the conditions in paragraphs 16A and 16B or paragraphs 16C and 16D to be classified as an equity instrument, amended paragraphs 11, 16, 17–19, 22, 23, 25, AG13, AG14 and AG27, and inserted paragraphs 16A–16F, 22A, 96B, 96C, 97C, AG14A–AG14J and AG29A. An entity shall apply those amendments for annual periods beginning on or after 1 January 2009. Earlier application is permitted. If an entity applies the changes for an earlier period, it shall disclose that fact and apply the related amendments to IAS 1, IAS 39, IFRS 7 and IFRIC 2 at the same time.

96B   *Puttable Financial Instruments and Obligations Arising on Liquidation* introduced a limited scope exception; therefore, an entity shall not apply the exception by analogy.

96C   The classification of instruments under this exception shall be restricted to the accounting for such an instrument under IAS 1, IAS 32, IAS 39 and IFRS 7. The instrument shall not be considered an equity instrument under other guidance, for example IFRS 2 *Share-based Payment*.

97   **This Standard shall be applied retrospectively.**

97A   **IAS 1 (as revised in 2007) amended the terminology used throughout IFRSs. In addition it amended paragraph 40. An entity shall apply those amendments for annual periods beginning on or after 1 January 2009. If an entity applies IAS 1 (revised 2007) for an earlier period, the amendments shall be applied for that earlier period.**

97B   IFRS 3 (as revised in 2008) deleted paragraph 4(c). An entity shall apply that amendment for annual periods beginning on or after 1 July 2009. If an entity applies IFRS 3 (revised 2008) for an earlier period, the amendment shall also be applied for that earlier period. However, the amendment does not apply to contingent consideration that arose from a business combination for which the acquisition date preceded the application of IFRS 3 (revised 2008). Instead, an entity shall account for such consideration in accordance with paragraphs 65A–65E of IFRS 3 (as amended in 2010).

97C   When applying the amendments described in paragraph 96A, an entity is required to split a compound financial instrument with an obligation to deliver to another party a pro rata share of the net assets of the entity only on liquidation into separate liability and equity components. If the liability component is no longer outstanding, a retrospective application of those amendments to IAS 32 would involve separating two components of equity. The first component would be in retained earnings and represent the cumulative interest accreted on the liability component. The other component would represent the original equity component. Therefore, an entity need not separate these two components if the liability component is no longer outstanding at the date of application of the amendments.

97D   Paragraph 4 was amended by *Improvements to IFRSs* issued in May 2008. An entity shall apply that amendment for annual periods beginning on or after 1 January 2009. Earlier application is permitted. If an entity applies the amendment for an earlier period it shall disclose that fact and apply for that earlier period the amendments to paragraph 3 of IFRS 7, paragraph 1 of IAS 28 and paragraph 1 of IAS 31 issued in May 2008. An entity is permitted to apply the amendment prospectively.

97E   Paragraphs 11 and 16 were amended by Classification of Rights Issues issued in October 2009. An entity shall apply that amendment for annual periods beginning on or after 1 February 2010. Earlier application is permitted. If an entity applies the amendment for an earlier period, it shall disclose that fact.

97G   Paragraph 97B was amended by *Improvements to IFRSs* issued in May 2010. An entity shall apply that amendment for annual periods beginning on or after 1 July 2010. Earlier application is permitted.

97K   *Presentation of Items of Other Comprehensive Income* (Amendments to IAS 1), issued in June 2011, amended paragraph 40. An entity shall apply that amendment when it applies IAS 1 as amended in June 2011.

Withdrawal of other pronouncements

98   This Standard supersedes IAS 32 *Financial Instruments: Disclosure and Presentation* revised in 2000.[*]

99   This Standard supersedes the following Interpretations:

(a)   SIC-5 *Classification of Financial Instruments—Contingent Settlement Provisions*;

(b)   SIC-16 *Share Capital—Reacquired Own Equity Instruments (Treasury Shares)*; and

(c)   SIC-17 *Equity—Costs of an Equity Transaction.*

100   This Standard withdraws draft SIC Interpretation D34 *Financial Instruments—Instruments or Rights Redeemable by the Holder.*

---

[*]   In August 2005 the IASB relocated all disclosures relating to financial instruments to IFRS 7 *Financial Instruments: Disclosures.*

Appendix
Application Guidance
IAS 32 *Financial Instruments: Presentation*

This appendix is an integral part of the Standard.

AG1   This Application Guidance explains the application of particular aspects of the Standard.

AG2   The Standard does not deal with the recognition or measurement of financial instruments. Requirements about the recognition and measurement of financial assets and financial liabilities are set out in IAS 39.

Definitions (paragraphs 11–14)

Financial assets and financial liabilities

AG3   Currency (cash) is a financial asset because it represents the medium of exchange and is therefore the basis on which all transactions are measured and recognised in financial statements. A deposit of cash with a bank or similar financial institution is a financial asset because it represents the contractual right of the depositor to obtain cash from the institution or to draw a cheque or similar instrument against the balance in favour of a creditor in payment of a financial liability.

AG4   Common examples of financial assets representing a contractual right to receive cash in the future and corresponding financial liabilities representing a contractual obligation to deliver cash in the future are:

(a)   trade accounts receivable and payable;

(b)   notes receivable and payable;

(c)   loans receivable and payable; and

(d)   bonds receivable and payable.

In each case, one party's contractual right to receive (or obligation to pay) cash is matched by the other party's corresponding obligation to pay (or right to receive).

AG5   Another type of financial instrument is one for which the economic benefit to be received or given up is a financial asset other than cash. For example, a note payable in government bonds gives the holder the contractual right to receive and the issuer the contractual obligation to deliver government bonds, not cash. The bonds are financial assets because they represent obligations of the issuing government to pay cash. The note is, therefore, a financial asset of the note holder and a financial liability of the note issuer.

AG6   'Perpetual' debt instruments (such as 'perpetual' bonds, debentures and capital notes) normally provide the holder with the contractual right to receive payments on account of interest at fixed dates extending into the indefinite future, either with no right to receive a return of principal or a right to a return of principal under terms that make it very unlikely or very far in the future. For example, an entity may issue a financial instrument requiring it to make annual payments in perpetuity equal to a stated interest rate of 8 per cent applied to a stated par or principal amount of CU1,000.[3] Assuming 8 per cent to be the market rate of interest for the instrument when issued, the issuer assumes a contractual obligation to make a stream of future interest payments having a fair value (present value) of CU1,000 on initial recognition. The holder and issuer of the instrument have a financial asset and a financial liability, respectively.

---

[3]   In this guidance, monetary amounts are denominated in 'currency units' (CU).

AG7　A contractual right or contractual obligation to receive, deliver or exchange financial instruments is itself a financial instrument. A chain of contractual rights or contractual obligations meets the definition of a financial instrument if it will ultimately lead to the receipt or payment of cash or to the acquisition or issue of an equity instrument.

AG8　The ability to exercise a contractual right or the requirement to satisfy a contractual obligation may be absolute, or it may be contingent on the occurrence of a future event. For example, a financial guarantee is a contractual right of the lender to receive cash from the guarantor, and a corresponding contractual obligation of the guarantor to pay the lender, if the borrower defaults. The contractual right and obligation exist because of a past transaction or event (assumption of the guarantee), even though the lender's ability to exercise its right and the requirement for the guarantor to perform under its obligation are both contingent on a future act of default by the borrower. A contingent right and obligation meet the definition of a financial asset and a financial liability, even though such assets and liabilities are not always recognised in the financial statements. Some of these contingent rights and obligations may be insurance contracts within the scope of IFRS 4.

AG9　Under IAS 17 *Leases* a finance lease is regarded as primarily an entitlement of the lessor to receive, and an obligation of the lessee to pay, a stream of payments that are substantially the same as blended payments of principal and interest under a loan agreement. The lessor accounts for its investment in the amount receivable under the lease contract rather than the leased asset itself. An operating lease, on the other hand, is regarded as primarily an uncompleted contract committing the lessor to provide the use of an asset in future periods in exchange for consideration similar to a fee for a service. The lessor continues to account for the leased asset itself rather than any amount receivable in the future under the contract. Accordingly, a finance lease is regarded as a financial instrument and an operating lease is not regarded as a financial instrument (except as regards individual payments currently due and payable).

AG10　Physical assets (such as inventories, property, plant and equipment), leased assets and intangible assets (such as patents and trademarks) are not financial assets. Control of such physical and intangible assets creates an opportunity to generate an inflow of cash or another financial asset, but it does not give rise to a present right to receive cash or another financial asset.

AG11　Assets (such as prepaid expenses) for which the future economic benefit is the receipt of goods or services, rather than the right to receive cash or another financial asset, are not financial assets. Similarly, items such as deferred revenue and most warranty obligations are not financial liabilities because the outflow of economic benefits associated with them is the delivery of goods and services rather than a contractual obligation to pay cash or another financial asset.

AG12　Liabilities or assets that are not contractual (such as income taxes that are created as a result of statutory requirements imposed by governments) are not financial liabilities or financial assets. Accounting for income taxes is dealt with in IAS 12. Similarly, constructive obligations, as defined in IAS 37 *Provisions, Contingent Liabilities and Contingent Assets*, do not arise from contracts and are not financial liabilities.

Equity instruments

AG13　Examples of equity instruments include non-puttable ordinary shares, some puttable instruments (see paragraphs 16A and 16B), some instruments that impose on the entity an obligation to deliver to another party a pro rata share of the net assets of the entity only on liquidation (see paragraphs 16C and 16D), some types of preference shares (see paragraphs AG25 and AG26), and warrants or written call options that allow the holder to subscribe for or purchase a fixed number of non-puttable ordinary shares in the issuing entity in exchange for a fixed amount of cash or another financial asset. An entity's obligation to issue or purchase a fixed number of its own equity instruments in exchange for a fixed amount of cash or another financial asset is an equity instrument of the entity (except as stated in paragraph 22A). However, if such a contract contains an obligation for the entity to pay cash or another financial asset (other than a contract classified as equity in accordance with paragraphs 16A and 16B or paragraphs 16C and 16D), it also gives rise to a liability for the present value of the redemption amount (see paragraph AG27(a)). An issuer of non-puttable ordinary shares assumes a liability when it formally acts to make a distribution and becomes legally obliged to the shareholders to do so. This may be the case following the declaration of a dividend or when the entity is being wound up and any assets remaining after the satisfaction of liabilities become distributable to shareholders.

AG14　A purchased call option or other similar contract acquired by an entity that gives it the right to reacquire a fixed number of its own equity instruments in exchange for delivering a fixed amount of cash or another financial asset is not a financial asset of the entity (except as stated in paragraph 22A). Instead, any consideration paid for such a contract is deducted from equity.

The class of instruments that is subordinate to all other classes (paragraphs 16A(b) and 16C(b))

AG14A One of the features of paragraphs 16A and 16C is that the financial instrument is in the class of instruments that is subordinate to all other classes.

AG14B When determining whether an instrument is in the subordinate class, an entity evaluates the instrument's claim on liquidation as if it were to liquidate on the date when it classifies the instrument. An entity shall reassess the classification if there is a change in relevant circumstances. For example, if the entity issues or redeems another financial instrument, this may affect whether the instrument in question is in the class of instruments that is subordinate to all other classes.

AG14C An instrument that has a preferential right on liquidation of the entity is not an instrument with an entitlement to a pro rata share of the net assets of the entity. For example, an instrument has a preferential right on liquidation if it entitles the holder to a fixed dividend on liquidation, in addition to a share of the entity's net assets, when other instruments in the subordinate class with a right to a pro rata share of the net assets of the entity do not have the same right on liquidation.

AG14D If an entity has only one class of financial instruments, that class shall be treated as if it were subordinate to all other classes.

Total expected cash flows attributable to the instrument over the life of the instrument (paragraph 16A(e))

AG14E The total expected cash flows of the instrument over the life of the instrument must be substantially based on the profit or loss, change in the recognised net assets or fair value of the recognised and unrecognised net assets of the entity over the life of the instrument. Profit or loss and the change in the recognised net assets shall be measured in accordance with relevant IFRSs.

Transactions entered into by an instrument holder other than as owner of the entity (paragraphs 16A and 16C)

AG14F The holder of a puttable financial instrument or an instrument that imposes on the entity an obligation to deliver to another party a pro rata share of the net assets of the entity only on liquidation may enter into transactions with the entity in a role other than that of an owner. For example, an instrument holder may also be an employee of the entity. Only the cash flows and the contractual terms and conditions of the instrument that relate to the instrument holder as an owner of the entity shall be considered when assessing whether the instrument should be classified as equity under paragraph 16A or paragraph 16C.

AG14G An example is a limited partnership that has limited and general partners. Some general partners may provide a guarantee to the entity and may be remunerated for providing that guarantee. In such situations, the guarantee and the associated cash flows relate to the instrument holders in their role as guarantors and not in their roles as owners of the entity. Therefore, such a guarantee and the associated cash flows would not result in the general partners being considered subordinate to the limited partners, and would be disregarded when assessing whether the contractual terms of the limited partnership instruments and the general partnership instruments are identical.

AG14H Another example is a profit or loss sharing arrangement that allocates profit or loss to the instrument holders on the basis of services rendered or business generated during the current and previous years. Such arrangements are transactions with instrument holders in their role as non-owners and should not be considered when assessing the features listed in paragraph 16A or paragraph 16C. However, profit or loss sharing arrangements that allocate profit or loss to instrument holders based on the nominal amount of their instruments relative to others in the class represent transactions with the instrument holders in their roles as owners and should be considered when assessing the features listed in paragraph 16A or paragraph 16C.

AG14I   The cash flows and contractual terms and conditions of a transaction between the instrument holder (in the role as a non-owner) and the issuing entity must be similar to an equivalent transaction that might occur between a non-instrument holder and the issuing entity.

No other financial instrument or contract with total cash flows that substantially fixes or restricts the residual return to the instrument holder (paragraphs 16B and 16D)

AG14J   A condition for classifying as equity a financial instrument that otherwise meets the criteria in paragraph 16A or paragraph 16C is that the entity has no other financial instrument or contract that has (a) total cash flows based substantially on the profit or loss, the change in the recognised net assets or the change in the fair value of the recognised and unrecognised net assets of the entity and (b) the effect of substantially restricting or fixing the residual return. The following instruments, when entered into on normal commercial terms with unrelated parties, are unlikely to prevent instruments that otherwise meet the criteria in paragraph 16A or paragraph 16C from being classified as equity:

(a)   instruments with total cash flows substantially based on specific assets of the entity.

(b)   instruments with total cash flows based on a percentage of revenue.

(c)   contracts designed to reward individual employees for services rendered to the entity.

(d)   contracts requiring the payment of an insignificant percentage of profit for services rendered or goods provided.

Derivative financial instruments

AG15   Financial instruments include primary instruments (such as receivables, payables and equity instruments) and derivative financial instruments (such as financial options, futures and forwards, interest rate swaps and currency swaps). Derivative financial instruments meet the definition of a financial instrument and, accordingly, are within the scope of this Standard.

AG16   Derivative financial instruments create rights and obligations that have the effect of transferring between the parties to the instrument one or more of the financial risks inherent in an underlying primary financial instrument. On inception, derivative financial instruments give one party a contractual right to exchange financial assets or financial liabilities with another party under conditions that are potentially favourable, or a contractual obligation to exchange financial assets or financial liabilities with another party under conditions that are potentially unfavourable. However, they generally[4] do not result in a transfer of the underlying primary financial instrument on inception of the contract, nor does such a transfer necessarily take place on maturity of the contract. Some instruments embody both a right and an obligation to make an exchange. Because the terms of the exchange are determined on inception of the derivative instrument, as prices in financial markets change those terms may become either favourable or unfavourable.

AG17   A put or call option to exchange financial assets or financial liabilities (ie financial instruments other than an entity's own equity instruments) gives the holder a right to obtain potential future economic benefits associated with changes in the fair value of the financial instrument underlying the contract. Conversely, the writer of an option assumes an obligation to forgo potential future economic benefits or bear potential losses of economic benefits associated with changes in the fair value of the underlying financial instrument. The contractual right of the holder and obligation of the writer meet the definition of a financial asset and a financial liability, respectively. The financial instrument underlying an option contract may be any financial asset, including shares in other entities and interest-bearing instruments. An option may require the writer to issue a debt instrument, rather than transfer a financial asset, but the instrument underlying the option would constitute a financial asset of the holder if the option were exercised. The option-holder's right to exchange the financial asset under potentially favourable conditions and the writer's obligation to exchange the financial asset under potentially unfavourable conditions are distinct from the underlying financial asset to be

---

[4]   This is true of most, but not all derivatives, eg in some cross-currency interest rate swaps principal is exchanged on inception (and re-exchanged on maturity).

exchanged upon exercise of the option. The nature of the holder's right and of the writer's obligation are not affected by the likelihood that the option will be exercised.

AG18   Another example of a derivative financial instrument is a forward contract to be settled in six months' time in which one party (the purchaser) promises to deliver CU1,000,000 cash in exchange for CU1,000,000 face amount of fixed rate government bonds, and the other party (the seller) promises to deliver CU1,000,000 face amount of fixed rate government bonds in exchange for CU1,000,000 cash. During the six months, both parties have a contractual right and a contractual obligation to exchange financial instruments. If the market price of the government bonds rises above CU1,000,000, the conditions will be favourable to the purchaser and unfavourable to the seller; if the market price falls below CU1,000,000, the effect will be the opposite. The purchaser has a contractual right (a financial asset) similar to the right under a call option held and a contractual obligation (a financial liability) similar to the obligation under a put option written; the seller has a contractual right (a financial asset) similar to the right under a put option held and a contractual obligation (a financial liability) similar to the obligation under a call option written. As with options, these contractual rights and obligations constitute financial assets and financial liabilities separate and distinct from the underlying financial instruments (the bonds and cash to be exchanged). Both parties to a forward contract have an obligation to perform at the agreed time, whereas performance under an option contract occurs only if and when the holder of the option chooses to exercise it.

AG19   Many other types of derivative instruments embody a right or obligation to make a future exchange, including interest rate and currency swaps, interest rate caps, collars and floors, loan commitments, note issuance facilities and letters of credit. An interest rate swap contract may be viewed as a variation of a forward contract in which the parties agree to make a series of future exchanges of cash amounts, one amount calculated with reference to a floating interest rate and the other with reference to a fixed interest rate. Futures contracts are another variation of forward contracts, differing primarily in that the contracts are standardised and traded on an exchange.

Contracts to buy or sell non-financial items (paragraphs 8–10)

AG20   Contracts to buy or sell non-financial items do not meet the definition of a financial instrument because the contractual right of one party to receive a non-financial asset or service and the corresponding obligation of the other party do not establish a present right or obligation of either party to receive, deliver or exchange a financial asset. For example, contracts that provide for settlement only by the receipt or delivery of a non-financial item (eg an option, futures or forward contract on silver) are not financial instruments. Many commodity contracts are of this type. Some are standardised in form and traded on organised markets in much the same fashion as some derivative financial instruments. For example, a commodity futures contract may be bought and sold readily for cash because it is listed for trading on an exchange and may change hands many times. However, the parties buying and selling the contract are, in effect, trading the underlying commodity. The ability to buy or sell a commodity contract for cash, the ease with which it may be bought or sold and the possibility of negotiating a cash settlement of the obligation to receive or deliver the commodity do not alter the fundamental character of the contract in a way that creates a financial instrument. Nevertheless, some contracts to buy or sell non-financial items that can be settled net or by exchanging financial instruments, or in which the non-financial item is readily convertible to cash, are within the scope of the Standard as if they were financial instruments (see paragraph 8).

AG21   A contract that involves the receipt or delivery of physical assets does not give rise to a financial asset of one party and a financial liability of the other party unless any corresponding payment is deferred past the date on which the physical assets are transferred. Such is the case with the purchase or sale of goods on trade credit.

AG22   Some contracts are commodity-linked, but do not involve settlement through the physical receipt or delivery of a commodity. They specify settlement through cash payments that are determined according to a formula in the contract, rather than through payment of fixed amounts. For example, the principal amount of a bond may be calculated by applying the market price of oil prevailing at the maturity of the bond to a fixed quantity of oil. The principal is indexed by reference to a commodity price, but is settled only in cash. Such a contract constitutes a financial instrument.

AG23   The definition of a financial instrument also encompasses a contract that gives rise to a non-financial asset or non-financial liability in addition to a financial asset or financial liability. Such financial instruments often give one party an option to exchange a financial asset for a non-financial asset. For example, an oil-linked bond may give the holder the right to receive a stream of fixed periodic interest payments and a fixed amount of cash on maturity, with the option to exchange the principal amount for a fixed quantity of oil. The desirability of exercising this option will vary from time to time depending on the fair value of oil relative to the exchange ratio of cash for oil (the exchange price) inherent in the bond. The intentions of the bondholder concerning the exercise of the option do not affect the substance of the component assets. The financial asset of the holder and the financial liability of the issuer make the bond a financial instrument, regardless of the other types of assets and liabilities also created.

AG24   [Deleted]

Presentation

Liabilities and equity (paragraphs 15–27)

No contractual obligation to deliver cash or another financial asset (paragraphs 17–20)

AG25   Preference shares may be issued with various rights. In determining whether a preference share is a financial liability or an equity instrument, an issuer assesses the particular rights attaching to the share to determine whether it exhibits the fundamental characteristic of a financial liability. For example, a preference share that provides for redemption on a specific date or at the option of the holder contains a financial liability because the issuer has an obligation to transfer financial assets to the holder of the share. The potential inability of an issuer to satisfy an obligation to redeem a preference share when contractually required to do so, whether because of a lack of funds, a statutory restriction or insufficient profits or reserves, does not negate the obligation. An option of the issuer to redeem the shares for cash does not satisfy the definition of a financial liability because the issuer does not have a present obligation to transfer financial assets to the shareholders. In this case, redemption of the shares is solely at the discretion of the issuer. An obligation may arise, however, when the issuer of the shares exercises its option, usually by formally notifying the shareholders of an intention to redeem the shares.

AG26   When preference shares are non-redeemable, the appropriate classification is determined by the other rights that attach to them. Classification is based on an assessment of the substance of the contractual arrangements and the definitions of a financial liability and an equity instrument. When distributions to holders of the preference shares, whether cumulative or non-cumulative, are at the discretion of the issuer, the shares are equity instruments. The classification of a preference share as an equity instrument or a financial liability is not affected by, for example:

(a)   a history of making distributions;

(b)   an intention to make distributions in the future;

(c)   a possible negative impact on the price of ordinary shares of the issuer if distributions are not made (because of restrictions on paying dividends on the ordinary shares if dividends are not paid on the preference shares);

(d)   the amount of the issuer's reserves;

(e)   an issuer's expectation of a profit or loss for a period; or

(f)   an ability or inability of the issuer to influence the amount of its profit or loss for the period.

Settlement in the entity's own equity instruments (paragraphs 21–24)

AG27   The following examples illustrate how to classify different types of contracts on an entity's own equity instruments:

(a)   A contract that will be settled by the entity receiving or delivering a fixed number of its own shares for no future consideration, or exchanging a fixed number of its own shares for a fixed amount of cash or another financial asset, is an equity instrument (except as stated in paragraph 22A).

Accordingly, any consideration received or paid for such a contract is added directly to or deducted directly from equity. One example is an issued share option that gives the counterparty a right to buy a fixed number of the entity's shares for a fixed amount of cash. However, if the contract requires the entity to purchase (redeem) its own shares for cash or another financial asset at a fixed or determinable date or on demand, the entity also recognises a financial liability for the present value of the redemption amount (with the exception of instruments that have all the features and meet the conditions in paragraphs 16A and 16B or paragraphs 16C and 16D). One example is an entity's obligation under a forward contract to repurchase a fixed number of its own shares for a fixed amount of cash.

(b)   An entity's obligation to purchase its own shares for cash gives rise to a financial liability for the present value of the redemption amount even if the number of shares that the entity is obliged to repurchase is not fixed or if the obligation is conditional on the counterparty exercising a right to redeem (except as stated in paragraphs 16A and 16B or paragraphs 16C and 16D). One example of a conditional obligation is an issued option that requires the entity to repurchase its own shares for cash if the counterparty exercises the option.

(c)   A contract that will be settled in cash or another financial asset is a financial asset or financial liability even if the amount of cash or another financial asset that will be received or delivered is based on changes in the market price of the entity's own equity (except as stated in paragraphs 16A and 16B or paragraphs 16C and 16D). One example is a net cash-settled share option.

(d)   A contract that will be settled in a variable number of the entity's own shares whose value equals a fixed amount or an amount based on changes in an underlying variable (eg a commodity price) is a financial asset or a financial liability. An example is a written option to buy gold that, if exercised, is settled net in the entity's own instruments by the entity delivering as many of those instruments as are equal to the value of the option contract. Such a contract is a financial asset or financial liability even if the underlying variable is the entity's own share price rather than gold. Similarly, a contract that will be settled in a fixed number of the entity's own shares, but the rights attaching to those shares will be varied so that the settlement value equals a fixed amount or an amount based on changes in an underlying variable, is a financial asset or a financial liability.

Contingent settlement provisions (paragraph 25)

AG28   Paragraph 25 requires that if a part of a contingent settlement provision that could require settlement in cash or another financial asset (or in another way that would result in the instrument being a financial liability) is not genuine, the settlement provision does not affect the classification of a financial instrument. Thus, a contract that requires settlement in cash or a variable number of the entity's own shares only on the occurrence of an event that is extremely rare, highly abnormal and very unlikely to occur is an equity instrument. Similarly, settlement in a fixed number of an entity's own shares may be contractually precluded in circumstances that are outside the control of the entity, but if these circumstances have no genuine possibility of occurring, classification as an equity instrument is appropriate.

Treatment in consolidated financial statements

AG29   In consolidated financial statements, an entity presents non-controllng interests—ie the interests of other parties in the equity and income of its subsidiaries—in accordance with IAS 1 and IAS 27. When classifying a financial instrument (or a component of it) in consolidated financial statements, an entity considers all terms and conditions agreed between members of the group and the holders of the instrument in determining whether the group as a whole has an obligation to deliver cash or another financial asset in respect of the instrument or to settle it in a manner that results in liability classification. When a subsidiary in a group issues a financial instrument and a parent or other group entity agrees additional terms directly with the holders of the instrument (eg a guarantee), the group may not have discretion over distributions or redemption. Although the subsidiary may appropriately classify the instrument without regard to these additional terms in its individual financial statements, the effect of other agreements between members of the group and the holders of the instrument is considered in order to ensure that consolidated financial statements reflect the contracts and transactions entered into by the group as a whole. To the extent that there is such an obligation or settlement provision, the instrument (or the component of it that is subject to the obligation) is classified as a financial liability in consolidated financial statements.

AG29A Some types of instruments that impose a contractual obligation on the entity are classified as equity instruments in accordance with paragraphs 16A and 16B or paragraphs 16C and 16D. Classification in accordance with those paragraphs is an exception to the principles otherwise applied in this Standard to the classification of an instrument. This exception is not extended to the classification of non-controlling interests in the consolidated financial statements. Therefore, instruments classified as equity instruments in accordance with either paragraphs 16A and 16B or paragraphs 16C and 16D in the separate or individual financial statements that are non-controlling interests are classified as liabilities in the consolidated financial statements of the group.

Compound financial instruments (paragraphs 28–32)

AG30 Paragraph 28 applies only to issuers of non-derivative compound financial instruments. Paragraph 28 does not deal with compound financial instruments from the perspective of holders. IAS 39 deals with the separation of embedded derivatives from the perspective of holders of compound financial instruments that contain debt and equity features.

AG31 A common form of compound financial instrument is a debt instrument with an embedded conversion option, such as a bond convertible into ordinary shares of the issuer, and without any other embedded derivative features. Paragraph 28 requires the issuer of such a financial instrument to present the liability component and the equity component separately in the statement of financial position, as follows:

(a) The issuer's obligation to make scheduled payments of interest and principal is a financial liability that exists as long as the instrument is not converted. On initial recognition, the fair value of the liability component is the present value of the contractually determined stream of future cash flows discounted at the rate of interest applied at that time by the market to instruments of comparable credit status and providing substantially the same cash flows, on the same terms, but without the conversion option.

(b) The equity instrument is an embedded option to convert the liability into equity of the issuer. The fair value of the option comprises its time value and its intrinsic value, if any. This option has value on initial recognition even when it is out of the money.

AG32 On conversion of a convertible instrument at maturity, the entity derecognises the liability component and recognises it as equity. The original equity component remains as equity (although it may be transferred from one line item within equity to another). There is no gain or loss on conversion at maturity.

AG33 When an entity extinguishes a convertible instrument before maturity through an early redemption or repurchase in which the original conversion privileges are unchanged, the entity allocates the consideration paid and any transaction costs for the repurchase or redemption to the liability and equity components of the instrument at the date of the transaction. The method used in allocating the consideration paid and transaction costs to the separate components is consistent with that used in the original allocation to the separate components of the proceeds received by the entity when the convertible instrument was issued, in accordance with paragraphs 28–32.

AG34 Once the allocation of the consideration is made, any resulting gain or loss is treated in accordance with accounting principles applicable to the related component, as follows:

(a) the amount of gain or loss relating to the liability component is recognised in profit or loss; and

(b) the amount of consideration relating to the equity component is recognised in equity.

AG35 An entity may amend the terms of a convertible instrument to induce early conversion, for example by offering a more favourable conversion ratio or paying other additional consideration in the event of conversion before a specified date. The difference, at the date the terms are amended, between the fair value of the consideration the holder receives on conversion of the instrument under the revised terms and the fair value of the consideration the holder would have received under the original terms is recognised as a loss in profit or loss.

Treasury shares (paragraphs 33 and 34)

AG36   An entity's own equity instruments are not recognised as a financial asset regardless of the reason for which they are reacquired. Paragraph 33 requires an entity that reacquires its own equity instruments to deduct those equity instruments from equity. However, when an entity holds its own equity on behalf of others, eg a financial institution holding its own equity on behalf of a client, there is an agency relationship and as a result those holdings are not included in the entity's statement of financial position.

Interest, dividends, losses and gains (paragraphs 35–41)

AG37   The following example illustrates the application of paragraph 35 to a compound financial instrument. Assume that a non-cumulative preference share is mandatorily redeemable for cash in five years, but that dividends are payable at the discretion of the entity before the redemption date. Such an instrument is a compound financial instrument, with the liability component being the present value of the redemption amount. The unwinding of the discount on this component is recognised in profit or loss and classified as interest expense. Any dividends paid relate to the equity component and, accordingly, are recognised as a distribution of profit or loss. A similar treatment would apply if the redemption was not mandatory but at the option of the holder, or if the share was mandatorily convertible into a variable number of ordinary shares calculated to equal a fixed amount or an amount based on changes in an underlying variable (eg commodity). However, if any unpaid dividends are added to the redemption amount, the entire instrument is a liability. In such a case, any dividends are classified as interest expense.

Offsetting a financial asset and a financial liability (paragraphs 42–50)

AG38   To offset a financial asset and a financial liability, an entity must have a currently enforceable legal right to set off the recognised amounts. An entity may have a conditional right to set off recognised amounts, such as in a master netting agreement or in some forms of non-recourse debt, but such rights are enforceable only on the occurrence of some future event, usually a default of the counterparty. Thus, such an arrangement does not meet the conditions for offset.

AG39   The Standard does not provide special treatment for so-called 'synthetic instruments', which are groups of separate financial instruments acquired and held to emulate the characteristics of another instrument. For example, a floating rate long-term debt combined with an interest rate swap that involves receiving floating payments and making fixed payments synthesises a fixed rate long-term debt. Each of the individual financial instruments that together constitute a 'synthetic instrument' represents a contractual right or obligation with its own terms and conditions and each may be transferred or settled separately. Each financial instrument is exposed to risks that may differ from the risks to which other financial instruments are exposed. Accordingly, when one financial instrument in a 'synthetic instrument' is an asset and another is a liability, they are not offset and presented in an entity's statement of financial position on a net basis unless they meet the criteria for offsetting in paragraph 42.

Disclosure

Financial assets and financial liabilities at fair value through profit or loss (paragraph 94(f))

AG40   [Deleted]

IAS 32 – Financial Instruments: Presentation

Übersicht

	Rn
I. Regelungsgehalt	1 – 4
II. Normzweck und Anwendungsbereich	5 – 7
III. Begriffe	8 – 15
IV. Ausweis	16 – 46
1. Kassainstrumente	20 – 26
2. Derivate	27 – 33
3. Sonderfall: Kündbare Instrumente	34 – 42
4. Sonderfall: Unternehmen mit fester Lebensdauer	43 – 45
V. Hybride Finanzinstrumente	46 – 51
VI. Eigene Anteile	52 – 53
VII. Dividenden, Zinsen, Gewinne und Verluste	54 – 55
VIII. Saldierung	56 – 59
IX. Inkrafttreten und Übergangsvorschriften	60 – 65
X. IFRS für kleine und mittelgroße Unternehmen	66 – 76
XI. Ausblick	77

I. Regelungsgehalt. IAS 32 *Financial Instruments: Presentation* regelt im Wesentlichen die Abgrenzung von Eigen- und Fremdkapital eines Unternehmens für emittierte Finanzinstrumente. Daneben enthält IAS 32 auch Regelungen zur Bilanzierung von hybriden Finanzinstrumenten (zB Wandelanleihen), zum Ausweis von eigenen Anteilen im Bestand, Zinsen, Dividenden und sonstigen Gewinnen und Verlusten sowie zur Aufrechnung von finanziellen Vermögenswerten und Verbindlichkeiten. IAS 32 regelt nicht die Bewertung von emittierten Finanzinstrumenten, die als Konsequenz seiner Vorschriften als finanzielle Verbindlichkeit klassifiziert wurden. Diese ist in IAS 39 *Financial Instruments: Recognition and Measurement* bzw. künftig in IFRS 9 *Financial Instruments*[1] geregelt. Obwohl IAS 32 ursprünglich auch Angabevorschriften für Finanzinstrumente enthielt, wurde dieser Abschnitt mit der Veröffentlichung von IFRS 7 *Financial Instruments: Disclosures* gestrichen. Interpretiert wird IAS 32 durch IFRIC 2 *Members' Shares in Co-operative Entities and Similar Instruments* sowie IFRIC 19 *Extinguishing Financial Liabilities with Equity Instruments*.[2] Daneben enthält IAS 32 einige wichtige Definitionen, die für IAS 39, IFRS 7 und IFRS 9 von Bedeutung sind.

1

Die Abgrenzung zwischen Eigen- und Fremdkapital ist von Bedeutung für divese Kennzahlen in der Bilanzanalyse wie zB den Verschuldungsgrad (*leverage ratio*) eines Unternehmens oder bestimmte kapitalbezogene Kreditauflagen (*debt covenants*). Aufgrund der Bedeutung für Investoren und andere Anwender (zB Banken) liegt die Abgrenzung zwischen Eigen- und Fremdkapital regelmäßig im Fokus der Enforcement-Behörden, in Deutschland die Deutsche Prüfstelle für Rechnungslegung e.V. – DPR.[3]

2

---

1 IFRS 9 wird IAS 32 und IAS 39 phasenweise vollständig ersetzen. Momentan sind jedoch die Regeln zur Bilanzierung von Finanzinstrumenten abschließend in IAS 32 und IAS 39 geregelt.
2 Diese Interpretation wird im Abschnitt zu IAS 39 in diesem Band beschrieben.
3 Vgl. *PwC (Hrsg.)* Manual of Accounting, 7001.

Bei Ausgabe (Emission) eines Finanzinstruments muss ein Unternehmen bei erstmaligem Ansatz eine Klassifizierung des Vertrags (bzw. unter bestimmten Umständen seiner Komponenten) entweder als Fremd- oder Eigenkapital für Ausweiszwecke vornehmen. Dabei hat die Klassifizierung auf Grundlage des wirtschaftlichen Gehalts der vertraglichen Vereinbarungen zu erfolgen – die rechtliche Form bzw. Bezeichnung ist dabei nicht von Relevanz und entfaltet bestenfalls indikative Wirkung. Grundsätzlich darf ein Instrument keine vertraglichen Zahlungsverpflichtungen beinhalten, um sich als Eigenkapitalinstrument im IFRS-Abschluss zu qualifizieren. Für derivative Finanzinstrumente, welche Eigenkapitalinstrumente des Unternehmens zum Basiswert haben, gelten zusätzliche Vorschriften. Im deutschen Rechtsraum ergeben sich Unterschiede zur handelsrechtlichen Bilanzierung, insbesondere im Bereich der Personenhandelsgesellschaften, obwohl das IASB mit einer Änderung der Vorschriften in IAS 32 im Jahr 2008 die Klassifizierung der Anteile an diesem Gesellschaftstyp überarbeitete.

3 Ebenfalls von großer Bedeutung in IAS 32 sind die Vorschriften für hybride Finanzinstrumente auf Seiten des Emittenten (die Bilanzierung aus Sicht des Inhabers regelt IAS 39). Als hybride Finanzinstrumente bezeichnet man im Kontext von IAS 32 Kombinationen aus Eigen- und Fremdkapitalinstrumenten, die in einem Vertrag niedergelegt sind. Liegt ein hybrides Finanzinstrument vor, ist dieses in seine Komponenten zu trennen. Dabei erfolgt die Zerlegung nach dem Restwertverfahren, bei dem zuerst der Wert der Fremdkapitalkomponente ermittelt wird und danach, durch Subtraktion vom Gesamtwert des Instruments, der Wert der Eigenkapitalkomponente.

4 Letztendlich ist noch hervorzuheben, dass IAS 32 einen Ansatz von Eigenkapitanteilen im eigenen Bestand als Aktivposten ablehnt. Somit ist jede Rücknahme von eigenen Anteilen als Abzug vom Eigenkapital des Unternehmens zu bilanzieren.

5 **II. Normzweck und Anwendungsbereich.** Gemäß IAS 32.2 ist Zielsetzung des Standards, Prinzipien für den Ausweis von Finanzinstrumenten als Schulden oder Eigenkapital in der Bilanz des Emittenten sowie wie für die Aufrechnung von Finanzaktiva und -passiva aufzustellen. Dabei ergänzen die Vorschriften in IAS 32 diejenigen in IAS 39 und IFRS 7 (vgl. IAS 32.3).

6 Die Vorschriften in IAS 32 sind von allen Unternehmen, unabhängig von Branchenzugehörigkeit, Größe oder Rechtsform, für alle Finanzinstrumente (gemäß der Definition in IAS 32.11) anzuwenden. Dabei bestehen insgesamt fünf Ausnahmen vom Anwendungsbereich (vgl. IAS 32.4):

- Anteile an verbundenen und assoziierten Unternehmen sowie Joint Ventures, die nach den Vorschriften in IAS 27 *Consolidated and Separate Financial Statements*, IAS 28 *Investments in Associates* bzw. IAS 31 *Interests in Joint Ventures* bilanziert werden (vgl. IAS 32.4(a)). Davon ausgenommen sind diejenigen Anteile, bei denen diese Standards eine Bilanzierung nach den Vorschriften von IAS 39 zulassen. In diesen Fällen sind auch die Vorschriften von IAS 32 anzuwenden. Darüber hinaus sind die Regelungen ausnahmslos auf alle Derivate über solche Anteile anzuwenden.
- Gemäß IAS 19 *Employee Benefits* zu bilanzierende **Rechte und Pflichten eines Arbeitgebers aus Leistungsplänen** gegenüber Arbeitnehmern (vgl. IAS 32.4(b)).
- **Versicherungsverträge** (wie in IFRS 4 *Insurance Contracts* definiert; vgl. IAS 32.4(d)). Jedoch sind die Vorschriften auf eingebettete Derivate, bei denen IAS 39 eine Trennung vorsieht, anzuwenden. Hat sich der Emittent einer Finanzgarantie entschieden, die Vorschriften von IAS 39 anzuwenden, so ist IAS 32 auch hier einschlägig.

- **Finanzinstrumente mit ermessensabhängigen Überschussbeteiligungen**, die im Anwendungsbereich von IFRS 4 sind (vgl. IAS 32.4(e)). Hier ist das berichtende Unternehmen von den Regelungen in IAS 32.15-32 sowie IAS 32.AG25-35[4] befreit, muss aber alle anderen Anforderungen von IAS 32 beachten. Daneben ist der Standard auf eingebettete und nach IAS 39 abgespaltene Derivate anzuwenden.
- Finanzinstrumente, Verträge und Pflichten aus anteilsbasierten Vergütungen, auf die IFRS 2 Share-based Payment Anwendung findet (vgl. IAS 32.4(f)). Davon ausgenommen sind wiederum Verträge über bestimmte nicht-finanzielle Posten, falls die Regeln inIAS 32.8-10 diese Verträge in den Anwendungsbereich von IAS 32 bringen. Daneben sind IAS 32.33-34 auf eigene Anteile anzuwenden, die im Rahmen von Vereinbarungen über anteilsbasierte Vergütungen erworben, verkauft, emittiert oder eingezogen werden.

Der Standard ist zudem anzuwenden auf Warenterminkontrakte, die nicht in die Eigenbedarfsausnahme fallen (vgl. IAS 32.8-10 und AG20-AG24; siehe dazu die Ausführungen zu IAS 39 in diesem Band).   7

III. Begriffe. IAS 32.11 definiert sechs Termini, die nachfolgend näher erläutert werden.   8

Ein **Finanzinstrument** (*financial instrument*) ist ein **Vertrag**, der bei einer Vertragspartei einen finanziellen Vermögenswert und bei der anderen Vertragspartei eine finanzielle Verbindlichkeit bzw. ein Eigenkapitalinstrument begründet. Dingliche, immaterielle oder im Rahmen einer Leasingvereinbarung gehaltene Vermögenswerte gelten nicht als Finanzinstrumente (vgl. IAS 32.AG10), da sie kein unmittelbares Recht zum Erhalt von Zahlungsmitteln oder anderen finanziellen Vermögenswerten darstellen.[5] Wesentlich für die Erfüllung der Definition ist das **Bestehen eines Vertrags**. Gemäß IAS 32.13 bezieht sich der Begriff des „Vertrags" (bzw. „vertraglich") auf eine Vereinbarung zwischen zwei oder mehr Parteien, die **eindeutige wirtschaftliche Konsequenzen** nach sich zieht. Diesen Konsequenzen können sich die Vertragsparteien in der Regel nicht entziehen, da die Vertragsbedingungen meist **rechtlich durchsetzbar** sind. Die **Schriftform** ist für das Erfüllen der Definition eines Vertrags grundsätzlich **nicht erforderlich** (wenn auch üblich). Auch eine Kombination mehrerer Verträge, an deren Ende ein Austausch von liquiden Mitteln oder anderen finanziellen Vermögenswerten steht, stellt ein Finanzinstrument dar (vgl. IAS 32.AG7). Vermögenswerte oder Schulden, denen kein Vertragsverhältnis zu Grunde liegt, beispielsweise aus hoheitlichen Vorschriften, sind keine finanziellen Vermögenswerte oder finanziellen Verbindlichkeiten und liegen somit nicht im Anwendungsbereich von IAS 32 (vgl. IAS 32.AG12). Dies gilt zB für **Ertragsteuern** (auf die dann jedoch IAS 12 Income Taxes Anwendung findet). Falls es sich bei dem zu beurteilenden Vertrag um ein **Leasingverhältnis** handelt, so ist IAS 32 anzuwenden, wenn eine Einstufung als Finanzierungsleasingverhältnis (*finance lease*) erfolgt ist (vgl. IAS 32.AG9). Handelt es sich um ein Mietleasingverhältnis (*operating lease*), ist dieses als schwebendes Dauerschuldverhältnis aufzufassen und somit, mit Ausnahme der jeweils fälligen Zahlungen, kein Finanzinstrument (vgl. IAS 32.AG9).   9

IAS 32 betrachtet die folgenden Vermögenswerte als **finanzielle Vermögenswerte** (*financial assets*):   10
- Zahlungsmittel,
- **Eigenkapitalinstrumente** eines anderen Unternehmens,
- Vertragliche Rechte zum **Erhalt** von Zahlungsmitteln oder anderen finanziellen Vermögenswerten von einem anderen Unternehmen bzw. zum **Tausch** von finanziellen Vermögenswerten oder finanziellen Verbindlichkeiten zu möglicherweise vorteilhaften Bedingungen,

---

4   Diese Rn regeln die Trennung nach Eigen- und Fremdkapital.
5   Finanzinstrumente generieren aus sich heraus Zahlungsmittel bzw. andere finanzielle Vermögenswerte. Bei ihnen ist somit kein unmittelbarer Wertschöpfungsprozess notwendig wie zB bei einer Maschine.

- Verträge, die in eigenen Anteilen des Unternehmens erfüllt werden (können) und im Falle von Kassainstrumenten den Erhalt einer variablen Anzahl von eigenen Anteilen vorsehen. Bei derivativen Finanzinstrumenten muss mindestens eine der Komponenten „Gegenleistung" oder „Anzahl eigener Anteile" variabel sein, damit eine Klassifizierung als finanzieller Vermögenswert in Betracht kommt. Kündbare Instrumente iSv. IAS 32.16A und 16B, Anteile an Unternehmen mit begrenzter Lebensdauer iSv. IAS 32.16C und 16D sowie Verträge über den künftigen Erhalt oder die Abgabe von eigenen Anteilen stellen für die Zwecke dieser Abgrenzung keine eigenen Anteile dar.

Daneben stellen geleistete Anzahlungen keine finanziellen Vermögenswerte dar, weil deren zukünftiger Nutzen im Erhalt von Gütern oder Dienstleistungen liegt und regelmäßig nicht im Erhalt von Zahlungsmitteln oder finanziellen Vermögenswerten (vgl. IAS 32.AG11).

11   Die Definition einer **finanziellen Verbindlichkeit** (*financial liability*) ist i.W. spiegelbildlich zur Begriffsabgrenzung eines finanziellen Vermögenswerts. Als Ausnahme zu der Definition stellen Instrumente, die vollständig entweder die Bedingung in IAS 32.16A und 16B oder IAS 32.16C und 16D erfüllen, gewillkürte Eigenkapitalinstrumente dar, obwohl sie die Definition einer finanziellen Verbindlichkeit erfüllen. Des Weiteren hat das IASB im Oktober 2009 eine Änderung an IAS 32 vorgenommen, die Rechte, Optionen und Bezugsrechte zum Erhalt einer festen Anzahl eigener Eigenkapitalinstrumente gegen einen festen Betrag in beliebiger Währung betrifft und diese zu Eigenkapital willkürt, falls diese Instrumente allen derzeitigen Anteilsnehmern in derselben Klasse von nicht-derivativen Eigenkapitalinstrumenten offeriert werden.[6] Ursprünglich wurden solche Derivate als Fremdkapital klassifiziert, wenn die Vertragswährung von der funktionalen Währung des berichtenden Unternehmens abwich.[7]

12   Ein **Eigenkapitalinstrument** (equity instrument) ist ein Vertrag, der einen Anspruch auf das Residualvermögen eines Unternehmens begründet, also einen Anspruch auf das Nettoreinvermögen (Vermögenswerte abzüglich Schulden). Auch wenn IAS 32 Eigenkapital als Restgröße definiert, muss man diese Definition im Kontext der Definitionen eines finanziellen Vermögenswerts und insbesondere einer finanziellen Verbindlichkeit sehen. Nur ein Finanzinstrument, das definitionsgemäß weder ein finanzieller Vermögenswert noch eine finanzielle Verbindlichkeit darstellt, kann als Eigenkapitalinstrument klassifiziert werden (und somit im Eigenkapital ausgewiesen werden). Somit ist die Definition eines Eigenkapitalinstruments für sich genommen bedeutungslos für die Anwendung von IAS 32, hilft aber bei der Auslegung der Vorschriften.

13   Der **beizulegende Zeitwert** (fair value) ist der Betrag, zu dem zwischen sachverständigen, vertragswilligen und voneinander unabhängigen Geschäftspartnern ein Vermögenswert getauscht oder eine Schuld beglichen werden könnte. Dabei ist festzuhalten, dass es sich beim beizulegenden Zeitwert um ein **Bewertungskonzept** handelt und nicht um einen **konkreten Wert**. Diesem Bewertungskonzept liegt eine hypothetische Transaktion zum Bewertungsstichtag zugrunde. Dabei ist der Wertbegriff des beizulegenden Zeitwerts in den IFRS regelmäßig als sog. *exit price* ausgestaltet,[8] der eine Veräußerung eines Vermögenswerts bzw. die Übertragung einer Schuld an einen Dritten als Grundlage für die Bewertung heranzieht.

14   **Kündbare Instrumente** sind Finanzinstrumente, die vom Inhaber gegen Übertragung von Zahlungsmitteln oder anderen finanziellen Vermögenswerten an den Emittenten zurückgegeben werden können (also eine eingebettete Put-Option besitzen). Daneben umfasst die Definition auch Finanzinstrumente, die eine automatische Ausübung des Kündigungsrechts bei Eintritt eines unsicheren zukünftigen Ereignisses oder dem Tod bzw. der Verrentung des Inhabers vorsehen. Obwohl solche kündbaren

---

6   Vgl. *Deloitte (Hrsg.)* iGAAP, 247ff.
7   Vgl. IFRS Update April 2005, 2.
8   Das IASB Projekt *Fair Value Measurement*, das zum Ziel hat, die Bewertungsvorschriften für beizulegende Zeitwerte zu bündeln, postuliert ebenfalls ein *exit price*-Konzept.

Instrumente aufgrund der inhärenten Zahlungsverpflichtung des emittierenden Unternehmens die Definition eines Eigenkapitalinstruments iSv. IAS 32.16 nicht erfüllen, stellen sie aufgrund einer Änderung der ursprünglichen Fassung von IAS 32 im Jahr 2008 nunmehr unter bestimmten Voraussetzungen gewillkürtes Eigenkapital für Ausweis- und Bewertungszwecke nach IFRS dar.

Daneben werden die bestehenden Definitionen aus IAS 39 für 16 weitere Begriffe übernommen (vgl. IAS 32.12):

- Fortgeführte Anschaffungskosten eines finanziellen Vermögenswerts oder einer finanziellen Verbindlichkeit (*amortised cost of a financial asset or financial liability*),
- Ausbuchung (*derecognition*),
- Derivat (*derivative*),
- Effektivzinsmethode (*effective interest method*),
- Finanzieller Vermögenswert oder finanzielle Verbindlichkeit, die erfolgswirksam zum beizulegenden Zeitwert bewertet wird (*financial asset or financial liability at fair value through profit or loss*),
- Finanzgarantie (*financial guarantee contract*),
- Feste Verpflichtung (*firm commitment*),
- Geplante Transaktion (*forecast transaction*);
- Wirksamkeit eines Sicherungsgeschäfts (*hedge effectiveness*),
- Gesichertes Grundgeschäft (*hedged item*),
- Sicherungsinstrument (*hedging instrument*),
- Bis zur Endfälligkeit zu haltende Finanzinvestitionen (*held-to-maturity investments*),
- Kredite und Forderungen (*loans and receivables*),
- Marktüblicher Kauf oder Verkauf (*regular way purchase or sale*),
- Transaktionskosten (*transaction costs*).

Der im Standard verwendete Begriff „Unternehmen" umfasst sämtliche Einzelpersonen, Personengesellschaften, Kapitalgesellschaften, Treuhänder und öffentliche Institutionen (vgl. IAS 32.14). 15

IV. Ausweis. IAS 32.15-27 regeln die Abgrenzung von Eigen- und Fremdkapitalinstrumenten für Ausweiszwecke. Die Vorschriften werden durch die Anwendungsleitlinien IAS 32.AG13-14J sowie AG25-29A ergänzt und erläutert. 16

Gemäß IAS 32.15 ist ein Finanzinstrument zum Zeitpunkt des erstmaligen Ansatzes entweder als finanzielle Verbindlichkeit (also Fremdkapital) oder Eigenkapital einzustufen und entsprechend in der Bilanz auszuweisen. Diese Klassifizierung hat neben einer Ausweiskonsequenz auch Bewertungskonsequenzen, da finanzielle Verbindlichkeiten in den Anwendungsbereich von IAS 39 gelangen und somit einer regelmäßigen Folgebewertung zu fortgeführten Anschaffungskosten bzw. zum beizulegenden Zeitwert unterliegen, während bei Verbleib im Anwendungsbereich von IAS 32 keine Folgebewertung stattfindet. Bei Eigenkapitalderivaten kommt auch ein Ausweis als finanzieller Vermögenswert in Betracht (bei positivem beizulegendem Zeitwert). Die Beurteilung wird im Zeitpunkt des erstmaligen Ansatzes vorgenommen und nachträglich nicht mehr revidiert, es sein denn, die vertraglichen Bedingungen werden substanziell geändert bzw. in den Anwendungsfällen von IAS 39.16A-D kommt es zu einer Änderung der Rahmenbedingungen. 17

Obwohl bei der Beurteilung eines emittierten Finanzinstruments die Vertragsbedingungen eine herausragende Bedeutung einnehmen (bestimmen sie doch letztendlich die aus einem Instrument ggf. resultierende Verpflichtung zur Zahlung/Übertragung anderer Finanzinstrumente), ist immer primär auf den **wirtschaftlichen Gehalt** des Vertrags abzustellen (vgl. IAS 32.18). Somit ist die Bezeichnung oder juristische Einstufung ohne Relevanz für den bilanziellen Ausweis. Entscheidendes Kriterium für die 18

Abgrenzung zwischen Eigen- und Fremdkapital ist das (Nicht-)Bestehen einer Zahlungsverpflichtung (bzw. Pflicht zur Übertragung von finanziellen Vermögenswerten) des Emittenten – diese kann auch bedingter Natur sein. Dabei sind folgende Sachverhalte unbeachtlich (vgl. IAS 32.AG26):

- die Vornahme von Ausschüttungen in der Vergangenheit,
- die Absicht, künftig Ausschüttungen vorzunehmen,
- eine mögliche nachteilige Auswirkung auf den Kurs der Stammaktien des Emittenten, falls keine Ausschüttungen vorgenommen werden (aufgrund von Beschränkungen hinsichtlich der Zahlung von Dividenden auf Stammaktien, wenn keine Dividenden auf Vorzugsaktien gezahlt werden),
- die Höhe der Rücklagen des Emittenten,
- eine Gewinn- oder Verlusterwartung des Emittenten für eine Berichtsperiode oder
- die Fähigkeit oder Unfähigkeit des Emittenten, die Höhe seines Gewinns oder Verlusts zu beeinflussen.

Für Derivate gibt es weiterführende Vorschriften (s.u.). Daneben sind die Ausnahmen in IAS 32.16A-D zu beachten.

19   Nachfolgend werden die Vorschriften in IAS 32 für Kassainstrumente, Derivate sowie die Sonderfälle „Kündbare Instrumente" und „Unternehmen mit fester Lebensdauer" dargestellt.

20   **1. Kassainstrumente.** Bei einem Kassainstrument (zB aufgenommenes Darlehen) ist für die Einstufung als Eigen- oder Fremdkapital für Zwecke der IFRS entscheidend, ob eine **vertragliche Verpflichtung des Emittenten zur Übertragung flüssiger Mittel bzw. anderer finanzieller Vermögenswerte** besteht. Dabei müssen Zahlungen nicht *ex ante* ausgeschlossen sein, sie müssen jedoch im Ermessen des Unternehmens stehen. Deutlich wird dies am Beispiel der klassischen Aktie, wo auf Beschluss der Hauptversammlung eine Ausschüttung (also eine Auszahlung) innerhalb des gesetzlichen Rahmens vorgenommen werden kann, falls keine besonderen Vertragsklauseln bestehen. Solche Aktien stellen Eigenkapital iSv. IAS 32 dar, da keine vertragliche Verpflichtung zur Zahlung bzw. Übertragung finanzieller Vermögenswerte besteht.[9] Entsteht jedoch die Verpflichtung durch Ausübung eines Rechts des Inhabers des Instruments, dann liegt ein Ressourcenabfluss nicht im Ermessen des Emittenten und das Instrument ist als finanzielle Verbindlichkeit zu klassifizieren (vgl. IAS 32.19(b)). Bei der Beurteilung ist es nicht von Bedeutung, ob ein ökonomischer Zwang besteht, eine Zahlung bzw. eine Übertragung von finanziellen Vermögenswerten vorzunehmen (sog. *economic compulsion*), falls sich aus dem Vertrag selbst keine Auszahlungspflicht ergibt. Diese Auffassung hat das IFRIC in einer Agendaentscheidung bestätigt.[10] Dabei stellt das IFRIC klar, dass eine vertragliche Zahlungsverpflichtung entweder direkt oder indirekt festgelegt sein kann – jedoch muss sich die Verpflichtung zwingend aus dem zugrundeliegenden Vertragsverhältnis ergeben.

Beispielhaft sei hier eine ewig laufende Anleihe genannt, die keine Auszahlungspflicht von Zinsen vorsieht, die nicht gezahlten Zinsen jedoch kumuliert und ein Emittentenkündigungsrecht alle drei Jahre einräumt. Bei Nichtausübung erfolgt jedoch eine Zinserhöhung von jeweils 10%. Wegen der fehlenden vertraglichen Auszahlungspflicht sehen die IFRS einen Ausweis als Eigenkapital vor, obwohl die Zinssprungklausel (*step up clause*) den Emittenten wirtschaftlich in der ganz überwiegenden Anzahl der Fälle dazu zwingen wird, die Anleihe zu tilgen. Die Wahrscheinlichkeit der Ausübung des Kündigungsrechts ist hierbei für die Beurteilung ohne Belang.

21   Bedingte Erfüllungsvereinbarungen (sog. *contingent settlement provisions*) führen idR. zu einem Fremdkapitalausweis, da die Zahlungsverpflichtung nicht im Ermessen des Unternehmens oder der Gegenpartei steht (vgl. IAS 32.25). Beispiele für solche bedingten Erfüllungsvereinbarungen sind:

- Entwicklung eines Aktien- oder Rohstoffindex,

---

9   Vgl. *KPMG (Hrsg.)* Insights, Rn 3.11.80.20.
10   Vgl. IFRIC Update Mai 2006, 5.

- Entwicklung eines Verbraucherpreisindex,
- Änderungen in den steuerlichen Rahmenbedingungen,
- Künftiger Umsatz des Emittenten,
- Künftiges Jahresergebnis des Emittenten,
- Künftiger Verschuldungsgrad

Jedoch regelt IAS 32.25 auch drei **Ausnahmen** von der Anwendbarkeit der Vorschrift. Die erste bezieht sich auf den materiellen Gehalt einer solchen Vereinbarung. Falls diese wirklichkeitsfremd (*not genuine*) ist, dann ist die Klausel nicht zu berücksichtigen (vgl. IAS 32.25(a)). Der IASB sieht eine Klausel dann als wirklichkeitsfremd an, wenn der Eintritt der Bedingung extrem selten, höchst ungewöhnlich und sehr unwahrscheinlich ist (vgl. IAS 32.AG28). Aus der Einschätzung der Wahrscheinlichkeit lässt sich jedoch keine Analogie auf andere Sachverhalte ableiten. Dabei ist insbesondere auf die Eintrittswahrscheinlichkeit der Bedingung abzustellen, mithin greift diese Regelung nur in sehr seltenen Fällen (Beispiel: Die Bedingung sieht eine Zahlung für den Fall vor, dass der Mond in den nächsten fünf Jahren auf die Erde fällt). Des Weiteren ist eine Verpflichtung zur Übertragung von Zahlungsmitteln oder anderen finanziellen Vermögenswerten für die Klassifizierung als Eigenkapital unschädlich, falls sie sich nur im Falle der Liquidation des Unternehmenes (jedoch nicht bei Insolvenz, da diese nicht zwingend zur Beendigung des Unternehmens führt) ergibt (vgl. IAS 32.25(b)). Zudem werden kündbare Instrumente iSv. IAS 32.16A und 16B von den Vorschriften zu bedingten Erfüllungsvereinbarungen ausgenommen (vgl. IAS 32.25(c)).

Des Weiteren ist für die Beurteilung unerheblich, ob der Emittent seinen vertraglichen Verpflichtungen nachkommen kann (vgl. IAS 32.19). Als Beispiele nennt der Standard das Nichtvorhandensein von Devisen zur Tilgung einer finanziellen Verbindlichkeit in fremder Währung oder die Notwendigkeit zur Einholung einer behördlichen Genehmigung zur Übertragung von Zahlungsmitteln. Hier wird wiederum deutlich, dass die Vertragskonditionen das dominierende Element in der Beurteilung sind, denn auch hier steht die vertragliche Pflicht zur Auskehrung dem Grunde nach nicht in Frage. Von den Vorgaben in IAS 32.19 sind kündbare Instrumente iSv. IAS 32.16A und 16B und von Unternehmen mit begrenzter Lebensdauer emittierte Instrumente iSv. IAS 32.16C und 16D ausgenommen.

22

Auch **implizite Auszahlungsverpflichtungen** sind in die Abgrenzungsentscheidung einzubeziehen. IAS 32.20 nennt hierzu zwei Beispiele:

23

- Ein Finanzinstrument kann eine nicht-finanzielle Verpflichtung enthalten, die nur dann erfüllt werden muss, wenn das Unternehmen keine Ausschüttungen vornimmt oder das Instrument nicht zurücknimmt. Wenn ein Unternehmen also die Übertragung von Zahlungsmitteln oder finanziellen Vermögenswerten nur durch Erfüllung der nicht-finanziellen Verpflichtung vermeiden kann, dann stellt das Finanzinstrument eine finanzielle Verbindlichkeit dar.
- Ein Finanzinstrument räumt bei Fälligkeit ein Wahlrecht ein, es entweder in Zahlungsmitteln oder anderen finanziellen Vermögenswerten oder in eigenen Anteilen zu erfüllen. Dabei wird der Wert der zu liefernden eigenen Anteile so ermittelt, dass er deutlich über der Baralternative liegt. Auch hier liegt nach Ansicht des IASB eine finanzielle Verbindlichkeit vor, da die Erfüllung immer in Zahlungsmitteln oder anderen finanziellen Vermögenswerten erfolgen wird.

Umgekehrt kann sich implizit auch eine Verneinung einer Zahlungsverpflichtung ergeben, wenn Satzung oder Gesetz einen Transfer von Zahlungsmitteln oder anderen finanziellen Vermögenswerten beschränken oder untersagen. So kann das Gesetz das Vorhalten eines bestimmten Mindestkapitals vorsehen und eine Erfüllung des Instruments würde zur Unterschreitung des Mindestkapitals führen (vgl. auch IFRIC 2). Hier ist eine Einzelfallprüfung angezeigt. Es sei darauf hingewiesen, dass mangelnde Liquidität eine Einstufung als Fremdkapital nicht verhindert.

24

25   Kassainstrumente, die eine **Erfüllung in eigenen Eigenkapitalinstrumenten** vorsehen, sind nur dann als Eigenkapital nach IAS 32 zu klassifizieren, wenn sie keine vertragliche Verpflichtung zur Erfüllung in einer variablen Anzahl an eigenen Eigenkapitalinstrumenten enthalten. Mithin qualifizieren sich also nur solche Instrumente, die ein festes Umtauschverhältnis vorsehen. Geleistete oder empfangene Leistungen im Kontrahierungszeitpunkt sind dabei unmittelbar und ohne Erfolgswirkung im Eigenkapital zu erfassen (vgl. IAS 32.21 und AG27(a)).

26   Für die typischen deutschen Gesellschaftsformen lässt sich die tendenzielle Einstufung als Fremd- oder Eigenkapital wie folgt darstellen – jedoch ist immer für den Einzelfall zu prüfen, ob die Tendenzaussage zutrifft:

Gesellschaftsform	Tendenzielle Einstufung	Bemerkung
Aktiengesellschaft (AG)	Eigenkapital	Gilt für Grundkapital, Kapitalrücklage, Gewinnrücklagen, Gewinnvortrag und Jahresüberschuss. Bei Vorzugsaktien kann sich eine Verbindlichkeit iHd. Barwerts der erwarteten Vorzugsdividenden ergeben[11]
Europäische Aktiengesellschaft (SE)	Eigenkapital	Gilt für Grundkapital, Kapitalrücklage, Gewinnrücklagen, Gewinnvortrag und Jahresüberschuss
Kommanditgesellschaft auf Aktien (KGaA)	Kommanditkapital in Aktien: Eigenkapital Anderes Kommanditkapital sowie Komplementärkapital: EK/FK	Anderes Kommanditkapital sowie Komplementärkapital muss auf die Vorschriften in IAS 32.16A und 16B hin untersucht werden
Gesellschaft mit beschränkter Haftung (GmbH)	Stammkapital: EK	
Genossenschaft (eG)	Geschäftsguthaben: FK Rücklagen: EK	
Personenhandelsgesellschaften (OHG, KG)	EK/FK	Bei Erfüllung der Kriterien in IAS 32.16A und 16B: EK Bei Nichterfüllung der Kriterien in IAS 32.16A und 16B: FK

27   **2. Derivate.** Die Regelungen zum Ausweis von derivativen Finanzinstrumenten (Derivaten) als Fremd- oder Eigenkapital, deren Basiswert (*underlying*) eigene Anteile sind, gestalten sich komplex und sind sicherlich auch von Missbrauchsüberlegungen getrieben, da bei Einstufung als Eigenkapitalinstrument kein Aufwand aus der Folgebewertung entstehen kann. Auf Konzernebene gilt zu beachten, dass solche Derivate auch Derivate über Anteile von Tochterunternehmen umfassen.[12]

---

11   Vgl. *KPMG (Hrsg.)* Eigenkapital vs Fremdkapital nach IFRS, 77ff.
12   Vgl. *Deloitte (Hrsg.)* iGAAP, 165.

Grundsätzlich kommt eine Einwertung eines Eigenkapitalderivats als Eigenkapital nur dann infrage, wenn die Erfüllung durch Lieferung (Erhalt) einer **festen** Anzahl eigener Eigenkapitalinstrumente erfolgt und die Gegenleistung im Erhalt (oder in der Zahlung) eines **festen** Betrags an Geldmitteln oder einem anderen finanziellen Vermögenswert besteht (vgl. IAS 32.16). Dabei ist bei der Analyse, ob es sich um einen festen Betrag handelt, grundsätzlich von der funktionalen Währung des Berichtsunternehmens iSv. IAS 21 auszugehen. Dh sollte die Vertragswährung ungleich der funktionalen Berichtswährung sein, scheidet eine Klassifizierung als Eigenkapital aus. Jedoch hat das IASB diese Regelung im Oktober 2009 abgeändert, so dass bestimmte Bezugsrechte diese Regelung nicht zu erfüllen brauchen, falls die Rechte anteilsproportional für eine Klasse von Eigenkapitalinstrumenten emittiert an die bisherigen Anteilseigner werden (vgl. IAS 32.11(b)(ii) idF. vom Oktober 2009). Eine analoge Anwendung auf andere Sachverhalte ist nicht zulässig.

Im Fall der Einstufung eines Eigenkapitalderivats als Eigenkapital wird eine eventuell erhaltene Prämie als Eigenkapitalerhöhung bilanziert, eine gezahlte als Eigenkapitalherabsetzung. In der Folge finden Änderungen im beizulegenden Zeitwert keinen Niederschlag in der Bilanz oder GuV – damit wird hier vom sonst üblichen Gebot der Zeitwertbilanzierung von Derivaten abgewichen. Dies ist aber nur konsequent, da Eigenkapital als Restgröße definiert ist und somit selbst keiner Bewertung unterworfen ist.

Eine **Ausnahme** vom Grundsatz, dass Derivate in ihrer Gesamtheit entweder Eigenkapital oder einen finanziellen Vermögenswert oder eine Schuld darstellen, stellt die Bilanzierung folgender Derivatetypen dar: 28

- Geschriebener Terminverkaufskontrakt über eigene Eigenkapitalinstrumente ohne Erfüllungsalternativen.
- Geschriebener Terminverkaufskontrakt über eigene Eigenkapitalinstrumente mit Erfüllungsalternativen, wobei eine der Alternativen die Erfüllung durch Lieferung der eigenen Eigenkapitalinstrumente ist.
- Geschriebene Verkaufsoption über eigene Eigenkapitalinstrumente ohne Erfüllungsalternativen.
- Geschriebene Verkaufsoption über eigene Eigenkapitalinstrumente mit Erfüllungsalternativen, wobei eine der Alternativen die Erfüllung durch Lieferung der eigenen Eigenkapitalinstrumente ist.

Für die o.g. Instrumente ist in Höhe des Barwerts der impliziten Verpflichtung eine finanzielle Verbindlichkeit anzusetzen, welche gemäß den Vorschriften von IAS 39 zu bewerten ist. Die Gegenbuchung erfolgt im Eigenkapital (vgl. IAS 32.23). Bilanziell stellt sich damit der Erwerb von Anteilen als bereits vollzogen dar.[13] Daher wird oftmals von einer synthetischen Verbindlichkeit gesprochen (vgl. IAS 32. DO1).[14]

Sieht ein derivatives Finanzinstrument **Erfüllungsalternativen** für eine der Vertragsparteien vor (zB   29 Nettoerfüllung in bar oder Lieferung der eigenen Anteile), dann ist das gesamte Instrument als finanzieller Vermögenswert oder finanzielle Verbindlichkeit zu klassifizieren (vgl. IAS 32.26). Davon ausgenommen sind Verträge, bei denen alle Erfüllungsalternativen zu einer Eigenkapitalklassifizierung führen würden.

Falls ein Derivat nicht als Eigenkapitalinstrument iSv. IAS 32 klassifiziert wird, ist eine Bilanzierung   30 nach den Vorschriften von IAS 39 angezeigt, was idR. eine erfolgswirksame Bewertung zum beizulegenden Zeitwert nach sich zieht.

---

13   Vgl. *Deloitte (Hrsg.)* iGAAP, 235.
14   Vgl. *KPMG (Hrsg.)* Eigenkapital vs Fremdkapital nach IFRS, 38.

31   **Beispiel**

Ein Unternehmen erwirbt am 10. März 201X 500 Kaufoptionen über seine eigenen Aktien. Die funktionale Währung des Unternehmens sei mit der Vertragswährung identisch. Der Ausübungspreis beträgt € 30 je Aktie. Es handelt sich um eine Option europäischen Typs, deren Fälligkeitszeitpunkt der 10. Oktober 201X ist. Bei Ausübung findet eine physische Lieferung der Anteile gegen Leistung des Ausübungspreises statt.

Es handelt sich um ein Derivat über eigene Eigenkapitalinstrumente, welches die Bedingungen in IAS 32.16(b) erfüllt. Damit ist ein Ausweis als Eigenkapital nach IFRS angezeigt.

32   **Beispiel**

Ein Unternehmen erwirbt am 10. März 201X 500 Kaufoptionen über seine eigenen Aktien. Die funktionale Währung des Unternehmens sei mit der Vertragswährung identisch. Der Ausübungspreis beträgt € 30 je Aktie. Es handelt sich um eine Option europäischen Typs, deren Fälligkeitszeitpunkt der 10. Oktober 201X ist. Bei Ausübung findet eine Nettoerfüllung durch Zahlung des inneren Werts der Option statt.

Es handelt sich um ein Derivat über eigene Eigenkapitalinstrumente, welches die Bedingungen in IAS 32.16(b) nicht erfüllt. Damit ist ein Ausweis als Fremdkapital nach IFRS angezeigt. Für Bewertungszwecke ist IAS 39 einschlägig, was eine erfolgswirksame Folgebewertung zum beizulegenden Zeitwert nach sich zieht.

33   **Beispiel**

Ein Unternehmen schreibt am 10. März 201X 500 Verkaufsoptionen über seine eigenen Aktien. Die funktionale Währung des Unternehmens sei mit der Vertragswährung identisch. Der Ausübungspreis beträgt 30 EUR je Aktie. Es handelt sich um eine Option europäischen Typs, deren Fälligkeitszeitpunkt der 10. Oktober 201X ist. Bei Ausübung findet eine physische Lieferung der Anteile gegen Leistung des Ausübungspreises statt.

Es handelt sich um ein Derivat über eigene Eigenkapitalinstrumente iSv. IAS 32.23. Es ist somit eine finanzielle Verbindlichkeit in Höhe des Barwerts des Glattstellungsbetrags zu erfassen, wobei die Gegenbuchung im Eigenkapital erfolgt. In der Folge ist die finanzielle Verbindlichkeit gemäß den Vorschriften in IAS 39 zu bilanzieren.

34   **3. Sonderfall: Kündbare Instrumente.** In Deutschland führten die Vorschriften in IAS 32 insbesondere bei **Personenhandelsgesellschaften** zu dem Phänomen, dass diese kein Eigenkapital nach IFRS ausweisen konnten, da die zugrundeliegenden Verträge idR. ein nicht ausschließbares Kündigungsrecht des Gesellschafters vorsehen. Dies hat nicht nur Konsequenzen für den Ausweis der Gesellschafteranteile in der Bilanz – durch die Klassifizierung als finanzielle Verbindlichkeit gelangen diese auch in den Anwendungsbereich von IAS 39 und sind fortlaufend zu bewerten. Da der Rückzahlungsbetrag mit dem Unternehmenserfolg schwankt, hilft auch nicht die Bilanzierung zu fortgeführten Anschaffungskosten, weil IAS 39.49 bei kündbaren Instrumenten einen Ansatz mit dem (ggf. diskutierten) Rückzahlungsbetrag zum frühestmöglichen Kündigungszeitpunkt vorsieht. Auch in anderen Ländern ergaben sich vergleichbare Probleme und das IASB sah sich mit steigender Kritik an den damals geltenden Regelungen konfrontiert.

35   Das IASB hat diese Kritik zum Anlass genommen, die Vorschriften in IAS 32 zu kündbaren Instrumenten zu überarbeiten. Im Februar 2008 wurden dann Änderungen an IAS 32 veröffentlicht, die auch bei kündbaren Instrumenten unter eng definierten Umständen einen Eigenkapitalausweis ermöglichen – es handelt sich hier ganz klar um eine Ausnahme, da kündbare Instrumente die Definition einer finanziellen Verbindlichkeit erfüllen. Der zugrundeliegende Gedanke der Regelung ist der ansonsten

bestehende Eigenkapitalcharakter des Instruments, wenn man das Kündigungsrecht ausklammert. Die Ausnahme iF. einer Willkürung zu Eigenkapital gilt, wenn kumulativ fünf Bedingungen erfüllt werden (vgl. IAS 32.16A):

(a) Das Instrument sichert dem Inhaber einen anteiligen Anspruch auf das Reinvermögen des Unternehmens im Falle der Liquidation zu.

(b) Das Instrument gehört der nachrangigsten Klasse von Instrumenten an, dh das Instrument wird im Falle der Abwicklung nicht vorrangig bedient.

(c) Alle Instrumente der Klasse weisen dieselben Ausstattungsmerkmale auf.

(d) Es bestehen mit Ausnahme der Verpflichtung bei Kündigung keine weiteren Verpflichtungen zur Zahlung, zur Übertragung von finanziellen Vermögenswerten, zum Tausch von Finanzinstrumenten unter potenziell nachteiligen Bedingungen oder zur Erfüllung in eigenen Anteilen.

(e) Die Summe aller aus dem Instrument erwarteten zukünftigen Zahlungen entspricht im Wesentlichen der Ergebnisentwicklung des Unternehmens, der Veränderung im bilanzierten Reinvermögen oder dem Zeitwert des bilanzierten und nicht-bilanzierten Reinvermögens.

Die hier genannten Bedingungen werden nachfolgend erörtert.

a) Anspruch auf das Reinvermögen des Unternehmens im Falle der Liquidation. Das kündbare Instrument muss einen beteiligungsproportionalen Anspruch auf das Reinvermögen für den Fall einräumen, dass das Unternehmen liquidiert wird (vgl. IAS 32.16A(a)). Dabei ist der beteiligungsproportionale Anspruch auf folgende Weise zu ermitteln: **36**

$$\textit{Nettoreinvermögen des Unternehmens bei Liquidation} \quad \times \quad \frac{\textit{Anzahl der durch den Kapitalgeber gehaltenen Anteile}}{\textit{Gesamtanzahl der Anteile}}$$

Der Referenzpunkt ist hier idR. das vereinbarte Kapital (also geleistete und noch ausstehende Einlagen). Weitere bestehende Ansprüche des Gesellschafters sind hier nicht zu berücksichtigen. Dabei sind auch weitere Zahlungsansprüche eines Gesellschafters aus anderen Verträgen, die sich nicht aus der Kapitalgeberstellung ergeben, für die Beurteilung nicht relevant (z.B. Arbeitsverträge). Dies ist im deutschen Rechtsraum etwa für die Kommanditgesellschaft einschlägig. Hier kommt das IASB zum Schluss, dass der zusätzliche Vergütungsanspruch des Komplementärs im Vergleich zum Kommanditisten sich aus der zusätzlichen Übernahme der unbegrenzten Haftung ergibt und somit nicht in die Evaluierung der Proportionalität einbezogen werden sollte (vgl. IAS 32.AG14G). Die vorrangige Bedienung eines Kapitalanteils im Falle der Liquidation ist hingegen schädlich für einen Eigenkapitalausweis (vgl. IAS 32.AG14C).

b) Zugehörigkeit zur nachrangigsten Kapitalklasse. Des Weiteren muss das zu beurteilende Instrument der nachrangigsten Kapitalklasse des Unternehmens angehören (vgl. IAS 32.16A(b)(i)). Relevant ist hierbei der Rang auf Basis einer angenommenen Abwicklung zum Bilanzstichtag. Dabei darf zuvor keine Umwandlung notwendig sein, um in die nachrangigste Kapitalklasse zu gelangen (vgl. IAS 32.16A(b)(ii)).   **37**

c) Gleiche Ausstattungsmerkmale. Daneben müssen alle Instrumente in der nachrangigsten Klasse die gleichen (*identical*) Ausstattungsmerkmale aufweisen (vgl. IAS 32.16A(c)). Die hM. in Deutschland geht hier davon aus, dass bei der Betrachtung ausschließlich auf die Vertragsteile abgestellt werden soll, welche die Beteiligung am Erfolg bzw. Liquidationsüberschuss regeln – reine Informationsrechte können somit aus der Analyse ausgeklammert werden. Diese müssen dann jedoch in der Tat identisch sein, es genügt nicht, dass die Ausstattungsmerkmale „vergleichbar" oder „ähnlich" sind.   **38**

39   **d) Keine weiteren Zahlungsverpflichtungen.** Als viertes Kriterium dürfen sich aus dem Instrument, mit Ausnahme der Rückzahlungsverpflichtung bei Rückgabe, keine weiteren Zahlungsverpflichtungen ergeben (vgl. IAS 32.16A(d)). Davon ausgenommen sind jedoch Zahlungsansprüche, die sich nicht aus der Gesellschafterstellung heraus ergeben und einem Drittvergleich standhalten (vgl. IAS 32.AG14I). Es besteht gemäß IAS 32.AG14J für folgende Vertragstypen die Einstandsvermutung, dass diese für eine Eigenkapitalklassifizierung unschädlich sind:

40   ▪ Instrumente, deren gesamte Zahlungsströme im Wesentlichen auf einzelnen Vermögenswerten des Unternehmens basieren,

▪ Instrumente, deren gesamte Zahlungsströme auf einem Prozentsatz vom Unternehmensumsatz basieren,

▪ Verträge, die zum Ziel haben, einzelne Mitarbeiter für die von ihnen erbrachten Dienstleistungen zu entlohnen,

▪ Verträge, die eine Zahlung eines nicht signifikanten Anteils des Jahresüberschusses für erbrachte Dienstleistungen bzw. gelieferte Güter vorsehen.

Jegliche darüber hinaus bestehende Zahlungsverpflichtung führt zu einem Ausweis des Vertrags als finanzielle Verbindlichkeit.

41   **e) Summe der erwarteten Zahlungsströme entspricht der Unternehmensentwicklung.** Als letzte Bedingung fordert das IASB, dass die Summe der zukünftig erwarteten Zahlungsströme aus dem Instrument im Wesentlichen den Erfolg, die Veränderung des bilanzierten Reinvermögens oder des Unternehmenswerts über die Laufzeit widerspiegeln muss (vgl. IAS 32.16A(e)). Falls bilanzielle Größen Grundlage für die Ermittlung des Abfindungsanspruchs sind, müssen diese Ergebnisgrößen nach IFRS berechnet werden, was in der Praxis häufig nicht der Fall sein dürfte (vgl. IAS 32.AG14E) – ein Rückgriff auf die Rechnungslegung nach nationalen Regeln ist nur im Ausnahmefall möglich, wenn die Unterschiede zu einer IFRS-Bilanzierung von untergeordneter Bedeutung sind. Auch dies wird in Deutschland trotz der Annäherung des HGB an die IFRS durch das BilMoG nur in Ausnahmen der Fall sein. Daneben ist die Auslegung des Terminus „im Wesentlichen" (*substantially*) von Bedeutung. Auch wenn der Begriff vom IASB nicht weiter konkretisiert wird, so interpretiert die Praxis den in anderen Standards verwandten Begriff „*substantially all*" als „ca. 90%", was als Referenzpunkt für die Auslegung im Kontext von IAS 32.16A(e) herangezogen werden kann.[15] Eine weitere Frage ergibt sich aus der Betrachtungsebene. IdR. basieren Abfindungsvereinbarungen auf den bilanziellen Größen bzw. dem Unternehmenswert des einzelnen Unternehmens (und nicht des Konzerns). Somit ist fraglich, ob eine Klassifizierung auf Ebene des Einzelabschlusses für den Konzern beibehalten werden kann. Auch wenn sich die IFRS hierzu nicht explizit äußern, ist von einer erneuten Überprüfung der Kriterien auf Konzernebene auszugehen (aA. Blaum 2009, Rz. 36).

42   **f) Umgliederungen.** Grundsätzlich ist die Einwertung eines emittierten Finanzinstruments als Eigen- oder Fremdkapital einmalig bei Zugang vorzunehmen (vgl. IAS 32.15). Für kündbare Instrumente gilt abweichend davon, dass eine Umgliederung in Eigenkapital vorzunehmen ist, sobald diese die Bedingungen in IAS 32.16A und 16B erfüllen (vgl. IAS 32.16E). Sollten sich jedoch die Bedingungen ändern bzw. nicht mehr erfüllt sein, dann hat eine Umgliederung in die finanziellen Verbindlichkeiten zu erfolgen.

43   **Beispiel**

Unternehmen A hat im Jahr 2000 Stammaktien emittiert. Diese stellen die nachrangigste Klasse an Kapitalien dar. 2001 emittiert das Unternehmen kündbare Anteile, die alle Bedingungen in IAS 32.16A und 16B mit Ausnahme der Bedingung in IAS 32.16A(b) erfüllen, da die Stammaktien

---

15 Vgl Deloitte (Hrsg), iGAAP, 503.

die nachrangigste Kapitalklasse bilden. In 2004 kauft Unternehmen A alle Stammaktien zurück. Ab diesem Zeitpunkt erfüllen die kündbaren Instrumente die Bedingung in IAS 32.16A(b) und die Instrumente sind in das Eigenkapital umzugliedern.

Eine Umgliederung von Fremd- in Eigenkapital hat dabei (erfolgsneutral) zum Buchwert im Zeitpunkt der Umgliederung zu erfolgen (vgl. IAS 32.16F(b)). Ist eine Umgliederung von Eigen- in Fremdkapital angezeigt, so hat diese zum beizulegenden Zeitwert zu erfolgen. Dabei ist die Differenz zwischen beizulegendem Zeitwert und Buchwert im Umgliederungszeitpunkt erfolgsneutral im Eigenkapital zu erfassen (vgl. IAS 32.16F(a)).

4. Sonderfall: Unternehmen mit fester Lebensdauer. Manche Unternehmen werden mit einer *ex*   44
ante definierten Lebensdauer gegründet (sog. *limited life entities* – zB zur Abwicklung eines bestimmten Projekts). Somit liegt eine vorab definierte Rückzahlungsverpflichtung des Emittenten vor, nämlich bei Abwicklung des Unternehmens nach Ablauf der vereinbarten Lebensdauer. Auch hier sieht IAS 32 eine **Ausnahme** vor, um einen Ausweis als Eigenkapital zu ermöglichen. Wie für die kündbaren Instrumente ist der Eigenkapitalausweis an bestimmte Kriterien gebunden (vgl. IAS 32.16C):

- Der Inhaber hat einen anteiligen Anspruch auf das Reinvermögen des Unternehmens im Falle der   45
(vorab vereinbarten) Liquidation – dabei hat die anteilige Ermittlung auf der gleichen Basis zu erfolgen wie bei den kündbaren Instrumenten.
- Das Instrument gehört zur nachrangigsten Klasse von Instrumenten (keine vorrangige Bedienung bei Liquidation), wobei keine vorherige Wandlung vonnöten sein darf, um zu dieser Klasse zu gehören.
- Alle Instrumente müssen hinsichtlich der vertraglichen Verpflichtung zur Auskehrung des anteiligen Reinvermögens identisch sein.

Zur Vermeidung von Missbrauch der Vorschriften dürfen daneben keine Instrumente vorhanden sein, welche die Reinvermögensmehrungen des Unternehmens zu Lasten der o.g. Instrumente beschränken. Dazu führt IAS 32.16D aus, dass keine anderen Instrumente emittiert sein dürfen:

- deren gesamte Zahlungsströme im Wesentlichen auf dem Jahreserfolg, der Änderung im bilanzierten Reinvermögen oder der Änderung des Unternehmenswerts basieren (unter Ausschluss der Auswirkungen des Instruments) sowie
- den Residualanspruch der Inhaber des Instruments beschränken bzw. fixieren.

Auch hier sind mit den Inhabern geschlossene nicht-finanzielle Verträge von der Berücksichtigung ausgenommen, solange sie dem Drittvergleich standhalten.

Auch für Kapitalien bei Unternehmen mit fester Lebensdauer gelten die Vorschriften zur Umglie-   46
derung in IAS 32.16F. An dieser Stelle wird auf die entsprechenden Ausführungen im Abschnitt zu den kündbaren Instrumenten verwiesen.

V. Hybride Finanzinstrumente. Unter hybriden Finanzinstrumenten (*compound financial instru-*   47
ments – in Abgrenzung zum strukturierten Produkt, welches im Englischen als *hybrid instrument* bezeichnet wird) versteht man Verträge, die sowohl Eigen- als auch Fremdkapitalkomponenten enthalten. Nach IAS 32.28 muss der Emittent (und nur für diesen gelten diese Vorschriften – aus Sicht des Inhabers handelt es sich immer um ein strukturiertes Produkt im Anwendungsbereich von IAS 39 – vgl. IAS 32. AG30) eines Kassainstruments prüfen, ob es sich um ein solches hybrides Finanzinstrument handelt. Ist dies der Fall, muss **das Instrument in seine Bestandteile aufgespalten und jeweils dem Eigen- und Fremdkapital zugeschlüsselt werden.** Die Zerlegungspflicht wird vom IASB damit begründet, dass auch einzelne Instrumente mit der gleichen ökonomischen Wirkung hätten emittiert werden können und eine getrennte Bilanzierung daher sachgerecht ist (vgl. IAS 32.29). Klassisches Beispiel für ein Instrument, dass einer solchen Prüfung unterzogen werden muss, ist die Wandelanleihe, welche dem Inhaber das

Recht (manchmal auch die Pflicht) einräumt, den Nennbetrag in Aktien zu erhalten (vgl. auch IAS 32. AG31). Dabei ist die vermeintliche Eigenkapitalkomponente daraufhin zu untersuchen, ob sie die Eigenkapitalbedingungen in IAS 32 erfüllt. Ist dem nicht so, muss das gesamte Instrument als finanzielle Verbindlichkeit klassifiziert werden. In den überwiegenden Fällen liegt dann aus Sicht von IAS 39 ein strukturiertes Produkt vor, welches ein eingebettetes Derivat enthält, das aufgrund der unterschiedlichen Risikoprofile (Eigenkapitalrisiko vs. Zinsänderungs- und Bonitätsrisiko) trennungspflichtig ist. Daneben ist auch bei einer abgetrennten Fremdkapitalkomponente im Rahmen der Bilanzierung nach IAS 39 zu prüfen, ob weitere trennungspflichtige eingebettete Derivate vorliegen.

48   Die Einwertung eines hybriden Finanzinstruments erfolgt einmalig, insbesondere sind Änderungen in der Ausübungswahrscheinlichkeit von Wandeloptionen nicht von Relevanz (vgl. IAS 32.30).

49   Ist ein hybrides Instrument als aufspaltungspflichtig iSv. IAS 32.28 identifiziert worden, kommt das sog. **Restwertverfahren** zur Anwendung (vgl. IAS 32.31). Dabei wird nach IAS 32.32 in einem ersten Schritt der beizulegende Zeitwert der Fremdkapitalkomponente (einschließlich etwaiger anderer eingebetteter Derivate, die keine Eigenkapitalinstrumente sind) ermittelt – dieser bildet den Buchwert der Fremdkapitalkomponenten bei Erstansatz.[16] Die Fremdkapitalkomponente fällt in den Anwendungsbereich von IAS 39 und wird dementsprechend folgebewertet. Dabei werden zur Ermittlung des beizulegenden Zeitwerts der Fremdkapitalkomponente die vertraglichen Zahlungsströme mit einem Zinssatz diskontiert, der die Marktrendite für ein Instrument gleicher Ausstattung (einschließlich Bonität) ohne ein entsprechendes Wandlungsrecht widerspiegelt. In einem zweiten Schritt wird der so ermittelte Wert vom beizulegenden Zeitwert des Gesamtinstruments abgezogen. Die Differenz bildet den Wert der Eigenkapitalkomponente ab – diese unterliegt keiner Folgebewertung, da sie im Anwendungsbereich von IAS 32 verbleibt. Das Verfahren spiegelt den Residualcharakter von Eigenkapital in der Definition des IASB wider (vgl. IAS 32.31).

50   Bei Ausübung eines Wandlungsrechts ist die Verbindlichkeitskomponente in das Eigenkapital umzubuchen (vgl. IAS 32.AG32). Die ursprüngliche Eigenkapitalkomponente (Optionsprämie für das gewährte Wandlungsrecht) verbleibt im Eigenkapital, kann jedoch ggf. in einen anderen Posten im Eigenkapital umgebucht werden. Dabei darf kein Gewinn oder Verlust entstehen. Bei vorzeitiger Rücknahme des Instruments ist das Entgelt (nebst Transaktionskosten) genauso aufzuteilen, wie bei der ursprünglichen Aufspaltung der Instrumente (vgl. IAS 32.AG33). Falls nach der Aufteilung des Entgelts eine Differenz verbleibt, ist diese ebenfalls im gleichen Verhältnis aufzuteilen und erfolgsneutral (Eigenkapitalkomponente) bzw. erfolgswirksam (Fremdkapitalkomponente) zu erfassen (vgl. IAS 32.AG34).

Bei Wandelanleihen stellt sich regelmäßig die Frage, ob das Wandlungsrecht (ein Derivat in Form einer geschriebenen Kaufoption) die Definition eines Eigenkapitalinstruments erfüllt (*fixed-for-fixed*-Regelung). Oftmals sehen die Anleihebedingungen für bestimmte Fälle eine Anpassung des Wandlungsverhältnisses vor. Typische Fälle sind:

- Aktiensplits bzw. -zusammenlegungen,
- Bar- oder Aktiendividenden,
- Kapitalerhöhungen,
- Bezugsrechte für Altaktionäre,
- Ausgabe weiterer Wandlungsanleihen,
- Change-of-Control-Klauseln.

---

16   Vgl. *Deloitte (Hrsg.)* iGAAP, 195.

Viele dieser Anpassungsklauseln dienen dem Schutz der Anleiheinhaber vor Verwässerung ihrer potenziellen Anteile.[17] Wenn Anpassungen des Wandlungsverhältnisses die ökonomische Position des Inhabers einer Wandelanleihe nicht verändern, ist dies nicht als Verletzung der *fixed-for-fixed*-Regelung zu werten.[18] Somit stehen solche Klauseln einer Klassifizierung des Wandlungsrechts als Eigenkapital nicht entgegen.

Ist eine Wandelanleihe in einer von der funktionalen Währung des Berichtsunternehmens abweichenden Währung denominiert, so hat dies eine Klassifizierung des gesamten hybriden Instruments als Fremdkapital zur Folge.[19]   51

Für den Fall, dass ein Unternehmen die Konversion einer Wandelanleihe forcieren möchte, wird oftmals das Wandlungsverhältnis nachträglich zu Gunsten des Inhabers der Wandelanleihe angepasst bzw. ein zusätzliches Entgelt bei vorzeitiger Wandlung geboten (auch Kombinationen daraus sind möglich). Bei solchen Konstellationen ist die Differenz, zum Zeitpunkt der Änderung der Bedingungen, zwischen dem beizulegenden Zeitwert des Entgelts, dass der Inhaber bei Wandlung des Instruments gemäß den geänderten Bedingungen erhält, und dem beizulegenden Zeitwert des Entgelts, dass der Inhaber gemäß den ursprünglichen Bedingungen erhalten hätte, als Aufwand zu erfassen (vgl. IAS 39.AG35).   52

VI. Eigene Anteile. Erwirbt ein Unternehmen eigene Anteile zurück, welche als Eigenkapital nach IAS 32 ausgewiesen worden sind, so sind diese **vom Eigenkapital in Abzug zu bringen** (Tilgung) (vgl. IAS 32.33). Dieser Vorgang ist erfolgsneutral abzubilden. Ein Ausweis als „eigene Anteile im Bestand" auf der Aktivseite kommt nicht in Betracht,[20] insbesondere da gehaltene eigene Anteile nicht die Definition eines Vermögenswerts im Rahmenkonzept erfüllen.[21] Der Betrag der gehaltenen eigenen Anteile ist jedoch für jede Klasse gesondert in der Bilanz oder im Anhang anzugeben (vgl. IAS 32.34 iVm. IAS 1.79(a)(iv)). Daneben sind Angaben zu machen für den Fall, dass eigene Anteile von nahestehenden Personen bzw. Unternehmen iSv. IAS 24 erworben wurden.[22] Treuhänderisch gehaltene eigene Anteile (zB erwerben Kreditinstitute regelmäßig ihre eigenen Aktien im Auftrag ihrer Kunden) sind jedoch nicht als Rücknahme abzubilden, mithin also nicht vom Eigenkapital in Abzug zu bringen (vgl. IAS 32.AG36). Der Rückerwerb eigener Anteile mit Handelsabsicht ist ebenfalls als Rücknahme abzubilden.[23]   53

Erfolgt zu einem späteren Zeitpunkt eine erneute Ausgabe der Anteile, sind diese wie eine Neuemission zu behandeln, also alle Schritte in IAS 32 erneut zu durchlaufen.   54

VII. Dividenden, Zinsen, Gewinne und Verluste. Der Ausweis einer Erfolgskomponente ist unmittelbar abhängig von der **Einwertung** des betroffenen Instruments als Eigen- oder Fremdkapital (vgl. IAS 32.36). Ist ein Finanzinstrument als **Fremdkapital** (finanzielle Verbindlichkeit) klassifiziert worden, so müssen Zinsen, Dividenden, Gewinne und Verluste in der GuV erfasst werden (vgl. IAS 32.35 iVm. IAS 32.41). Im Gegensatz dazu sind Auskehrungen an Inhaber von **Eigenkapitalinstrumenten** in Form von Dividenden direkt als Eigenkapitalminderung zu erfassen. Bei Dividendenbeschluss ist gemäß IAS 10.12 eine finanzielle Verbindlichkeit zu erfassen (Gegenbuchung zur Eigenkapitalminderung). Die rechtliche Beurteilung des Instruments spielt dabei keine Rolle – ebenso nicht die Bezeichnung.   55

Transaktionskosten (unter Berücksichtigung etwaiger Ertragsteuervorteile) für die Emission oder den Rückerwerb von Eigenkapitalinstrumenten sind vom Eigenkapital in Abzug zu bringen (vgl. IAS 32.37). Dabei muss es sich jedoch um inkrementelle Kosten handeln, also um Kosten, die vermeidbar wären, würde die Transaktion nicht durchgeführt werden. Hierunter fallen typischerweise Aufwendun-   56

---

17 Vgl. IDW HFA 9, Rn 34.
18 Vgl. *Deloitte (Hrsg.)* iGAAP, 220.
19 Vgl. *Deloitte (Hrsg.)* iGAAP, 215f.
20 Vgl. IDW HFA 9, Rn 41.
21 Vgl. *KPMG (Hrsg.)* Eigenkapital vs Fremdkapital nach IFRS, 37.
22 Vgl. *Deloitte (Hrsg.)* iGAAP, 231.
23 Vgl. IFRIC Update August 2002, 3.

gen wie Emissionskosten, Beratungskosten oder Registrierungskosten. Kosten für eine fehlgeschlagene Eigenkapitaltransaktion sind sofort als Aufwand zu erfassen. Für hybride Finanzinstrumente ist eine Aufteilung der Transaktionskosten auf die jeweiligen Eigen- und Fremdkapitalkomponenten notwendig. Hierbei ist das gleiche Verhältnis zu wählen wie bei der Aufteilung des aufgenommenen Kapitals aus der Transaktion. Beziehen sich die Kosten auf mehr als eine Transaktion (zB eine Privatplatzierung eines Teils des Kapitals mit gleichzeitiger Börsennotierung eines anderen Teils) so ist eine rationale Allokationsbasis zu wählen, die konsistent mit vergleichbaren Transaktionen ist (vgl. IAS 32.38). In Einklang mit IAS 1 sind die vom Eigenkapital in Abzug gebrachten Transaktionskosten offenzulegen (vgl. IAS 32.39). Ebenso sind die direkt im Eigenkapital erfassten Ertragsteuern gemäß IAS 12 offenzulegen. Hierbei sind die im Eigenkapital erfassten laufenden und latenten Steuern einzubeziehen.

57   **VIII. Saldierung.** Grundsätzlich besteht innerhalb der IFRS ein **Saldierungsverbot** (vgl. IAS 1.32), außer ein spezifischer IFRS sieht eine Saldierung zwingend oder wahlweise vor. IAS 32 enthält eine solche Ausnahmeregelung (vgl. IAS 32.42). Danach ist ein finanzieller Vermögenswert mit einer finanziellen Verbindlichkeit zwingend zu verrechnen, falls:

- das Unternehmen einen gegenwärtig einklagbaren Rechtsanspruch besitzt, die erfassten Beträge gegeneinander aufzurechnen und
- das Unternehmen beabsichtigt, eine solche Aufrechnung herbeizuführen bzw. den finanziellen Vermögenswert und die finanzielle Verbindlichkeit zum gleichen Zeitpunkt zu verwerten.

Diese Regelungen gelten jedoch nicht für fehlgeschlagene Ausbuchungen gemäß IAS 39.36. Der dabei verbleibende finanzielle Vermögenswert und die damit zusammenhängende finanzielle Verbindlichkeit dürfen nicht miteinander verrechnet werden.

Es muss betont werden, dass o.g. Kriterien kumulativ erfüllt sein müssen. Selbst bei der rechtlichen Möglichkeit zur Saldierung muss auch die Absicht bestehen, diese durchzuführen (vgl. IAS 32.46). Des Weiteren gilt es zu beachten, dass der Rechtsanspruch zur Aufrechnung nicht aufschiebend bedingt sein darf, also zum Berichtsstichtag rechtlich durchsetzbar sein muss.

58   Die Saldierung wird nur dann als sachgerecht angesehen, wenn der Nettoausweis den wirtschaftlichen Gehalt iSe. Abbildung der künftigen Zahlungsströme widerspiegelt (vgl. IAS 32.43). In Abgrenzung zur Ausbuchung kann aus einer Saldierung von Finanzinstrumenten kein Gewinn oder Verlust resultieren (vgl. IAS 32.44).

59   **Globalaufrechnungsvereinbarungen** (*master netting arrangements*), die häufig im Finanzdienstleistungssektor Anwendung finden (v.a. bei Derivaten), sind nicht hinreichend für eine Aufrechnung, da es sich dabei nicht um einen gegenwärtigen durchsetzbaren Anspruch handelt (vgl. IAS 32.50). Vielmehr sind diese Vereinbarungen bedingte Ansprüche zur Aufrechnung für den Fall des Ausfalls bzw. der Kündigung eines Instruments durch die Gegenpartei mit dem Ziel der Ausfallrisikominimierung.

60   IAS 32.49 nennt weitere Situationen, in denen eine Saldierung aufgrund der Nichterfüllung der Bedingungen in IAS 32.42 nicht statthaft ist:

- **Synthetische Finanzinstrumente:** mittels mehrerer Finanzinstrumente sollen die Eigenschaften eines einzelnen Finanzinstruments nachgebildet werden (zB Nachbildung eines Festsatzkredits mittels eines variabel verzinslichen Darlehens und eines Zinsswaps).
- **Risikoidentität:** Finanzielle Vermögenswerte und Verbindlichkeiten, die zwar die gleichen Risikoeigenschaften besitzen, jedoch mit unterschiedlichen Vertragsparteien abgeschlossen wurden (bspw. Swapportfolien).
- **Sicherheiten:** Vermögenswerte, die als Sicherheit für eine finanzielle Verbindlichkeit ohne Rückgriffmöglichkeit (*non-recourse financial liability*) gestellt wurden.

- Finanzielle Vermögenswerte, die innerhalb eines **Treuhandvermögens** zur Begleichung einer Schuld abgegrenzt wurden, ohne dass der Gläubiger diese als erfüllend angenommen hat.
- **Versicherungsansprüche:** Aus verlustverursachenden Ereignissen entstandene Verpflichtung, bei der erwartet wird, dass sie durch einen Versicherungsanspruch kompensiert wird.

IX. Inkrafttreten und Übergangsvorschriften. Die ursprüngliche Fassung von IAS 32 war für Geschäftsjahre beginnend am oder nach dem **1. Januar 2005** anzuwenden. Eine vorzeitige Anwendung war zulässig, sofern dies im Anhang offengelegt wurde. Die erstmalige Anwendung war retrospektiv vorzunehmen.   61

Die Änderungen zu kündbaren Instrumenten sowie Unternehmen mit begrenzter Lebensdauer (veröffentlicht im Februar 2008) waren für Geschäftsjahre beginnend am oder nach dem **1. Januar 2009** anzuwenden. Eine vorzeitige Anwendung war zulässig, sofern dies im Anhang offengelegt wurde und gleichzeitig alle Änderungen an IAS 1, IAS 39, IFRS 7 und IFRIC 2 vorzeitig angewendet wurden. Die erstmalige Anwendung war retrospektiv vorzunehmen.   62

Durch die in 2007 überarbeitete Fassung von IAS 1 wurden Folgeänderungen an IAS 32 vorgenommen, die für Geschäftsjahre beginnend am oder nach dem 1. Januar 2009 anzuwenden waren. IFRS 3 (überarbeitet in 2008) hat die ursprüngliche Textziffer 4(c) gelöscht. Diese Änderung war für Geschäftsjahre beginnend ab dem 1. Juli 2009 anzuwenden.   63

Die Änderungen aus den jährlichen Verbesserungen 2008 waren erstmals in der ersten Berichtsperiode eines am **1. Januar 2009** oder danach beginnenden Geschäftsjahres anzuwenden. Eine frühere Anwendung war zulässig. Falls ein Unternehmen diese Änderungen auf eine frühere Periode angewendet, so hatte es diese Tatsache anzugeben und die entsprechenden Änderungen von Paragraph 3 des IFRS 7, Paragraph 1 des IAS 28 und Paragraph 1 des IAS 31 und (überarbeitet Mai 2008) gleichzeitig anzuwenden. Ein Unternehmen konnte die Änderungen prospektiv anwenden.   64

Die Änderungen zur Bilanzierung von Bezugsrechten aus Oktober 2009 war für Geschäftsjahre beginnend ab dem 1. Januar 2010 anzuwenden. Eine vorzeitige Anwendung war erlaubt, sofern dies im Anhang offengelegt wird.   65

Die aus IFRS 9 resultierenden Änderungen sind dann anzuwenden, wenn IFRS 9 erstmalig Anwendung findet.   66

X. IFRS für kleine und mittelgroße Unternehmen. IFRS-SMEs Abschnitt 22 *Liabilities and Equity* regelt die Abgrenzung zwischen Eigen- und Fremdkapital nach dem IFRS für kleine und mittelständische Unternehmen.   67

Dabei ist das **Grundprinzip** der Abgrenzung dasselbe wie in IAS 32. Eigenkapital ist der Anspruch an den Vermögenswerten nach Abzug aller Schulden des Unternehmens, mithin das Nettoreinvermögen (vgl. IFRS-SMEs Abschnitt 22.3). Dabei wird Eigenkapital jedoch positiv definiert als: 68
- Einlagen der Eigner des Unternehmens,
- zuzüglich der Vermögensmehrungen durch Jahresüberschüsse, die im Unternehmen verbleiben,
- abzüglich der Vermögensminderungen durch Jahresfehlbeträge,
- abzüglich der Ausschüttungen an die Eigner des Unternehmens.

Auch im IFRS-SMEs existiert **gewillkürtes Eigenkapital**, das die Definition in IFRS-SMEs Abschnitt 22.3 nicht erfüllt. IFRS-SMEs Abschnitt 22.4 legt diese Liste abschließend fest: 69
- Kündbare Instrumente, die dem Inhaber ein Recht zur Rückgabe des Instruments an das Unternehmen gegen liquide Mittel oder sonstige finanzielle Vermögenswerte einräumen bzw. die bei Eintritt eines ungewissen künftigen Ereignisses bzw. dem Tod oder der Verrentung des Inhabers automatisch zurückgenommen(-erworben) werden. Dabei sind Nebenbedingungen zu erfüllen, die mit denen in IAS 32 zu kündbaren Instrumenten enthaltenen vergleichbar sind.

- Instrumente bzw. Teile von Instrumenten, die nachrangig gegenüber allen anderen Kapitalklassen sind, wenn eine Pflicht zur Auskehrung eines beteiligungsproportionalen Anteils am Nettoreinvermögen nur bei Liquidation des Unternehmens besteht.

70   Für Genossenschaftsanteile ist eine Eigenkapitalklassifizierung nur dann möglich, wenn das Unternehmen ein unbedingtes Recht zur Verweigerung der Rücknahme hat oder die Rücknahme durch Gesetz, Regulierung oder die Satzung verboten ist (vgl. IFRS-SMEs Abschnitt 22.6).

71   Ein Unternehmen hat dann eine Eigenkapitalerhöhung zu bilanzieren, falls die Instrumente emittiert sind und die Gegenpartei zur Leistung von liquiden Mitteln oder sonstigen Ressourcen an das Unternehmen verpflichtet ist (vgl. IFRS SMEs Abschnitt 22.7). Dabei hat die Bewertung zum beizulegenden Zeitwert der liquiden Mittel bzw. der sonstigen erhaltenen oder zu erhaltenden Ressourcen zu erfolgen. Bei späterer Erfüllung der Leistung ist der Barwert anzusetzen, sofern der Abzinsungseffekt wesentlich ist (vgl. IFRS-SMEs Abschnitt 22.8). Transaktionskosten sind in Abzug vom Eigenkapital zu bringen. Dabei ist ein Ertragsteuervorteil zu berücksichtigen (vgl. IFRS-SMEs Abschnitt 22.9). Die Darstellung einer Kapitalerhöhung überlässt der IFRS-SMEs den jeweiligen Landesgesetzen (vgl. IFRS-SMEs Abschnitt 22.10).

72   Für die Emission von Optionen, Bezugsrechten, Bezugsscheinen sowie vergleichbaren Instrumenten gelten die gleichen Vorschriften wie für Kassaemissionen (vgl. IFRS-SMEs Abschnitt 22.11).

73   Anteilsdividenden sowie Anteilssplits ändern nicht den Gesamtbetrag des ausgewiesenen Eigenkapitals, jedoch ist eine kraft gesetzlicher Vorschriften notwendige Umgliederung im Eigenkapital statthaft (vgl. IFRS-SMEs Abschnitt 22.12).

74   **Wandelanleihen und vergleichbare zusammengesetzte Finanzinstrumente** sind wie in IAS 32 in ihre Eigen- und Fremdkapitalkomponenten zu zerlegen. Auch hier kommt das Restwertverfahren zum Einsatz. Transaktionskosten sind auf Basis der relativen beizulegenden Zeitwerte von Eigen- und Fremdkapitalkomponente aufzuteilen (vgl. IFRS-SMEs Abschnitt 22.13). Die Aufteilung ist in Folgeperioden nicht anzupassen (vgl. IFRS-SMEs Abschnitt 22.14). Die Differenz zwischen dem Buchwert der Fremdkapitalkomponente und dem Nominalbetrag ist nach der Effektivzinsmethode über die Laufzeit zu verteilen (vgl. IFRS-SMEs Abschnitt 22.15).

75   **Eigene Anteile** im Bestand sind vom Eigenkapital bei Rückerwerb in Abzug zu bringen (vgl. IFRS-SMEs Abschnitt 22.16). Der vom Eigenkapital abzuziehende Betrag bemisst sich am beizulegenden Zeitwert der hingegebenen Gegenleistung. Es darf dabei kein Gewinn oder Verlust entstehen.

76   Ausschüttungen an die Anteilseigner vermindern das Eigenkapital, dabei ist ein Ertragsteuervorteil zu berücksichtigen (vgl. IFRS-SMEs Abschnitt 22.17). Sachdividenden sind mit Beschluss als Verbindlichkeit zu erfassen (vgl. IFRS-SMEs Abschnitt 22.18). Dabei ist die Verbindlichkeit mit dem beizulegenden Zeitwert der auszukehrenden Vermögenswerte zu bemessen. Dieser Wert ist zu jedem Berichtsstichtag und im Zeitpunkt der Erfüllung der Sachdividendenverpflichtung in Höhe der Änderungen des beizulegenden Zeitwerts anzupassen. Dabei erfolgt die Gegenbuchung im Eigenkapital.

77   Der IFRS-SMEs stellt auch klar, dass im **Konzernabschluss** Minderheiten im Eigenkapital auszuweisen sind (vgl. IFRS-SMEs Abschnitt 22.19). Transaktionen zwischen Mehrheitsanteilseignern und Minderheiten, die nicht in einem Kontrollverlust münden, sind als Transaktionen zwischen Anteilseignern zu bilanzieren. Das hat zur Folge, dass bei solchen Transaktionen kein Gewinn oder Verlust bzw. Änderungen in den Buchwerten von Vermögenswerten (einschließlich dem Goodwill) erfasst werden dürfen.

XI. Ausblick. Das IASB überabeitet derzeit in einem **gemeinsamen Projekt** mit dem US-amerika- 78
nischen Rechnungslegungsgremium FASB die Vorschriften zur Abgrenzung von Eigen- und Fremdkapital. Das Projekt wurde im Herbst 2010 unterbrochen, um Ressourcen für Konvergenzprojekte mit
höherer Priorität freizusetzen. Mit einer Wiederaufnahme des gemeinsamen Projektes ist derzeit nicht
vor Mitte 2011 zu rechnen.

International Accounting Standard 39
Financial Instruments: Recognition and Measurement

Objective

1 The objective of this Standard is to establish principles for recognising and measuring financial assets, financial liabilities and some contracts to buy or sell non-financial items. Requirements for presenting information about financial instruments are in IAS 32 *Financial Instruments: Presentation*. Requirements for disclosing information about financial instruments are in IFRS 7 *Financial Instruments: Disclosures*.

Scope

2 This Standard shall be applied by all entities to all types of financial instruments except:

(a) those interests in subsidiaries, associates and joint ventures that are accounted for under IAS 27 *Consolidated and Separate Financial Statements*, IAS 28 *Investments in Associates* or IAS 31 *Interests in Joint Ventures*. However, entities shall apply this Standard to an interest in a subsidiary, associate or joint venture that according to IAS 27, IAS 28 or IAS 31 is accounted for under this Standard. Entities shall also apply this Standard to derivatives on an interest in a subsidiary, associate or joint venture unless the derivative meets the definition of an equity instrument of the entity in IAS 32.

(b) rights and obligations under leases to which IAS 17 *Leases* applies. However:

(i) lease receivables recognised by a lessor are subject to the derecognition and impairment provisions of this Standard (see paragraphs 15–37, 58, 59, 63–65 and Appendix A paragraphs AG36–AG52 and AG84–AG93);

(ii) finance lease payables recognised by a lessee are subject to the derecognition provisions of this Standard (see paragraphs 39–42 and Appendix A paragraphs AG57–AG63); and

(iii) derivatives that are embedded in leases are subject to the embedded derivatives provisions of this Standard (see paragraphs 10–13 and Appendix A paragraphs AG27–AG33).

(c) employers' rights and obligations under employee benefit plans, to which IAS 19 *Employee Benefits* applies.

(d) financial instruments issued by the entity that meet the definition of an equity instrument in IAS 32 (including options and warrants) or that are required to be classified as an equity instrument in accordance with paragraphs 16A and 16B or paragraphs 16C and 16D of IAS 32.. However, the holder of such equity instruments shall apply this Standard to those instruments, unless they meet the exception in (a) above.

(e) rights and obligations arising under (i) an insurance contract as defined in IFRS 4 *Insurance Contracts*, other than an issuer's rights and obligations arising under an insurance contract that meets the definition of a financial guarantee contract in paragraph 9, or (ii) a contract that is within the scope of IFRS 4 because it contains a discretionary participation feature. However, this Standard applies to a derivative that is embedded in a contract within the scope of IFRS 4 if the derivative is not itself a contract within the scope of IFRS 4 (see paragraphs 10–13 and Appendix A paragraphs AG27–AG33 of this Standard). Moreover, if an issuer of financial guarantee contracts has previously asserted explicitly that it regards such contracts as insurance contracts and has used accounting applicable to insurance contracts, the issuer may elect to apply either this Standard or IFRS 4 to such financial guarantee contracts (see paragraphs AG4 and AG4A). The issuer may make that election contract by contract, but the election for each contract is irrevocable.

(f)   [deleted]

(g)   any forward contract between an acquirer and a selling shareholder to buy or sell an acquiree that will result in a business combination at a future acquisition date. The term of the forward contract should not exceed a reasonable period normally necessary to obtain any required approvals and to complete the transaction. (h)   loan commitments other than those loan commitments described in paragraph 4. An issuer of loan commitments shall apply IAS 37 *Provisions, Contingent Liabilities and Contingent Assets* to loan commitments that are not within the scope of this Standard. However, all loan commitments are subject to the derecognition provisions of this Standard (see paragraphs 15–42 and Appendix A paragraphs AG36–AG63).

(i)   financial instruments, contracts and obligations under share-based payment transactions to which IFRS 2 *Share-based Payment* applies, except for contracts within the scope of paragraphs 5–7 of this Standard, to which this Standard applies.

(j)   rights to payments to reimburse the entity for expenditure it is required to make to settle a liability that it recognises as a provision in accordance with IAS 37, or for which, in an earlier period, it recognised a provision in accordance with IAS 37.

3   [Deleted]

4   The following loan commitments are within the scope of this Standard:

(a)   loan commitments that the entity designates as financial liabilities at fair value through profit or loss. An entity that has a past practice of selling the assets resulting from its loan commitments shortly after origination shall apply this Standard to all its loan commitments in the same class.

(b)   loan commitments that can be settled net in cash or by delivering or issuing another financial instrument. These loan commitments are derivatives. A loan commitment is not regarded as settled net merely because the loan is paid out in instalments (for example, a mortgage construction loan that is paid out in instalments in line with the progress of construction).

(c)   commitments to provide a loan at a below-market interest rate. Paragraph 47(d) specifies the subsequent measurement of liabilities arising from these loan commitments.

5   This Standard shall be applied to those contracts to buy or sell a non-financial item that can be settled net in cash or another financial instrument, or by exchanging financial instruments, as if the contracts were financial instruments, with the exception of contracts that were entered into and continue to be held for the purpose of the receipt or delivery of a non-financial item in accordance with the entity's expected purchase, sale or usage requirements.

6   There are various ways in which a contract to buy or sell a non-financial item can be settled net in cash or another financial instrument or by exchanging financial instruments. These include:

(a)   when the terms of the contract permit either party to settle it net in cash or another financial instrument or by exchanging financial instruments;

(b)   when the ability to settle net in cash or another financial instrument, or by exchanging financial instruments, is not explicit in the terms of the contract, but the entity has a practice of settling similar contracts net in cash or another financial instrument or by exchanging financial instruments (whether with the counterparty, by entering into offsetting contracts or by selling the contract before its exercise or lapse);

(c)   when, for similar contracts, the entity has a practice of taking delivery of the underlying and selling it within a short period after delivery for the purpose of generating a profit from short-term fluctuations in price or dealer's margin; and

(d)   when the non-financial item that is the subject of the contract is readily convertible to cash.

A contract to which (b) or (c) applies is not entered into for the purpose of the receipt or delivery of the non-financial item in accordance with the entity's expected purchase, sale or usage requirements and, accordingly, is within the scope of this Standard. Other contracts to which paragraph 5 applies are evaluated to determine whether they were entered into and continue to be held for the purpose of the receipt or delivery of the non-financial item in accordance with the entity's expected purchase, sale or usage requirements and, accordingly, whether they are within the scope of this Standard.

7   A written option to buy or sell a non-financial item that can be settled net in cash or another financial instrument, or by exchanging financial instruments, in accordance with paragraph 6(a) or (d) is within the scope of this Standard. Such a contract cannot be entered into for the purpose of the receipt or delivery of the non-financial item in accordance with the entity's expected purchase, sale or usage requirements.

Definitions

8   The terms defined in IAS 32 are used in this Standard with the meanings specified in paragraph 11 of IAS 32. IAS 32 defines the following terms:

   •   financial instrument

   •   financial asset

   •   financial liability

   •   equity instrument

and provides guidance on applying those definitions.

9   **The following terms are used in this Standard with the meanings specified:**

Definition of a derivative

A *derivative* **is a financial instrument or other contract within the scope of this Standard (see paragraphs 2–7) with all three of the following characteristics:**

(a)   **its value changes in response to the change in a specified interest rate, financial instrument price, commodity price, foreign exchange rate, index of prices or rates, credit rating or credit index, or other variable, provided in the case of a non-financial variable that the variable is not specific to a party to the contract (sometimes called the 'underlying');**

(b)   **it requires no initial net investment or an initial net investment that is smaller than would be required for other types of contracts that would be expected to have a similar response to changes in market factors; and**

(c)   **it is settled at a future date.**

Definitions of four categories of financial instruments

A *financial asset or financial liability at fair value through profit or loss* **is a financial asset or financial liability that meets either of the following conditions.**

(a)   **It is classified as held for trading. A financial asset or financial liability is classified as held for trading if:**

   (i)   **it is acquired or incurred principally for the purpose of selling or repurchasing it in the near term;**

   (ii)   **on initial recognition it is part of a portfolio of identified financial instruments that are managed together and for which there is evidence of a recent actual pattern of short-term profit-taking; or**

(iii)   it is a derivative (except for a derivative that is a financial guarantee contract or a designated and effective hedging instrument).

(b)   Upon initial recognition it is designated by the entity as at fair value through profit or loss. An entity may use this designation only when permitted by paragraph 11A, or when doing so results in more relevant information, because either

(i)   it eliminates or significantly reduces a measurement or recognition inconsistency (sometimes referred to as 'an accounting mismatch') that would otherwise arise from measuring assets or liabilities or recognising the gains and losses on them on different bases; or

(ii)   a group of financial assets, financial liabilities or both is managed and its performance is evaluated on a fair value basis, in accordance with a documented risk management or investment strategy, and information about the group is provided internally on that basis to the entity's key management personnel (as defined in IAS 24 *Related Party Disclosures* (as revised in 2003)), for example the entity's board of directors and chief executive officer.

In IFRS 7, paragraphs 9–11 and B4 require the entity to provide disclosures about financial assets and financial liabilities it has designated as at fair value through profit or loss, including how it has satisfied these conditions. For instruments qualifying in accordance with (ii) above, that disclosure includes a narrative description of how designation as at fair value through profit or loss is consistent with the entity's documented risk management or investment strategy.

Investments in equity instruments that do not have a quoted market price in an active market, and whose fair value cannot be reliably measured (see paragraph 46(c) and Appendix A paragraphs AG80 and AG81), shall not be designated as at fair value through profit or loss.

It should be noted that paragraphs 48, 48A, 49 and Appendix A paragraphs AG69–AG82, which set out requirements for determining a reliable measure of the fair value of a financial asset or financial liability, apply equally to all items that are measured at fair value, whether by designation or otherwise, or whose fair value is disclosed.

Held-to-maturity investments are non-derivative financial assets with fixed or determinable payments and fixed maturity that an entity has the positive intention and ability to hold to maturity (see Appendix A paragraphs AG16–AG25) other than:

(a)   those that the entity upon initial recognition designates as at fair value through profit or loss;

(b)   those that the entity designates as available for sale; and

(c)   those that meet the definition of loans and receivables.

An entity shall not classify any financial assets as held to maturity if the entity has, during the current financial year or during the two preceding financial years, sold or reclassified more than an insignificant amount of held-to-maturity investments before maturity (more than insignificant in relation to the total amount of held-to-maturity investments) other than sales or reclassifications that:

(i)   are so close to maturity or the financial asset's call date (for example, less than three months before maturity) that changes in the market rate of interest would not have a significant effect on the financial asset's fair value;

(ii)   occur after the entity has collected substantially all of the financial asset's original principal through scheduled payments or prepayments; or

(iii)   are attributable to an isolated event that is beyond the entity's control, is non-recurring and could not have been reasonably anticipated by the entity.

Loans and receivables are non-derivative financial assets with fixed or determinable payments that are not quoted in an active market, other than:

(a)   those that the entity intends to sell immediately or in the near term, which shall be classified as held for trading, and those that the entity upon initial recognition designates as at fair value through profit or loss;

(b)   those that the entity upon initial recognition designates as available for sale; or

(c)   those for which the holder may not recover substantially all of its initial investment, other than because of credit deterioration, which shall be classified as available for sale.

An interest acquired in a pool of assets that are not loans or receivables (for example, an interest in a mutual fund or a similar fund) is not a loan or receivable.

Available-for-sale financial assets are those non-derivative financial assets that are designated as available for sale or are not classified as (a) loans and receivables, (b) held-to-maturity investments or (c) financial assets at fair value through profit or loss.

Definition of a financial guarantee contract

A *financial guarantee contract* is a contract that requires the issuer to make specified payments to reimburse the holder for a loss it incurs because a specified debtor fails to make payment when due in accordance with the original or modified terms of a debt instrument.

Definitions relating to recognition and measurement

The *amortised cost of a financial asset or financial liability* is the amount at which the financial asset or financial liability is measured at initial recognition minus principal repayments, plus or minus the cumulative amortisation using the effective interest method of any difference between that initial amount and the maturity amount, and minus any reduction (directly or through the use of an allowance account) for impairment or uncollectibility.

The *effective interest method* is a method of calculating the amortised cost of a financial asset or a financial liability (or group of financial assets or financial liabilities) and of allocating the interest income or interest expense over the relevant period. The *effective interest rate* is the rate that exactly discounts estimated future cash payments or receipts through the expected life of the financial instrument or, when appropriate, a shorter period to the net carrying amount of the financial asset or financial liability. When calculating the effective interest rate, an entity shall estimate cash flows considering all contractual terms of the financial instrument (for example, prepayment, call and similar options) but shall not consider future credit losses. The calculation includes all fees and points paid or received between parties to the contract that are an integral part of the effective interest rate (see IAS 18 *Revenue*), transaction costs, and all other premiums or discounts. There is a presumption that the cash flows and the expected life of a group of similar financial instruments can be estimated reliably. However, in those rare cases when it is not possible to estimate reliably the cash flows or the expected life of a financial instrument (or group of financial instruments), the entity shall use the contractual cash flows over the full contractual term of the financial instrument (or group of financial instruments).

Derecognition is the removal of a previously recognised financial asset or financial liability from an entity's statement of financial position.

Fair value is the amount for which an asset could be exchanged, or a liability settled, between knowledgeable, willing parties in an arm's length transaction.*

A *regular way purchase or sale* is a purchase or sale of a financial asset under a contract whose terms require delivery of the asset within the time frame established generally by regulation or convention in the marketplace concerned.

Transaction costs are incremental costs that are directly attributable to the acquisition, issue or disposal of a financial asset or financial liability (see Appendix A paragraph AG13). An incremental cost is one that would not have been incurred if the entity had not acquired, issued or disposed of the financial instrument.

---

*   Paragraphs 48–49 and AG69–AG82 of Appendix A contain requirements for determining the fair value of a financial asset or financial liability.

Definitions relating to hedge accounting

A *firm commitment* is a binding agreement for the exchange of a specified quantity of resources at a specified price on a specified future date or dates.

A *forecast transaction* is an uncommitted but anticipated future transaction.

A *hedging instrument* is a designated derivative or (for a hedge of the risk of changes in foreign currency exchange rates only) a designated non-derivative financial asset or non-derivative financial liability whose fair value or cash flows are expected to offset changes in the fair value or cash flows of a designated hedged item (paragraphs 72–77 and Appendix A paragraphs AG94–AG97 elaborate on the definition of a hedging instrument).

A *hedged item* is an asset, liability, firm commitment, highly probable forecast transaction or net investment in a foreign operation that (a) exposes the entity to risk of changes in fair value or future cash flows and (b) is designated as being hedged (paragraphs 78–84 and Appendix A paragraphs AG98–AG101 elaborate on the definition of hedged items).

Hedge effectiveness is the degree to which changes in the fair value or cash flows of the hedged item that are attributable to a hedged risk are offset by changes in the fair value or cash flows of the hedging instrument (see Appendix A paragraphs AG105–AG113).

Embedded derivatives

10   An embedded derivative is a component of a hybrid (combined) instrument that also includes a non-derivative host contract—with the effect that some of the cash flows of the combined instrument vary in a way similar to a stand-alone derivative. An embedded derivative causes some or all of the cash flows that otherwise would be required by the contract to be modified according to a specified interest rate, financial instrument price, commodity price, foreign exchange rate, index of prices or rates, credit rating or credit index, or other variable, provided in the case of a non-financial variable that the variable is not specific to a party to the contract. A derivative that is attached to a financial instrument but is contractually transferable independently of that instrument, or has a different counterparty from that instrument, is not an embedded derivative, but a separate financial instrument.

11   An embedded derivative shall be separated from the host contract and accounted for as a derivative under this Standard if, and only if:

(a)   the economic characteristics and risks of the embedded derivative are not closely related to the economic characteristics and risks of the host contract (see Appendix A paragraphs AG30 and AG33);

(b)   a separate instrument with the same terms as the embedded derivative would meet the definition of a derivative; and

(c)   the hybrid (combined) instrument is not measured at fair value with changes in fair value recognised in profit or loss (ie a derivative that is embedded in a financial asset or financial liability at fair value through profit or loss is not separated).

If an embedded derivative is separated, the host contract shall be accounted for under this Standard if it is a financial instrument, and in accordance with other appropriate Standards if it is not a financial instrument. This Standard does not address whether an embedded derivative shall be presented separately in the statement of financial position.

11A   Notwithstanding paragraph 11, if a contract contains one or more embedded derivatives, an entity may designate the entire hybrid (combined) contract as a financial asset or financial liability at fair value through profit or loss unless:

(a)   the embedded derivative(s) does not significantly modify the cash flows that otherwise would be required by the contract; or

(b)   it is clear with little or no analysis when a similar hybrid (combined) instrument is first considered that separation of the embedded derivative(s) is prohibited, such as a prepayment

> option embedded in a loan that permits the holder to prepay the loan for approximately its amortised cost.

12 If an entity is required by this Standard to separate an embedded derivative from its host contract, but is unable to measure the embedded derivative separately either at acquisition or at the end of a subsequent financial reporting period, it shall designate the entire hybrid (combined) contract as at fair value through profit or loss. Similarly, if an entity is unable to measure separately the embedded derivative that would have to be separated on reclassification of a hybrid (combined) contract out of the fair value through profit or loss category, that reclassification is prohibited. In such circumstances the hybrid (combined) contract remains classified as at fair value through profit or loss in its entirety.13   If an entity is unable to determine reliably the fair value of an embedded derivative on the basis of its terms and conditions (for example, because the embedded derivative is based on an unquoted equity instrument), the fair value of the embedded derivative is the difference between the fair value of the hybrid (combined) instrument and the fair value of the host contract, if those can be determined under this Standard. If the entity is unable to determine the fair value of the embedded derivative using this method, paragraph 12 applies and the hybrid (combined) instrument is designated as at fair value through profit or loss.

Recognition and derecognition

Initial recognition

14 **An entity shall recognise a financial asset or a financial liability in its statement of financial position when, and only when, the entity becomes a party to the contractual provisions of the instrument. (See paragraph 38 with respect to regular way purchases of financial assets.)**

Derecognition of a financial asset

15 In consolidated financial statements, paragraphs 16–23 and Appendix A paragraphs AG34–AG52 are applied at a consolidated level. Hence, an entity first consolidates all subsidiaries in accordance with IAS 27 and SIC-12 *Consolidation—Special Purpose Entities* and then applies paragraphs 16–23 and Appendix A paragraphs AG34–AG52 to the resulting group.

16 **Before evaluating whether, and to what extent, derecognition is appropriate under paragraphs 17–23, an entity determines whether those paragraphs should be applied to a part of a financial asset (or a part of a group of similar financial assets) or a financial asset (or a group of similar financial assets) in its entirety, as follows.**

   (a) **Paragraphs 17–23 are applied to a part of a financial asset (or a part of a group of similar financial assets) if, and only if, the part being considered for derecognition meets one of the following three conditions.**

      (i) **The part comprises only specifically identified cash flows from a financial asset (or a group of similar financial assets). For example, when an entity enters into an interest rate strip whereby the counterparty obtains the right to the interest cash flows, but not the principal cash flows from a debt instrument, paragraphs 17–23 are applied to the interest cash flows.**

      (ii) **The part comprises only a fully proportionate (pro rata) share of the cash flows from a financial asset (or a group of similar financial assets). For example, when an entity enters into an arrangement whereby the counterparty obtains the rights to a 90 per cent share of all cash flows of a debt instrument, paragraphs 17–23 are applied to 90 per cent of those cash flows. If there is more than one counterparty, each counterparty is not required to have a proportionate share of the cash flows provided that the transferring entity has a fully proportionate share.**

      (iii) **The part comprises only a fully proportionate (pro rata) share of specifically identified cash flows from a financial asset (or a group of similar financial assets). For example, when an entity enters into an arrangement whereby the counterparty obtains the rights to a 90 per cent share of interest cash flows from a financial asset,** paragraphs 17–23 are applied to 90 per cent of those interest cash flows. If there is more than one counterparty, each counterparty is not required to have a proportionate share of the specifically identified cash flows provided that the transferring entity has a fully proportionate share.

(b)   In all other cases, paragraphs 17–23 are applied to the financial asset in its entirety (or to the group of similar financial assets in their entirety). For example, when an entity transfers (i) the rights to the first or the last 90 per cent of cash collections from a financial asset (or a group of financial assets), or (ii) the rights to 90 per cent of the cash flows from a group of receivables, but provides a guarantee to compensate the buyer for any credit losses up to 8 per cent of the principal amount of the receivables, paragraphs 17–23 are applied to the financial asset (or a group of similar financial assets) in its entirety.

In paragraphs 17–26, the term 'financial asset' refers to either a part of a financial asset (or a part of a group of similar financial assets) as identified in (a) above or, otherwise, a financial asset (or a group of similar financial assets) in its entirety.

17   An entity shall derecognise a financial asset when, and only when:

(a)   the contractual rights to the cash flows from the financial asset expire; or

(b)   it transfers the financial asset as set out in paragraphs 18 and 19 and the transfer qualifies for derecognition in accordance with paragraph 20.

(See paragraph 38 for regular way sales of financial assets.)

18   An entity transfers a financial asset if, and only if, it either:

(a)   transfers the contractual rights to receive the cash flows of the financial asset; or

(b)   retains the contractual rights to receive the cash flows of the financial asset, but assumes a contractual obligation to pay the cash flows to one or more recipients in an arrangement that meets the conditions in paragraph 19.

19   When an entity retains the contractual rights to receive the cash flows of a financial asset (the 'original asset'), but assumes a contractual obligation to pay those cash flows to one or more entities (the 'eventual recipients'), the entity treats the transaction as a transfer of a financial asset if, and only if, all of the following three conditions are met.

(a)   The entity has no obligation to pay amounts to the eventual recipients unless it collects equivalent amounts from the original asset. Short-term advances by the entity with the right of full recovery of the amount lent plus accrued interest at market rates do not violate this condition.

(b)   The entity is prohibited by the terms of the transfer contract from selling or pledging the original asset other than as security to the eventual recipients for the obligation to pay them cash flows.

(c)   The entity has an obligation to remit any cash flows it collects on behalf of the eventual recipients without material delay. In addition, the entity is not entitled to reinvest such cash flows, except for investments in cash or cash equivalents (as defined in IAS 7 *Statement of cash flows*) during the short settlement period from the collection date to the date of required remittance to the eventual recipients, and interest earned on such investments is passed to the eventual recipients.

20   When an entity transfers a financial asset (see paragraph 18), it shall evaluate the extent to which it retains the risks and rewards of ownership of the financial asset. In this case:

(a)   if the entity transfers substantially all the risks and rewards of ownership of the financial asset, the entity shall derecognise the financial asset and recognise separately as assets or liabilities any rights and obligations created or retained in the transfer.

(b)   if the entity retains substantially all the risks and rewards of ownership of the financial asset, the entity shall continue to recognise the financial asset.

(c)   if the entity neither transfers nor retains substantially all the risks and rewards of ownership of the financial asset, the entity shall determine whether it has retained control of the financial asset. In this case:

   (i)   if the entity has not retained control, it shall derecognise the financial asset and recognise separately as assets or liabilities any rights and obligations created or retained in the transfer.

   (ii)   if the entity has retained control, it shall continue to recognise the financial asset to the extent of its continuing involvement in the financial asset (see paragraph 30).

21   The transfer of risks and rewards (see paragraph 20) is evaluated by comparing the entity's exposure, before and after the transfer, with the variability in the amounts and timing of the net cash flows of the transferred asset. An entity has retained substantially all the risks and rewards of ownership of a financial asset if its exposure to the variability in the present value of the future net cash flows from the financial asset does not change significantly as a result of the transfer (eg because the entity has sold a financial asset subject to an agreement to buy it back at a fixed price or the sale price plus a lender's return). An entity has transferred substantially all the risks and rewards of ownership of a financial asset if its exposure to such variability is no longer significant in relation to the total variability in the present value of the future net cash flows associated with the financial asset (eg because the entity has sold a financial asset subject only to an option to buy it back at its fair value at the time of repurchase or has transferred a fully proportionate share of the cash flows from a larger financial asset in an arrangement, such as a loan sub-participation, that meets the conditions in paragraph 19).

22   Often it will be obvious whether the entity has transferred or retained substantially all risks and rewards of ownership and there will be no need to perform any computations. In other cases, it will be necessary to compute and compare the entity's exposure to the variability in the present value of the future net cash flows before and after the transfer. The computation and comparison is made using as the discount rate an appropriate current market interest rate. All reasonably possible variability in net cash flows is considered, with greater weight being given to those outcomes that are more likely to occur.

23   Whether the entity has retained control (see paragraph 20(c)) of the transferred asset depends on the transferee's ability to sell the asset. If the transferee has the practical ability to sell the asset in its entirety to an unrelated third party and is able to exercise that ability unilaterally and without needing to impose additional restrictions on the transfer, the entity has not retained control. In all other cases, the entity has retained control.

Transfers that qualify for derecognition (see paragraph 20(a) and (c)(i))

24   If an entity transfers a financial asset in a transfer that qualifies for derecognition in its entirety and retains the right to service the financial asset for a fee, it shall recognise either a servicing asset or a servicing liability for that servicing contract. If the fee to be received is not expected to compensate the entity adequately for performing the servicing, a servicing liability for the servicing obligation shall be recognised at its fair value. If the fee to be received is expected to be more than adequate compensation for the servicing, a servicing asset shall be recognised for the servicing right at an amount determined on the basis of an allocation of the carrying amount of the larger financial asset in accordance with paragraph 27.

25   If, as a result of a transfer, a financial asset is derecognised in its entirety but the transfer results in the entity obtaining a new financial asset or assuming a new financial liability, or a servicing liability, the entity shall recognise the new financial asset, financial liability or servicing liability at fair value.

26   On derecognition of a financial asset in its entirety, the difference between:

(a)   the carrying amount and

(b)   the sum of (i) the consideration received (including any new asset obtained less any new liability assumed) and (ii) any cumulative gain or loss that had been recognised in other comprehensive income (see paragraph 55(b))

shall be recognised in profit or loss.

27 If the transferred asset is part of a larger financial asset (eg when an entity transfers interest cash flows that are part of a debt instrument, see paragraph 16(a)) and the part transferred qualifies for derecognition in its entirety, the previous carrying amount of the larger financial asset shall be allocated between the part that continues to be recognised and the part that is derecognised, based on the relative fair values of those parts on the date of the transfer. For this purpose, a retained servicing asset shall be treated as a part that continues to be recognised. The difference between:

(a) the carrying amount allocated to the part derecognised and

(b) the sum of (i) the consideration received for the part derecognised (including any new asset obtained less any new liability assumed) and (ii) any cumulative gain or loss allocated to it that had been recognised in other comprehensive income (see paragraph 55(b))

shall be recognised in profit or loss. A cumulative gain or loss that had been recognised in other comprehensive income is allocated between the part that continues to be recognised and the part that is derecognised, based on the relative fair values of those parts.

28 When an entity allocates the previous carrying amount of a larger financial asset between the part that continues to be recognised and the part that is derecognised, the fair value of the part that continues to be recognised needs to be determined. When the entity has a history of selling parts similar to the part that continues to be recognised or other market transactions exist for such parts, recent prices of actual transactions provide the best estimate of its fair value. When there are no price quotes or recent market transactions to support the fair value of the part that continues to be recognised, the best estimate of the fair value is the difference between the fair value of the larger financial asset as a whole and the consideration received from the transferee for the part that is derecognised.

Transfers that do not qualify for derecognition (see paragraph 20(b))

29 If a transfer does not result in derecognition because the entity has retained substantially all the risks and rewards of ownership of the transferred asset, the entity shall continue to recognise the transferred asset in its entirety and shall recognise a financial liability for the consideration received. In subsequent periods, the entity shall recognise any income on the transferred asset and any expense incurred on the financial liability.

Continuing involvement in transferred assets (see paragraph 20(c)(ii))

30 If an entity neither transfers nor retains substantially all the risks and rewards of ownership of a transferred asset, and retains control of the transferred asset, the entity continues to recognise the transferred asset to the extent of its continuing involvement. The extent of the entity's continuing involvement in the transferred asset is the extent to which it is exposed to changes in the value of the transferred asset. For example:

(a) when the entity's continuing involvement takes the form of guaranteeing the transferred asset, the extent of the entity's continuing involvement is the lower of (i) the amount of the asset and (ii) the maximum amount of the consideration received that the entity could be required to repay ('the guarantee amount').

(b) when the entity's continuing involvement takes the form of a written or purchased option (or both) on the transferred asset, the extent of the entity's continuing involvement is the amount of the transferred asset that the entity may repurchase. However, in case of a written put option on an asset that is measured at fair value, the extent of the entity's continuing involvement is limited to the lower of the fair value of the transferred asset and the option exercise price (see paragraph AG48).

(c) when the entity's continuing involvement takes the form of a cash-settled option or similar provision on the transferred asset, the extent of the entity's continuing involvement is measured in the same way as that which results from non-cash settled options as set out in (b) above.

31   When an entity continues to recognise an asset to the extent of its continuing involvement, the entity also recognises an associated liability. Despite the other measurement requirements in this Standard, the transferred asset and the associated liability are measured on a basis that reflects the rights and obligations that the entity has retained. The associated liability is measured in such a way that the net carrying amount of the transferred asset and the associated liability is:

      (a)   the amortised cost of the rights and obligations retained by the entity, if the transferred asset is measured at amortised cost; or

      (b)   equal to the fair value of the rights and obligations retained by the entity when measured on a stand-alone basis, if the transferred asset is measured at fair value.

32   The entity shall continue to recognise any income arising on the transferred asset to the extent of its continuing involvement and shall recognise any expense incurred on the associated liability.

33   For the purpose of subsequent measurement, recognised changes in the fair value of the transferred asset and the associated liability are accounted for consistently with each other in accordance with paragraph 55, and shall not be offset.

34   If an entity's continuing involvement is in only a part of a financial asset (eg when an entity retains an option to repurchase part of a transferred asset, or retains a residual interest that does not result in the retention of substantially all the risks and rewards of ownership and the entity retains control), the entity allocates the previous carrying amount of the financial asset between the part it continues to recognise under continuing involvement, and the part it no longer recognises on the basis of the relative fair values of those parts on the date of the transfer. For this purpose, the requirements of paragraph 28 apply. The difference between:

      (a)   the carrying amount allocated to the part that is no longer recognised; and

      (b)   the sum of (i) the consideration received for the part no longer recognised and (ii) any cumulative gain or loss allocated to it that had been recognised in other comprehensive income (see paragraph 55(b))

      shall be recognised in profit or loss. A cumulative gain or loss that had been recognised in other comprehensive income is allocated between the part that continues to be recognised and the part that is no longer recognised on the basis of the relative fair values of those parts.

35   If the transferred asset is measured at amortised cost, the option in this Standard to designate a financial liability as at fair value through profit or loss is not applicable to the associated liability.

All transfers

36   If a transferred asset continues to be recognised, the asset and the associated liability shall not be offset. Similarly, the entity shall not offset any income arising from the transferred asset with any expense incurred on the associated liability (see IAS 32 paragraph 42).

37   If a transferor provides non-cash collateral (such as debt or equity instruments) to the transferee, the accounting for the collateral by the transferor and the transferee depends on whether the transferee has the right to sell or repledge the collateral and on whether the transferor has defaulted. The transferor and transferee shall account for the collateral as follows:

      (a)   If the transferee has the right by contract or custom to sell or repledge the collateral, then the transferor shall reclassify that asset in its statement of financial position (eg as a loaned asset, pledged equity instruments or repurchase receivable) separately from other assets.

      (b)   If the transferee sells collateral pledged to it, it shall recognise the proceeds from the sale and a liability measured at fair value for its obligation to return the collateral.

      (c)   If the transferor defaults under the terms of the contract and is no longer entitled to redeem the collateral, it shall derecognise the collateral, and the transferee shall recognise the collateral as its asset initially measured at fair value or, if it has already sold the collateral, derecognise its obligation to return the collateral.

(d)   Except as provided in (c), the transferor shall continue to carry the collateral as its asset, and the transferee shall not recognise the collateral as an asset.

Regular way purchase or sale of a financial asset

38   A regular way purchase or sale of financial assets shall be recognised and derecognised, as applicable, using trade date accounting or settlement date accounting (see Appendix A paragraphs AG53–AG56).

Derecognition of a financial liability

39   An entity shall remove a financial liability (or a part of a financial liability) from its statement of financial position when, and only when, it is extinguished—ie when the obligation specified in the contract is discharged or cancelled or expires.

40   An exchange between an existing borrower and lender of debt instruments with substantially different terms shall be accounted for as an extinguishment of the original financial liability and the recognition of a new financial liability. Similarly, a substantial modification of the terms of an existing financial liability or a part of it (whether or not attributable to the financial difficulty of the debtor) shall be accounted for as an extinguishment of the original financial liability and the recognition of a new financial liability.

41   The difference between the carrying amount of a financial liability (or part of a financial liability) extinguished or transferred to another party and the consideration paid, including any non-cash assets transferred or liabilities assumed, shall be recognised in profit or loss.

42   If an entity repurchases a part of a financial liability, the entity shall allocate the previous carrying amount of the financial liability between the part that continues to be recognised and the part that is derecognised based on the relative fair values of those parts on the date of the repurchase. The difference between (a) the carrying amount allocated to the part derecognised and (b) the consideration paid, including any non-cash assets transferred or liabilities assumed, for the part derecognised shall be recognised in profit or loss.

Measurement

Initial measurement of financial assets and financial liabilities

43   When a financial asset or financial liability is recognised initially, an entity shall measure it at its fair value plus, in the case of a financial asset or financial liability not at fair value through profit or loss, transaction costs that are directly attributable to the acquisition or issue of the financial asset or financial liability.

44   When an entity uses settlement date accounting for an asset that is subsequently measured at cost or amortised cost, the asset is recognised initially at its fair value on the trade date (see Appendix A paragraphs AG53–AG56).

Subsequent measurement of financial assets

45   For the purpose of measuring a financial asset after initial recognition, this Standard classifies financial assets into the following four categories defined in paragraph 9:

(a)   financial assets at fair value through profit or loss;

(b)   held-to-maturity investments;

(c)   loans and receivables; and

(d)   available-for-sale financial assets.

These categories apply to measurement and profit or loss recognition under this Standard. The entity may use other descriptors for these categories or other categorisations when presenting information in the financial statements. The entity shall disclose in the notes the information required by IFRS 7.

46 After initial recognition, an entity shall measure financial assets, including derivatives that are assets, at their fair values, without any deduction for transaction costs it may incur on sale or other disposal, except for the following financial assets:

(a) loans and receivables as defined in paragraph 9, which shall be measured at amortised cost using the effective interest method;

(b) held-to-maturity investments as defined in paragraph 9, which shall be measured at amortised cost using the effective interest method; and

(c) investments in equity instruments that do not have a quoted market price in an active market and whose fair value cannot be reliably measured and derivatives that are linked to and must be settled by delivery of such unquoted equity instruments, which shall be measured at cost (see Appendix A paragraphs AG80 and AG81).

Financial assets that are designated as hedged items are subject to measurement under the hedge accounting requirements in paragraphs 89–102. All financial assets except those measured at fair value through profit or loss are subject to review for impairment in accordance with paragraphs 58–70 and Appendix A paragraphs AG84–AG93.

Subsequent measurement of financial liabilities

47 After initial recognition, an entity shall measure all financial liabilities at amortised cost using the effective interest method, except for:

(a) financial liabilities at fair value through profit or loss. Such liabilities, including derivatives that are liabilities, shall be measured at fair value except for a derivative liability that is linked to and must be settled by delivery of an unquoted equity instrument whose fair value cannot be reliably measured, which shall be measured at cost.

(b) financial liabilities that arise when a transfer of a financial asset does not qualify for derecognition or when the continuing involvement approach applies. Paragraphs 29 and 31 apply to the measurement of such financial liabilities.

(c) financial guarantee contracts as defined in paragraph 9. After initial recognition, an issuer of such a contract shall (unless paragraph 47(a) or (b) applies) measure it at the higher of:

(i) the amount determined in accordance with IAS 37; and

(ii) the amount initially recognised (see paragraph 43) less, when appropriate, cumulative amortisation recognised in accordance with IAS 18.

(d) commitments to provide a loan at a below-market interest rate. After initial recognition, an issuer of such a commitment shall (unless paragraph 47(a) applies) measure it at the higher of:

(i) the amount determined in accordance with IAS 37; and

(ii) the amount initially recognised (see paragraph 43) less, when appropriate, cumulative amortisation recognised in accordance with IAS 18.

Financial liabilities that are designated as hedged items are subject to the hedge accounting requirements in paragraphs 89–102.

Fair value measurement considerations

48 In determining the fair value of a financial asset or a financial liability for the purpose of applying this Standard, IAS 32 or IFRS 7, an entity shall apply paragraphs AG69–AG82 of Appendix A.

48A   The best evidence of fair value is quoted prices in an active market. If the market for a financial instrument is not active, an entity establishes fair value by using a valuation technique. The objective of using a valuation technique is to establish what the transaction price would have been on the measurement date in an arm's length exchange motivated by normal business considerations. Valuation techniques include using recent arm's length market transactions between knowledgeable, willing parties, if available, reference to the current fair value of another instrument that is substantially the same, discounted cash flow analysis and option pricing models. If there is a valuation technique commonly used by market participants to price the instrument and that technique has been demonstrated to provide reliable estimates of prices obtained in actual market transactions, the entity uses that technique. The chosen valuation technique makes maximum use of market inputs and relies as little as possible on entity-specific inputs. It incorporates all factors that market participants would consider in setting a price and is consistent with accepted economic methodologies for pricing financial instruments. Periodically, an entity calibrates the valuation technique and tests it for validity using prices from any observable current market transactions in the same instrument (ie without modification or repackaging) or based on any available observable market data.

49   The fair value of a financial liability with a demand feature (eg a demand deposit) is not less than the amount payable on demand, discounted from the first date that the amount could be required to be paid.

Reclassifications

50   An entity:

(a)   shall not reclassify a derivative out of the fair value through profit or loss category while it is held or issued;

(b)   shall not reclassify any financial instrument out of the fair value through profit or loss category if upon initial recognition it was designated by the entity as at fair value through profit or loss; and

(c)   may, if a financial asset is no longer held for the purpose of selling or repurchasing it in the near term (notwithstanding that the financial asset may have been acquired or incurred principally for the purpose of selling or repurchasing it in the near term), reclassify that financial asset out of the fair value through profit or loss category if the requirements in paragraph 50B or 50D are met.

An entity shall not reclassify any financial instrument into the fair value through profit or loss category after initial recognition.

50A   The following changes in circumstances are not reclassifications for the purposes of paragraph 50:

(a)   a derivative that was previously a designated and effective hedging instrument in a cash flow hedge or net investment hedge no longer qualifies as such;

(b)   a derivative becomes a designated and effective hedging instrument in a cash flow hedge or net investment hedge;

(c)   financial assets are reclassified when an insurance company changes its accounting policies in accordance with paragraph 45 of IFRS 4.

50B   A financial asset to which paragraph 50(c) applies (except a financial asset of the type described in paragraph 50D) may be reclassified out of the fair value through profit or loss category only in rare circumstances.

50C   If an entity reclassifies a financial asset out of the fair value through profit or loss category in accordance with paragraph 50B, the financial asset shall be reclassified at its fair value on the date of reclassification. Any gain or loss already recognised in profit or loss shall not be reversed. The fair value of the financial asset on the date of reclassification becomes its new cost or amortised cost, as applicable.

50D   A financial asset to which paragraph 50(c) applies that would have met the definition of loans and receivables (if the financial asset had not been required to be classified as held for trading at initial recognition) may be reclassified out of the fair value through profit or loss category if the entity has the intention and ability to hold the financial asset for the foreseeable future or until maturity.

50E   A financial asset classified as available for sale that would have met the definition of loans and receivables (if it had not been designated as available for sale) may be reclassified out of the available-for-sale category to the loans and receivables category if the entity has the intention and ability to hold the financial asset for the foreseeable future or until maturity.

50F   If an entity reclassifies a financial asset out of the fair value through profit or loss category in accordance with paragraph 50D or out of the available-for-sale category in accordance with paragraph 50E, it shall reclassify the financial asset at its fair value on the date of reclassification. For a financial asset reclassified in accordance with paragraph 50D, any gain or loss already recognised in profit or loss shall not be reversed. The fair value of the financial asset on the date of reclassification becomes its new cost or amortised cost, as applicable. For a financial asset reclassified out of the available-for-sale category in accordance with paragraph 50E, any previous gain or loss on that asset that has been recognised in other comprehensive income in accordance with paragraph 55(b) shall be accounted for in accordance with paragraph 54.

51   **If, as a result of a change in intention or ability, it is no longer appropriate to classify an investment as held to maturity, it shall be reclassified as available for sale and remeasured at fair value, and the difference between its carrying amount and fair value shall be accounted for in accordance with paragraph 55(b).**

52   **Whenever sales or reclassification of more than an insignificant amount of held-to-maturity investments do not meet any of the conditions in paragraph 9, any remaining held-to-maturity investments shall be reclassified as available for sale. On such reclassification, the difference between their carrying amount and fair value shall be accounted for in accordance with paragraph 55(b).**

53   **If a reliable measure becomes available for a financial asset or financial liability for which such a measure was previously not available, and the asset or liability is required to be measured at fair value if a reliable measure is available (see paragraphs 46(c) and 47), the asset or liability shall be remeasured at fair value, and the difference between its carrying amount and fair value shall be accounted for in accordance with paragraph 55.**

54   **If, as a result of a change in intention or ability or in the rare circumstance that a reliable measure of fair value is no longer available (see paragraphs 46(c) and 47) or because the 'two preceding financial years' referred to in paragraph 9 have passed, it becomes appropriate to carry a financial asset or financial liability at cost or amortised cost rather than at fair value, the fair value carrying amount of the financial asset or the financial liability on that date becomes its new cost or amortised cost, as applicable. Any previous gain or loss on that asset that has been recognised in other comprehensive income in accordance with paragraph 55(b) shall be accounted for as follows:**

       (a)   **In the case of a financial asset with a fixed maturity, the gain or loss shall be amortised to profit or loss over the remaining life of the held-to-maturity investment using the effective interest method. Any difference between the new amortised cost and maturity amount shall also be amortised over the remaining life of the financial asset using the effective interest method, similar to the amortisation of a premium and a discount. If the financial asset is subsequently impaired, any gain or loss that has been recognised in other comprehensive income is reclassified from equity to profit or loss in accordance with paragraph 67.**

       (b)   **In the case of a financial asset that does not have a fixed maturity, the gain or loss shall recognised in profit or loss when the financial asset is sold or otherwise disposed of. If the financial asset is subsequently impaired any previous gain or loss that has been recognised in other comprehensive income is reclassified from equity to profit or loss in accordance with paragraph 67.**

Gains and losses

55   **A gain or loss arising from a change in the fair value of a financial asset or financial liability that is not part of a hedging relationship (see paragraphs 89–102), shall be recognised, as follows.**

       (a)   **A gain or loss on a financial asset or financial liability classified as at fair value through profit or loss shall be recognised in profit or loss.**

       (b)   **A gain or loss on an available-for-sale financial asset shall be recognised in other comprehensive income, except for impairment losses (see paragraphs 67–70) and foreign exchange gains and losses (see Appendix A paragraph AG83), until the financial asset is** derecognized. At that time, the cumulative gain or loss previously recognised in other comprehensive income shall be reclassified from equity to profit or loss as a reclassification adjustment (see IAS 1 *Presentation of Financial Statements* (as revised in 2007)). However, interest calculated using the effective interest method (see paragraph 9) is recognised in profit or loss (see IAS 18). Dividends on an available-for-sale equity instrument are recognised in profit or loss when the entity's right to receive payment is established (see IAS 18).

56   For financial assets and financial liabilities carried at amortised cost (see paragraphs 46 and 47), a gain or loss is recognised in profit or loss when the financial asset or financial liability is derecognised or impaired, and through the amortisation process. However, for financial assets or financial liabilities that are hedged items (see paragraphs 78–84 and Appendix A paragraphs AG98–AG101) the accounting for the gain or loss shall follow paragraphs 89–102.

57   If an entity recognises financial assets using settlement date accounting (see paragraph 38 and Appendix A paragraphs AG53 and AG56), any change in the fair value of the asset to be received during the period between the trade date and the settlement date is not recognised for assets carried at cost or amortised cost (other than impairment losses). For assets carried at fair value, however, the change in fair value shall be recognised in profit or loss or in equity, as appropriate under paragraph 55.

Impairment and uncollectibility of financial assets

58   An entity shall assess at the end of each reporting period whether there is any objective evidence that a financial asset or group of financial assets is impaired. If any such evidence exists, the entity shall apply paragraph 63 (for financial assets carried at amortised cost), paragraph 66 (for financial assets carried at cost) or paragraph 67 (for available-for-sale financial assets) to determine the amount of any impairment loss.

59   A financial asset or a group of financial assets is impaired and impairment losses are incurred if, and only if, there is objective evidence of impairment as a result of one or more events that occurred after the initial recognition of the asset (a 'loss event') and that loss event (or events) has an impact on the estimated future cash flows of the financial asset or group of financial assets that can be reliably estimated. It may not be possible to identify a single, discrete event that caused the impairment. Rather the combined effect of several events may have caused the impairment. Losses expected as a result of future events, no matter how likely, are not recognised. Objective evidence that a financial asset or group of assets is impaired includes observable data that comes to the attention of the holder of the asset about the following loss events:

(a)   significant financial difficulty of the issuer or obligor;

(b)   a breach of contract, such as a default or delinquency in interest or principal payments;

(c)   the lender, for economic or legal reasons relating to the borrower's financial difficulty, granting to the borrower a concession that the lender would not otherwise consider;

(d)   it becoming probable that the borrower will enter bankruptcy or other financial reorganisation;

(e)   the disappearance of an active market for that financial asset because of financial difficulties; or

(f)   observable data indicating that there is a measurable decrease in the estimated future cash flows from a group of financial assets since the initial recognition of those assets, although the decrease cannot yet be identified with the individual financial assets in the group, including:

    (i)   adverse changes in the payment status of borrowers in the group (eg an increased number of delayed payments or an increased number of credit card borrowers who have reached their credit limit and are paying the minimum monthly amount); or

    (ii)   national or local economic conditions that correlate with defaults on the assets in the group (eg an increase in the unemployment rate in the geographical area of the borrowers, a decrease in property prices for mortgages in the relevant area, a decrease in oil prices for loan assets to oil producers, or adverse changes in industry conditions that affect the borrowers in the group).

60   The disappearance of an active market because an entity's financial instruments are no longer publicly traded is not evidence of impairment. A downgrade of an entity's credit rating is not, of itself, evidence of impairment, although it may be evidence of impairment when considered with other available information. A decline in the fair value of a financial asset below its cost or amortised cost is not necessarily evidence of impairment (for example, a decline in the fair value of an investment in a debt instrument that results from an increase in the risk-free interest rate).

61   In addition to the types of events in paragraph 59, objective evidence of impairment for an investment in an equity instrument includes information about significant changes with an adverse effect that have taken place in the technological, market, economic or legal environment in which the issuer operates, and indicates that the cost of the investment in the equity instrument may not be recovered. A significant or prolonged decline in the fair value of an investment in an equity instrument below its cost is also objective evidence of impairment.

62   In some cases the observable data required to estimate the amount of an impairment loss on a financial asset may be limited or no longer fully relevant to current circumstances. For example, this may be the case when a borrower is in financial difficulties and there are few available historical data relating to similar borrowers. In such cases, an entity uses its experienced judgement to estimate the amount of any impairment loss. Similarly an entity uses its experienced judgement to adjust observable data for a group of financial assets to reflect current circumstances (see paragraph AG89). The use of reasonable estimates is an essential part of the preparation of financial statements and does not undermine their reliability.

Financial assets carried at amortised cost

63   **If there is objective evidence that an impairment loss on loans and receivables or held-to-maturity investments carried at amortised cost has been incurred, the amount of the loss is measured as the difference between the asset's carrying amount and the present value of estimated future cash flows (excluding future credit losses that have not been incurred) discounted at the financial asset's original effective interest rate (ie the effective interest rate computed at initial recognition). The carrying amount of the asset shall be reduced either directly or through use of an allowance account. The amount of the loss shall be recognised in profit or loss.**

64   An entity first assesses whether objective evidence of impairment exists individually for financial assets that are individually significant, and individually or collectively for financial assets that are not individually significant (see paragraph 59). If an entity determines that no objective evidence of impairment exists for an individually assessed financial asset, whether significant or not, it includes the asset in a group of financial assets with similar credit risk characteristics and collectively assesses them for impairment. Assets that are individually assessed for impairment and for which an impairment loss is or continues to be recognised are not included in a collective assessment of impairment.

65   **If, in a subsequent period, the amount of the impairment loss decreases and the decrease can be related objectively to an event occurring after the impairment was recognised (such as an improvement in the debtor's credit rating), the previously recognised impairment loss shall be reversed either directly or by adjusting an allowance account. The reversal shall not result in a carrying amount of the financial asset that exceeds what the amortised cost would have been had the impairment not been recognised at the date the impairment is reversed. The amount of the reversal shall be recognised in profit or loss.**

Financial assets carried at cost

66   **If there is objective evidence that an impairment loss has been incurred on an unquoted equity instrument that is not carried at fair value because its fair value cannot be reliably measured, or on a derivative asset that is linked to and must be settled by delivery of such an unquoted equity instrument, the amount of the impairment loss is measured as the difference between the carrying amount of the financial asset and the present value of estimated future cash flows discounted at the current market rate of return for a similar financial asset (see paragraph 46(c) and Appendix A paragraphs AG80 and AG81). Such impairment losses shall not be reversed.**

Available-for-sale financial assets

67 When a decline in the fair value of an available-for-sale financial asset has been recognised in other comprehensive income and there is objective evidence that the asset is impaired (see paragraph 59), the cumulative loss that had been recognised in other comprehensive income shall be reclassified from equity to profit or loss as a reclassification adjustment even though the financial asset has not been derecognised.

68 The amount of the cumulative loss that is reclassified from equity to profit or loss under paragraph 67 shall be the difference between the acquisition cost (net of any principal repayment and amortisation) and current fair value, less any impairment loss on that financial asset previously recognised in profit or loss.

69 Impairment losses recognised in profit or loss for an investment in an equity instrument classified as available for sale shall not be reversed through profit or loss.

70 If, in a subsequent period, the fair value of a debt instrument classified as available for sale increases and the increase can be objectively related to an event occurring after the impairment loss was recognised in profit or loss, the impairment loss shall be reversed, with the amount of the reversal recognised in profit or loss.

Hedging

71 If there is a designated hedging relationship between a hedging instrument and a hedged item as described in paragraphs 85–88 and Appendix A paragraphs AG102–AG104, accounting for the gain or loss on the hedging instrument and the hedged item shall follow paragraphs 89–102.

Hedging instruments

Qualifying instruments

72 This Standard does not restrict the circumstances in which a derivative may be designated as a hedging instrument provided the conditions in paragraph 88 are met, except for some written options (see Appendix A paragraph AG94). However, a non-derivative financial asset or non-derivative financial liability may be designated as a hedging instrument only for a hedge of a foreign currency risk.

73 For hedge accounting purposes, only instruments that involve a party external to the reporting entity (ie external to the group or individual entity that is being reported on) can be designated as hedging instruments. Although individual entities within a consolidated group or divisions within an entity may enter into hedging transactions with other entities within the group or divisions within the entity, any such intragroup transactions are eliminated on consolidation. Therefore, such hedging transactions do not qualify for hedge accounting in the consolidated financial statements of the group. However, they may qualify for hedge accounting in the individual or separate financial statements of individual entities within the group provided that they are external to the individual entity that is being reported on.

Designation of hedging instruments

74 There is normally a single fair value measure for a hedging instrument in its entirety, and the factors that cause changes in fair value are co-dependent. Thus, a hedging relationship is designated by an entity for a hedging instrument in its entirety. The only exceptions permitted are:

(a) separating the intrinsic value and time value of an option contract and designating as the hedging instrument only the change in intrinsic value of an option and excluding change in its time value; and

(b) separating the interest element and the spot price of a forward contract.

These exceptions are permitted because the intrinsic value of the option and the premium on the forward can generally be measured separately. A dynamic hedging strategy that assesses both the intrinsic value and time value of an option contract can qualify for hedge accounting.

75 A proportion of the entire hedging instrument, such as 50 per cent of the notional amount, may be designated as the hedging instrument in a hedging relationship. However, a hedging relationship may not be designated for only a portion of the time period during which a hedging instrument remains outstanding.

76 A single hedging instrument may be designated as a hedge of more than one type of risk provided that (a) the risks hedged can be identified clearly; (b) the effectiveness of the hedge can be demonstrated; and (c) it is possible to ensure that there is specific designation of the hedging instrument and different risk positions.

77 Two or more derivatives, or proportions of them (or, in the case of a hedge of currency risk, two or more non-derivatives or proportions of them, or a combination of derivatives and non-derivatives or proportions of them), may be viewed in combination and jointly designated as the hedging instrument, including when the risk(s) arising from some derivatives offset(s) those arising from others. However, an interest rate collar or other derivative instrument that combines a written option and a purchased option does not qualify as a hedging instrument if it is, in effect, a net written option (for which a net premium is received). Similarly, two or more instruments (or proportions of them) may be designated as the hedging instrument only if none of them is a written option or a net written option.

Hedged items

Qualifying items

78 A hedged item can be a recognised asset or liability, an unrecognised firm commitment, a highly probable forecast transaction or a net investment in a foreign operation. The hedged item can be (a) a single asset, liability, firm commitment, highly probable forecast transaction or net investment in a foreign operation, (b) a group of assets, liabilities, firm commitments, highly probable forecast transactions or net investments in foreign operations with similar risk characteristics or (c) in a portfolio hedge of interest rate risk only, a portion of the portfolio of financial assets or financial liabilities that share the risk being hedged.

79 Unlike loans and receivables, a held-to-maturity investment cannot be a hedged item with respect to interest-rate risk or prepayment risk because designation of an investment as held to maturity requires an intention to hold the investment until maturity without regard to changes in the fair value or cash flows of such an investment attributable to changes in interest rates. However, a held-to-maturity investment can be a hedged item with respect to risks from changes in foreign currency exchange rates and credit risk.

80 For hedge accounting purposes, only assets, liabilities, firm commitments or highly probable forecast transactions that involve a party external to the entity can be designated as hedged items. It follows that hedge accounting can be applied to transactions between entities in the same group only in the individual or separate financial statements of those entities and not in the consolidated financial statements of the group. As an exception, the foreign currency risk of an intragroup monetary item (eg a payable/receivable between two subsidiaries) may qualify as a hedged item in the consolidated financial statements if it results in an exposure to foreign exchange rate gains or losses that are not fully eliminated on consolidation in accordance with IAS 21 *The Effects of Changes in Foreign Exchange Rates*. In accordance with IAS 21, foreign exchange rate gains and losses on intragroup monetary items are not fully eliminated on consolidation when the intragroup monetary item is transacted between two group entities that have different functional currencies. In addition, the foreign currency risk of a highly probable forecast intragroup transaction may qualify as a hedged item in consolidated financial statements provided that the transaction is denominated in a currency other than the functional currency of the entity entering into that transaction and the foreign currency risk will affect consolidated profit or loss.

Designation of financial items as hedged items

81 If the hedged item is a financial asset or financial liability, it may be a hedged item with respect to the risks associated with only a portion of its cash flows or fair value (such as one or more selected contractual cash flows or portions of them or a percentage of the fair value) provided that effectiveness can be measured. For example, an identifiable and separately measurable portion of the interest rate exposure of an interest-bearing asset or interest-bearing liability may be designated as the hedged risk (such as a risk-free

interest rate or benchmark interest rate component of the total interest rate exposure of a hedged financial instrument).

81A   In a fair value hedge of the interest rate exposure of a portfolio of financial assets or financial liabilities (and only in such a hedge), the portion hedged may be designated in terms of an amount of a currency (eg an amount of dollars, euro, pounds or rand) rather than as individual assets (or liabilities). Although the portfolio may, for risk management purposes, include assets and liabilities, the amount designated is an amount of assets or an amount of liabilities. Designation of a net amount including assets and liabilities is not permitted. The entity may hedge a portion of the interest rate risk associated with this designated amount. For example, in the case of a hedge of a portfolio containing prepayable assets, the entity may hedge the change in fair value that is attributable to a change in the hedged interest rate on the basis of expected, rather than contractual, repricing dates. [...].

Designation of non-financial items as hedged items

82   **If the hedged item is a non-financial asset or non-financial liability, it shall be designated as a hedged item (a) for foreign currency risks, or (b) in its entirety for all risks, because of the difficulty of isolating and measuring the appropriate portion of the cash flows or fair value changes attributable to specific risks other than foreign currency risks.**

Designation of groups of items as hedged items

83   Similar assets or similar liabilities shall be aggregated and hedged as a group only if the individual assets or individual liabilities in the group share the risk exposure that is designated as being hedged. Furthermore, the change in fair value attributable to the hedged risk for each individual item in the group shall be expected to be approximately proportional to the overall change in fair value attributable to the hedged risk of the group of items.

84   Because an entity assesses hedge effectiveness by comparing the change in the fair value or cash flow of a hedging instrument (or group of similar hedging instruments) and a hedged item (or group of similar hedged items), comparing a hedging instrument with an overall net position (eg the net of all fixed rate assets and fixed rate liabilities with similar maturities), rather than with a specific hedged item, does not qualify for hedge accounting.

Hedge accounting

85   Hedge accounting recognises the offsetting effects on profit or loss of changes in the fair values of the hedging instrument and the hedged item.

86   **Hedging relationships are of three types:**

   (a)   *fair value hedge*: **a hedge of the exposure to changes in fair value of a recognised asset or liability or an unrecognised firm commitment, or an identified portion of such an asset, liability or firm commitment, that is attributable to a particular risk and could affect profit or loss.**

   (b)   *cash flow hedge*: **a hedge of the exposure to variability in cash flows that (i) is attributable to a particular risk associated with a recognised asset or liability (such as all or some future interest payments on variable rate debt) or a highly probable forecast transaction and (ii) could affect profit or loss.**

   (c)   *hedge of a net investment in a foreign operation* **as defined in IAS 21.**

87   A hedge of the foreign currency risk of a firm commitment may be accounted for as a fair value hedge or as a cash flow hedge.

88   **A hedging relationship qualifies for hedge accounting under paragraphs 89–102 if, and only if, all of the following conditions are met.**

   (a)   **At the inception of the hedge there is formal designation and documentation of the hedging relationship and the entity's risk management objective and strategy for undertaking the hedge. That documentation shall include identification of the hedging instrument, the hedged** item or transaction, the nature of the risk being hedged and how the entity will assess the hedging instrument's effectiveness in offsetting the exposure to changes in the hedged item's fair value or cash flows attributable to the hedged risk.

(b)   The hedge is expected to be highly effective (see Appendix A paragraphs AG105–AG113) in achieving offsetting changes in fair value or cash flows attributable to the hedged risk, consistently with the originally documented risk management strategy for that particular hedging relationship.

(c)   For cash flow hedges, a forecast transaction that is the subject of the hedge must be highly probable and must present an exposure to variations in cash flows that could ultimately affect profit or loss.

(d)   The effectiveness of the hedge can be reliably measured, ie the fair value or cash flows of the hedged item that are attributable to the hedged risk and the fair value of the hedging instrument can be reliably measured (see paragraphs 46 and 47 and Appendix A paragraphs AG80 and AG81 for guidance on determining fair value).

(e)   The hedge is assessed on an ongoing basis and determined actually to have been highly effective throughout the financial reporting periods for which the hedge was designated.

Fair value hedges

89   If a fair value hedge meets the conditions in paragraph 88 during the period, it shall be accounted for as follows:

(a)   the gain or loss from remeasuring the hedging instrument at fair value (for a derivative hedging instrument) or the foreign currency component of its carrying amount measured in accordance with IAS 21 (for a non-derivative hedging instrument) shall be recognised in profit or loss; and

(b)   the gain or loss on the hedged item attributable to the hedged risk shall adjust the carrying amount of the hedged item and be recognised in profit or loss. This applies if the hedged item is otherwise measured at cost. Recognition of the gain or loss attributable to the hedged risk in profit or loss applies if the hedged item is an available-for-sale financial asset.

89A   For a fair value hedge of the interest rate exposure of a portion of a portfolio of financial assets or financial liabilities (and only in such a hedge), the requirement in paragraph 89(b) may be met by presenting the gain or loss attributable to the hedged item either:

(a)   in a single separate line item within assets, for those repricing time periods for which the hedged item is an asset; or

(b)   in a single separate line item within liabilities, for those repricing time periods for which the hedged item is a liability.

The separate line items referred to in (a) and (b) above shall be presented next to financial assets or financial liabilities. Amounts included in these line items shall be removed from the statement of financial position when the assets or liabilities to which they relate are derecognised.

90   If only particular risks attributable to a hedged item are hedged, recognised changes in the fair value of the hedged item unrelated to the hedged risk are recognised as set out in paragraph 55.

91   An entity shall discontinue prospectively the hedge accounting specified in paragraph 89 if:

(a)   the hedging instrument expires or is sold, terminated or exercised (for this purpose, the replacement or rollover of a hedging instrument into another hedging instrument is not an expiration or termination if such replacement or rollover is part of the entity's documented hedging strategy);

(b)   the hedge no longer meets the criteria for hedge accounting in paragraph 88; or

(c)   the entity revokes the designation.

92   Any adjustment arising from paragraph 89(b) to the carrying amount of a hedged financial instrument for which the effective interest method is used (or, in the case of a portfolio hedge of interest rate risk, to the separate line item in the statement of financial position described in paragraph 89A) shall be amortised to profit or loss. Amortisation may begin as soon as an adjustment exists and shall begin no later than when the hedged item ceases to be adjusted for changes in its fair value attributable to the risk being hedged. The adjustment is based on a recalculated effective interest rate at the date amortisation begins. However, if, in the case of a fair value hedge of the interest rate exposure of a portfolio of financial assets or financial liabilities (and only in such a hedge), amortising using a recalculated effective interest rate is not practicable, the adjustment shall be amortised using a straight-line method. The adjustment shall be amortised fully by maturity of the financial instrument or, in the case of a portfolio hedge of interest rate risk, by expiry of the relevant repricing time period.

93   When an unrecognised firm commitment is designated as a hedged item, the subsequent cumulative change in the fair value of the firm commitment attributable to the hedged risk is recognised as an asset or liability with a corresponding gain or loss recognised in profit or loss (see paragraph 89(b)). The changes in the fair value of the hedging instrument are also recognised in profit or loss.

94   When an entity enters into a firm commitment to acquire an asset or assume a liability that is a hedged item in a fair value hedge, the initial carrying amount of the asset or liability that results from the entity meeting the firm commitment is adjusted to include the cumulative change in the fair value of the firm commitment attributable to the hedged risk that was recognised in the statement of financial position.

Cash flow hedges

95   If a cash flow hedge meets the conditions in paragraph 88 during the period, it shall be accounted for as follows:

(a)   the portion of the gain or loss on the hedging instrument that is determined to be an effective hedge (see paragraph 88) shall be recognized in other comprehensive income; and

(b)   the ineffective portion of the gain or loss on the hedging instrument shall be recognised in profit or loss.

96   More specifically, a cash flow hedge is accounted for as follows:

(a)   the separate component of equity associated with the hedged item is adjusted to the lesser of the following (in absolute amounts):

(i)   the cumulative gain or loss on the hedging instrument from inception of the hedge; and

(ii)   the cumulative change in fair value (present value) of the expected future cash flows on the hedged item from inception of the hedge;

(b)   any remaining gain or loss on the hedging instrument or designated component of it (that is not an effective hedge) is recognised in profit or loss; and

(c)   if an entity's documented risk management strategy for a particular hedging relationship excludes from the assessment of hedge effectiveness a specific component of the gain or loss or related cash flows on the hedging instrument (see paragraphs 74, 75 and 88(a)), that excluded component of gain or loss is recognised in accordance with paragraph 55.

97   If a hedge of a forecast transaction subsequently results in the recognition of a financial asset or a financial liability, the associated gains or losses that were recognised in other comprehensive income in accordance with paragraph 95 shall be reclassified from equity to profit or loss as a reclassification adjustment (see IAS 1 (as revised in 2007)) in the same period or periods during which the hedged forecast cash flows affect profit or loss (such as in the periods that interest income or interest expense is recognised). However, if an entity expects that all or a portion of a loss recognised in other comprehensive income will not be recovered in one or more future periods, it shall reclassify into profit or loss as a reclassification adjustment the amount that is not expected to be recovered.

98   If a hedge of a forecast transaction subsequently results in the recognition of a non-financial asset or a non-financial liability, or a forecast transaction for a non-financial asset or non-financial liability

becomes a firm commitment for which fair value hedge accounting is applied, then the entity shall adopt (a) or (b) below:

(a)   It reclassifies the associated gains and losses that were recognised in other comprehensive income in accordance with paragraph 95 into profit or loss as a reclassification adjustment (see IAS 1 (revised 2007)) in the same period or periods during which the asset acquired or liability assumed affects profit or loss (such as in the periods that depreciation expense or cost of sales is recognised). However, if an entity expects that all or a portion of a loss recognised in other comprehensive income will not be recovered in one or more future periods, it shall reclassifyfrom equity to profit or loss as a reclassification adjustment the amount that is not expected to be recovered.

(b)   It removes the associated gains and losses that were recognised in other comprehensive income in accordance with paragraph 95, and includes them in the initial cost or other carrying amount of the asset or liability.

99   An entity shall adopt either (a) or (b) in paragraph 98 as its accounting policy and shall apply it consistently to all hedges to which paragraph 98 relates.

100   For cash flow hedges other than those covered by paragraphs 97 and 98, amounts that had been recognised in other comprehensive income shall be reclassified from equity to profit or loss as a reclassification adjustment (see IAS 1 (revised 2007)) in the same period or periods during which the hedged forecast cash flows affect profit or loss (for example, when a forecast sale occurs).

101   In any of the following circumstances an entity shall discontinue prospectively the hedge accounting specified in paragraphs 95–100:

(a)   The hedging instrument expires or is sold, terminated or exercised (for this purpose, the replacement or rollover of a hedging instrument into another hedging instrument is not an expiration or termination if such replacement or rollover is part of the entity's documented hedging strategy). In this case, the cumulative gain or loss on the hedging instrument that has been recognized in other comprehensive income from the period when the hedge was effective (see paragraph 95(a)) shall remain separately in equity until the forecast transaction occurs. When the transaction occurs, paragraph 97, 98 or 100 applies.

(b)   The hedge no longer meets the criteria for hedge accounting in paragraph 88. In this case, the cumulative gain or loss on the hedging instrument that has been recognized in other comprehensive income from the period when the hedge was effective (see paragraph 95(a)) shall remain separately in equity until the forecast transaction occurs. When the transaction occurs, paragraph 97, 98 or 100 applies.

(c)   The forecast transaction is no longer expected to occur, in which case any related cumulative gain or loss on the hedging instrument that has been recognized in other comprehensive income from the period when the hedge was effective (see paragraph 95(a)) shall be reclassified from equity to profit or loss as a reclassification adjustment. A forecast transaction that is no longer highly probable (see paragraph 88(c)) may still be expected to occur.

(d)   The entity revokes the designation. For hedges of a forecast transaction, the cumulative gain or loss on the hedging instrument that has been recognized in other comprehensive income from the period when the hedge was effective (see paragraph 95(a)) shall remain separately in equity until the forecast transaction occurs or is no longer expected to occur. When the transaction occurs, paragraph 97, 98 or 100 applies. If the transaction is no longer expected to occur, the cumulative gain or loss that had been recognised in other comprehensive income shall be reclassified from equity to profit or loss as a reclassification adjustment.

Hedges of a net investment

102   Hedges of a net investment in a foreign operation, including a hedge of a monetary item that is accounted for as part of the net investment (see IAS 21), shall be accounted for similarly to cash flow hedges:

(a)   the portion of the gain or loss on the hedging instrument that is determined to be an effective hedge (see paragraph 88) shall be recognised in other comprehensive income; and

(b)   the ineffective portion shall be recognised in profit or loss.

The gain or loss on the hedging instrument relating to the effective portion of the hedge that has been recognised in other comprehensive income shall be reclassified from equity to profit or loss as a reclassification adjustment (see IAS 1 (revised 2007)) in accordance with paragraphs 48–49 of IAS 21 on the disposal or partial disposal of the foreign operation.

Effective date and transition

103   An entity shall apply this Standard (including the amendments issued in March 2004) for annual periods beginning on or after 1 January 2005. Earlier application is permitted. An entity shall not apply this Standard (including the amendments issued in March 2004) for annual periods beginning before 1 January 2005 unless it also applies IAS 32 (issued December 2003). If an entity applies this Standard for a period beginning before 1 January 2005, it shall disclose that fact.

103A   An entity shall apply the amendment in paragraph 2(j) for annual periods beginning on or after 1 January 2006. If an entity applies IFRIC 5 *Rights to Interests arising from Decommissioning, Restoration and Environmental Rehabilitation Funds* for an earlier period, this amendment shall be applied for that earlier period.

103B   *Financial Guarantee Contracts* (Amendments to IAS 39 and IFRS 4), issued in August 2005, amended paragraphs 2(e) and (h), 4, 47 and AG4, added paragraph AG4A, added a new definition of financial guarantee contracts in paragraph 9, and deleted paragraph 3. An entity shall apply those amendments for annual periods beginning on or after 1 January 2006. Earlier application is encouraged. If an entity applies these changes for an earlier period, it shall disclose that fact and apply the related amendments to IAS 32* and IFRS 4 at the same time.

103C   IAS 1 (as revised in 2007) amended the terminology used throughout IFRSs. In addition it amended paragraphs 26, 27, 34, 54, 55, 57, 67, 68, 95(a), 97, 98, 100, 102, 105, 108, AG4D, AG4E(d)(i), AG56, AG67, AG83 and AG99B. An entity shall apply those amendments for annual periods beginning on or after 1 January 2009. If an entity applies IAS 1 (revised 2007) for an earlier period, the amendments shall be applied for that earlier period.

103D   IFRS 3 (as revised in 2008) deleted paragraph 2(f). An entity shall apply that amendment for annual periods beginning on or after 1 July 2009. If an entity applies IFRS 3 (revised 2008) for an earlier period, the amendment shall also be applied for that earlier period. However, the amendment does not apply to contingent consideration that arose from a business combination for which the acquisition date preceded the application of IFRS 3 (revised 2008). Instead, an entity shall account for such consideration in accordance with paragraphs 65A–65E of IFRS 3 (as amended in 2010).

103E   IAS 27 (as amended by the International Accounting Standards Board in 2008) amended paragraph 102. An entity shall apply that amendment for annual periods beginning on or after 1 July 2009. If an entity applies IAS 27 (amended 2008) for an earlier period, the amendment shall be applied for that earlier period.

103F   An entity shall apply the amendment in paragraph 2 for annual periods beginning on or after 1 January 2009. If an entity applies *Puttable Financial Instruments and Obligations Arising on Liquidation* (Amendments to IAS 32 and IAS 1), issued in February 2008, for an earlier period, the amendment in paragraph 2 shall be applied for that earlier period.103G   An entity shall apply paragraphs AG99BA, AG99E, AG99F, AG110A and AG110B retrospectively for annual periods beginning on or after 1 July 2009, in accordance with IAS 8 Accounting Policies, Changes in Accounting Estimates and Errors. Earlier application is permitted. If an entity applies Eligible Hedged Items (Amendment to IAS 39) for periods beginning before 1 July 2009, it shall disclose that fact.

103H   *Reclassification of Financial Assets* (Amendments to IAS 39 and IFRS 7), issued in October 2008, amended paragraphs 50 and AG8, and added paragraphs 50B–50F. An entity shall apply those amendments on or after 1 July 2008. An entity shall not reclassify a financial asset in accordance with paragraph 50B, 50D or

*   When an entity applies IFRS 7, the reference to IAS 32 is replaced by a reference to IFRS 7.

50E before 1 July 2008. Any reclassification of a financial asset made on or after 1 November 2008 shall take effect only from the date when the reclassification is made. Any reclassification of a financial asset in accordance with paragraph 50B, 50D or 50E shall not be applied retrospectively before 1 July 2008.

103I   *Reclassification of Financial Assets—Effective Date and Transition* (Amendments to IAS 39 and IFRS 7), issued in November 2008, amended paragraph 103H. An entity shall apply that amendment on or after 1 July 2008.104   This Standard shall be applied retrospectively except as specified in paragraphs 105–108. The opening balance of retained earnings for the earliest prior period presented and all other comparative amounts shall be adjusted as if this Standard had always been in use unless restating the information would be impracticable. If restatement is impracticable, the entity shall disclose that fact and indicate the extent to which the information was restated.

103J   An entity shall apply paragraph 12, as amended by *Embedded Derivatives* (Amendments to IFRIC 9 and IAS 39), issued in March 2009, for annual periods ending on or after 30 June 2009.

103K   *Improvements to IFRSs* issued in April 2009 amended paragraphs 2(g), 97, 100 and AG30(g). An entity shall apply the amendments to paragraphs 2(g), 97 and 100 prospectively to all unexpired contracts for annual periods beginning on or after 1 January 2010. An entity shall apply the amendment to paragraph AG30(g) for annual periods beginning on or after 1 January 2010. Earlier application is permitted. If an entity applies the amendment for an earlier period it shall disclose that fact.

103N   Paragraph 103D was amended by *Improvements to IFRSs* issued in May 2010. An entity shall apply that amendment for annual periods beginning on or after 1 July 2010. Earlier application is permitted.

105   When this Standard is first applied, an entity is permitted to designate a previously recognised financial asset as available for sale. For any such financial asset the entity shall recognise all cumulative changes in fair value in a separate component of equity until subsequent derecognition or impairment, when the entity shall reclassify that cumulative gain or loss from equity to profit or loss as a reclassification adjustment (see IAS 1 (revised 2007)). The entity shall also:

(a)   restate the financial asset using the new designation in the comparative financial statements; and

(b)   disclose the fair value of the financial assets at the date of designation and their classification and carrying amount in the previous financial statements.

105A   An entity shall apply paragraphs 11A, 48A, AG4B–AG4K, AG33A and AG33B and the 2005 amendments in paragraphs 9, 12 and 13 for annual periods beginning on or after 1 January 2006. Earlier application is encouraged.

105B   An entity that first applies paragraphs 11A, 48A, AG4B–AG4K, AG33A and AG33B and the 2005 amendments in paragraphs 9, 12 and 13 in its annual period beginning before 1 January 2006

(a)   is permitted, when those new and amended paragraphs are first applied, to designate as at fair value through profit or loss any previously recognised financial asset or financial liability that then qualifies for such designation. When the annual period begins before 1 September 2005, such designations need not be completed until 1 September 2005 and may also include financial assets and financial liabilities recognised between the beginning of that annual period and 1 September 2005. Notwithstanding paragraph 91, any financial assets and financial liabilities designated as at fair value through profit or loss in accordance with this subparagraph that were previously designated as the hedged item in fair value hedge accounting relationships shall be de-designated from those relationships at the same time they are designated as at fair value through profit or loss.

(b)   shall disclose the fair value of any financial assets or financial liabilities designated in accordance with subparagraph (a) at the date of designation and their classification and carrying amount in the previous financial statements.

(c)   shall de-designate any financial asset or financial liability previously designated as at fair value through profit or loss if it does not qualify for such designation in accordance with those new and amended paragraphs. When a financial asset or financial liability will be measured at amortised cost after de-designation, the date of de-designation is deemed to be its date of initial recognition.

(d)   **shall disclose the fair value of any financial assets or financial liabilities de-designated in accordance with subparagraph (c) at the date of de-designation and their new classifications.**

105C   **An entity that first applies paragraphs 11A, 48A, AG4B–AG4K, AG33A and AG33B and the 2005 amendments in paragraphs 9, 12 and 13 in its annual period beginning on or after 1 January 2006**

(a)   **shall de-designate any financial asset or financial liability previously designated as at fair value through profit or loss only if it does not qualify for such designation in accordance with those new and amended paragraphs. When a financial asset or financial liability will be measured at amortised cost after de-designation, the date of de-designation is deemed to be its date of initial recognition.**

(b)   **shall not designate as at fair value through profit or loss any previously recognised financial assets or financial liabilities.**

(c)   **shall disclose the fair value of any financial assets or financial liabilities de-designated in accordance with subparagraph (a) at the date of de-designation and their new classifications.**

105D   **An entity shall restate its comparative financial statements using the new designations in paragraph 105B or 105C provided that, in the case of a financial asset, financial liability, or group of financial assets, financial liabilities or both, designated as at fair value through profit or loss, those items or groups would have met the criteria in paragraph 9(b)(i), 9(b)(ii) or 11A at the beginning of the comparative period or, if acquired after the beginning of the comparative period, would have met the criteria in paragraph 9(b)(i), 9(b)(ii) or 11A at the date of initial recognition.**

106   **Except as permitted by paragraph 107, an entity shall apply the derecognition requirements in paragraphs 15–37 and Appendix A paragraphs AG36–AG52 prospectively. Accordingly, if an entity derecognised financial assets under IAS 39 (revised 2000) as a result of a transaction that occurred before 1 January 2004 and those assets would not have been derecognised under this Standard, it shall not recognise those assets.**

107   **Notwithstanding paragraph 106, an entity may apply the derecognition requirements in paragraphs 15–37 and Appendix A paragraphs AG36–AG52 retrospectively from a date of the entity's choosing, provided that the information needed to apply IAS 39 to assets and liabilities derecognised as a result of past transactions was obtained at the time of initially accounting for those transactions.**

107A   Notwithstanding paragraph 104, an entity may apply the requirements in the last sentence of paragraph AG76, and paragraph AG76A, in either of the following ways:

(a)   prospectively to transactions entered into after 25 October 2002; or

(b)   prospectively to transactions entered into after 1 January 2004.

108   An entity shall not adjust the carrying amount of non-financial assets and non-financial liabilities to exclude gains and losses related to cash flow hedges that were included in the carrying amount before the beginning of the financial year in which this Standard is first applied. At the beginning of the financial period in which this Standard is first applied, any amount recognised outside profit or loss (in other comprehensive income or directly in equity) for a hedge of a firm commitment that under this Standard is accounted for as a fair value hedge shall be reclassified as an asset or liability, except for a hedge of foreign currency risk that continues to be treated as a cash flow hedge.

108A   An entity shall apply the last sentence of paragraph 80, and paragraphs AG99A and AG99B, for annual periods beginning on or after 1 January 2006. Earlier application is encouraged. If an entity has designated as the hedged item an external forecast transaction that

(a)   is denominated in the functional currency of the entity entering into the transaction,

(b)   gives rise to an exposure that will have an effect on consolidated profit or loss (ie is denominated in a currency other than the group's presentation currency), and

(c)   would have qualified for hedge accounting had it not been denominated in the functional currency of the entity entering into it,

it may apply hedge accounting in the consolidated financial statements in the period(s) before the date of application of the last sentence of paragraph 80, and paragraphs AG99A and AG99B.

108B   An entity need not apply paragraph AG99B to comparative information relating to periods before the date of application of the last sentence of paragraph 80 and paragraph AG99A.

108C   Paragraphs 9, 73 and AG8 were amended and paragraph 50A added by *Improvements to IFRSs* issued in May 2008. Paragraph 80 was amended by *Improvements to IFRSs* issued in April 2009. An entity shall apply those amendments for annual periods beginning on or after 1 January 2009. An entity shall apply the amendments in paragraphs 9 and 50A as of the date and in the manner it applied the 2005 amendments described in paragraph 105A. Earlier application of all the amendments is permitted. If an entity applies the amendments for an earlier period it shall disclose that fact.

Withdrawal of other pronouncements

109   This Standard supersedes IAS 39 *Financial Instruments: Recognition and Measurement* revised in October 2000.

110   This Standard and the accompanying Implementation Guidance supersede the Implementation Guidance issued by the IAS 39 Implementation Guidance Committee, established by the former IASC.

Appendix A
Application guidance

This appendix is an integral part of the Standard.

Scope (paragraphs 2–7)

AG1 Some contracts require a payment based on climatic, geological or other physical variables. (Those based on climatic variables are sometimes referred to as 'weather derivatives'.) If those contracts are not within the scope of IFRS 4, they are within the scope of this Standard.

AG2 This Standard does not change the requirements relating to employee benefit plans that comply with IAS 26 *Accounting and Reporting by Retirement Benefit Plans* and royalty agreements based on the volume of sales or service revenues that are accounted for under IAS 18.

AG3 Sometimes, an entity makes what it views as a 'strategic investment' in equity instruments issued by another entity, with the intention of establishing or maintaining a long-term operating relationship with the entity in which the investment is made. The investor entity uses IAS 28 to determine whether the equity method of accounting is appropriate for such an investment. Similarly, the investor entity uses IAS 31 to determine whether proportionate consolidation or the equity method is appropriate for such an investment. If neither the equity method nor proportionate consolidation is appropriate, the entity applies this Standard to that strategic investment.

AG3A This Standard applies to the financial assets and financial liabilities of insurers, other than rights and obligations that paragraph 2(e) excludes because they arise under contracts within the scope of IFRS 4.

AG4 Financial guarantee contracts may have various legal forms, such as a guarantee, some types of letter of credit, a credit default contract or an insurance contract. Their accounting treatment does not depend on their legal form. The following are examples of the appropriate treatment (see paragraph 2(e)):

(a) Although a financial guarantee contract meets the definition of an insurance contract in IFRS 4 if the risk transferred is significant, the issuer applies this Standard. Nevertheless, if the issuer has previously asserted explicitly that it regards such contracts as insurance contracts and has used accounting applicable to insurance contracts, the issuer may elect to apply either this Standard or IFRS 4 to such financial guarantee contracts. If this Standard applies, paragraph 43 requires the issuer to recognise a financial guarantee contract initially at fair value. If the financial guarantee contract was issued to an unrelated party in a stand-alone arm's length transaction, its fair value at inception is likely to equal the premium received, unless there is evidence to the contrary. Subsequently, unless the financial guarantee contract was designated at inception as at fair value through profit or loss or unless paragraphs 29–37 and AG47–AG52 apply (when a transfer of a financial asset does not qualify for derecognition or the continuing involvement approach applies), the issuer measures it at the higher of:

(i) the amount determined in accordance with IAS 37; and

(ii) the amount initially recognised less, when appropriate, cumulative amortisation recognised in accordance with IAS 18 (see paragraph 47(c)).

(b) Some credit-related guarantees do not, as a precondition for payment, require that the holder is exposed to, and has incurred a loss on, the failure of the debtor to make payments on the guaranteed asset when due. An example of such a guarantee is one that requires payments in response to changes in a specified credit rating or credit index. Such guarantees are not financial guarantee contracts, as defined in this Standard, and are not insurance contracts, as defined in IFRS 4. Such guarantees are derivatives and the issuer applies this Standard to them.

(c) If a financial guarantee contract was issued in connection with the sale of goods, the issuer applies IAS 18 in determining when it recognises the revenue from the guarantee and from the sale of goods.

AG4A   Assertions that an issuer regards contracts as insurance contracts are typically found throughout the issuer's communications with customers and regulators, contracts, business documentation and financial statements. Furthermore, insurance contracts are often subject to accounting requirements that are distinct from the requirements for other types of transaction, such as contracts issued by banks or commercial companies. In such cases, an issuer's financial statements typically include a statement that the issuer has used those accounting requirements.

Definitions (paragraphs 8 and 9)

Designation as at fair value through profit or loss

AG4B   Paragraph 9 of this Standard allows an entity to designate a financial asset, a financial liability, or a group of financial instruments (financial assets, financial liabilities or both) as at fair value through profit or loss provided that doing so results in more relevant information.

AG4C   The decision of an entity to designate a financial asset or financial liability as at fair value through profit or loss is similar to an accounting policy choice (although, unlike an accounting policy choice, it is not required to be applied consistently to all similar transactions). When an entity has such a choice, paragraph 14(b) of IAS 8 *Accounting Policies, Changes in Accounting Estimates and Errors* requires the chosen policy to result in the financial statements providing reliable and more relevant information about the effects of transactions, other events and conditions on the entity's financial position, financial performance or cash flows. In the case of designation as at fair value through profit or loss, paragraph 9 sets out the two circumstances when the requirement for more relevant information will be met. Accordingly, to choose such designation in accordance with paragraph 9, the entity needs to demonstrate that it falls within one (or both) of these two circumstances.

Paragraph 9(b)(i): Designation eliminates or significantly reduces a measurement or recognition inconsistency that would otherwise arise

AG4D   Under IAS 39, measurement of a financial asset or financial liability and classification of recognised changes in its value are determined by the item's classification and whether the item is part of a designated hedging relationship. Those requirements can create a measurement or recognition inconsistency (sometimes referred to as an 'accounting mismatch') when, for example, in the absence of designation as at fair value through profit or loss, a financial asset would be classified as available for sale (with most changes in fair value recognised in other comprehensive income) and a liability the entity considers related would be measured at amortised cost (with changes in fair value not recognised). In such circumstances, an entity may conclude that its financial statements would provide more relevant information if both the asset and the liability were classified as at fair value through profit or loss.

AG4E   The following examples show when this condition could be met. In all cases, an entity may use this condition to designate financial assets or financial liabilities as at fair value through profit or loss only if it meets the principle in paragraph 9(b)(i).

(a)   An entity has liabilities whose cash flows are contractually based on the performance of assets that would otherwise be classified as available for sale. For example, an insurer may have liabilities containing a discretionary participation feature that pay benefits based on realised and/or unrealised investment returns of a specified pool of the insurer's assets. If the measurement of those liabilities reflects current market prices, classifying the assets as at fair value through profit or loss means that changes in the fair value of the financial assets are recognised in profit or loss in the same period as related changes in the value of the liabilities.

(b)   An entity has liabilities under insurance contracts whose measurement incorporates current information (as permitted by IFRS 4, paragraph 24), and financial assets it considers related that would otherwise be classified as available for sale or measured at amortised cost.

(c)   An entity has financial assets, financial liabilities or both that share a risk, such as interest rate risk, that gives rise to opposite changes in fair value that tend to offset each other. However, only some of the instruments would be measured at fair value through profit or loss (ie are derivatives, or are classified as held for trading). It may also be the case that the requirements for hedge accounting are not met, for example because the requirements for effectiveness in paragraph 88 are not met.

(d) An entity has financial assets, financial liabilities or both that share a risk, such as interest rate risk, that gives rise to opposite changes in fair value that tend to offset each other and the entity does not qualify for hedge accounting because none of the instruments is a derivative. Furthermore, in the absence of hedge accounting there is a significant inconsistency in the recognition of gains and losses. For example:

(i) the entity has financed a portfolio of fixed rate assets that would otherwise be classified as available for sale with fixed rate debentures whose changes in fair value tend to offset each other. Reporting both the assets and the debentures at fair value through profit or loss corrects the inconsistency that would otherwise arise from measuring the assets at fair value with changes recognised in other comprehensive income and the debentures at amortised cost.

(ii) the entity has financed a specified group of loans by issuing traded bonds whose changes in fair value tend to offset each other. If, in addition, the entity regularly buys and sells the bonds but rarely, if ever, buys and sells the loans, reporting both the loans and the bonds at fair value through profit or loss eliminates the inconsistency in the timing of recognition of gains and losses that would otherwise result from measuring them both at amortised cost and recognising a gain or loss each time a bond is repurchased.

AG4F   In cases such as those described in the preceding paragraph, to designate, at initial recognition, the financial assets and financial liabilities not otherwise so measured as at fair value through profit or loss may eliminate or significantly reduce the measurement or recognition inconsistency and produce more relevant information. For practical purposes, the entity need not enter into all of the assets and liabilities giving rise to the measurement or recognition inconsistency at exactly the same time. A reasonable delay is permitted provided that each transaction is designated as at fair value through profit or loss at its initial recognition and, at that time, any remaining transactions are expected to occur.

AG4G   It would not be acceptable to designate only some of the financial assets and financial liabilities giving rise to the inconsistency as at fair value through profit or loss if to do so would not eliminate or significantly reduce the inconsistency and would therefore not result in more relevant information. However, it would be acceptable to designate only some of a number of similar financial assets or similar financial liabilities if doing so achieves a significant reduction (and possibly a greater reduction than other allowable designations) in the inconsistency. For example, assume an entity has a number of similar financial liabilities that sum to CU100* and a number of similar financial assets that sum to CU50 but are measured on a different basis. The entity may significantly reduce the measurement inconsistency by designating at initial recognition all of the assets but only some of the liabilities (for example, individual liabilities with a combined total of CU45) as at fair value through profit or loss. However, because designation as at fair value through profit or loss can be applied only to the whole of a financial instrument, the entity in this example must designate one or more liabilities in their entirety. It could not designate either a component of a liability (eg changes in value attributable to only one risk, such as changes in a benchmark interest rate) or a proportion (ie percentage) of a liability.

Paragraph 9(b)(ii): A group of financial assets, financial liabilities or both is managed and its performance is evaluated on a fair value basis, in accordance with a documented risk management or investment strategy

AG4H   An entity may manage and evaluate the performance of a group of financial assets, financial liabilities or both in such a way that measuring that group at fair value through profit or loss results in more relevant information. The focus in this instance is on the way the entity manages and evaluates performance, rather than on the nature of its financial instruments.

AG4I   The following examples show when this condition could be met. In all cases, an entity may use this condition to designate financial assets or financial liabilities as at fair value through profit or loss only if it meets the principle in paragraph 9(b)(ii).

(a) The entity is a venture capital organisation, mutual fund, unit trust or similar entity whose business is investing in financial assets with a view to profiting from their total return in the form of interest or dividends and changes in fair value. IAS 28 and IAS 31 allow such investments to be excluded from their scope provided they are measured at fair value through profit or loss. An entity may

---

*   In this Standard, monetary amounts are denominated in 'currency units' (CU).

apply the same accounting policy to other investments managed on a total return basis but over which its influence is insufficient for them to be within the scope of IAS 28 or IAS 31.

(b)   The entity has financial assets and financial liabilities that share one or more risks and those risks are managed and evaluated on a fair value basis in accordance with a documented policy of asset and liability management. An example could be an entity that has issued 'structured products' containing multiple embedded derivatives and manages the resulting risks on a fair value basis using a mix of derivative and non-derivative financial instruments. A similar example could be an entity that originates fixed interest rate loans and manages the resulting benchmark interest rate risk using a mix of derivative and non-derivative financial instruments.

(c)   The entity is an insurer that holds a portfolio of financial assets, manages that portfolio so as to maximise its total return (ie interest or dividends and changes in fair value), and evaluates its performance on that basis. The portfolio may be held to back specific liabilities, equity or both. If the portfolio is held to back specific liabilities, the condition in paragraph 9(b)(ii) may be met for the assets regardless of whether the insurer also manages and evaluates the liabilities on a fair value basis. The condition in paragraph 9(b)(ii) may be met when the insurer's objective is to maximise total return on the assets over the longer term even if amounts paid to holders of participating contracts depend on other factors such as the amount of gains realised in a shorter period (eg a year) or are subject to the insurer's discretion.

AG4J   As noted above, this condition relies on the way the entity manages and evaluates performance of the group of financial instruments under consideration. Accordingly, (subject to the requirement of designation at initial recognition) an entity that designates financial instruments as at fair value through profit or loss on the basis of this condition shall so designate all eligible financial instruments that are managed and evaluated together.

AG4K   Documentation of the entity's strategy need not be extensive but should be sufficient to demonstrate compliance with paragraph 9(b)(ii). Such documentation is not required for each individual item, but may be on a portfolio basis. For example, if the performance management system for a department—as approved by the entity's key management personnel—clearly demonstrates that its performance is evaluated on a total return basis, no further documentation is required to demonstrate compliance with paragraph 9(b)(ii).

Effective interest rate

AG5   In some cases, financial assets are acquired at a deep discount that reflects incurred credit losses. Entities include such incurred credit losses in the estimated cash flows when computing the effective interest rate.

AG6   When applying the effective interest method, an entity generally amortises any fees, points paid or received, transaction costs and other premiums or discounts included in the calculation of the effective interest rate over the expected life of the instrument. However, a shorter period is used if this is the period to which the fees, points paid or received, transaction costs, premiums or discounts relate. This will be the case when the variable to which the fees, points paid or received, transaction costs, premiums or discounts relate is repriced to market rates before the expected maturity of the instrument. In such a case, the appropriate amortisation period is the period to the next such repricing date. For example, if a premium or discount on a floating rate instrument reflects interest that has accrued on the instrument since interest was last paid, or changes in market rates since the floating interest rate was reset to market rates, it will be amortised to the next date when the floating interest is reset to market rates. This is because the premium or discount relates to the period to the next interest reset date because, at that date, the variable to which the premium or discount relates (ie interest rates) is reset to market rates. If, however, the premium or discount results from a change in the credit spread over the floating rate specified in the instrument, or other variables that are not reset to market rates, it is amortised over the expected life of the instrument.

AG7   For floating rate financial assets and floating rate financial liabilities, periodic re-estimation of cash flows to reflect movements in market rates of interest alters the effective interest rate. If a floating rate financial asset or floating rate financial liability is recognised initially at an amount equal to the principal receivable or payable on maturity, re-estimating the future interest payments normally has no significant effect on the carrying amount of the asset or liability.

AG8   If an entity revises its estimates of payments or receipts, the entity shall adjust the carrying amount of the financial asset or financial liability (or group of financial instruments) to reflect actual and revised estimated cash flows. The entity recalculates the carrying amount by computing the present value of estimated future cash flows at the financial instrument's original effective interest rate or, when applicable, the revised effective interest rate calculated in accordance with paragraph 92.. The adjustment is recognised in profit or loss as income or expense. If a financial asset is reclassified in accordance with paragraph 50B, 50D or 50E, and the entity subsequently increases its estimates of future cash receipts as a result of increased recoverability of those cash receipts, the effect of that increase shall be recognised as an adjustment to the effective interest rate from the date of the change in estimate rather than as an adjustment to the carrying amount of the asset at the date of the change in estimate.

Derivatives

AG9   Typical examples of derivatives are futures and forward, swap and option contracts. A derivative usually has a notional amount, which is an amount of currency, a number of shares, a number of units of weight or volume or other units specified in the contract. However, a derivative instrument does not require the holder or writer to invest or receive the notional amount at the inception of the contract. Alternatively, a derivative could require a fixed payment or payment of an amount that can change (but not proportionally with a change in the underlying) as a result of some future event that is unrelated to a notional amount. For example, a contract may require a fixed payment of CU1,000* if six-month LIBOR increases by 100 basis points. Such a contract is a derivative even though a notional amount is not specified.

AG10   The definition of a derivative in this Standard includes contracts that are settled gross by delivery of the underlying item (eg a forward contract to purchase a fixed rate debt instrument). An entity may have a contract to buy or sell a non-financial item that can be settled net in cash or another financial instrument or by exchanging financial instruments (eg a contract to buy or sell a commodity at a fixed price at a future date). Such a contract is within the scope of this Standard unless it was entered into and continues to be held for the purpose of delivery of a non-financial item in accordance with the entity's expected purchase, sale or usage requirements (see paragraphs 5–7).

AG11   One of the defining characteristics of a derivative is that it has an initial net investment that is smaller than would be required for other types of contracts that would be expected to have a similar response to changes in market factors. An option contract meets that definition because the premium is less than the investment that would be required to obtain the underlying financial instrument to which the option is linked. A currency swap that requires an initial exchange of different currencies of equal fair values meets the definition because it has a zero initial net investment.

AG12   A regular way purchase or sale gives rise to a fixed price commitment between trade date and settlement date that meets the definition of a derivative. However, because of the short duration of the commitment it is not recognised as a derivative financial instrument. Rather, this Standard provides for special accounting for such regular way contracts (see paragraphs 38 and AG53–AG56).

AG12A   The definition of a derivative refers to non-financial variables that are not specific to a party to the contract. These include an index of earthquake losses in a particular region and an index of temperatures in a particular city. Non-financial variables specific to a party to the contract include the occurrence or non-occurrence of a fire that damages or destroys an asset of a party to the contract. A change in the fair value of a non-financial asset is specific to the owner if the fair value reflects not only changes in market prices for such assets (a financial variable) but also the condition of the specific non-financial asset held (a non-financial variable). For example, if a guarantee of the residual value of a specific car exposes the guarantor to the risk of changes in the car's physical condition, the change in that residual value is specific to the owner of the car.

Transaction costs

AG13   Transaction costs include fees and commissions paid to agents (including employees acting as selling agents), advisers, brokers and dealers, levies by regulatory agencies and securities exchanges, and transfer taxes and duties. Transaction costs do not include debt premiums or discounts, financing costs or internal administrative or holding costs.

---

*   In this Standard, monetary amounts are denominated in 'currency units' (CU).

Financial assets and financial liabilities held for trading

AG14   Trading generally reflects active and frequent buying and selling, and financial instruments held for trading generally are used with the objective of generating a profit from short-term fluctuations in price or dealer's margin.

AG15   Financial liabilities held for trading include:

(a)   derivative liabilities that are not accounted for as hedging instruments;

(b)   obligations to deliver financial assets borrowed by a short seller (ie an entity that sells financial assets it has borrowed and does not yet own);

(c)   financial liabilities that are incurred with an intention to repurchase them in the near term (eg a quoted debt instrument that the issuer may buy back in the near term depending on changes in its fair value); and

(d)   financial liabilities that are part of a portfolio of identified financial instruments that are managed together and for which there is evidence of a recent pattern of short-term profit-taking.

The fact that a liability is used to fund trading activities does not in itself make that liability one that is held for trading.

Held-to-maturity investments

AG16   An entity does not have a positive intention to hold to maturity an investment in a financial asset with a fixed maturity if:

(a)   the entity intends to hold the financial asset for an undefined period;

(b)   the entity stands ready to sell the financial asset (other than if a situation arises that is non-recurring and could not have been reasonably anticipated by the entity) in response to changes in market interest rates or risks, liquidity needs, changes in the availability of and the yield on alternative investments, changes in financing sources and terms or changes in foreign currency risk; or

(c)   the issuer has a right to settle the financial asset at an amount significantly below its amortised cost.

AG17   A debt instrument with a variable interest rate can satisfy the criteria for a held-to-maturity investment. Equity instruments cannot be held-to-maturity investments either because they have an indefinite life (such as ordinary shares) or because the amounts the holder may receive can vary in a manner that is not predetermined (such as for share options, warrants and similar rights). With respect to the definition of held-to-maturity investments, fixed or determinable payments and fixed maturity mean that a contractual arrangement defines the amounts and dates of payments to the holder, such as interest and principal payments. A significant risk of non-payment does not preclude classification of a financial asset as held to maturity as long as its contractual payments are fixed or determinable and the other criteria for that classification are met. If the terms of a perpetual debt instrument provide for interest payments for an indefinite period, the instrument cannot be classified as held to maturity because there is no maturity date.

AG18   The criteria for classification as a held-to-maturity investment are met for a financial asset that is callable by the issuer if the holder intends and is able to hold it until it is called or until maturity and the holder would recover substantially all of its carrying amount. The call option of the issuer, if exercised, simply accelerates the asset's maturity. However, if the financial asset is callable on a basis that would result in the holder not recovering substantially all of its carrying amount, the financial asset cannot be classified as a held-to-maturity investment. The entity considers any premium paid and capitalised transaction costs in determining whether the carrying amount would be substantially recovered.

AG19   A financial asset that is puttable (ie the holder has the right to require that the issuer repay or redeem the financial asset before maturity) cannot be classified as a held-to-maturity investment because paying for a put feature in a financial asset is inconsistent with expressing an intention to hold the financial asset until maturity.

AG20   For most financial assets, fair value is a more appropriate measure than amortised cost. The held-to-maturity classification is an exception, but only if the entity has a positive intention and the ability to hold the investment to maturity. When an entity's actions cast doubt on its intention and ability to hold such investments to maturity, paragraph 9 precludes the use of the exception for a reasonable period of time.

AG21   A disaster scenario that is only remotely possible, such as a run on a bank or a similar situation affecting an insurer, is not something that is assessed by an entity in deciding whether it has the positive intention and ability to hold an investment to maturity.

AG22   Sales before maturity could satisfy the condition in paragraph 9—and therefore not raise a question about the entity's intention to hold other investments to maturity—if they are attributable to any of the following:

     (a)   a significant deterioration in the issuer's creditworthiness. For example, a sale following a downgrade in a credit rating by an external rating agency would not necessarily raise a question about the entity's intention to hold other investments to maturity if the downgrade provides evidence of a significant deterioration in the issuer's creditworthiness judged by reference to the credit rating at initial recognition. Similarly, if an entity uses internal ratings for assessing exposures, changes in those internal ratings may help to identify issuers for which there has been a significant deterioration in creditworthiness, provided the entity's approach to assigning internal ratings and changes in those ratings give a consistent, reliable and objective measure of the credit quality of the issuers. If there is evidence that a financial asset is impaired (see paragraphs 58 and 59), the deterioration in creditworthiness is often regarded as significant.

     (b)   a change in tax law that eliminates or significantly reduces the tax-exempt status of interest on the held-to-maturity investment (but not a change in tax law that revises the marginal tax rates applicable to interest income).

     (c)   a major business combination or major disposition (such as a sale of a segment) that necessitates the sale or transfer of held-to-maturity investments to maintain the entity's existing interest rate risk position or credit risk policy (although the business combination is an event within the entity's control, the changes to its investment portfolio to maintain an interest rate risk position or credit risk policy may be consequential rather than anticipated).

     (d)   a change in statutory or regulatory requirements significantly modifying either what constitutes a permissible investment or the maximum level of particular types of investments, thereby causing an entity to dispose of a held-to-maturity investment.

     (e)   a significant increase in the industry's regulatory capital requirements that causes the entity to downsize by selling held-to-maturity investments.

     (f)   a significant increase in the risk weights of held-to-maturity investments used for regulatory risk-based capital purposes.

AG23   An entity does not have a demonstrated ability to hold to maturity an investment in a financial asset with a fixed maturity if:

     (a)   it does not have the financial resources available to continue to finance the investment until maturity; or

     (b)   it is subject to an existing legal or other constraint that could frustrate its intention to hold the financial asset to maturity. (However, an issuer's call option does not necessarily frustrate an entity's intention to hold a financial asset to maturity—see paragraph AG18.)

AG24   Circumstances other than those described in paragraphs AG16–AG23 can indicate that an entity does not have a positive intention or the ability to hold an investment to maturity.

AG25   An entity assesses its intention and ability to hold its held-to-maturity investments to maturity not only when those financial assets are initially recognised, but also at the end of each subsequent reporting period.

Loans and receivables

AG26   Any non-derivative financial asset with fixed or determinable payments (including loan assets, trade receivables, investments in debt instruments and deposits held in banks) could potentially meet the definition of loans and receivables. However, a financial asset that is quoted in an active market (such as a quoted debt instrument, see paragraph AG71) does not qualify for classification as a loan or receivable. Financial assets that do not meet the definition of loans and receivables may be classified as held-to-maturity investments if they meet the conditions for that classification (see paragraphs 9 and AG16–AG25). On initial recognition of a financial asset that would otherwise be classified as a loan or receivable, an entity may designate it as a financial asset at fair value through profit or loss, or available for sale.

Embedded derivatives (paragraphs 10–13)

AG27   If a host contract has no stated or predetermined maturity and represents a residual interest in the net assets of an entity, then its economic characteristics and risks are those of an equity instrument, and an embedded derivative would need to possess equity characteristics related to the same entity to be regarded as closely related. If the host contract is not an equity instrument and meets the definition of a financial instrument, then its economic characteristics and risks are those of a debt instrument.

AG28   An embedded non-option derivative (such as an embedded forward or swap) is separated from its host contract on the basis of its stated or implied substantive terms, so as to result in it having a fair value of zero at initial recognition. An embedded option-based derivative (such as an embedded put, call, cap, floor or swaption) is separated from its host contract on the basis of the stated terms of the option feature. The initial carrying amount of the host instrument is the residual amount after separating the embedded derivative.

AG29   Generally, multiple embedded derivatives in a single instrument are treated as a single compound embedded derivative. However, embedded derivatives that are classified as equity (see IAS 32) are accounted for separately from those classified as assets or liabilities. In addition, if an instrument has more than one embedded derivative and those derivatives relate to different risk exposures and are readily separable and independent of each other, they are accounted for separately from each other.

AG30   The economic characteristics and risks of an embedded derivative are not closely related to the host contract (paragraph 11(a)) in the following examples. In these examples, assuming the conditions in paragraph 11(b) and (c) are met, an entity accounts for the embedded derivative separately from the host contract.

(a)   A put option embedded in an instrument that enables the holder to require the issuer to reacquire the instrument for an amount of cash or other assets that varies on the basis of the change in an equity or commodity price or index is not closely related to a host debt instrument.

(b)   A call option embedded in an equity instrument that enables the issuer to reacquire that equity instrument at a specified price is not closely related to the host equity instrument from the perspective of the holder (from the issuer's perspective, the call option is an equity instrument provided it meets the conditions for that classification under IAS 32, in which case it is excluded from the scope of this Standard).

(c)   An option or automatic provision to extend the remaining term to maturity of a debt instrument is not closely related to the host debt instrument unless there is a concurrent adjustment to the approximate current market rate of interest at the time of the extension. If an entity issues a debt instrument and the holder of that debt instrument writes a call option on the debt instrument to a third party, the issuer regards the call option as extending the term to maturity of the debt instrument provided the issuer can be required to participate in or facilitate the remarketing of the debt instrument as a result of the call option being exercised.

(d)   Equity-indexed interest or principal payments embedded in a host debt instrument or insurance contract—by which the amount of interest or principal is indexed to the value of equity instruments—are not closely related to the host instrument because the risks inherent in the host and the embedded derivative are dissimilar.

(e)   Commodity-indexed interest or principal payments embedded in a host debt instrument or insurance contract—by which the amount of interest or principal is indexed to the price of a commodity (such as gold)—are not closely related to the host instrument because the risks inherent in the host and the embedded derivative are dissimilar.

(f)   An equity conversion feature embedded in a convertible debt instrument is not closely related to the host debt instrument from the perspective of the holder of the instrument (from the issuer's perspective, the equity conversion option is an equity instrument and excluded from the scope of this Standard provided it meets the conditions for that classification under IAS 32).

(g)   A call, put, or prepayment option embedded in a host debt contract or host insurance contract is not closely related to the host contract unless:

    (i)   the option's exercise price is approximately equal on each exercise date to the amortised cost of the host debt instrument or the carrying amount of the host insurance contract; or

    (ii)   the exercise price of a prepayment option reimburses the lender for an amount up to the approximate present value of lost interest for the remaining term of the host contract. Lost interest is the product of the principal amount prepaid multiplied by the interest rate differential. The interest rate differential is the excess of the effective interest rate of the host contract over the effective interest rate the entity would receive at the prepayment date if it reinvested the principal amount prepaid in a similar contract for the remaining term of the host contract.

The assessment of whether the call or put option is closely related to the host debt contract is made before separating the equity element of a convertible debt instrument in accordance with IAS 32.

(h)   Credit derivatives that are embedded in a host debt instrument and allow one party (the 'beneficiary') to transfer the credit risk of a particular reference asset, which it may not own, to another party (the 'guarantor') are not closely related to the host debt instrument. Such credit derivatives allow the guarantor to assume the credit risk associated with the reference asset without directly owning it.

AG31   An example of a hybrid instrument is a financial instrument that gives the holder a right to put the financial instrument back to the issuer in exchange for an amount of cash or other financial assets that varies on the basis of the change in an equity or commodity index that may increase or decrease (a 'puttable instrument'). Unless the issuer on initial recognition designates the puttable instrument as a financial liability at fair value through profit or loss, it is required to separate an embedded derivative (ie the indexed principal payment) under paragraph 11 because the host contract is a debt instrument under paragraph AG27 and the indexed principal payment is not closely related to a host debt instrument under paragraph AG30(a). Because the principal payment can increase and decrease, the embedded derivative is a non-option derivative whose value is indexed to the underlying variable.

AG32   In the case of a puttable instrument that can be put back at any time for cash equal to a proportionate share of the net asset value of an entity (such as units of an open-ended mutual fund or some unit-linked investment products), the effect of separating an embedded derivative and accounting for each component is to measure the combined instrument at the redemption amount that is payable at the end of the reporting period if the holder exercised its right to put the instrument back to the issuer.

AG33   The economic characteristics and risks of an embedded derivative are closely related to the economic characteristics and risks of the host contract in the following examples. In these examples, an entity does not account for the embedded derivative separately from the host contract.

(a)   An embedded derivative in which the underlying is an interest rate or interest rate index that can change the amount of interest that would otherwise be paid or received on an interest-bearing host debt contract or insurance contract is closely related to the host contract unless the combined instrument can be settled in such a way that the holder would not recover substantially all of its recognised investment or the embedded derivative could at least double the holder's initial rate of return on the host contract and could result in a rate of return that is at least twice what the market return would be for a contract with the same terms as the host contract.

(b)   An embedded floor or cap on the interest rate on a debt contract or insurance contract is closely related to the host contract, provided the cap is at or above the market rate of interest and the floor is at or below the market rate of interest when the contract is issued, and the cap or floor is not leveraged in relation to the host contract. Similarly, provisions included in a contract to purchase or sell an asset (eg a commodity) that establish a cap and a floor on the price to be paid or received for the asset are closely related to the host contract if both the cap and floor were out of the money at inception and are not leveraged.

(c)   An embedded foreign currency derivative that provides a stream of principal or interest payments that are denominated in a foreign currency and is embedded in a host debt instrument (eg a dual currency bond) is closely related to the host debt instrument. Such a derivative is not separated from the host instrument because IAS 21 requires foreign currency gains and losses on monetary items to be recognised in profit or loss.

(d)   An embedded foreign currency derivative in a host contract that is an insurance contract or not a financial instrument (such as a contract for the purchase or sale of a non-financial item where the price is denominated in a foreign currency) is closely related to the host contract provided it is not leveraged, does not contain an option feature, and requires payments denominated in one of the following currencies:

   (i)   the functional currency of any substantial party to that contract;

   (ii)   the currency in which the price of the related good or service that is acquired or delivered is routinely denominated in commercial transactions around the world (such as the US dollar for crude oil transactions); or

   (iii) a currency that is commonly used in contracts to purchase or sell non-financial items in the economic environment in which the transaction takes place (eg a relatively stable and liquid currency that is commonly used in local business transactions or external trade).

(e)   An embedded prepayment option in an interest-only or principal-only strip is closely related to the host contract provided the host contract (i) initially resulted from separating the right to receive contractual cash flows of a financial instrument that, in and of itself, did not contain an embedded derivative, and (ii) does not contain any terms not present in the original host debt contract.

(f)   An embedded derivative in a host lease contract is closely related to the host contract if the embedded derivative is (i) an inflation-related index such as an index of lease payments to a consumer price index (provided that the lease is not leveraged and the index relates to inflation in the entity's own economic environment), (ii) contingent rentals based on related sales or (iii) contingent rentals based on variable interest rates.

(g)   A unit-linking feature embedded in a host financial instrument or host insurance contract is closely related to the host instrument or host contract if the unit-denominated payments are measured at current unit values that reflect the fair values of the assets of the fund. A unit-linking feature is a contractual term that requires payments denominated in units of an internal or external investment fund.

(h)   A derivative embedded in an insurance contract is closely related to the host insurance contract if the embedded derivative and host insurance contract are so interdependent that an entity cannot measure the embedded derivative separately (ie without considering the host contract).

Instruments containing embedded derivatives

AG33A   When an entity becomes a party to a hybrid (combined) instrument that contains one or more embedded derivatives, paragraph 11 requires the entity to identify any such embedded derivative, assess whether it is required to be separated from the host contract and, for those that are required to be separated, measure the derivatives at fair value at initial recognition and subsequently. These requirements can be more complex, or result in less reliable measures, than measuring the entire instrument at fair value through profit or loss. For that reason this Standard permits the entire instrument to be designated as at fair value through profit or loss.

AG33B   Such designation may be used whether paragraph 11 requires the embedded derivatives to be separated from the host contract or prohibits such separation. However, paragraph 11A would not justify designating the hybrid (combined) instrument as at fair value through profit or loss in the cases set out in paragraph 11A(a) and (b) because doing so would not reduce complexity or increase reliability.

Recognition and derecognition (paragraphs 14–42)

Initial recognition (paragraph 14)

AG34   As a consequence of the principle in paragraph 14, an entity recognises all of its contractual rights and obligations under derivatives in its statement of financial position as assets and liabilities, respectively, except for derivatives that prevent a transfer of financial assets from being accounted for as a sale (see paragraph AG49). If a transfer of a financial asset does not qualify for derecognition, the transferee does not recognise the transferred asset as its asset (see paragraph AG50).

AG35   The following are examples of applying the principle in paragraph 14:

(a)   unconditional receivables and payables are recognised as assets or liabilities when the entity becomes a party to the contract and, as a consequence, has a legal right to receive or a legal obligation to pay cash.

(b)   assets to be acquired and liabilities to be incurred as a result of a firm commitment to purchase or sell goods or services are generally not recognised until at least one of the parties has performed under the agreement. For example, an entity that receives a firm order does not generally recognise an asset (and the entity that places the order does not recognise a liability) at the time of the commitment but, rather, delays recognition until the ordered goods or services have been shipped, delivered or rendered. If a firm commitment to buy or sell non-financial items is within the scope of this Standard under paragraphs 5–7, its net fair value is recognised as an asset or liability on the commitment date (see (c) below). In addition, if a previously unrecognised firm commitment is designated as a hedged item in a fair value hedge, any change in the net fair value attributable to the hedged risk is recognised as an asset or liability after the inception of the hedge (see paragraphs 93 and 94).

(c)   a forward contract that is within the scope of this Standard (see paragraphs 2–7) is recognised as an asset or a liability on the commitment date, rather than on the date on which settlement takes place. When an entity becomes a party to a forward contract, the fair values of the right and obligation are often equal, so that the net fair value of the forward is zero. If the net fair value of the right and obligation is not zero, the contract is recognised as an asset or liability.

(d)   option contracts that are within the scope of this Standard (see paragraphs 2–7) are recognised as assets or liabilities when the holder or writer becomes a party to the contract.

(e)   planned future transactions, no matter how likely, are not assets and liabilities because the entity has not become a party to a contract.

Derecognition of a financial asset (paragraphs 15–37)

AG36 The following flow chart illustrates the evaluation of whether and to what extent a financial asset is derecognised.

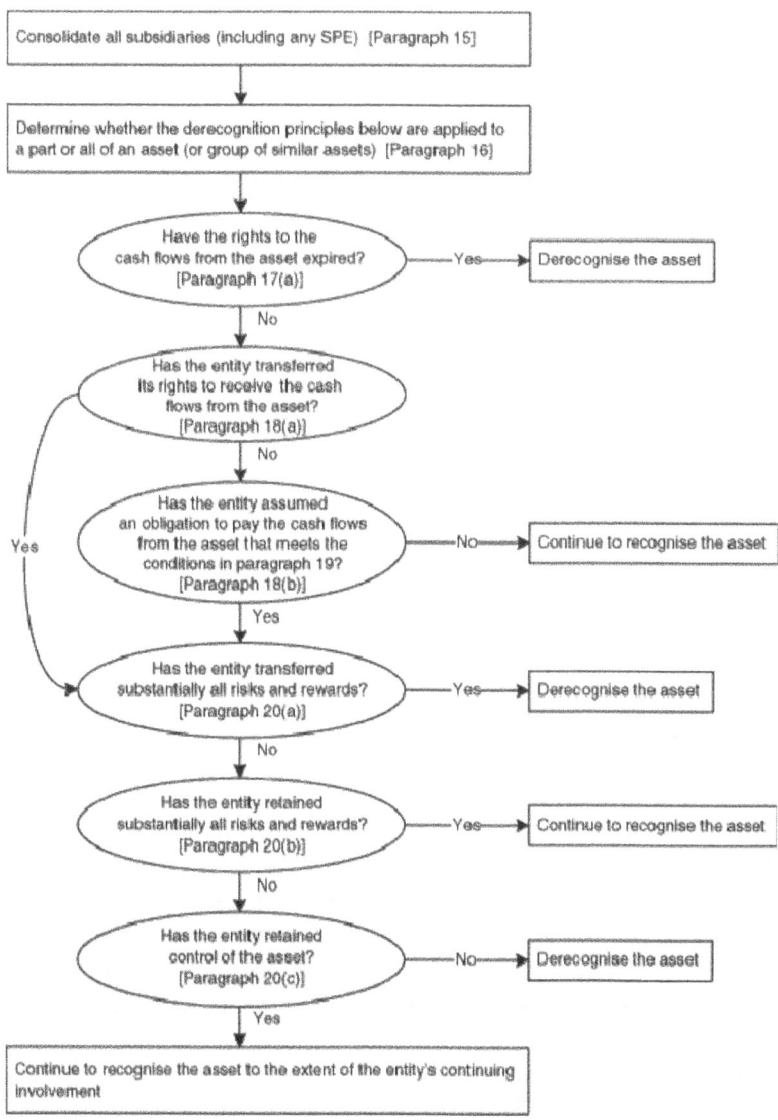

Arrangements under which an entity retains the contractual rights to receive the cash flows of a financial asset, but assumes a contractual obligation to pay the cash flows to one or more recipients (paragraph 18(b))

AG37 The situation described in paragraph 18(b) (when an entity retains the contractual rights to receive the cash flows of the financial asset, but assumes a contractual obligation to pay the cash flows to one or more recipients) occurs, for example, if the entity is a special purpose entity or trust, and issues to investors beneficial interests in the underlying financial assets that it owns and provides servicing of those financial assets. In that case, the financial assets qualify for derecognition if the conditions in paragraphs 19 and 20 are met.

AG38   In applying paragraph 19, the entity could be, for example, the originator of the financial asset, or it could be a group that includes a consolidated special purpose entity that has acquired the financial asset and passes on cash flows to unrelated third party investors.

Evaluation of the transfer of risks and rewards of ownership (paragraph 20)

AG39   Examples of when an entity has transferred substantially all the risks and rewards of ownership are:

(a)   an unconditional sale of a financial asset;

(b)   a sale of a financial asset together with an option to repurchase the financial asset at its fair value at the time of repurchase; and

(c)   a sale of a financial asset together with a put or call option that is deeply out of the money (ie an option that is so far out of the money it is highly unlikely to go into the money before expiry).

AG40   Examples of when an entity has retained substantially all the risks and rewards of ownership are:

(a)   a sale and repurchase transaction where the repurchase price is a fixed price or the sale price plus a lender's return;

(b)   a securities lending agreement;

(c)   a sale of a financial asset together with a total return swap that transfers the market risk exposure back to the entity;

(d)   a sale of a financial asset together with a deep in-the-money put or call option (ie an option that is so far in the money that it is highly unlikely to go out of the money before expiry); and

(e)   a sale of short-term receivables in which the entity guarantees to compensate the transferee for credit losses that are likely to occur.

AG41   If an entity determines that as a result of the transfer, it has transferred substantially all the risks and rewards of ownership of the transferred asset, it does not recognise the transferred asset again in a future period, unless it reacquires the transferred asset in a new transaction.

Evaluation of the transfer of control

AG42   An entity has not retained control of a transferred asset if the transferee has the practical ability to sell the transferred asset. An entity has retained control of a transferred asset if the transferee does not have the practical ability to sell the transferred asset. A transferee has the practical ability to sell the transferred asset if it is traded in an active market because the transferee could repurchase the transferred asset in the market if it needs to return the asset to the entity. For example, a transferee may have the practical ability to sell a transferred asset if the transferred asset is subject to an option that allows the entity to repurchase it, but the transferee can readily obtain the transferred asset in the market if the option is exercised. A transferee does not have the practical ability to sell the transferred asset if the entity retains such an option and the transferee cannot readily obtain the transferred asset in the market if the entity exercises its option.

AG43   The transferee has the practical ability to sell the transferred asset only if the transferee can sell the transferred asset in its entirety to an unrelated third party and is able to exercise that ability unilaterally and without imposing additional restrictions on the transfer. The critical question is what the transferee is able to do in practice, not what contractual rights the transferee has concerning what it can do with the transferred asset or what contractual prohibitions exist. In particular:

(a)   a contractual right to dispose of the transferred asset has little practical effect if there is no market for the transferred asset; and

(b)   an ability to dispose of the transferred asset has little practical effect if it cannot be exercised freely. For that reason:

       (i)   the transferee's ability to dispose of the transferred asset must be independent of the actions of others (ie it must be a unilateral ability); and

       (ii)   the transferee must be able to dispose of the transferred asset without needing to attach restrictive conditions or 'strings' to the transfer (eg conditions about how a loan asset is serviced or an option giving the transferee the right to repurchase the asset).

AG44   That the transferee is unlikely to sell the transferred asset does not, of itself, mean that the transferor has retained control of the transferred asset. However, if a put option or guarantee constrains the transferee from selling the transferred asset, then the transferor has retained control of the transferred asset. For example, if a put option or guarantee is sufficiently valuable it constrains the transferee from selling the transferred asset because the transferee would, in practice, not sell the transferred asset to a third party without attaching a similar option or other restrictive conditions. Instead, the transferee would hold the transferred asset so as to obtain payments under the guarantee or put option. Under these circumstances the transferor has retained control of the transferred asset.

Transfers that qualify for derecognition

AG45   An entity may retain the right to a part of the interest payments on transferred assets as compensation for servicing those assets. The part of the interest payments that the entity would give up upon termination or transfer of the servicing contract is allocated to the servicing asset or servicing liability. The part of the interest payments that the entity would not give up is an interest-only strip receivable. For example, if the entity would not give up any interest upon termination or transfer of the servicing contract, the entire interest spread is an interest-only strip receivable. For the purposes of applying paragraph 27, the fair values of the servicing asset and interest-only strip receivable are used to allocate the carrying amount of the receivable between the part of the asset that is derecognised and the part that continues to be recognised. If there is no servicing fee specified or the fee to be received is not expected to compensate the entity adequately for performing the servicing, a liability for the servicing obligation is recognised at fair value.

AG46   In estimating the fair values of the part that continues to be recognised and the part that is derecognised for the purposes of applying paragraph 27, an entity applies the fair value measurement requirements in paragraphs 48-49 and AG69–AG82 in addition to paragraph 28.

Transfers that do not qualify for derecognition

AG47   The following is an application of the principle outlined in paragraph 29. If a guarantee provided by the entity for default losses on the transferred asset prevents a transferred asset from being derecognised because the entity has retained substantially all the risks and rewards of ownership of the transferred asset, the transferred asset continues to be recognised in its entirety and the consideration received is recognised as a liability.

Continuing involvement in transferred assets

AG48   The following are examples of how an entity measures a transferred asset and the associated liability under paragraph 30.

All assets

(a)   If a guarantee provided by an entity to pay for default losses on a transferred asset prevents the transferred asset from being derecognised to the extent of the continuing involvement, the transferred asset at the date of the transfer is measured at the lower of (i) the carrying amount of the asset and (ii) the maximum amount of the consideration received in the transfer that the entity could be required to repay ('the guarantee amount'). The associated liability is initially measured at the guarantee amount plus the fair value of the guarantee (which is normally the consideration received for the guarantee). Subsequently, the initial fair value of the guarantee is recognised in profit or loss on a time proportion basis (see IAS 18) and the carrying value of the asset is reduced by any impairment losses.

Assets measured at amortised cost

(b) If a put option obligation written by an entity or call option right held by an entity prevents a transferred asset from being derecognised and the entity measures the transferred asset at amortised cost, the associated liability is measured at its cost (ie the consideration received) adjusted for the amortisation of any difference between that cost and the amortised cost of the transferred asset at the expiration date of the option. For example, assume that the amortised cost and carrying amount of the asset on the date of the transfer is CU98 and that the consideration received is CU95. The amortised cost of the asset on the option exercise date will be CU100. The initial carrying amount of the associated liability is CU95 and the difference between CU95 and CU100 is recognised in profit or loss using the effective interest method. If the option is exercised, any difference between the carrying amount of the associated liability and the exercise price is recognised in profit or loss.

Assets measured at fair value

(c) If a call option right retained by an entity prevents a transferred asset from being derecognised and the entity measures the transferred asset at fair value, the asset continues to be measured at its fair value. The associated liability is measured at (i) the option exercise price less the time value of the option if the option is in or at the money, or (ii) the fair value of the transferred asset less the time value of the option if the option is out of the money. The adjustment to the measurement of the associated liability ensures that the net carrying amount of the asset and the associated liability is the fair value of the call option right. For example, if the fair value of the underlying asset is CU80, the option exercise price is CU95 and the time value of the option is CU5, the carrying amount of the associated liability is CU75 (CU80 – CU5) and the carrying amount of the transferred asset is CU80 (ie its fair value).

(d) If a put option written by an entity prevents a transferred asset from being derecognised and the entity measures the transferred asset at fair value, the associated liability is measured at the option exercise price plus the time value of the option. The measurement of the asset at fair value is limited to the lower of the fair value and the option exercise price because the entity has no right to increases in the fair value of the transferred asset above the exercise price of the option. This ensures that the net carrying amount of the asset and the associated liability is the fair value of the put option obligation. For example, if the fair value of the underlying asset is CU120, the option exercise price is CU100 and the time value of the option is CU5, the carrying amount of the associated liability is CU105 (CU100 + CU5) and the carrying amount of the asset is CU100 (in this case the option exercise price).

(e) If a collar, in the form of a purchased call and written put, prevents a transferred asset from being derecognised and the entity measures the asset at fair value, it continues to measure the asset at fair value. The associated liability is measured at (i) the sum of the call exercise price and fair value of the put option less the time value of the call option, if the call option is in or at the money, or (ii) the sum of the fair value of the asset and the fair value of the put option less the time value of the call option if the call option is out of the money. The adjustment to the associated liability ensures that the net carrying amount of the asset and the associated liability is the fair value of the options held and written by the entity. For example, assume an entity transfers a financial asset that is measured at fair value while simultaneously purchasing a call with an exercise price of CU120 and writing a put with an exercise price of CU80. Assume also that the fair value of the asset is CU100 at the date of the transfer. The time value of the put and call are CU1 and CU5 respectively. In this case, the entity recognises an asset of CU100 (the fair value of the asset) and a liability of CU96 [(CU100 + CU1) – CU5]. This gives a net asset value of CU4, which is the fair value of the options held and written by the entity.

All transfers

AG49 To the extent that a transfer of a financial asset does not qualify for derecognition, the transferor's contractual rights or obligations related to the transfer are not accounted for separately as derivatives if recognising both the derivative and either the transferred asset or the liability arising from the transfer would result in recognising the same rights or obligations twice. For example, a call option retained by the transferor may prevent a transfer of financial assets from being accounted for as a sale. In that case, the call option is not separately recognised as a derivative asset.

AG50   To the extent that a transfer of a financial asset does not qualify for derecognition, the transferee does not recognise the transferred asset as its asset. The transferee derecognises the cash or other consideration paid and recognises a receivable from the transferor. If the transferor has both a right and an obligation to reacquire control of the entire transferred asset for a fixed amount (such as under a repurchase agreement), the transferee may account for its receivable as a loan or receivable.

Examples

AG51   The following examples illustrate the application of the derecognition principles of this Standard.

(a)   *Repurchase agreements and securities lending.* If a financial asset is sold under an agreement to repurchase it at a fixed price or at the sale price plus a lender's return or if it is loaned under an agreement to return it to the transferor, it is not derecognised because the transferor retains substantially all the risks and rewards of ownership. If the transferee obtains the right to sell or pledge the asset, the transferor reclassifies the asset in its statement of financial position, for example, as a loaned asset or repurchase receivable.

(b)   *Repurchase agreements and securities lending—assets that are substantially the same.* If a financial asset is sold under an agreement to repurchase the same or substantially the same asset at a fixed price or at the sale price plus a lender's return or if a financial asset is borrowed or loaned under an agreement to return the same or substantially the same asset to the transferor, it is not derecognised because the transferor retains substantially all the risks and rewards of ownership.

(c)   *Repurchase agreements and securities lending—right of substitution.* If a repurchase agreement at a fixed repurchase price or a price equal to the sale price plus a lender's return, or a similar securities lending transaction, provides the transferee with a right to substitute assets that are similar and of equal fair value to the transferred asset at the repurchase date, the asset sold or lent under a repurchase or securities lending transaction is not derecognised because the transferor retains substantially all the risks and rewards of ownership.

(d)   *Repurchase right of first refusal at fair value.* If an entity sells a financial asset and retains only a right of first refusal to repurchase the transferred asset at fair value if the transferee subsequently sells it, the entity derecognises the asset because it has transferred substantially all the risks and rewards of ownership.

(e)   *Wash sale transaction.* The repurchase of a financial asset shortly after it has been sold is sometimes referred to as a wash sale. Such a repurchase does not preclude derecognition provided that the original transaction met the derecognition requirements. However, if an agreement to sell a financial asset is entered into concurrently with an agreement to repurchase the same asset at a fixed price or the sale price plus a lender's return, then the asset is not derecognised.

(f)   *Put options and call options that are deeply in the money.* If a transferred financial asset can be called back by the transferor and the call option is deeply in the money, the transfer does not qualify for derecognition because the transferor has retained substantially all the risks and rewards of ownership. Similarly, if the financial asset can be put back by the transferee and the put option is deeply in the money, the transfer does not qualify for derecognition because the transferor has retained substantially all the risks and rewards of ownership.

(g)   *Put options and call options that are deeply out of the money.* A financial asset that is transferred subject only to a deep out-of-the-money put option held by the transferee or a deep out-of-the-money call option held by the transferor is derecognised. This is because the transferor has transferred substantially all the risks and rewards of ownership.

(h)   *Readily obtainable assets subject to a call option that is neither deeply in the money nor deeply out of the money.* If an entity holds a call option on an asset that is readily obtainable in the market and the option is neither deeply in the money nor deeply out of the money, the asset is derecognised. This is because the entity (i) has neither retained nor transferred substantially all the risks and rewards of ownership, and (ii) has not retained control. However, if the asset is not readily obtainable in the market, derecognition is precluded to the extent of the amount of the asset that is subject to the call option because the entity has retained control of the asset.

(i)   *A not readily obtainable asset subject to a put option written by an entity that is neither deeply in the money nor deeply out of the money.* If an entity transfers a financial asset that is not readily obtainable in the market, and writes a put option that is not deeply out of the money, the entity neither retains nor transfers substantially all the risks and rewards of ownership because of the written put option. The entity retains control of the asset if the put option is sufficiently valuable to prevent the transferee from selling the asset, in which case the asset continues to be recognised to the extent of the transferor's continuing involvement (see paragraph AG44). The entity transfers control of the asset if the put option is not sufficiently valuable to prevent the transferee from selling the asset, in which case the asset is derecognised.

(j)   *Assets subject to a fair value put or call option or a forward repurchase agreement.* A transfer of a financial asset that is subject only to a put or call option or a forward repurchase agreement that has an exercise or repurchase price equal to the fair value of the financial asset at the time of repurchase results in derecognition because of the transfer of substantially all the risks and rewards of ownership.

(k)   *Cash settled call or put options.* An entity evaluates the transfer of a financial asset that is subject to a put or call option or a forward repurchase agreement that will be settled net in cash to determine whether it has retained or transferred substantially all the risks and rewards of ownership. If the entity has not retained substantially all the risks and rewards of ownership of the transferred asset, it determines whether it has retained control of the transferred asset. That the put or the call or the forward repurchase agreement is settled net in cash does not automatically mean that the entity has transferred control (see paragraphs AG44 and (g), (h) and (i) above).

(l)   *Removal of accounts provision.* A removal of accounts provision is an unconditional repurchase (call) option that gives an entity the right to reclaim assets transferred subject to some restrictions. Provided that such an option results in the entity neither retaining nor transferring substantially all the risks and rewards of ownership, it precludes derecognition only to the extent of the amount subject to repurchase (assuming that the transferee cannot sell the assets). For example, if the carrying amount and proceeds from the transfer of loan assets are CU100,000 and any individual loan could be called back but the aggregate amount of loans that could be repurchased could not exceed CU10,000, CU90,000 of the loans would qualify for derecognition.

(m)   *Clean-up calls.* An entity, which may be a transferor, that services transferred assets may hold a clean-up call to purchase remaining transferred assets when the amount of outstanding assets falls to a specified level at which the cost of servicing those assets becomes burdensome in relation to the benefits of servicing. Provided that such a clean-up call results in the entity neither retaining nor transferring substantially all the risks and rewards of ownership and the transferee cannot sell the assets, it precludes derecognition only to the extent of the amount of the assets that is subject to the call option.

(n)   *Subordinated retained interests and credit guarantees.* An entity may provide the transferee with credit enhancement by subordinating some or all of its interest retained in the transferred asset. Alternatively, an entity may provide the transferee with credit enhancement in the form of a credit guarantee that could be unlimited or limited to a specified amount. If the entity retains substantially all the risks and rewards of ownership of the transferred asset, the asset continues to be recognised in its entirety. If the entity retains some, but not substantially all, of the risks and rewards of ownership and has retained control, derecognition is precluded to the extent of the amount of cash or other assets that the entity could be required to pay.

(o)   *Total return swaps.* An entity may sell a financial asset to a transferee and enter into a total return swap with the transferee, whereby all of the interest payment cash flows from the underlying asset are remitted to the entity in exchange for a fixed payment or variable rate payment and any increases or declines in the fair value of the underlying asset are absorbed by the entity. In such a case, derecognition of all of the asset is prohibited.

(p)   *Interest rate swaps.* An entity may transfer to a transferee a fixed rate financial asset and enter into an interest rate swap with the transferee to receive a fixed interest rate and pay a variable interest rate based on a notional amount that is equal to the principal amount of the transferred financial asset. The interest rate swap does not preclude derecognition of the transferred asset provided the payments on the swap are not conditional on payments being made on the transferred asset.

(q)   *Amortising interest rate swaps.* An entity may transfer to a transferee a fixed rate financial asset that is paid off over time, and enter into an amortising interest rate swap with the transferee to receive a fixed interest rate and pay a variable interest rate based on a notional amount. If the notional amount of the swap amortises so that it equals the principal amount of the transferred financial asset outstanding at any point in time, the swap would generally result in the entity retaining substantial prepayment risk, in which case the entity either continues to recognise all of the transferred asset or continues to recognise the transferred asset to the extent of its continuing involvement. Conversely, if the amortisation of the notional amount of the swap is not linked to the principal amount outstanding of the transferred asset, such a swap would not result in the entity retaining prepayment risk on the asset. Hence, it would not preclude derecognition of the transferred asset provided the payments on the swap are not conditional on interest payments being made on the transferred asset and the swap does not result in the entity retaining any other significant risks and rewards of ownership on the transferred asset.

AG52　This paragraph illustrates the application of the continuing involvement approach when the entity's continuing involvement is in a part of a financial asset.

Assume an entity has a portfolio of prepayable loans whose coupon and effective interest rate is 10 per cent and whose principal amount and amortised cost is CU10,000. It enters into a transaction in which, in return for a payment of CU9,115, the transferee obtains the right to CU9,000 of any collections of principal plus interest thereon at 9.5 per cent. The entity retains rights to CU1,000 of any collections of principal plus interest thereon at 10 per cent, plus the excess spread of 0.5 per cent on the remaining CU9,000 of principal. Collections from prepayments are allocated between the entity and the transferee proportionately in the ratio of 1:9, but any defaults are deducted from the entity's interest of CU1,000 until that interest is exhausted. The fair value of the loans at the date of the transaction is CU10,100 and the estimated fair value of the excess spread of 0.5 per cent is CU40.

The entity determines that it has transferred some significant risks and rewards of ownership (for example, significant prepayment risk) but has also retained some significant risks and rewards of ownership (because of its subordinated retained interest) and has retained control. It therefore applies the continuing involvement approach.

To apply this Standard, the entity analyses the transaction as (a) a retention of a fully proportionate retained interest of CU1,000, plus (b) the subordination of that retained interest to provide credit enhancement to the transferee for credit losses.

The entity calculates that CU9,090 (90 per cent × CU10,100) of the consideration received of CU9,115 represents the consideration for a fully proportionate 90 per cent share. The remainder of the consideration received (CU25) represents consideration received for subordinating its retained interest to provide credit enhancement to the transferee for credit losses. In addition, the excess spread of 0.5 per cent represents consideration received for the credit enhancement. Accordingly, the total consideration received for the credit enhancement is CU65 (CU25 + CU40).

The entity calculates the gain or loss on the sale of the 90 per cent share of cash flows. Assuming that separate fair values of the 90 per cent part transferred and the 10 per cent part retained are not available at the date of the transfer, the entity allocates the carrying amount of the asset in accordance with paragraph 28 as follows:

	Estimated fair value	Percentage	Allocated carrying amount
Portion transferred	9,090	90%	9,000
Portion retained	1,010	10%	1,000
Total	**10,100**		**10,000**

The entity computes its gain or loss on the sale of the 90 per cent share of the cash flows by deducting the allocated carrying amount of the portion transferred from the consideration received, ie CU90 (CU9,090 – CU9,000). The carrying amount of the portion retained by the entity is CU1,000.

In addition, the entity recognises the continuing involvement that results from the subordination of its retained interest for credit losses. Accordingly, it recognises an asset of CU1,000 (the maximum amount of the cash flows it would not receive under the subordination), and an associated liability of CU1,065 (which is the maximum amount of the cash flows it would not receive under the subordination, ie CU1,000 plus the fair value of the subordination of CU65).

The entity uses all of the above information to account for the transaction as follows:

	Debit	Credit
Original asset	–	9,000
Asset recognised for subordination or the residual interest	1,000	–
Asset for the consideration received in the form of excess spread	40	–
Profit or loss (gain on transfer)	–	90
Liability	–	1,065
Cash received	9,115	–
Total	**10,155**	**10,155**

Immediately following the transaction, the carrying amount of the asset is CU2,040 comprising CU1,000, representing the allocated cost of the portion retained, and CU1,040, representing the entity's additional continuing involvement from the subordination of its retained interest for credit losses (which includes the excess spread of CU40).

In subsequent periods, the entity recognises the consideration received for the credit enhancement (CU65) on a time proportion basis, accrues interest on the recognised asset using the effective interest method and recognises any credit impairment on the recognised assets. As an example of the latter, assume that in the following year there is a credit impairment loss on the underlying loans of CU300. The entity reduces its recognised asset by CU600 (CU300 relating to its retained interest and CU300 relating to the additional continuing involvement that arises from the subordination of its retained interest for credit losses), and reduces its recognised liability by CU300. The net result is a charge to profit or loss for credit impairment of CU300.

Regular way purchase or sale of a financial asset (paragraph 38)

AG53   A regular way purchase or sale of financial assets is recognised using either trade date accounting or settlement date accounting as described in paragraphs AG55 and AG56. The method used is applied consistently for all purchases and sales of financial assets that belong to the same category of financial assets defined in paragraph 9. For this purpose assets that are held for trading form a separate category from assets designated at fair value through profit or loss.

AG54   A contract that requires or permits net settlement of the change in the value of the contract is not a regular way contract. Instead, such a contract is accounted for as a derivative in the period between the trade date and the settlement date.

AG55   The trade date is the date that an entity commits itself to purchase or sell an asset. Trade date accounting refers to (a) the recognition of an asset to be received and the liability to pay for it on the trade date, and (b) derecognition of an asset that is sold, recognition of any gain or loss on disposal and the recognition of a receivable from the buyer for payment on the trade date. Generally, interest does not start to accrue on the asset and corresponding liability until the settlement date when title passes.

AG56 The settlement date is the date that an asset is delivered to or by an entity. Settlement date accounting refers to (a) the recognition of an asset on the day it is received by the entity, and (b) the derecognition of an asset and recognition of any gain or loss on disposal on the day that it is delivered by the entity. When settlement date accounting is applied an entity accounts for any change in the fair value of the asset to be received during the period between the trade date and the settlement date in the same way as it accounts for the acquired asset. In other words, the change in value is not recognised for assets carried at cost or amortised cost; it is recognised in profit or loss for assets classified as financial assets at fair value through profit or loss; and it is recognised in other comprehensive income for assets classified as available for sale.

Derecognition of a financial liability (paragraphs 39–42)

AG57 A financial liability (or part of it) is extinguished when the debtor either:

(a) discharges the liability (or part of it) by paying the creditor, normally with cash, other financial assets, goods or services; or

(b) is legally released from primary responsibility for the liability (or part of it) either by process of law or by the creditor. (If the debtor has given a guarantee this condition may still be met.)

AG58 If an issuer of a debt instrument repurchases that instrument, the debt is extinguished even if the issuer is a market maker in that instrument or intends to resell it in the near term.

AG59 Payment to a third party, including a trust (sometimes called 'in-substance defeasance'), does not, by itself, relieve the debtor of its primary obligation to the creditor, in the absence of legal release.

AG60 If a debtor pays a third party to assume an obligation and notifies its creditor that the third party has assumed its debt obligation, the debtor does not derecognise the debt obligation unless the condition in paragraph AG57(b) is met. If the debtor pays a third party to assume an obligation and obtains a legal release from its creditor, the debtor has extinguished the debt. However, if the debtor agrees to make payments on the debt to the third party or direct to its original creditor, the debtor recognises a new debt obligation to the third party.

AG61 Although legal release, whether judicially or by the creditor, results in derecognition of a liability, the entity may recognise a new liability if the derecognition criteria in paragraphs 15–37 are not met for the financial assets transferred. If those criteria are not met, the transferred assets are not derecognised, and the entity recognises a new liability relating to the transferred assets.

AG62 For the purpose of paragraph 40, the terms are substantially different if the discounted present value of the cash flows under the new terms, including any fees paid net of any fees received and discounted using the original effective interest rate, is at least 10 per cent different from the discounted present value of the remaining cash flows of the original financial liability. If an exchange of debt instruments or modification of terms is accounted for as an extinguishment, any costs or fees incurred are recognised as part of the gain or loss on the extinguishment. If the exchange or modification is not accounted for as an extinguishment, any costs or fees incurred adjust the carrying amount of the liability and are amortised over the remaining term of the modified liability.

AG63 In some cases, a creditor releases a debtor from its present obligation to make payments, but the debtor assumes a guarantee obligation to pay if the party assuming primary responsibility defaults. In this circumstance the debtor:

(a) recognises a new financial liability based on the fair value of its obligation for the guarantee; and

(b) recognises a gain or loss based on the difference between (i) any proceeds paid and (ii) the carrying amount of the original financial liability less the fair value of the new financial liability.

Measurement (paragraphs 43–70)

Initial measurement of financial assets and financial liabilities (paragraph 43)

AG64   The fair value of a financial instrument on initial recognition is normally the transaction price (ie the fair value of the consideration given or received, see also paragraph AG76). However, if part of the consideration given or received is for something other than the financial instrument, the fair value of the financial instrument is estimated, using a valuation technique (see paragraphs AG74–AG79). For example, the fair value of a long-term loan or receivable that carries no interest can be estimated as the present value of all future cash receipts discounted using the prevailing market rate(s) of interest for a similar instrument (similar as to currency, term, type of interest rate and other factors) with a similar credit rating. Any additional amount lent is an expense or a reduction of income unless it qualifies for recognition as some other type of asset.

AG65   If an entity originates a loan that bears an off-market interest rate (eg 5 per cent when the market rate for similar loans is 8 per cent), and receives an up-front fee as compensation, the entity recognises the loan at its fair value, ie net of the fee it receives. The entity accretes the discount to profit or loss using the effective interest rate method.

Subsequent measurement of financial assets (paragraphs 45 and 46)

AG66   If a financial instrument that was previously recognised as a financial asset is measured at fair value and its fair value falls below zero, it is a financial liability measured in accordance with paragraph 47.

AG67   The following example illustrates the accounting for transaction costs on the initial and subsequent measurement of an available-for-sale financial asset. An asset is acquired for CU100 plus a purchase commission of CU2. Initially, the asset is recognised at CU102. The end of the reporting period occurs one day later, when the quoted market price of the asset is CU100. If the asset were sold, a commission of CU3 would be paid. On that date, the asset is measured at CU100 (without regard to the possible commission on sale) and a loss of CU2 is recognised in other comprehensive income. If the available-for-sale financial asset has fixed or determinable payments, the transaction costs are amortised to profit or loss using the effective interest method. If the available-for-sale financial asset does not have fixed or determinable payments, the transaction costs are recognised in profit or loss when the asset is derecognised or becomes impaired.

AG68   Instruments that are classified as loans and receivables are measured at amortised cost without regard to the entity's intention to hold them to maturity.

Fair value measurement considerations (paragraphs 48–49)

AG69   Underlying the definition of fair value is a presumption that an entity is a going concern without any intention or need to liquidate, to curtail materially the scale of its operations or to undertake a transaction on adverse terms. Fair value is not, therefore, the amount that an entity would receive or pay in a forced transaction, involuntary liquidation or distress sale. However, fair value reflects the credit quality of the instrument.

AG70   This Standard uses the terms 'bid price' and 'asking price' (sometimes referred to as 'current offer price') in the context of quoted market prices, and the term 'the bid-ask spread' to include only transaction costs. Other adjustments to arrive at fair value (eg for counterparty credit risk) are not included in the term 'bid-ask spread'.

Active market: quoted price

AG71   A financial instrument is regarded as quoted in an active market if quoted prices are readily and regularly available from an exchange, dealer, broker, industry group, pricing service or regulatory agency, and those prices represent actual and regularly occurring market transactions on an arm's length basis. Fair value is defined in terms of a price agreed by a willing buyer and a willing seller in an arm's length transaction. The objective of determining fair value for a financial instrument that is traded in an active market is to arrive at the price at which a transaction would occur at the end of the reporting period in that instrument (ie without modifying or repackaging the instrument) in the most advantageous active market to which the entity has immediate access. However, the entity adjusts the price in the more advantageous market to reflect any differences in counterparty credit risk between instruments traded in that market and the one being valued. The existence of published price quotations in an active market is the best evidence of fair value and when they exist they are used to measure the financial asset or financial liability.

AG72   The appropriate quoted market price for an asset held or liability to be issued is usually the current bid price and, for an asset to be acquired or liability held, the asking price. When an entity has assets and liabilities with offsetting market risks, it may use mid-market prices as a basis for establishing fair values for the offsetting risk positions and apply the bid or asking price to the net open position as appropriate. When current bid and asking prices are unavailable, the price of the most recent transaction provides evidence of the current fair value as long as there has not been a significant change in economic circumstances since the time of the transaction. If conditions have changed since the time of the transaction (eg a change in the risk-free interest rate following the most recent price quote for a corporate bond), the fair value reflects the change in conditions by reference to current prices or rates for similar financial instruments, as appropriate. Similarly, if the entity can demonstrate that the last transaction price is not fair value (eg because it reflected the amount that an entity would receive or pay in a forced transaction, involuntary liquidation or distress sale), that price is adjusted. The fair value of a portfolio of financial instruments is the product of the number of units of the instrument and its quoted market price. If a published price quotation in an active market does not exist for a financial instrument in its entirety, but active markets exist for its component parts, fair value is determined on the basis of the relevant market prices for the component parts.

AG73   If a rate (rather than a price) is quoted in an active market, the entity uses that market-quoted rate as an input into a valuation technique to determine fair value. If the market-quoted rate does not include credit risk or other factors that market participants would include in valuing the instrument, the entity adjusts for those factors.

No active market: valuation technique

AG74   If the market for a financial instrument is not active, an entity establishes fair value by using a valuation technique. Valuation techniques include using recent arm's length market transactions between knowledgeable, willing parties, if available, reference to the current fair value of another instrument that is substantially the same, discounted cash flow analysis and option pricing models. If there is a valuation technique commonly used by market participants to price the instrument and that technique has been demonstrated to provide reliable estimates of prices obtained in actual market transactions, the entity uses that technique.

AG75   The objective of using a valuation technique is to establish what the transaction price would have been on the measurement date in an arm's length exchange motivated by normal business considerations. Fair value is estimated on the basis of the results of a valuation technique that makes maximum use of market inputs, and relies as little as possible on entity-specific inputs. A valuation technique would be expected to arrive at a realistic estimate of the fair value if (a) it reasonably reflects how the market could be expected to price the instrument and (b) the inputs to the valuation technique reasonably represent market expectations and measures of the risk-return factors inherent in the financial instrument.

AG76   Therefore, a valuation technique (a) incorporates all factors that market participants would consider in setting a price and (b) is consistent with accepted economic methodologies for pricing financial instruments. Periodically, an entity calibrates the valuation technique and tests it for validity using prices from any observable current market transactions in the same instrument (ie without modification or repackaging) or based on any available observable market data. An entity obtains market data consistently in the same market where the instrument was originated or purchased. The best evidence of the fair value of a financial instrument at initial recognition is the transaction price (ie the fair value of the consideration given or received) unless the fair value of that instrument is evidenced by comparison with other observable current market transactions in the same instrument (ie without modification or repackaging) or based on a valuation technique whose variables include only data from observable markets.

AG76A   The subsequent measurement of the financial asset or financial liability and the subsequent recognition of gains and losses shall be consistent with the requirements of this Standard. The application of paragraph AG76 may result in no gain or loss being recognised on the initial recognition of a financial asset or financial liability. In such a case, IAS 39 requires that a gain or loss shall be recognised after initial recognition only to the extent that it arises from a change in a factor (including time) that market participants would consider in setting a price.

AG77 The initial acquisition or origination of a financial asset or incurrence of a financial liability is a market transaction that provides a foundation for estimating the fair value of the financial instrument. In particular, if the financial instrument is a debt instrument (such as a loan), its fair value can be determined by reference to the market conditions that existed at its acquisition or origination date and current market conditions or interest rates currently charged by the entity or by others for similar debt instruments (ie similar remaining maturity, cash flow pattern, currency, credit risk, collateral and interest basis). Alternatively, provided there is no change in the credit risk of the debtor and applicable credit spreads after the origination of the debt instrument, an estimate of the current market interest rate may be derived by using a benchmark interest rate reflecting a better credit quality than the underlying debt instrument, holding the credit spread constant, and adjusting for the change in the benchmark interest rate from the origination date. If conditions have changed since the most recent market transaction, the corresponding change in the fair value of the financial instrument being valued is determined by reference to current prices or rates for similar financial instruments, adjusted as appropriate, for any differences from the instrument being valued.

AG78 The same information may not be available at each measurement date. For example, at the date that an entity makes a loan or acquires a debt instrument that is not actively traded, the entity has a transaction price that is also a market price. However, no new transaction information may be available at the next measurement date and, although the entity can determine the general level of market interest rates, it may not know what level of credit or other risk market participants would consider in pricing the instrument on that date. An entity may not have information from recent transactions to determine the appropriate credit spread over the basic interest rate to use in determining a discount rate for a present value computation. It would be reasonable to assume, in the absence of evidence to the contrary, that no changes have taken place in the spread that existed at the date the loan was made. However, the entity would be expected to make reasonable efforts to determine whether there is evidence that there has been a change in such factors. When evidence of a change exists, the entity would consider the effects of the change in determining the fair value of the financial instrument.

AG79 In applying discounted cash flow analysis, an entity uses one or more discount rates equal to the prevailing rates of return for financial instruments having substantially the same terms and characteristics, including the credit quality of the instrument, the remaining term over which the contractual interest rate is fixed, the remaining term to repayment of the principal and the currency in which payments are to be made. Short-term receivables and payables with no stated interest rate may be measured at the original invoice amount if the effect of discounting is immaterial.

No active market: equity instruments

AG80 The fair value of investments in equity instruments that do not have a quoted market price in an active market and derivatives that are linked to and must be settled by delivery of such an unquoted equity instrument (see paragraphs 46(c) and 47) is reliably measurable if (a) the variability in the range of reasonable fair value estimates is not significant for that instrument or (b) the probabilities of the various estimates within the range can be reasonably assessed and used in estimating fair value.

AG81 There are many situations in which the variability in the range of reasonable fair value estimates of investments in equity instruments that do not have a quoted market price and derivatives that are linked to and must be settled by delivery of such an unquoted equity instrument (see paragraphs 46(c) and 47) is likely not to be significant. Normally it is possible to estimate the fair value of a financial asset that an entity has acquired from an outside party. However, if the range of reasonable fair value estimates is significant and the probabilities of the various estimates cannot be reasonably assessed, an entity is precluded from measuring the instrument at fair value.

Inputs to valuation techniques

AG82 An appropriate technique for estimating the fair value of a particular financial instrument would incorporate observable market data about the market conditions and other factors that are likely to affect the instrument's fair value. The fair value of a financial instrument will be based on one or more of the following factors (and perhaps others).

(a)   *The time value of money (ie interest at the basic or risk-free rate).* Basic interest rates can usually be derived from observable government bond prices and are often quoted in financial publications. These rates typically vary with the expected dates of the projected cash flows along a yield curve of interest rates for different time horizons. For practical reasons, an entity may use a well-accepted and readily observable general rate, such as LIBOR or a swap rate, as the benchmark rate. (Because a rate such as LIBOR is not the risk-free interest rate, the credit risk adjustment appropriate to the particular financial instrument is determined on the basis of its credit risk in relation to the credit risk in this benchmark rate.) In some countries, the central government's bonds may carry a significant credit risk and may not provide a stable benchmark basic interest rate for instruments denominated in that currency. Some entities in these countries may have a better credit standing and a lower borrowing rate than the central government. In such a case, basic interest rates may be more appropriately determined by reference to interest rates for the highest rated corporate bonds issued in the currency of that jurisdiction.

(b)   *Credit risk.* The effect on fair value of credit risk (ie the premium over the basic interest rate for credit risk) may be derived from observable market prices for traded instruments of different credit quality or from observable interest rates charged by lenders for loans of various credit ratings.

(c)   *Foreign currency exchange prices.* Active currency exchange markets exist for most major currencies, and prices are quoted daily in financial publications.

(d)   *Commodity prices.* There are observable market prices for many commodities.

(e)   *Equity prices.* Prices (and indexes of prices) of traded equity instruments are readily observable in some markets. Present value based techniques may be used to estimate the current market price of equity instruments for which there are no observable prices.

(f)   *Volatility (ie magnitude of future changes in price of the financial instrument or other item).* Measures of the volatility of actively traded items can normally be reasonably estimated on the basis of historical market data or by using volatilities implied in current market prices.

(g)   *Prepayment risk and surrender risk.* Expected prepayment patterns for financial assets and expected surrender patterns for financial liabilities can be estimated on the basis of historical data. (The fair value of a financial liability that can be surrendered by the counterparty cannot be less than the present value of the surrender amount—see paragraph 49.)

(h)   *Servicing costs for a financial asset or a financial liability.* Costs of servicing can be estimated using comparisons with current fees charged by other market participants. If the costs of servicing a financial asset or financial liability are significant and other market participants would face comparable costs, the issuer would consider them in determining the fair value of that financial asset or financial liability. It is likely that the fair value at inception of a contractual right to future fees equals the origination costs paid for them, unless future fees and related costs are out of line with market comparables.

Gains and losses (paragraphs 55–57)

AG83   An entity applies IAS 21 to financial assets and financial liabilities that are monetary items in accordance with IAS 21 and denominated in a foreign currency. Under IAS 21, any foreign exchange gains and losses on monetary assets and monetary liabilities are recognised in profit or loss. An exception is a monetary item that is designated as a hedging instrument in either a cash flow hedge (see paragraphs 95–101) or a hedge of a net investment (see paragraph 102). For the purpose of recognising foreign exchange gains and losses under IAS 21, a monetary available-for-sale financial asset is treated as if it were carried at amortised cost in the foreign currency. Accordingly, for such a financial asset, exchange differences resulting from changes in amortised cost are recognised in profit or loss and other changes in carrying amount are recognised in accordance with paragraph 55(b). For available-for-sale financial assets that are not monetary items under IAS 21 (for example, equity instruments), the gain or loss that is recognised in other comprehensive income under paragraph 55(b) includes any related foreign exchange component. If there is a hedging relationship between a non-derivative monetary asset and a non-derivative monetary liability, changes in the foreign currency component of those financial instruments are recognised in profit or loss.

Impairment and uncollectibility of financial assets (paragraphs 58–70)

Financial assets carried at amortised cost (paragraphs 63–65)

AG84   Impairment of a financial asset carried at amortised cost is measured using the financial instrument's original effective interest rate because discounting at the current market rate of interest would, in effect, impose fair value measurement on financial assets that are otherwise measured at amortised cost. If the terms of a loan, receivable or held-to-maturity investment are renegotiated or otherwise modified because of financial difficulties of the borrower or issuer, impairment is measured using the original effective interest rate before the modification of terms. Cash flows relating to short-term receivables are not discounted if the effect of discounting is immaterial. If a loan, receivable or held-to-maturity investment has a variable interest rate, the discount rate for measuring any impairment loss under paragraph 63 is the current effective interest rate(s) determined under the contract. As a practical expedient, a creditor may measure impairment of a financial asset carried at amortised cost on the basis of an instrument's fair value using an observable market price. The calculation of the present value of the estimated future cash flows of a collateralised financial asset reflects the cash flows that may result from foreclosure less costs for obtaining and selling the collateral, whether or not foreclosure is probable.

AG85   The process for estimating impairment considers all credit exposures, not only those of low credit quality. For example, if an entity uses an internal credit grading system it considers all credit grades, not only those reflecting a severe credit deterioration.

AG86   The process for estimating the amount of an impairment loss may result either in a single amount or in a range of possible amounts. In the latter case, the entity recognises an impairment loss equal to the best estimate within the range[5] taking into account all relevant information available before the financial statements are issued about conditions existing at the end of the reporting period.

AG87   For the purpose of a collective evaluation of impairment, financial assets are grouped on the basis of similar credit risk characteristics that are indicative of the debtors' ability to pay all amounts due according to the contractual terms (for example, on the basis of a credit risk evaluation or grading process that considers asset type, industry, geographical location, collateral type, past-due status and other relevant factors). The characteristics chosen are relevant to the estimation of future cash flows for groups of such assets by being indicative of the debtors' ability to pay all amounts due according to the contractual terms of the assets being evaluated. However, loss probabilities and other loss statistics differ at a group level between (a) assets that have been individually evaluated for impairment and found not to be impaired and (b) assets that have not been individually evaluated for impairment, with the result that a different amount of impairment may be required. If an entity does not have a group of assets with similar risk characteristics, it does not make the additional assessment.

AG88   Impairment losses recognised on a group basis represent an interim step pending the identification of impairment losses on individual assets in the group of financial assets that are collectively assessed for impairment. As soon as information is available that specifically identifies losses on individually impaired assets in a group, those assets are removed from the group.

AG89   Future cash flows in a group of financial assets that are collectively evaluated for impairment are estimated on the basis of historical loss experience for assets with credit risk characteristics similar to those in the group. Entities that have no entity-specific loss experience or insufficient experience, use peer group experience for comparable groups of financial assets. Historical loss experience is adjusted on the basis of current observable data to reflect the effects of current conditions that did not affect the period on which the historical loss experience is based and to remove the effects of conditions in the historical period that do not exist currently. Estimates of changes in future cash flows reflect and are directionally consistent with changes in related observable data from period to period (such as changes in unemployment rates, property prices, commodity prices, payment status or other factors that are indicative of incurred losses in the group and their magnitude). The methodology and assumptions used for estimating future cash flows are reviewed regularly to reduce any differences between loss estimates and actual loss experience.

AG90   As an example of applying paragraph AG89, an entity may determine, on the basis of historical experience, that one of the main causes of default on credit card loans is the death of the borrower. The entity may

---

[5]   IAS 37, paragraph 39 contains guidance on how to determine the best estimate in a range of possible outcomes.

observe that the death rate is unchanged from one year to the next. Nevertheless, some of the borrowers in the entity's group of credit card loans may have died in that year, indicating that an impairment loss has occurred on those loans, even if, at the year-end, the entity is not yet aware which specific borrowers have died. It would be appropriate for an impairment loss to be recognised for these 'incurred but not reported' losses. However, it would not be appropriate to recognise an impairment loss for deaths that are expected to occur in a future period, because the necessary loss event (the death of the borrower) has not yet occurred.

AG91   When using historical loss rates in estimating future cash flows, it is important that information about historical loss rates is applied to groups that are defined in a manner consistent with the groups for which the historical loss rates were observed. Therefore, the method used should enable each group to be associated with information about past loss experience in groups of assets with similar credit risk characteristics and relevant observable data that reflect current conditions.

AG92   Formula-based approaches or statistical methods may be used to determine impairment losses in a group of financial assets (eg for smaller balance loans) as long as they are consistent with the requirements in paragraphs 63–65 and AG87–AG91. Any model used would incorporate the effect of the time value of money, consider the cash flows for all of the remaining life of an asset (not only the next year), consider the age of the loans within the portfolio and not give rise to an impairment loss on initial recognition of a financial asset.

Interest income after impairment recognition

AG93   Once a financial asset or a group of similar financial assets has been written down as a result of an impairment loss, interest income is thereafter recognised using the rate of interest used to discount the future cash flows for the purpose of measuring the impairment loss.

Hedging (paragraphs 71–102)

Hedging instruments (paragraphs 72–77)

Qualifying instruments (paragraphs 72 and 73)

AG94   The potential loss on an option that an entity writes could be significantly greater than the potential gain in value of a related hedged item. In other words, a written option is not effective in reducing the profit or loss exposure of a hedged item. Therefore, a written option does not qualify as a hedging instrument unless it is designated as an offset to a purchased option, including one that is embedded in another financial instrument (for example, a written call option used to hedge a callable liability). In contrast, a purchased option has potential gains equal to or greater than losses and therefore has the potential to reduce profit or loss exposure from changes in fair values or cash flows. Accordingly, it can qualify as a hedging instrument.

AG95   A held-to-maturity investment carried at amortised cost may be designated as a hedging instrument in a hedge of foreign currency risk.

AG96   An investment in an unquoted equity instrument that is not carried at fair value because its fair value cannot be reliably measured or a derivative that is linked to and must be settled by delivery of such an unquoted equity instrument (see paragraphs 46(c) and 47) cannot be designated as a hedging instrument.

AG97   An entity's own equity instruments are not financial assets or financial liabilities of the entity and therefore cannot be designated as hedging instruments.

Hedged items (paragraphs 78–84)

Qualifying items (paragraphs 78–80)

AG98   A firm commitment to acquire a business in a business combination cannot be a hedged item, except for foreign exchange risk, because the other risks being hedged cannot be specifically identified and measured. These other risks are general business risks.

AG99   An equity method investment cannot be a hedged item in a fair value hedge because the equity method recognises in profit or loss the investor's share of the associate's profit or loss, rather than changes in the investment's fair value. For a similar reason, an investment in a consolidated subsidiary cannot be a hedged item in a fair value hedge because consolidation recognises in profit or loss the subsidiary's profit or loss, rather than changes in the investment's fair value. A hedge of a net investment in a foreign operation is different because it is a hedge of the foreign currency exposure, not a fair value hedge of the change in the value of the investment.

AG99A Paragraph 80 states that in consolidated financial statements the foreign currency risk of a highly probable forecast intragroup transaction may qualify as a hedged item in a cash flow hedge, provided the transaction is denominated in a currency other than the functional currency of the entity entering into that transaction and the foreign currency risk will affect consolidated profit or loss. For this purpose an entity can be a parent, subsidiary, associate, joint venture or branch. If the foreign currency risk of a forecast intragroup transaction does not affect consolidated profit or loss, the intragroup transaction cannot qualify as a hedged item. This is usually the case for royalty payments, interest payments or management charges between members of the same group unless there is a related external transaction. However, when the foreign currency risk of a forecast intragroup transaction will affect consolidated profit or loss, the intragroup transaction can qualify as a hedged item. An example is forecast sales or purchases of inventories between members of the same group if there is an onward sale of the inventory to a party external to the group. Similarly, a forecast intragroup sale of plant and equipment from the group entity that manufactured it to a group entity that will use the plant and equipment in its operations may affect consolidated profit or loss. This could occur, for example, because the plant and equipment will be depreciated by the purchasing entity and the amount initially recognised for the plant and equipment may change if the forecast intragroup transaction is denominated in a currency other than the functional currency of the purchasing entity.

AG99B If a hedge of a forecast intragroup transaction qualifies for hedge accounting, any gain or loss that is recognised in other comprehensive income in accordance with paragraph 95(a) shall be reclassified from equity to profit or loss as a reclassification adjustment in the same period or periods during which the foreign currency risk of the hedged transaction affects consolidated profit or loss.

AG99BA   An entity can designate all changes in the cash flows or fair value of a hedged item in a hedging relationship. An entity can also designate only changes in the cash flows or fair value of a hedged item above or below a specified price or other variable (a one-sided risk). The intrinsic value of a purchased option hedging instrument (assuming that it has the same principal terms as the designated risk), but not its time value, reflects a one-sided risk in a hedged item. For example, an entity can designate the variability of future cash flow outcomes resulting from a price increase of a forecast commodity purchase. In such a situation, only cash flow losses that result from an increase in the price above the specified level are designated. The hedged risk does not include the time value of a purchased option because the time value is not a component of the forecast transaction that affects profit or loss (paragraph 86(b)).

Designation of financial items as hedged items (paragraphs 81 and 81A)

AG99C [...]The entity may designate all of the cash flows of the entire financial asset or financial liability as the hedged item and hedge them for only one particular risk (eg only for changes that are attributable to changes in LIBOR). For example, in the case of a financial liability whose effective interest rate is 100 basis points below LIBOR, an entity can designate as the hedged item the entire liability (ie principal plus interest at LIBOR minus 100 basis points) and hedge the change in the fair value or cash flows of that entire liability that is attributable to changes in LIBOR. The entity may also choose a hedge ratio of other than one to one in order to improve the effectiveness of the hedge as described in paragraph AG100.

AG99D   In addition, if a fixed rate financial instrument is hedged some time after its origination and interest rates have changed in the meantime, the entity can designate a portion equal to a benchmark rate [...].. For example, assume an entity originates a fixed rate financial asset of CU100 that has an effective interest rate of 6 per cent at a time when LIBOR is 4 per cent. It begins to hedge that asset some time later when LIBOR has increased to 8 per cent and the fair value of the asset has decreased to CU90. The entity calculates that if it had purchased the asset on the date it first designates it as the hedged item for its then fair value of CU90, the effective yield would have been 9.5 per cent. [...].The entity can designate a LIBOR portion of 8 per cent that consists partly of the contractual interest cash flows and partly of the difference between the current fair value (ie CU90) and the amount repayable on maturity (ie CU100).

AG99E   Paragraph 81 permits an entity to designate something other than the entire fair value change or cash flow variability of a financial instrument. For example:

(a)   all of the cash flows of a financial instrument may be designated for cash flow or fair value changes attributable to some (but not all) risks; or

(b)   some (but not all) of the cash flows of a financial instrument may be designated for cash flow or fair value changes attributable to all or only some risks (ie a 'portion' of the cash flows of the financial instrument may be designated for changes attributable to all or only some risks).

AG99F   To be eligible for hedge accounting, the designated risks and portions must be separately identifiable components of the financial instrument, and changes in the cash flows or fair value of the entire financial instrument arising from changes in the designated risks and portions must be reliably measurable. For example:

(a)   for a fixed rate financial instrument hedged for changes in fair value attributable to changes in a risk-free or benchmark interest rate, the risk-free or benchmark rate is normally regarded as both a separately identifiable component of the financial instrument and reliably measurable.

(b)   inflation is not separately identifiable and reliably measurable and cannot be designated as a risk or a portion of a financial instrument unless the requirements in (c) are met.

(c)   a contractually specified inflation portion of the cash flows of a recognised inflation-linked bond (assuming there is no requirement to account for an embedded derivative separately) is separately identifiable and reliably measurable as long as other cash flows of the instrument are not affected by the inflation portion.

Designation of non-financial items as hedged items (paragraph 82)

AG100   Changes in the price of an ingredient or component of a non-financial asset or non-financial liability generally do not have a predictable, separately measurable effect on the price of the item that is comparable to the effect of, say, a change in market interest rates on the price of a bond. Thus, a non-financial asset or non-financial liability is a hedged item only in its entirety or for foreign exchange risk. If there is a difference between the terms of the hedging instrument and the hedged item (such as for a hedge of the forecast purchase of Brazilian coffee using a forward contract to purchase Colombian coffee on otherwise similar terms), the hedging relationship nonetheless can qualify as a hedge relationship provided all the conditions in paragraph 88 are met, including that the hedge is expected to be highly effective. For this purpose, the amount of the hedging instrument may be greater or less than that of the hedged item if this improves the effectiveness of the hedging relationship. For example, a regression analysis could be performed to establish a statistical relationship between the hedged item (eg a transaction in Brazilian coffee) and the hedging instrument (eg a transaction in Colombian coffee). If there is a valid statistical relationship between the two variables (ie between the unit prices of Brazilian coffee and Colombian coffee), the slope of the regression line can be used to establish the hedge ratio that will maximise expected effectiveness. For example, if the slope of the regression line is 1.02, a hedge ratio based on 0.98 quantities of hedged items to 1.00 quantities of the hedging instrument maximises expected effectiveness. However, the hedging relationship may result in ineffectiveness that is recognised in profit or loss during the term of the hedging relationship.

Designation of groups of items as hedged items (paragraphs 83 and 84)

AG101 A hedge of an overall net position (eg the net of all fixed rate assets and fixed rate liabilities with similar maturities), rather than of a specific hedged item, does not qualify for hedge accounting. However, almost the same effect on profit or loss of hedge accounting for this type of hedging relationship can be achieved by designating as the hedged item part of the underlying items. For example, if a bank has CU100 of assets and CU90 of liabilities with risks and terms of a similar nature and hedges the net CU10 exposure, it can designate as the hedged item CU10 of those assets. This designation can be used if such assets and liabilities are fixed rate instruments, in which case it is a fair value hedge, or if they are variable rate instruments, in which case it is a cash flow hedge. Similarly, if an entity has a firm commitment to make a purchase in a foreign currency of CU100 and a firm commitment to make a sale in the foreign currency of CU90, it can hedge the net amount of CU10 by acquiring a derivative and designating it as a hedging instrument associated with CU10 of the firm purchase commitment of CU100.

Hedge accounting (paragraphs 85–102)

AG102 An example of a fair value hedge is a hedge of exposure to changes in the fair value of a fixed rate debt instrument as a result of changes in interest rates. Such a hedge could be entered into by the issuer or by the holder.

AG103 An example of a cash flow hedge is the use of a swap to change floating rate debt to fixed rate debt (ie a hedge of a future transaction where the future cash flows being hedged are the future interest payments).

AG104 A hedge of a firm commitment (eg a hedge of the change in fuel price relating to an unrecognised contractual commitment by an electric utility to purchase fuel at a fixed price) is a hedge of an exposure to a change in fair value. Accordingly, such a hedge is a fair value hedge. However, under paragraph 87 a hedge of the foreign currency risk of a firm commitment could alternatively be accounted for as a cash flow hedge.

Assessing hedge effectiveness

AG105 A hedge is regarded as highly effective only if both of the following conditions are met:

(a) At the inception of the hedge and in subsequent periods, the hedge is expected to be highly effective in achieving offsetting changes in fair value or cash flows attributable to the hedged risk during the period for which the hedge is designated. Such an expectation can be demonstrated in various ways, including a comparison of past changes in the fair value or cash flows of the hedged item that are attributable to the hedged risk with past changes in the fair value or cash flows of the hedging instrument, or by demonstrating a high statistical correlation between the fair value or cash flows of the hedged item and those of the hedging instrument. The entity may choose a hedge ratio of other than one to one in order to improve the effectiveness of the hedge as described in paragraph AG100.

(b) The actual results of the hedge are within a range of 80–125 per cent. For example, if actual results are such that the loss on the hedging instrument is CU120 and the gain on the cash instrument is CU100, offset can be measured by 120/100, which is 120 per cent, or by 100/120, which is 83 per cent. In this example, assuming the hedge meets the condition in (a), the entity would conclude that the hedge has been highly effective.

AG106 Effectiveness is assessed, at a minimum, at the time an entity prepares its annual or interim financial statements.

AG107 This Standard does not specify a single method for assessing hedge effectiveness. The method an entity adopts for assessing hedge effectiveness depends on its risk management strategy. For example, if the entity's risk management strategy is to adjust the amount of the hedging instrument periodically to reflect changes in the hedged position, the entity needs to demonstrate that the hedge is expected to be highly effective only for the period until the amount of the hedging instrument is next adjusted. In some cases, an entity adopts different methods for different types of hedges. An entity's documentation of its hedging strategy includes its procedures for assessing effectiveness. Those procedures state whether the assessment includes all of the gain or loss on a hedging instrument or whether the instrument's time value is excluded.

AG107A […].

AG108 If the principal terms of the hedging instrument and of the hedged asset, liability, firm commitment or highly probable forecast transaction are the same, the changes in fair value and cash flows attributable to the risk being hedged may be likely to offset each other fully, both when the hedge is entered into and afterwards. For example, an interest rate swap is likely to be an effective hedge if the notional and principal amounts, term, repricing dates, dates of interest and principal receipts and payments, and basis for measuring interest rates are the same for the hedging instrument and the hedged item. In addition, a hedge of a highly probable forecast purchase of a commodity with a forward contract is likely to be highly effective if:

    (a)   the forward contract is for the purchase of the same quantity of the same commodity at the same time and location as the hedged forecast purchase;

    (b)   the fair value of the forward contract at inception is zero; and

    (c)   either the change in the discount or premium on the forward contract is excluded from the assessment of effectiveness and recognised in profit or loss or the change in expected cash flows on the highly probable forecast transaction is based on the forward price for the commodity.

AG109 Sometimes the hedging instrument offsets only part of the hedged risk. For example, a hedge would not be fully effective if the hedging instrument and hedged item are denominated in different currencies that do not move in tandem. Also, a hedge of interest rate risk using a derivative would not be fully effective if part of the change in the fair value of the derivative is attributable to the counterparty's credit risk.

AG110 To qualify for hedge accounting, the hedge must relate to a specific identified and designated risk, and not merely to the entity's general business risks, and must ultimately affect the entity's profit or loss. A hedge of the risk of obsolescence of a physical asset or the risk of expropriation of property by a government is not eligible for hedge accounting; effectiveness cannot be measured because those risks are not measurable reliably.

AG110A Paragraph 74(a) permits an entity to separate the intrinsic value and time value of an option contract and designate as the hedging instrument only the change in the intrinsic value of the option contract. Such a designation may result in a hedging relationship that is perfectly effective in achieving offsetting changes in cash flows attributable to a hedged one-sided risk of a forecast transaction, if the principal terms of the forecast transaction and hedging instrument are the same.

AG110B If an entity designates a purchased option in its entirety as the hedging instrument of a one-sided risk arising from a forecast transaction, the hedging relationship will not be perfectly effective. This is because the premium paid for the option includes time value and, as stated in paragraph AG99BA, a designated one-sided risk does not include the time value of an option. Therefore, in this situation, there will be no offset between the cash flows relating to the time value of the option premium paid and the designated hedged risk.

AG111 In the case of interest rate risk, hedge effectiveness may be assessed by preparing a maturity schedule for financial assets and financial liabilities that shows the net interest rate exposure for each time period, provided that the net exposure is associated with a specific asset or liability (or a specific group of assets or liabilities or a specific portion of them) giving rise to the net exposure, and hedge effectiveness is assessed against that asset or liability.

AG112 In assessing the effectiveness of a hedge, an entity generally considers the time value of money. The fixed interest rate on a hedged item need not exactly match the fixed interest rate on a swap designated as a fair value hedge. Nor does the variable interest rate on an interest-bearing asset or liability need to be the same as the variable interest rate on a swap designated as a cash flow hedge. A swap's fair value derives from its net settlements. The fixed and variable rates on a swap can be changed without affecting the net settlement if both are changed by the same amount.

AG113 If an entity does not meet hedge effectiveness criteria, the entity discontinues hedge accounting from the last date on which compliance with hedge effectiveness was demonstrated. However, if the entity identifies the event or change in circumstances that caused the hedging relationship to fail the effectiveness criteria, and demonstrates that the hedge was effective before the event or change in circumstances occurred, the entity discontinues hedge accounting from the date of the event or change in circumstances.

Fair value hedge accounting for a portfolio hedge of interest rate risk

AG114 For a fair value hedge of interest rate risk associated with a portfolio of financial assets or financial liabilities, an entity would meet the requirements of this Standard if it complies with the procedures set out in (a)–(i) and paragraphs AG115–AG132 below.

(a) As part of its risk management process the entity identifies a portfolio of items whose interest rate risk it wishes to hedge. The portfolio may comprise only assets, only liabilities or both assets and liabilities. The entity may identify two or more portfolios (eg the entity may group its available-for-sale assets into a separate portfolio), in which case it applies the guidance below to each portfolio separately.

(b) The entity analyses the portfolio into repricing time periods based on expected, rather than contractual, repricing dates. The analysis into repricing time periods may be performed in various ways including scheduling cash flows into the periods in which they are expected to occur, or scheduling notional principal amounts into all periods until repricing is expected to occur.

(c) On the basis of this analysis, the entity decides the amount it wishes to hedge. The entity designates as the hedged item an amount of assets or liabilities (but not a net amount) from the identified portfolio equal to the amount it wishes to designate as being hedged. [...].

(d) The entity designates the interest rate risk it is hedging. This risk could be a portion of the interest rate risk in each of the items in the hedged position, such as a benchmark interest rate (eg LIBOR).

(e) The entity designates one or more hedging instruments for each repricing time period.

(f) Using the designations made in (c)–(e) above, the entity assesses at inception and in subsequent periods, whether the hedge is expected to be highly effective during the period for which the hedge is designated.

(g) Periodically, the entity measures the change in the fair value of the hedged item (as designated in (c)) that is attributable to the hedged risk (as designated in (d)), [...]. Provided that the hedge is determined actually to have been highly effective when assessed using the entity's documented method of assessing effectiveness, the entity recognises the change in fair value of the hedged item as a gain or loss in profit or loss and in one of two line items in the statement of financial position as described in paragraph 89A. The change in fair value need not be allocated to individual assets or liabilities.

(h) The entity measures the change in fair value of the hedging instrument(s) (as designated in (e)) and recognises it as a gain or loss in profit or loss. The fair value of the hedging instrument(s) is recognised as an asset or liability in the statement of financial position.

(i) Any ineffectiveness[6] will be recognised in profit or loss as the difference between the change in fair value referred to in (g) and that referred to in (h).

AG115 This approach is described in more detail below. The approach shall be applied only to a fair value hedge of the interest rate risk associated with a portfolio of financial assets or financial liabilities.

AG116 The portfolio identified in paragraph AG114(a) could contain assets and liabilities. Alternatively, it could be a portfolio containing only assets, or only liabilities. The portfolio is used to determine the amount of the assets or liabilities the entity wishes to hedge. However, the portfolio is not itself designated as the hedged item.

AG117 In applying paragraph AG114(b), the entity determines the expected repricing date of an item as the earlier of the dates when that item is expected to mature or to reprice to market rates. The expected repricing dates are estimated at the inception of the hedge and throughout the term of the hedge, based on historical experience and other available information, including information and expectations regarding prepayment rates, interest rates and the interaction between them. Entities that have no entity-specific experience or insufficient experience use peer group experience for comparable financial instruments. These estimates are reviewed periodically and updated in the light of experience. In the case of a fixed rate item that is prepayable, the expected repricing date is the date on which the item is expected to prepay unless it reprices to market rates on an earlier date. For a group of similar items, the analysis into time periods based on expected repricing

---

[6] The same materiality considerations apply in this context as apply throughout IFRSs.

dates may take the form of allocating a percentage of the group, rather than individual items, to each time period. An entity may apply other methodologies for such allocation purposes. For example, it may use a prepayment rate multiplier for allocating amortising loans to time periods based on expected repricing dates. However, the methodology for such an allocation shall be in accordance with the entity's risk management procedures and objectives.

AG118   As an example of the designation set out in paragraph AG114(c), if in a particular repricing time period an entity estimates that it has fixed rate assets of CU100 and fixed rate liabilities of CU80 and decides to hedge all of the net position of CU20, it designates as the hedged item assets in the amount of CU20 (a portion of the assets).7 The designation is expressed as an 'amount of a currency' (eg an amount of dollars, euro, pounds or rand) rather than as individual assets. It follows that all of the assets (or liabilities) from which the hedged amount is drawn—ie all of the CU100 of assets in the above example—must be items whose fair value changes in response to changes in the interest rate being hedged[…].

AG119   The entity also complies with the other designation and documentation requirements set out in paragraph 88(a). For a portfolio hedge of interest rate risk, this designation and documentation specifies the entity's policy for all of the variables that are used to identify the amount that is hedged and how effectiveness is measured, including the following:

(a)   which assets and liabilities are to be included in the portfolio hedge and the basis to be used for removing them from the portfolio.

(b)   how the entity estimates repricing dates, including what interest rate assumptions underlie estimates of prepayment rates and the basis for changing those estimates. The same method is used for both the initial estimates made at the time an asset or liability is included in the hedged portfolio and for any later revisions to those estimates.

(c)   the number and duration of repricing time periods.

(d)   how often the entity will test effectiveness […].

(e)   the methodology used by the entity to determine the amount of assets or liabilities that are designated as the hedged item […].

(f)   […]. whether the entity will test effectiveness for each repricing time period individually, for all time periods in aggregate, or by using some combination of the two.

The policies specified in designating and documenting the hedging relationship shall be in accordance with the entity's risk management procedures and objectives. Changes in policies shall not be made arbitrarily. They shall be justified on the basis of changes in market conditions and other factors and be founded on and consistent with the entity's risk management procedures and objectives.

AG120   The hedging instrument referred to in paragraph AG114(e) may be a single derivative or a portfolio of derivatives all of which contain exposure to the hedged interest rate risk designated in paragraph AG114(d) (eg a portfolio of interest rate swaps all of which contain exposure to LIBOR). Such a portfolio of derivatives may contain offsetting risk positions. However, it may not include written options or net written options, because the Standard[8] does not permit such options to be designated as hedging instruments (except when a written option is designated as an offset to a purchased option). If the hedging instrument hedges the amount designated in paragraph AG114(c) for more than one repricing time period, it is allocated to all of the time periods that it hedges. However, the whole of the hedging instrument must be allocated to those repricing time periods because the Standard[9] does not permit a hedging relationship to be designated for only a portion of the time period during which a hedging instrument remains outstanding.

AG121   When the entity measures the change in the fair value of a prepayable item in accordance with paragraph AG114(g), a change in interest rates affects the fair value of the prepayable item in two ways: it affects the fair value of the contractual cash flows and the fair value of the prepayment option that is contained in a prepayable item. Paragraph 81 of the Standard permits an entity to designate a portion of a financial asset or financial liability, sharing a common risk exposure, as the hedged item, provided effectiveness can be measured. […].

---

[7]   The Standard permits an entity to designate any amount of the available qualifying assets or liabilities, ie in this example any amount of assets between CU0 and CU100.

[8]   see paragraphs 77 and AG94

[9]   see paragraph 75

AG122   The Standard does not specify the techniques used to determine the amount referred to in paragraph AG114(g), namely the change in the fair value of the hedged item that is attributable to the hedged risk. [...]. It is not appropriate to assume that changes in the fair value of the hedged item equal changes in the value of the hedging instrument.

AG123   Paragraph 89A requires that if the hedged item for a particular repricing time period is an asset, the change in its value is presented in a separate line item within assets. Conversely, if the hedged item for a particular repricing time period is a liability, the change in its value is presented in a separate line item within liabilities. These are the separate line items referred to in paragraph AG114(g). Specific allocation to individual assets (or liabilities) is not required.

AG124   Paragraph AG114(i) notes that ineffectiveness arises to the extent that the change in the fair value of the hedged item that is attributable to the hedged risk differs from the change in the fair value of the hedging derivative. Such a difference may arise for a number of reasons, including:

   (a)   [...];

   (b)   items in the hedged portfolio becoming impaired or being derecognised;

   (c)   the payment dates of the hedging instrument and the hedged item being different; and

   (d)   other causes [...].

Such ineffectiveness[10] shall be identified and recognised in profit or loss.

AG125   Generally, the effectiveness of the hedge will be improved:

   (a)   if the entity schedules items with different prepayment characteristics in a way that takes account of the differences in prepayment behaviour.

   (b)   when the number of items in the portfolio is larger. When only a few items are contained in the portfolio, relatively high ineffectiveness is likely if one of the items prepays earlier or later than expected. Conversely, when the portfolio contains many items, the prepayment behaviour can be predicted more accurately.

   (c)   when the repricing time periods used are narrower (eg 1-month as opposed to 3-month repricing time periods). Narrower repricing time periods reduce the effect of any mismatch between the repricing and payment dates (within the repricing time period) of the hedged item and those of the hedging instrument.

   (d)   the greater the frequency with which the amount of the hedging instrument is adjusted to reflect changes in the hedged item (eg because of changes in prepayment expectations).

AG126   An entity tests effectiveness periodically. [...].

AG127   When measuring effectiveness, the entity distinguishes revisions to the estimated repricing dates of existing assets (or liabilities) from the origination of new assets (or liabilities), with only the former giving rise to ineffectiveness. [...].Once ineffectiveness has been recognised as set out above, the entity establishes a new estimate of the total assets (or liabilities) in each repricing time period, including new assets (or liabilities) that have been originated since it last tested effectiveness, and designates a new amount as the hedged item and a new percentage as the hedged percentage. [...].

AG128   Items that were originally scheduled into a repricing time period may be derecognised because of earlier than expected prepayment or write-offs caused by impairment or sale. When this occurs, the amount of change in fair value included in the separate line item referred to in paragraph AG114(g) that relates to the derecognised item shall be removed from the statement of financial position, and included in the gain or loss that arises on derecognition of the item. For this purpose, it is necessary to know the repricing time period(s) into which the derecognised item was scheduled, because this determines the repricing time period(s) from which to remove it and hence the amount to remove from the separate line item referred to in paragraph AG114(g). When an item is derecognised, if it can be determined in which time period it was included, it is removed from that time period. If not, it is removed from the earliest time period if the derecognition resulted

---

[10]   The same materiality considerations apply in this context as apply throughout IFRSs.

from higher than expected prepayments, or allocated to all time periods containing the derecognised item on a systematic and rational basis if the item was sold or became impaired.

AG129 In addition, any amount relating to a particular time period that has not been derecognised when the time period expires is recognised in profit or loss at that time (see paragraph 89A). [...]..

AG130 [...].

AG131 If the hedged amount for a repricing time period is reduced without the related assets (or liabilities) being derecognised, the amount included in the separate line item referred to in paragraph AG114(g) that relates to the reduction shall be amortised in accordance with paragraph 92.

AG132 An entity may wish to apply the approach set out in paragraphs AG114–AG131 to a portfolio hedge that had previously been accounted for as a cash flow hedge in accordance with IAS 39. Such an entity would revoke the previous designation of a cash flow hedge in accordance with paragraph 101(d), and apply the requirements set out in that paragraph. It would also redesignate the hedge as a fair value hedge and apply the approach set out in paragraphs AG114–AG131 prospectively to subsequent accounting periods.

Transition (paragraphs 103–108B)

AG133 An entity may have designated a forecast intragroup transaction as a hedged item at the start of an annual period beginning on or after 1 January 2005 (or, for the purpose of restating comparative information, the start of an earlier comparative period) in a hedge that would qualify for hedge accounting in accordance with this Standard (as amended by the last sentence of paragraph 80). Such an entity may use that designation to apply hedge accounting in consolidated financial statements from the start of the annual period beginning on or after 1 January 2005 (or the start of the earlier comparative period). Such an entity shall also apply paragraphs AG99A and AG99B from the start of the annual period beginning on or after 1 January 2005. However, in accordance with paragraph 108B, it need not apply paragraph AG99B to comparative information for earlier periods.

IAS 39 – Financial Instruments: Recognition and Measurement

Übersicht

	Rn
I. Regelungsgehalt	1 – 3
II. Normzweck und Anwendungsbereich	4 – 26
1. Ausnahmen aufgrund der Konkurrenz mit anderen IFRS	7
2. Ausnahmen bezüglich der Bilanzierung als schwebendes Geschäft	8 – 26
a) Ausnahme für bestimmte Verträge für Unternehmenszusammenschlüsse	9 – 12
b) Ausnahme für bestimmte Arten von Kreditzusagen	13 – 15
c) „Eigenbedarfsausnahme"	16 – 26
III. Bilanzierungseinheit	27 – 50
1. Definition eines Derivats	28 – 31
2. Eingebettete Derivate	32 – 45
a) Voraussetzung der Abtrennung vom Basisvertrag	33 – 41
b) Art und Weise der Abtrennung vom Basisvertrag	42 – 45
3. Zusammenfassung von Verträgen	46 – 47
4. Zweifelsfragen zur Bilanzierungseinheit	48 – 50
IV. Ansatz	51 – 52
V. Ausbuchung	53 – 101
1. Ausbuchung von finanziellen Vermögenswerten	54 – 89
a) Grundlegendes	54 – 56
b) Konsolidierung aller Tochtergesellschaften	57
c) Anwendung auf gesamten Vermögenswert oder Teile	58 – 61
d) Auslaufen der Ansprüche auf Zahlungsmittel	62
e) Übertragung der Rechte auf Zahlungsmittel	63 – 67
f) Übertragung aller wesentlichen Chancen und Risiken aus dem Vermögenswert	68 – 75
g) Rückbehalt der wesentlichen Chancen und Risiken	76 – 78
h) Keine Übertragung bzw. kein Rückbehalt der wesentlichen Chancen und Risiken	79 – 89
2. Ausbuchung von finanziellen Verbindlichkeiten	90 – 101
a) Allgemeine Vorschriften	90 – 95
b) Tilgung finanzieller Verbindlichkeiten durch Eigenkapitalinstrumente	96 – 101
VI. Kategorisierung	102 – 131

1. Kategorisierung nach IAS 39 .... 103 – 124

2. Kategorisierung nach IFRS 9 .... 125 – 128

3. Umgliederungen nach IAS 39 129

4. Umgliederungen nach IFRS 9 130

VII. Erstmalige Bewertung .... 132 – 135

VIII. Folgebewertung .... 136 – 171

1. Folgebewertung nach IAS 39 .... 136 – 142

   a) Finanzielle Vermögenswerte .... 136 – 139

   b) Finanzielle Verbindlichkeiten .... 140 – 142

2. Folgebewertung nach IFRS 9 143

3. Bewertungsmethoden zur Folgebewertung .... 144 – 153

   a) Beizulegender Zeitwert .... 144 – 145

   b) Fortgeführte Anschaffungskosten .... 146 – 153

4. Erfassung von Gewinnen und Verlusten .... 154 – 160

5. Wertminderungen .... 161 – 172

   a) Objektive Hinweise auf eine Wertminderung .... 162 – 164

   b) Bemessung einer Wertminderung und
      Wertaufholung .... 165 – 172

IX. Sicherungsgeschäfte (hedging) .... 173 – 248

1. Hintergrund .... 174 – 177

2. Sicherungsinstrumente .... 178 – 184

3. Gesicherte Grundgeschäfte .... 185 – 201

   a) Finanzielle Posten als gesichertes Grundgeschäft .... 192 – 196

   b) Nicht-finanzielle Posten als gesichertes
      Grundgeschäft .... 197 – 201

4. Die Bilanzierung von Sicherungsgeschäften .... 202 – 248

   a) Die verschiedenen Arten von
      Sicherungsgeschäften .... 202 – 205

   b) Die Voraussetzungen für die Bilanzierung
      von Sicherungsgeschäften .... 206 – 229

   c) Die Bilanzierung einer Absicherung des
      beizulegenden Zeitwerts .... 230 – 237

   d) Die Bilanzierung einer Absicherung von
      Zahlungsströmen .... 238 – 248

X. Inkrafttreten und Übergangsvorschriften .... 249 – 251

1. IAS 39 249

2. IFRS 9 .... 250 – 251

XI. IFRS für kleine und mittelgroße Unternehmen .... 252 – 260

1. Überblick über die Struktur der Vorschriften .... 252 – 254

2. Einfache Finanzinstrumente 255

3. Komplexe Finanzinstrumente .... 256 – 260

XII. Ausblick .... 261 – 263

XIII. Angaben gem. IFRS 7 264

1. Normzweck und Anwendungsbereich .... 264 – 266

2. Struktur und Art der Angaben .... 267 – 294

a) Bilanzbezogene Angaben .... 269 – 270

b) Auf die Gesamtergebnisrechnung bezogene ....

Angaben .... 272 – 273

c) Weitere Angaben .... 275 – 280

d) Angaben zu Risiken aus Finanzinstrumenten .... 281 – 294

I. Regelungsgehalt. Die Bilanzierung von Finanzinstrumenten wird derzeit durch das IASB umfassend neu geregelt. Auf der aktiven Agenda des IASB befinden sich derzeit Projekte bezüglich der Ausbuchung von Finanzinstrumenten (Derecognition), der Unterscheidung von Eigen- und Fremdkapitalinstrumenten sowie der Bilanzierung von Finanzinstrumenten im Allgemeinen. Das letztere Projekt – die Ablösung von IAS 39 *Financial Instruments: Recognition and Measurement* – ist in mehrere Phasen unterteilt. Die erste Phase bezüglich der Kategorisierung und Bewertung finanzieller Vermögenswerte ist im November 2009 mit der Veröffentlichung von IFRS 9 *Financial Instruments* abgeschlossen worden. Für die Kategorisierung und Bewertung finanzieller Verbindlichkeiten hat das IASB im Mai 2010 den Standardentwurf *Fair Value Option für finanzielle Verbindlichkeiten* mit dem Ziel einer Verabschiedung eines Standards im selben Jahr veröffentlicht. Die zweite Phase betrifft die Bilanzierung von Wertminderungen finanzieller Vermögenswerte. Im November 2009 hat das IASB daneben den Standardentwurf *Financial Instruments: Amortised Cost and Impairment* veröffentlicht. Die dritte Phase betrifft die Bilanzierung von Sicherungsgeschäften, für die ein Standardentwurf im zweiten Halbjahr 2010 erwartet wird.

Dieses Kapitel befasst sich mit dem Ansatz und der Bewertung von Finanzinstrumenten, einschließlich der Bilanzierung von Sicherungszusammenhängen. Die betreffenden Regelungen befinden sich in den Standards IAS 39 und IFRS 9. Obwohl sich IFRS 9 noch im Übernahmeprozess befindet und daher noch nicht in EU-Recht umgesetzt worden ist, werden die neuen Regelungen dieses Standards in dieses Kapitel einbezogen. Das berücksichtigt, dass es Unternehmen gibt, die ihren Abschluss nach den vom IASB verabschiedeten IFRS ohne etwaige Änderungen durch die EU im Rahmen des Übernahmeprozesses aufstellen. Die übrigen vom IASB geplanten Änderungen im Rahmen des Projekts zur Ablösung von IAS 39 sind noch nicht endgültig verabschiedet,[1] sondern befinden sich noch im Standardsetzungsprozess. Dieses Kapitel geht daher nicht auf diese geplanten Änderungen ein, da sie noch nicht verbindliche Regelungen darstellen und sich im Laufe des Standardsetzungsprozesses noch mit hoher Wahrscheinlichkeit ändern werden.

Die Unterscheidung von Eigen- und Fremdkapitalinstrumenten wird in einem anderen Kapitel (zu IAS 32 *Financial Instruments: Presentation*) behandelt. Dieses Kapital behandelt nicht die besonderen Regelungen im Rahmen der erstmaligen Anwendung von IFRS gemäß IFRS 1 *First-time Adoption of International Financial Reporting Standards*.

1

2

3

---

1   Zum Redaktionsschluss dieses Kapitels (Ende Mai 2010).

4   **II. Normzweck und Anwendungsbereich.** Der **Normzweck** von IAS 39 ist die Festlegung von Prinzipien für den Ansatz (und die Ausbuchung) und die Bewertung von finanziellen Vermögenswerten und Verbindlichkeiten sowie bzgl. bestimmter Verträge zum Kauf oder Verkauf nicht-finanzieller Posten. Dies schließt die Bilanzierung von Sicherungsgeschäften ein.

5   Der **Anwendungsbereich** von IAS 39 ist von zahlreichen Ausnahmen geprägt. Dies ist die Folge der sehr allgemein gehaltenen Definition des Begriffs Finanzinstrument: „Ein Finanzinstrument ist ein Vertrag, der gleichzeitig bei dem einen Unternehmen zu einem finanziellen Vermögenswert und bei dem anderen Unternehmen zu einer finanziellen Verbindlichkeit oder einem Eigenkapitalinstrument führt." (IAS 39.8 i.V.m. 32.11). Diese Definition ist der Ausgangspunkt des Anwendungsbereichs von IAS 39, der alle Finanzinstrumente umfasst, die nicht explizit ausgenommen sind. Umgekehrt sind bestimmte Verträge über den Kauf oder Verkauf nicht-finanzieller Posten, d.h. Güter und Dienstleistungen, in den Anwendungsbereich des IAS 39 einbezogen, obwohl sie die Definition des Finanzinstruments nicht erfüllen. Hierbei handelt es sich um solche Verträge, die durch Ausgleich in bar oder in anderen Finanzinstrumenten so erfüllt werden können, dass sie in ihrem wirtschaftlichen Gehalt Finanzinstrumenten gleichkommen (finanzieller Nettoausgleich). Für diese Art von Verträgen besteht jedoch wiederum eine Ausnahme von der Einbeziehung in den Anwendungsbereich von IAS 39, soweit der Vertrag dem Eigenbedarf des Unternehmens dient (im Folgenden Eigenbedarfsausnahme). Diese Ausnahme von der Einbeziehung wird in diesem Kapitel zusammen mit anderen Ausnahmen vom Anwendungsbereich behandelt, obwohl es sich konzeptionell betrachtet um eine Beschränkung der Einbeziehung von Nicht-Finanzinstrumenten in den Anwendungsbereich des IAS 39 handelt.

6   Die Ausnahmen vom Anwendungsbereich des IAS 39 lassen sich grob wie folgt kategorisieren:

- Ausnahmen aufgrund der Konkurrenz der Anwendung von IAS 39 mit anderen Standards.
- Ausnahmen, die der vereinfachten Bilanzierung einer Transaktion als schwebendes Geschäft dienen (einschließlich des Eigenbedarfs bezüglich Verträgen über den Kauf oder Verkauf nicht-finanzieller Posten mit finanziellem Nettoausgleich).

7   **1. Ausnahmen aufgrund der Konkurrenz mit anderen IFRS.** Der Anwendungsbereich von IAS 39 enthält Ausnahmen im Hinblick auf die Anwendung anderer IFRS, denen der Vorrang gegeben wird, um eine Überschneidung von Anwendungsbereichen und somit konkurrierende Vorschriften zu vermeiden. Finanzinstrumente, die aus Sicht des Emittenten als Eigenkapitalinstrumente gemäß IAS 32 bilanziert werden, sind daher vom Anwendungsbereich des IAS 39 ausgenommen (IAS 39.2(d)). Die übrigen Ausnahmen im Hinblick auf die Anwendung anderer IFRS entsprechen den Ausnahmen vom Anwendungsbereich des IAS 32, auf die daher verwiesen wird.

8   **2. Ausnahmen bezüglich der Bilanzierung als schwebendes Geschäft.** Die Ausnahmen von Finanzinstrumenten vom Anwendungsbereich des IAS 39, die zur Bilanzierung als schwebendes Geschäft führen, betreffen bestimmte Verträge für Unternehmenszusammenschlüsse, bestimmte Arten von Kreditzusagen und – für den Zweck der Gliederung dieses Kapitels – den Eigenbedarf bezüglich Verträgen über den Kauf oder Verkauf nicht-finanzieller Posten mit finanziellem Nettoausgleich.

9   **a) Ausnahme für bestimmte Verträge für Unternehmenszusammenschlüsse.** Die Ausnahme für bestimmte Verträge für Unternehmenszusammenschlüsse (IAS 39.2(g)) war für lange Zeit Gegenstand unterschiedlicher Interpretationen. Daher hat das IASB 2009 im Rahmen des „Annual Improvement" Prozesses IAS 39.2(g) geändert, um zwei Aspekte klarzustellen: erstens die Art von Vertrag und zweitens die Art von Unternehmenszusammenschluss, die jeweils unter die Ausnahme fallen.

10   Hinsichtlich der Vertragsart ist die Ausnahme nunmehr explizit auf solche Verträge beschränkt, die Termingeschäfte sind. Daher fallen Vereinbarungen, die als Optionsgeschäft ausgestaltet sind, in den Anwendungsbereich des IAS 39. Dadurch soll sicher gestellt werden, dass nur solche Vereinbarungen un-

ter die Ausnahme fallen, die definitiv zu einem Unternehmenszusammenschluss führen. Aufgrund der Diskussionen des IASB im Vorfeld der Verabschiedung der Änderung ist der Begriff Termingeschäft eng auszulegen. So ist z.B. ein „synthetisches Termingeschäft", d.h. die Kombination einer Call-Option und einer geschriebenen Put-Option mit jeweils gleichem Ausübungspreis, Ausübungsfrist und Bezugsgröße, nicht als Termingeschäft im Sinne von IAS 39.2(g) zu werten. Die enge Auslegung der Neuregelung hat insbesondere auch Auswirkung auf Vereinbarungen mit Zustimmungsvorbehalt bezüglich Organen (z.B. Aufsichtsrat oder Aktionärsversammlung) der beteiligten Vertragsparteien. Sofern diese nicht zeitgleich bei beiden Vertragsparteien erfolgt, wird ein Kaufvertrag mit Zustimmungsvorbehalt für den Zeitraum zwischen den Zustimmungszeitpunkten bei den Vertragsparteien zu einer Option. Dabei wird die Vertragspartei, die zuerst die erforderliche Zustimmung herbeiführt, zum Stillhalter der Option bis die andere Vertragspartei die ihrerseits die erforderliche Zustimmung herbeiführt. Die andere Vertragspartei ist entsprechend Inhaber der Option (Long Position). Erst nachdem alle erforderlichen Zustimmungen von beiden Vertragsparteien herbeigeführt worden sind, fällt der Vertrag unter die Ausnahme.

Die Neufassung des IAS 39.2(g) verlangt außerdem, dass die Laufzeit des Termingeschäfts nicht den Zeitraum überschreitet, der normalerweise erforderlich ist, um etwaige erforderliche Genehmigungen einzuholen und die Transaktion zu vollenden. Erforderliche Genehmigungen im Sinne dieser Vorschrift sind solche seitens Dritter, z.B. von Kartellbehörden. Wie zuvor ausgeführt, betrifft ein Zustimmungsvorbehalt auf Seiten der Vertragsparteien die Vertragsart und kann einer Qualifizierung als Termingeschäft entgegen stehen. 11

Die Neufassung des IAS 39.2(g) stellt ferner hinsichtlich der Art des Unternehmenszusammenschlusses, die unter die Ausnahme fällt, klar, dass es sich um einen Unternehmenszusammenschluss i.S.v. IFRS 3 *Business Combinations* handeln muss. Transaktionen, die den Erwerb von Anteilen an assoziierten Unternehmen betreffen, fallen daher in den Anwendungsbereich des IAS 39. 12

b) Ausnahme für bestimmte Arten von Kreditzusagen. Kreditzusagen sind feste Verpflichtungen, Darlehen unter vorab festgelegten Bedingungen zu gewähren. Kreditzusagen mit einem bestimmten (nicht notwendigerweise festen) Zinsatz für einen bestimmten Zeitraum sind Optionsgeschäfte, bei denen der potentielle Darlehensgeber als Stillhalter fungiert. Diese Kreditzusagen erfüllen die Definition eines Derivats und sind daher im Anwendungsbereich des IAS 39 es sei denn, sie fallen unter die Ausnahme vom Anwendungsbereich gemäß IAS 39.2(h). Für Kreditzusagen betrifft die Ausnahme jedoch nicht die Anwendung von IAS 39 insgesamt sondern ist in ihrem Umfang dahingehend beschränkt, dass die Vorschriften des IAS 39 zur Ausbuchung von Finanzinstrumenten in jedem Fall Anwendung finden. 13

Hintergrund der Ausnahme einiger Kreditzusagen vom Anwendungsbereich des IAS 39 ist die Bilanzierung der aus diesen Kreditzusagen resultierenden Darlehen zu fortgeführten Anschaffungskosten. Die Ausnahme bezweckt, dass für diese Kreditzusagen keine Änderungen des beizulegenden Zeitwerts aufgrund von Schwankungen des Markzinsniveaus oder des Risikoaufschlags erfasst werden. Entsprechend gilt die Ausnahme sowohl für das Unternehmen, das die Kreditzusage gewährt, als auch für die Gegenpartei (d.h. den potentiellen Darlehensnehmer). Allerdings unterliegen alle von der Ausnahme erfassten Kreditzusagen den Vorschriften des IAS 37 *Provisions, Contingent Liabilities and Contingent Assets*. Dies betrifft insbesondere die Rückstellungsbildung für belastende Verträge (IAS 37.66-69). Dies führt in der Praxis zu Problemen, weil das Kreditrisikomanagement von Unternehmen oft einheitliche Verfahren unabhängig davon hat, ob das Kreditrisiko sich auf eine noch nicht bilanzwirksame Kreditzusage oder eine bereits bilanzwirksame Forderung bezieht.[2] 14

Die Ausnahme umfasst alle Kreditzusagen die nicht in die folgenden drei Kategorien fallen: 15

---

2   Zur Bilanzierung von Wertminderungen von finanziellen Vermögenswerten siehe Rn 161-172.

(a) Kreditzusagen, die das die Zusage erteilende Unternehmen als Folge der Ausübung der Fair Value Option[3] (IAS 39.9) erfolgswirksam zum beizulegenden Zeitwert bewertet.[4] Sofern jedoch ein Unternehmen die finanziellen Vermögenswerte, die aus von ihm erteilten Kreditzusagen resultieren, in der Vergangenheit für gewöhnlich kurz nach deren Entstehung verkauft hat, ist die erfolgswirksame Bewertung zum beizulegenden Zeitwert für solche Kreditzusagen verpflichtend. Diese Verpflichtende Bilanzierung umfasst alle Kreditzusagen derselben Klasse. Der Begriff „Klasse" ist in IAS 39 nicht definiert. Im Hinblick auf Angabepflichten enthält IFRS 7 *Financial Instruments: Disclosures* Regelungen für die Bestimmung von „Klassen" von Finanzinstrumenten (IFRS 7.6 und B1-B3). Daraus lässt sich ableiten, dass eine Klasse eine Gruppierung ist, die zumindest zwischen Finanzinstrumenten unterscheidet, die verschiedenen Bewertungsmethoden (d.h. fortgeführte Anschaffungskosten und beizulegender Zeitwert) unterliegen. In der Praxis wird die Gruppierung in Klassen im Rahmen der Ausnahme für Kreditzusagen oft auf einer tieferen Ebene vorgenommen, z.B. auf Produktebene. Eine Bank, die regelmäßig Hypothekendarlehen für Gewerbeimmobilien kurz nach der Inanspruchnahme der Kreditzusage veräußert, kann diese Kreditzusagen als eine Klasse identifizieren, die in den Anwendungsbereich von IAS 39 fällt. Wenn dieselbe Bank Kreditzusagen für Wohnungsbaudarlehen gewährt und die daraus resultierenden Darlehen im Bankbuch hält, bilden diese Kreditzusagen eine eigene Klasse, die vom Anwendungsbereich des IAS 39 ausgenommen ist. Je nach Art und Umfang der Geschäftstätigkeit können sich auch verschiedene Klassen von Kreditzusagen innerhalb des Bereichs Gewerbeimmobilienfinanzierung ergeben.

(b) Kreditzusagen mit finanziellem Nettoausgleich, d.h. Verträge, die durch Ausgleich in bar oder in anderen Finanzinstrumenten so erfüllt werden können. Darunter fällt auch der Umstand, dass ein Unternehmen die aus seinen Kreditzusagen resultierenden finanziellen Vermögenswerte in der Vergangenheit für gewöhnlich kurz nach deren Entstehung verkauft hat.[5] Die Inanspruchnahme einer Kreditzusage in in Teilbeträgen (zB bei einer Kreditlinie) für sich genommen stellt keinen finanziellen Nettoausgleich dar.

(c) Kreditzusagen zu Zinskonditionen unterhalb des Marktzinssatzes. Für die Beurteilung, ob die Zinskonditionen dem Marktzinsniveau entsprechen ist, auf den Zeitpunkt der Gewährung der Kreditzusage abzustellen. Spätere Änderungen des Marktzinsniveaus haben dagegen keinen Einfluss auf die Ausnahme von Anwendungsbereich des IAS 39.[6]

Die Kreditzusagen in den Kategorien (a) und (b) sind als Derivate erfolgswirksam zum beizulegenden Zeitwert zu bilanzieren, es sei denn sie unterliegen als Sicherungsinstrument den besonderen Vorschriften für die Bilanzierung von Sicherungsgeschäften. Obwohl auch die Kreditzusagen in Kategorie (c). Derivate sind, unterliegen sie besonderen Vorschriften zur Folgebewertung (ähnlich derer für finanzielle Garantien).[7]

16   **c) Eigenbedarfsausnahme.** Grundsätzlich sind Verträge über den künftigen Kauf bzw. Verkauf von nicht-finanziellen Posten zu einem fest vereinbarten Preis (Warentermingeschäfte) vom Anwendungsbereich des IAS 39 ausgeschlossen (sog. „own use exemption" oder Eigenbedarfsausnahme), obwohl sie die Definition von Derivaten erfüllen:

1. Solche Verträge benötigen idR. keine Anfangsauszahlung.

2. Ihr Wert schwankt mit dem einer Basisvariablen (Waren).

---

3   Unterabschnitt (b) der Definition der Kategorie „erfolgswirksam zum beizulegenden Zeitwert bewertet".
4   Zur Fair Value Option siehe Rn 110.
5   Siehe Unterabschnitt (a). in dieser Randnummer.
6   Für vom Anwendungsbereich des IAS 39 ausgenommene Kreditzusagen kann ein späterer Anstieg des Markzinsniveaus jedoch Relevanz für die Beurteilung belastender Verträge gemäß IAS 37 haben (siehe Rn 14).
7   Zur Folgebewertung siehe Rn 141.

3. Sie werden zu einem späteren Zeitpunkt erfüllt.

Dieser Ausschluss gilt bis auf den Ausnahmetatbestand, dass Warentermingeschäfte durch Nettoausgleich erfüllt werden können[8] und gemäß IAS 39.5 als gewillkürte Finanzinstrumente (hier: Derivate) zu bilanzieren sind. Dabei umfasst ein Nettoausgleich die Erfüllung in bar, durch andere Finanzinstrumente oder den Tausch von Finanzinstrumenten. Ein möglicher Nettoausgleich ist jedoch unschädlich, wenn das Unternehmen nachweisen kann, dass die Warentermingeschäfte gemäß dem erwarteten Einkaufs-, Verkaufs- oder Nutzungsbedarf des Unternehmens abgeschlossen wurden und die Verträge weiterhin zu diesem Zwecke gehalten werden. Ziel der Regelung war es, Warentermingeschäfte, die ökonomisch und intentional eher Finanzinstrumente sind, in den Anwendungsbereich zu bringen, gleichzeitig aber übliche Warentermingeschäfte aus dem Anwendungsbereich auszuklammern. Somit ist die güterwirtschaftliche Wertschöpfung das wesentliche Abgrenzungskriterium für die Anwendbarkeit der Eigenbedarfsausnahme.[9] Die Eigenbedarfsausnahme stellt kein Wahlrecht dar.[10] Daneben sind für Warentermingeschäfte im Anwendungsbereich von IAS 39 auch die Angaben nach IFRS 7 erforderlich.[11]

Sofern ein Warentermingeschäft nicht im Anwendungsbereich von IAS 39 liegt, handelt es sich um   17
ein „normales" schwebendes Geschäft iSv. IAS 37.1 und 3. Dabei finden die Rückstellungsvorschriften in IAS 37 nur Anwendung auf belastende Verträge.[12] Ggf. sind jedoch eingebettete Derivate aus einem Warentermingeschäft abzutrennen, obwohl der Basisvertrag nicht im Anwendungsbereich von IAS 39 liegt.

IAS 39.6 identifiziert mögliche (alternative) Mechanismen eines Nettoausgleichs bei Warentermin-   18
geschäften:

(a) Die Vertragsbedingungen gestatten mindestens einem Kontrahenten, den Vertrag durch Ausgleich in bar oder einem anderen Finanzinstrument bzw. durch Tausch von Finanzinstrumenten zu erfüllen.

(b) Die Möglichkeit zu einem Ausgleich in bar oder einem anderen Finanzinstrument bzw. durch Tausch von Finanzinstrumenten ist zwar nicht explizit in den Vertragsbedingungen vorgesehen, doch erfüllt das Unternehmen ähnliche Verträge für gewöhnlich durch Ausgleich in bar oder einem anderen Finanzinstrument bzw. durch Tausch von Finanzinstrumenten (sei es mit der Vertragspartei, durch Abschluss gegenläufiger Verträge oder durch Verkauf des Vertrags vor dessen Ausübung oder Verfall).

(c) Bei ähnlichen Verträgen nimmt das Unternehmen den Vertragsgegenstand für gewöhnlich an und veräußert ihn kurz nach der Anlieferung wieder, um Gewinne aus kurzfristigen Schwankungen der Preise oder der Händlermargen zu erzielen.

(d) Der nicht finanzielle Posten, der Gegenstand des Vertrags ist, kann jederzeit in Zahlungsmittel umgewandelt werden.

Verträge, bei denen die Bedingungen in (b) oder (c) erfüllt sind, können niemals unter die Eigen-   19
bedarfsausnahme fallen, da bei ihnen (unwiderlegbar) davon ausgegangen wird, dass sie nicht für den Eigenbedarf abgeschlossen wurden (IAS 39.6).[13] In diesen Situationen wird der Vertrag als Derivat erfolgswirksam zum beizulegenden Zeitwert gemäß IAS 39 bilanziert.

Die Vertragstypen (b) und (c) unterscheiden sich im Wesentlichen darin, dass bei (c) im Gegensatz   20
zu (b) tatsächlich eine physische Lieferung des nicht-finanziellen Postens erfolgt, dieser jedoch kurz danach weiterveräußert wurde. Die kurzfristige Weiterveräußerung ist allerdings noch nicht hinreichend

---

8   Vgl. *PwC (Hrsg.)* IFRS Manual, 3012.
9   Vgl. IDW RS HFA 25, Rn. 13.
10   Vgl. IDW RS HFA 25, Rn. 6.
11   Vgl. *Deloitte (Hrsg.)* iGAAP 22 und Rn 266ii.
12   Vgl. IDW RS HFA 25, Rn. 4.
13   Vgl. *PwC (Hrsg.)* 3013.

für eine Bilanzierung nach IAS 39, vielmehr muss auch eine Intention zur Erzielung von Gewinnen aus kurzfristigen Schwankungen der Preise oder der Händlermargen bestehen. Diese Absicht kann nur durch eine Würdigung aller relevanten Faktoren beurteilt werden. Von Bedeutung können hier u.a. sein:[14]

- Art des operativen Geschäfts sowie dessen Steuerung – Findet eine güterwirtschaftliche Wertschöpfung statt?
  - Veredlung der Ware.
  - Losgrößentransformation.
  - Räumliche und zeitliche Transformation.
- Art der Erfolgsrealisierung – Was ist der primäre Treiber des Erfolgs?
  - Ausnutzung von kurzfristigen Preisschwankungen.
  - Realisierung von kurzfristigen Schwankungen in der Händlermarge.

21   Es gilt zu beachten, dass die Einordnung eines Vertrags als Typ (b) oder (c) für ähnliche Verträge gleich zu erfolgen hat. Demnach haben schädliche Verträge eine Abfärbewirkung auf ähnliche Verträge, außer es kann eine Änderung des Verhaltens nachgewiesen werden.[15] Daher ist es von besonderer Bedeutung, auf welcher Basis Verträge als „ähnlich" (similar) gruppiert werden, da auf diese grundsätzlich die gleiche Bilanzierung Anwendung findet. In der Literatur werden u.a. folgende Faktoren vorgeschlagen:[16]

- gleiche wirtschaftliche Zielsetzung;
- gleiche/gemeinsame Märkte für Güter;
- substitutionale Beziehungen zwischen den Gütern; und
- einheitliche organisatorische Verantwortlichkeit im Rahmen des Risikomanagements.

22   In der Literatur wird die Auffassung vertreten, dass gleiche Verträge mit unterschiedlicher Intention nicht ähnlich sind.[17] Durch Etablierung einer Buchstruktur (Eigenbedarfsbuch vs. Handelsbuch) kann dieser Nachweis *ex ante* geführt werden. Dabei muss jedoch eine Zuordnung zu den jeweiligen Büchern bei erstmaligem Ansatz erfolgen. Nachträgliche Umschichtungen von Verträgen zwischen den Büchern sind grundsätzlich schädlich.

23   Für den einzelnen Vertrag kann sich der Verwendungszweck ändern. Für den Fall, dass ein Warentermingeschäft außerhalb von IAS 39 bilanziert wurde, sich aber in der Folge der Verwendungszweck geändert hat, ist diese Zweckänderung prospektiv zu bilanzieren. D.h. ab dem Zeitpunkt der Zweckänderung ist der beizulegende Zeitwert des Vertrags erstmalig in der Bilanz zu erfassen und fortlaufend zu bewerten. Eine retrospektive Anpassung ist nicht zulässig, da es sich nicht um einen Bilanzierungsfehler handelt.[18]

24   Für Verträge vom Typ (a) und (d) kann das Unternehmen den Nachweis führen, dass die Verträge aus Eigenbedarfserwägungen geschlossen und gehalten werden. Davon ausgenommen sind jedoch geschriebene Optionen über den Kauf oder Verkauf eines nicht-finanziellen Postens mit Nettoerfüllungsmöglichkeit. Diese sind immer als Derivat im Sinne von IAS 39 erfolgswirksam zum beizulegenden Zeitwert anzusetzen und fortlaufend zu bewerten (IAS 39.7). Dies wird damit begründet, dass mit geschriebenen Optionen der Warenfluss und somit die güterwirtschaftliche Wertschöpfung nicht steuerbar ist.[19] Ebenso verhält es sich bei Verträgen vom Typ (a)* Liegt die Möglichkeit zur Nettoerfüllung bei der

---

14   Vgl. IDW RS HFA 25, Rn. 14.
15   Vgl. IDW RS HFA 25, Rn. 17.
16   Vgl. IDW RS HFA 25, Rn. 19.
17   Bspw. IDW RS HFA 25, Rn. 22; *Deloitte (Hrsg.)* iGAAP 31f.
18   Vgl. IDW RS HFA 25, Rn. 7.
19   Vgl. IDW RS HFA 25, Rn. 37.

Gegenpartei, muss davon ausgegangen werden, dass der Eigenbedarfsnachweis nicht erbracht werden kann und die Verträge in den Anwendungsbereich von IAS 39 fallen.[20] Dies heißt im Umkehrschluss, dass sich gekaufte Optionen grundsätzlich für die Eigenbedarfsausnahme eignen.[21]

Es stellt sich die Frage, ob jede Form der Optionalität, die durch das Unternehmen zugesagt wird, schädlich ist. Dies ist vor allem in der Energiebranche von Bedeutung, wo oftmals Optionalität in Form von Mehrmengenoptionen zugesagt wird (sog. volumetrische Flexibilität). Für Verträge mit Endkunden ist diese Frage bereits durch das IFRIC[22] geklärt worden. Dem IFRIC wurde die Frage gestellt, ob eine volumetrische Flexibilität in Energielieferverträgen zwischen Energieversorgern und Endkunden den Charakter einer geschriebenen Option hat und somit aus Sicht des Energieversorgers in den Anwendungsbereich von IAS 39 fällt. Zwar lehnte das IFRIC die Aufnahme der Fragestellung auf die Agenda ab, jedoch machte es in seiner Ablehnungsentscheidung klar, dass die genannten Verträge nicht in den Anwendungsbereich von IAS 39 fallen, da es den Endkunden an der konkreten Realisationsmöglichkeit der Option zur Gewinnerzielung mangelt, obwohl diese abstrakt vorliegt. Wie solche Verträge bei Gegenparteien zu beurteilen sind, die auch die konkrete Verwertungsfähigkeit haben, lässt das IFRIC offen. Es ist jedoch davon auszugehen, dass es sich hier um geschriebene Optionen iSd. Standards handelt und eine Derivatebilanzierung angezeigt ist.

25

Eine ähnlich gelagerte Problematik ergibt sich bei Verträgen, die eine Mindestabnahmemenge zu einem festen Preis vorsehen, jedoch als „Puffer" eine volumetrische Flexibilität ebenfalls zu einem festen Preis einräumen (z.B. Abnahme von mindestens 80KWh plus bis zu 20 zusätzliche KWh). Da IAS 39 Verträge idR. als ein einziges Bilanzierungsobjekt betrachtet, sofern spezifische Regelungen dem nicht entgegenstehen, ist davon auszugehen, dass auch solche Verträge, sofern man die optionale Komponente als geschriebene Option iSd. Standards betrachtet, in toto als Derivate zu bilanzieren sind.[23] Allerdings hat das IFRS Interpretations Committee zwischenzeitlich diese Frage in einer Agendaentscheidung behandelt und diese Frage ausdrücklich offen gelassen.[24]

26

III. Bilanzierungseinheit. Die Bestimmung der Bilanzierungseinheit hat besondere Bedeutung für die Bilanzierung von Finanzinstrumenten. Die Ursache liegt darin, dass sich Finanzinstrumente in besonderer Weise zur Strukturierung eignen. Daher enthält IAS 39 eigene Vorschriften zur Bilanzierung **eingebetteter Derivate** (embedded derivatives) um zu verhindern, dass die Ansatz und Bewertungsvorschriften für Derivate umgangen werden, indem Derivate in Verträge über nicht-derivative Transaktionen einbezogen werden (IAS 39.BC37). Im Gegensatz dazu liegt die Bedeutung eingebetteter Derivate für IFRS 9 allein darin, wie sie sich auf die Cashflow-bezogenen Vertragsmerkmale des Finanzinstruments auswirken.[25] Eine Abtrennung eingebetteter Derivate vom Basisvertrag erfolgt nach IFRS 9 nicht (IFRS 9.4.7).[26]

27

1. Definition eines Derivats. Die Definition eines eingebetteten Derivats beruht auf der Definition eines Derivats, auf die daher zuerst eingegangen wird. Ein **Derivat** ist ein Vertrag, der entweder ein Finanzinstrument oder ein Vertrag über den Kauf oder Verkauf nicht-finanzieller Posten mit finanziellem Nettoausgleich im Anwendungsbereich des IAS 39 ist,[27] und folgende Kriterien kumulativ erfüllt:

28

---

20 Vgl. *Deloitte (Hrsg.)* iGAAP 30f.
21 Vgl. auch *Deloitte (Hrsg.)* iGAAP, 30.
22 Das IFRIC wurde 2010 in „IFRS Interpretations Committee" umbenannt.
23 Vgl. *Deloitte (Hrsg.)* iGAAP 28f.
24 Siehe zur Bilanzierungseinheit in diesen Fällen Rn 49f.
25 Zur Auswirkung auf die Bilanzierung gemäß IFRS 9 siehe Rn 125-128.
26 Dies betrifft die Aktivseite, d.h. hybride Finanzinstrumente, deren Basisvertrag ein finanzieller Vermögenswert ist und damit im Anwendungsbereich von IFRS 9 liegt.
27 Siehe Rn 4.

(a) Der Wert des Vertrags ändert sich in Abhängigkeit einer festgelegten Bezugsgröße (Basis) wie z.B. einem Zinssatz, Rohstoffpreis, Wechselkurs, Bonitätsrating oder anderen Variablen (einschließlich von Indizes auf solche Variablen). Für die Beurteilung dieses Kriteriums umfassen die Bezugsgrößen jedoch keine nicht-finanziellen Variablen, die vertragsparteispezifisch sind.

(b) Bei Vertragsschluss ist entweder keine Nettoinvestition erforderlich oder sie ist geringer als für alternative Vertragstypen, deren Wert erwartungsgemäß ähnlich auf Änderungen der Marktbedingungen reagiert.

(c) Der Vertrag wird an einem späteren Datum erfüllt.

Diese Kriterien werden in den nachfolgenden Randnummern näher erläutert.

29   Für die Auslegung des ersten Kriteriums (a) der Definition eines Derivats hat die Fragestellung, wann eine Bezugsgröße eine nicht-finanzielle vertragsparteispezifische Variable ist, die größte Bedeutung in der Praxis. Erhebliche Unterschiede in der Interpretation beziehen sich auf zwei Aspekte. Erstens besteht die Frage, ob die Bezugnahme auf nicht-finanzielle vertragsparteispezifische Variablen bezweckt, lediglich Versicherungsverträge von der Definition eines Derivats auszuschließen. Zweitens besteht die Frage, ob Kennzahlen wie EBITDA, Umsatzerlöse oder ähnliche Größen als „nicht-finanziell" anzusehen sind. Das IFRIC hatte sich ursprünglich 2006 mit diesen Fragestellungen befasst und vorläufig entschieden, dass das Kriterium nicht lediglich Versicherungsverträge von der Definition eines Derivats ausschließt und dass die Formulierung des Kriteriums hinsichtlich der Beurteilung von Kennzahlen wie EBITDA, Umsatzerlöse oder ähnlicher Größen als „nicht-finanziell" unklar ist. Um die unterschiedliche Auslegung in der Praxis zu beenden, beschloss das IFRIC im Januar 2007, den Sachverhalt an das IASB zwecks Klarstellung mittels einer Anpassung von IAS 39 weiterzuleiten.[28] Das IASB schlug darauf hin eine Streichung der Bezugnahme auf nicht-finanzielle vertragsparteispezifische Variablen vor. Aufgrund der Stellungnahmen zu diesem Änderungsvorschlag wurde dieser jedoch nicht weiter verfolgt. Stattdessen beabsichtigt das IASB eine erneute Diskussion im Rahmen der Projekts zur Ablösung von IAS 39.[29] Vor diesem Hintergrund bleibt dieser Themenkreis weiterhin ungeklärt. Dabei ist zu beachten, dass Verträge, die Zahlungen in Abhängigkeit von Kennzahlen wie wie EBITDA oder Umsatzerlösen vorsehen, auch wenn sie nicht als Derivat bilanziert werden, dennoch Finanzinstrumente sein können, die in den Anwendungsbereich von IAS 39 fallen. Allerdings erfolgt dann gegebenenfalls die Folgebewertung zu fortgeführten Anschaffungskosten statt zum beizulegenden Zeitwert.[30]

30   Das zweite Kriterium (b) hinsichtlich der Nettoinvestition bei Vertragsschluss zielt auf die Hebelwirkung von Derivaten. Für Optionen ist der relevante Vergleichsmaßstab für die Nettoinvestition der Wert des Bezugsobjekts bei Abschluss des Optionsvertrags. Obwohl für Optionen oft die Optionsprämie bei Vertragsschluss (d.h. im Voraus) gezahlt wird, ist diese Nettoinvestition geringer als der Wert des Bezugsobjekts. Auch Verträge, die einen Austausch von Bezugsobjekten bei Vertragsschluss vorsehen (z.B. bestimmte Währungsswaps bei denen die Währungsbeträge zu Vertragsbeginn getauscht werden), erfüllen das Nettoinvestitionskriterium, da der Tausch zu keiner Investition auf Nettobasis führt (IAS 39. AG11). Sofern eine Vertragspartei erhebliche Vorauszahlungen bei Vertragsschluss leistet, ist sorgfältig zu prüfen, ob diese der Nettoinvestition in das Bezugsobjekt entsprechen. So erfordert z.B. ein im Voraus bezahltes Termingeschäft eine Nettoinvestition in Höhe des Kassapreises und erfüllt nicht die Definition eines Derivats (IAS 39 IG B.9). Etwaige Sicherheitsleistungen einschließlich sogenannter „Margin-Zahlungen" sind nicht als Teil der Nettoinvestition zu behandeln, sondern separat zu bilanzieren (IAS 39 IG B.10).

---

28   Siehe IFRIC Update vom Januar 2007, Seite 4.
29   Siehe Rn 1.
30   Siehe Rn 136-141.

Die Beurteilung des dritten Kriteriums (c) hinsichtlich der Vertragserfüllung an einem späteren Datum erfordert in der Regel kein Ermessen. Hierbei ist lediglich zu beachten, dass bei Optionsverträgen auch eine Nichtausübung durch den Inhaber eine Vertragserfüllung seitens des Stillhalters darstellt (IAS 39 IG B.7). Die Definition eines Derivats in IAS 39 umfasst sowohl Verträge mit Nettoausgleich (z.B. mittels Zahlung des beizulegenden Zeitwerts des Derivats bei Fälligkeit) als auch **Verträge mit Bruttoausgleich** (z.B. Erfüllung eines Termingeschäfts zum Erwerb einer Anleihe durch Übertragung der Anleihe gegen Zahlung des Terminkaufpreises) (IAS 39.AG10). Sofern es sich bei dem Derivat um einen Vertrag über den Kauf oder Verkauf nicht-finanzieller Posten mit finanziellem Nettoausgleich handelt,[31] ist zu prüfen, ob er aufgrund der Eigenbedarfsausnahme als schwebendes Geschäft zu behandeln ist. Falls das der Fall ist, erfüllt der Vertrag nicht die Definition eines Derivats, da er vom Anwendungsbereich des IAS 39 ausgenommen ist.[32]

2. Eingebettete Derivate. Ein eingebettetes Derivat unterscheidet sich von einem freistehenden Derivat dadurch, dass es ein integraler Bestandteil eines **strukturierten (hybriden) Finanzinstruments** mit einer nicht-derivativen Komponente – dem sogenannten **Basisvertrag** (host contract) – ist. Dadurch verändert sich ein Teil der Cashflows des strukturierten Finanzinstruments ähnlich wie die eines freistehenden Derivats. Ist ein Derivat unabhängig von anderen Vertragsbestandteilen übertragbar, so handelt es sich um ein freistehendes Derivat (z.B. ein Bezugsrecht, das separat von der Stammaktie handelbar ist). Gleiches gilt, wenn die verschiedenen Vertragsbestandteile mit verschiedenen Vertragsparteien abgeschlossen werden (IAS 39.10).

a) Voraussetzung der Abtrennung vom Basisvertrag. Ein eingebettetes Derivat ist getrennt vom Basisvertrag als eine eigene Bilanzierungseinheit zu behandeln, wenn folgende kumulative Kriterien erfüllt sind:

(a) Die wirtschaftlichen Merkmale und Risiken des eingebetteten Derivats sind nicht eng mit denen des Basisvertrags verbunden.

(b) Als freistehendes Instrument mit ansonsten denselben Vertragskonditionen würde das eingebettete Derivat die Definition eines Derivats erfüllen.

(c) Das eingebettete Derivat ist nicht Bestandteil eines strukturierten Finanzinstruments, das insgesamt erfolgswirksam zum beizulegenden Zeitwert bewertet wird.

Diese Kriterien werden in den nachfolgenden Randnummern näher erläutert.

Die Beurteilung, ob die wirtschaftlichen Merkmale und Risiken eines eingebetteten Derivats eng mit denen des Basisvertrags verbunden sind, gehört zu den komplexesten Bilanzierungsfragen. Dies liegt daran, dass dieses Kriterium eine Erleichterungsregel für eine auf die Verhinderung von Umgehungstatbeständen gerichtete Vorschrift ist. Hintergrund dieser Erleichterungsregel ist, dass bei einer engen wirtschaftlichen Beziehung zwischen eingebettetem Derivat und Basisvertrag die Wahrscheinlichkeit geringer ist, dass die Strukturierung des Finanzinstruments im Hinblick auf die bilanzielle Auswirkung erfolgte (IAS 39.BC37). Dieser Beweggrund führt zwangsläufig zu einem widersprüchlichen und willkürlichen Katalog von „Beispielen" (IAS 39.AG30 und AG33). Mangels eines klaren, logisch schlüssigen übergeordneten Normzwecks stellen diese Beispiele daher faktisch eine Liste von Regeln dar, die für Analogieschlüsse weitgehend unbrauchbar ist.

Generell gilt, dass bei einem Basisvertrag mit wirtschaftlichen Merkmalen und Risiken eines Eigenkapitalinstruments nur solche eingebetteten Derivate als eng verbunden gelten, die Eigenkapitalmerkmale bzgl. desselben Unternehmens (d.h. Emittenten) aufweisen (IAS 39.AG27).

---

31 Siehe Rn 4 und 16
32 Siehe Rn 28.

Die für die Praxis wichtigsten Beispiele einer engen Verbindung der wirtschaftlichen Merkmale und Risiken des eingebetteten Derivats mit denen des Basisvertrags sind:

(a) **Eingebettete Fremdwährungsderivate (IAS 39.AG33(d)).** Voraussetzung ist, dass diese in einen Versicherungsvertrag oder einen nicht-finanziellen Basisvertrag (z.B. ein schwebendes Geschäft hinsichtlich eines nicht-finanziellen Postens) eingebettet sind sowie weder Hebelwirkung noch Optionscharakter besitzen. Ferner müssen Zahlungen in einer der folgenden Währungen bedungen sein:

- der funktionalen Währung einer wesentlichen Vertragspartei; hier stellt sich in der Praxis das Problem, die funktionale Währung anderer Vertragsparteien zu ermitteln (z.B. für nicht nach IFRS bilanzierende Unternehmen, einzelne Konzerngesellschaften oder natürliche Personen).

- der Währung, in der nach IAS 39 IG C.8 auf weltweiter Basis regelmäßig der Preis des nicht-finanziellen Postens festgelegt wird; dies betrifft vor allem Rohstoffe (z.B. Rohöl, Gold, Silber, Kupfer, Eisenerz) sowie Großraumflugzeuge.[33]

- der Währung, die üblicherweise für Kaufverträge verwendet wird, die nicht-finanzielle Posten im wirtschaftlichen Gebiet, in dem das Geschäft erfolgt, betreffen; dies sind z.B. sogenannte „stabile“ oder „harte“ Währungen, die üblicherweise entweder statt der lokalen Währung im Binnenhandel oder im Außenhandel verwendet werden; in der Praxis erfordert die Beurteilung, ob eine solche Währung vorliegt, eine individuelle Analyse (wobei es mehr als eine solche Währung gleichzeitig je wirtschaftlichem Gebiet geben kann).[34]

(b) **Eingebettete Derivate in Leasingverträgen (IAS 39.AG33(f).** Voraussetzung ist, dass das eingebettete Derivat eine der drei folgenden Bezugsgrößen aufweist:

- einen Inflationsindex, der keine Hebelwirkung hat und sich auf Inflation im wirtschaftlichen Gebiet des jeweiligen Unternehmens bezieht.

- Bedingte Mietzahlung auf Basis von Umsätzen.

- Bedingte Mietzahlungen auf Basis variabler Zinssätze.

(c) **Eingebettete Caps und Floors (IAS 39.AG33(b)).** Caps und Floors sind Optionsgeschäfte, die Ober- bzw. Untergrenzen für Parameter (z.B. Preise, Zinssätze, Indizes) festlegen. Ein Collar ist eine Kombination aus Caps und Floors, d.h. sie legen eine Bandbreite fest, innerhalb derer sich ein Parameter bewegt. Ein Cap ist „im Geld“, wenn der relevante Parameter oberhalb der Obergrenze liegt (z.B. ein Strompreis-Cap mit einem Ausübungspreis von 70 €/MWh ist im Geld, sobald der Strompreis diesen Wert übersteigt). Entsprechend umgekehrt verhält es sich mit einem Floor (d.h. dieser ist im Geld, wenn der relevante Parameter unterhalb der Untergrenze liegt). Ein Collar ist dementsprechend im Geld, wenn der relevante Parameter außerhalb der durch Ober- und Untergrenze definierten Bandbreite liegt. Die wirtschaftlichen Merkmale und Risiken eines eingebetteten Caps oder Floors sind in folgenden Fällen eng mit denen des Basisvertrags verbunden:

- Die Caps oder Floors sind Zinsinstrumente ohne Hebelwirkung, deren Basisvertrag ein Schuldinstrument oder Versicherungsvertrag ist, und sind im Zeitpunkt des Abschlusses des Vertrags nicht im Geld. Für die Beurteilung, ob ein Zinscap oder -floor im Geld ist, wird in der Praxis auf den Kassawert des entsprechenden Referenzzinssatzes abgestellt.[35] Wenn z.B. die Terminzinssätze die Obergrenze eines Caps überschreiten, aber der Kassazins unterhalb oder auf der Obergrenze liegt, wird daher von einer engen Verbindung der wirtschaftlichen Merkmale und

---

33 Siehe z.B. *Deloitte (Hrsg.)*, iGAAP, 928 (mit Verweis auf Abstract EIC 169 des Canadian Institute of Chartered Accountants), *PwC (Hrsg.)* IFRS Manual – Financial instruments, Rn 5.87 und 5.87.3.
34 Siehe z.B. *Deloitte (Hrsg.)* iGAAP, 929; *PwC (Hrsg.)* IFRS Manual – Financial instruments, Rn 5.89f.
35 So auch *Ernst & Young (Hrsg.)* International GAAP, 2161.

Risiken des eingebetteten Caps mit denen des Basisvertrags ausgegangen. Da die Beurteilung im Zeitpunkt des Abschlusses des Basisvertrags erfolgt, ändert sich diese nicht aufgrund der nachfolgenden Zinsentwicklung.

- Die Caps oder Floors sind in Verträge über den Kauf oder Verkauf von Vermögenswerten wie z.B. Rohstoffen eingebettet, haben keine Hebelwirkung, und sind im Zeitpunkt des Abschlusses des Basisvertrags nicht im Geld. Bei diesen Verträgen handelt es sich oft um Termingeschäfte. In solchen fällen stellt sich die Frage, ob für die Beurteilung, ob Caps oder Floors im Geld sind, auf den Kassapreis oder den Terminpreis abzustellen ist. Die Bewertung von Terminkontrakten sowie der Regelungszweck der Vorschrift sprechen in diesen Fällen dafür, für die Beurteilung den Terminpreis heranzuziehen.

Obwohl in IAS 39 nur Caps und Floors ausdrücklich genannt sind, ist für Collars entsprechend zu verfahren.[36]

Neben den zuvor genannten Beispielen einer engen Verbindung der wirtschaftlichen Merkmale und Risiken des eingebetteten Derivats mit denen des Basisvertrags enthält IAS 39 noch weitere Beispiele für folgende Situationen:
- in Schuldinstrumente oder Versicherungsverträge eingebettete Zinsderivate mit Hebelwirkung (IAS 39.AG33(a)).
- in Doppelwährungsanleihen oder -darlehen eingebettete Fremdwährungsderivate (IAS 39.AG33(c)). Hier ist jedoch zu berücksichtigen, dass ungeachtet einer Beurteilung der wirtschaftlichen Merkmale und Risiken des eingebetteten Fremdwährungsderivats als eng verbunden mit denen des Basisvertrags eine separate Bilanzierung der beiden Währungskomponenten erforderlich ist.[37] Diese erfolgt jedoch nicht als Folge der Aufspaltung eines Basisvertrags nach den Regeln für eingebettete Derivate sondern im Rahmen der allgemeinen Bewertungsvorschriften in IAS 39 und IAS 21.
- Optionen zur vorzeitigen Rückzahlung, die in aus einem sogenannten „Bondstripping" entstandene Zins- oder Kapitalstrips eingebettet sind (IAS 39.AG33(e)).
- in Finanzinstrumente oder Versicherungsverträge eingebettete Derivate, die Zahlungen erfordern, deren Betrag in Anteilen an (internen oder externen) Investmentfonds bemessen ist (IAS 39. AG33(g)).
- in Versicherungsverträge eingebettete Derivate, die aufgrund der engen Verflechtung mit dem Basisvertrag nicht separat bewertet werden können (IAS 39.AG33(h)).

Umgekehrt enthält IAS 39 Beispiele, in denen die wirtschaftlichen Merkmale und Risiken des eingebetteten Derivats *nicht* eng mit denen des Basisvertrags verbunden sind. Die für die Praxis wichtigsten Beispiele sind:

(a) **Eingebettete Optionen bzgl. einer vorzeitigen Rückzahlung (IAS 39.AG30(g)).** Diese Derivate sind entweder in Schuldinstrumente oder Versicherungsverträge eingebettet. Neben einer Option zur vorzeitigen Rückzahlung können diese Derivate auch als Kauf- oder Verkaufoption ausgestaltet sein, die zu einer vorzeitigen Tilgung mittels Erwerb durch den Schuldner vor der Fälligkeit des Instruments führen. Als Ausnahme vom Grundsatz sind die wirtschaftlichen Merkmale und Risiken dieser eingebetteten Derivate jedoch dann eng mit denen des Basisvertrags verbunden sofern eine der folgenden Situationen vorliegt:
- der Ausübungspreis der Option an jedem möglichen Ausübungszeitpunkt annähernd entspricht den fortgeführten Anschaffungskosten (bei Schuldinstrumenten) oder dem Buchwert (bei Versicherungsverträgen) des Basisvertrags.

36

37

---

36 So auch *PwC (Hrsg.)* IFRS Manual – Financial instruments, Rn 5.40, 5.42 und 5.83.
37 Vgl. *PwC (Hrsg.)* IFRS Manual – Financial instruments, Rn 9.163.1ff.

- der Ausübungspreis der Option zur vorzeitigen Rückzahlung entschädigt den Gläubiger für etwaige entgangene Zinsen. Diese Entschädigung darf höchstens den ungefähren Barwert der entgangenen Zinsen für die Restlaufzeit des Basisvertrags betragen. Die entgangenen Zinsen werden berechnet als die auf den Darlehensbetrag entfallende Zinsdifferenz zwischen dem Effektivzinssatz des Basisvertrags und dem Zinssatz für eine Alternativinvestition in eine vergleichbare Anlage über die Restlaufzeit des Basisvertrags. Diese Ausnahme trägt den in der Praxis häufig vereinbarten Vorfälligkeitsentschädigungen Rechnung, die bei einer vorzeitigen Darlehenstilgung neben Darlehensbetrag und aufgelaufenen Zinsen zahlbar sind. Für die Beurteilung dieses Kriteriums ist in der Praxis zu beachten, dass die beschriebene Vorgehensweise Effekten aufgrund der Zinsstrukturkurve unterliegt. Wird z.B. ein Darlehen mit einer ursprünglichen Laufzeit von 10 Jahren zwei Jahre vor Fälligkeit getilgt, so weist die relevante Alternativinvestition einen Zinssatz in Abhängigkeit der Instrumente mit zweijähriger Laufzeit auf. Selbst wenn sich das Zinsniveau insgesamt nicht ändert, hat daher die Form der Zinsstrukturkurve Einfluss auf die Beurteilung.

  Bei wandelbaren Schuldinstrumenten nimmt der Schuldner die Beurteilung dieses Kriteriums vor der Aufspaltung in Eigen- und Fremdkapitalkomponente gemäß IAS 32 vor.

(b) **Eingebettete Regelungen zur Laufzeitverlängerung (IAS 39.AG30(c)).** Diese Derivate sind in Schuldinstrumente eingebettet und können entweder als Option oder als automatische Regelung zur Verlängerung der Restlaufzeit ausgestaltet sein. Wenn der Inhaber des Schuldinstruments geschriebene Call-Optionen auf dieses an Dritte ausgibt und der Emittent des Schuldinstruments dadurch bei Ausübung der Option verpflichtet werden kann, sich an der Vermarktung des Schuldinstruments zu beteiligen oder sie zu erleichtern, so ist die Call-Option aus Sicht des Emittenten als Verlängerungsoption zu behandeln. Als Ausnahme vom Grundsatz sind die wirtschaftlichen Merkmale und Risiken dieser eingebetteten Derivate jedoch dann eng mit denen des Basisvertrags verbunden sofern im Zeitpunkt der Laufzeitverlängerung eine näherungsweise Anpassung der Verzinsung an das dann herrschende Marktzinsniveau erfolgt. Teilweise wird die Auffassung vertreten, dass eine Verlängerungsoption als Kreditzusage betrachtet werden kann.[38] Folgt man dieser Auffassung, ist zu beachten, dass Kreditzusagen, die vom Anwendungsbereich des IAS 39 ausgenommen sind,[39] nicht die Definition eines Derivats erfüllen.[40] Folglich erfüllen eingebettete Regelungen zur Laufzeitverlängerung, die nach dieser Auffassung als Kreditzusagen außerhalb des Anwendungsbereichs von IAS 39 angesehen werden, auch nicht die Definition eines eingebetteten Derivats.[41] Ob diese Auffassung eine mögliche Interpretation von IAS 39 darstellt, ist mangels eines klaren, logisch schlüssigen übergeordneten Normzwecks der Regelungen zu eingebetteten Derivaten[42] schwer zu beurteilen. Es erscheint jedoch vertretbar, wenn als Ergebnis der Auslegung von IAS 39 eine Kreditzusage nicht allein aufgrund der Tatsache, dass sie in ein Schuldinstrument eingebettet ist, als Derivat nach IAS 39 bilanziert wird, während eine freistehende Kreditzusage mit ansonsten gleichen Konditionen nicht als Derivat bilanziert würde. Die Regelungen zu eingebetteten Derivaten zur Laufzeitverlängerung sind auch ein Beispiel für die Widersprüchlichkeit der Vorschriften für eingebettete Derivate.[43] Wirtschaftlich betrachtet sind z.B. Optionen zur Laufzeitverlängerung und zur vorzeitigen Rückzahlung[44] äquivalente Mechanismen, die sich nur dadurch unterscheiden, welche der vertraglich möglichen

---

38   Vgl. *PwC (Hrsg.)* IFRS Manual – Financial instruments, Rn 5.46.1.
39   Siehe Rn 15.
40   Siehe Rn 28.
41   Siehe Rn 33.
42   Siehe Rn 34.
43   Siehe Rn 34.
44   Siehe Unterabschnitt (a) in dieser Rn.

Fälligkeiten aus der Ausübung der Option oder deren Nichtausübung resultiert. Dennoch werden die wirtschaftlich gleichen Mechanismen nach IAS 39 allein nach ihrer rechtlichen Ausgestaltung verschieden behandelt.[45]

(c) **Eingebettete Regelungen zur Umwandlung in Eigenkapital (IAS 39.AG30(f)).** Diese Derivate sind in wandelbare Schuldinstrumente eingebettete Regelungen, die die Umwandlung des Schuldinstruments in Eigenkapitalinstrumente des Emittenten bewirken (z.B. die Umwandlungsoption in einer Wandelschuldverschreibung). Aus Sicht des Inhabers sind die wirtschaftlichen Merkmale und Risiken dieser eingebetteten Derivate nicht eng mit denen des Basisvertrags verbunden. Der Emittent hat dagegen zu beurteilen, ob das eingebettete Derivat ein Eigenkapitalinstrument gemäß IAS 32 darstellt. In diesem Fall ist das eingebettete Derivat unter Anwendung von IAS 32 von der Fremdkapitalkomponente des zusammengesetzten Finanzinstruments zu trennen. Derivate, die Eigenkapitalinstrumente darstellen, sind vom Anwendungsbereich des IAS 39 ausgenommen.[46]

Neben den zuvor genannten Beispielen, in denen die wirtschaftlichen Merkmale und Risiken des eingebetteten Derivats *nicht* eng mit denen des Basisvertrags verbunden sind, enthält IAS 39 noch weitere Beispiele für folgende Situationen: 38

- in Schuldinstrumente eingebettete Verkaufsoptionen mit einem variablen Ausübungspreis in Abhängigkeit von Preisen für oder Indizes auf Eigenkapitalinstrumente oder Rohstoffe, die den Emittenten zum Rückkauf des Instruments verpflichten (IAS 39.AG30(a)).
- in Eigenkapitalinstrumente eingebettete Kaufoptionen, die den Rückkauf durch den Emittenten zu einem festgelegten Preis erlauben(IAS 39.AG30(b)). Dies gilt aus Sicht des Inhabers. Der Emittent hat dagegen zu beurteilen, ob das eingebettete Derivat ein Eigenkapitalinstrument gemäß IAS 32 darstellt. In diesem Fall ist das eingebettete Derivat unter Anwendung von IAS 32 von der Fremdkapitalkomponente des zusammengesetzten Finanzinstruments zu trennen. Derivate, die Eigenkapitalinstrumente darstellen, sind vom Anwendungsbereich des IAS 39 ausgenommen.[47]
- in Schuldinstrumente oder Versicherungsverträge eingebettete Derivate, die den Betrag von Zinsoder Tilgungszahlungen und den Wert eines Eigenkapitalinstruments koppeln (IAS 39.AG30(d)).
- in Schuldinstrumente oder Versicherungsverträge eingebettete Derivate, die den Betrag von Zinsoder Tilgungszahlungen und den Wert eines Rohstoffes koppeln (IAS 39.AG30)).
- in Schuldinstrumente **eingebettete Kreditderivate**, die es dem Sicherungsnehmer ermöglichen, das Kreditrisiko von Finanzinstrumenten unabhängig davon, ob er diese besitzt, auf die andere Vertragspartei zu überwälzen (IAS 39.AG30(h)). Dieses betrifft z.B. sogenannte „**Credit Linked Notes**" (CLNs), d.h. Anleihen, deren Rückzahlung von der Kreditwürdigkeit von Referenzunternehmen (d.h. anderen Unternehmen als dem Emittenten) abhängt. Ferner hat dieses Beispiel Bedeutung für die Beurteilung sogenannter „**Collateralised Debt Obligations**" (CDOs). In der Praxis hat dieses Beispiel dazu geführt, dass für synthetische CDOs nach IFRS die wirtschaftlichen Merkmale und Risiken des eingebetteten Kreditderivats als *nicht* eng mit denen des Basisvertrags verbunden angesehen werden. Im Gegensatz wird in der Praxis bei sogenannten „Cash CDOs" von einer wirtschaftlich engen Verbindung ausgegangen.

Die zweite Voraussetzung für die Trennung eines eingebetteten Derivats vom Basisvertrag ist, dass es 39 als freistehendes Instrument mit ansonsten denselben Vertragskonditionen würde die Definition eines Derivats erfüllen würde.[48] Für diese Beurteilung wird daher auf die Ausführungen zur Definition eines Derivats in Rn. 28-31 verwiesen.

---

45 Vgl. *Deloitte (Hrsg.)* iGAAP, 895.
46 Siehe Rn 7.
47 Siehe Rn 7.
48 Siehe Rn 33(b).

40   Die dritte Voraussetzung für die Trennung eines eingebetteten Derivats vom Basisvertrag ist, dass das eingebettete Derivat nicht Bestandteil eines strukturierten Finanzinstruments ist, das insgesamt erfolgswirksam zum beizulegenden Zeitwert bewertet wird.[49] In der Praxis wird diese Voraussetzung aus Effizienzgesichtspunkten zuerst geprüft, da sie einfach zu beurteilen ist und die schwierigere Beurteilung der beiden anderen Voraussetzungen überflüssig macht, sofern das strukturierte Finanzinstrument erfolgswirksam zum beizulegenden Zeitwert bilanziert wird. Es besteht eine enge Verbindung dieser dritten Voraussetzung zur sogenannten „Fair Value Option", d.h. dem *Wahlrecht*, ein Finanzinstrument erfolgswirksam zum beizulegenden Zeitwert zu bilanzieren. Die Fair Value Option ist z.B. verfügbar, wenn ein strukturiertes Finanzinstrument ein oder mehrere eingebettete Derivate enthält und diese die andernfalls vertraglich bedingten Cashflows mehr als nur unwesentlich verändern und nicht bereits ohne aufwendige Analyse deutlich ist, dass ihre Abspaltung unzulässig ist (IAS 39.11A). Entsprechend erfüllen strukturierte Finanzinstrumente mit eingebetteten Derivaten, die explizit als Beispiel für eine enge Verbindung ihrer wirtschaftlichen Merkmale und Risiken mit denen des Basisvertrags aufgeführt sind, diese Voraussetzung nicht.

41   Die Beurteilung, ob ein eingebettetes Derivat vom seinem Basisvertrag zu trennen und separat als Derivat zu bilanzieren ist, erfolgt im Zeitpunkt, in dem das Unternehmen zum ersten Mal Vertragspartei wird. Diese Beurteilung wird nachfolgend nur dann überprüft, wenn es entweder zu einer Änderung der Vertragsbedingungen mit erheblicher Auswirkung auf die vertraglichen Cashflows kommt oder ein finanzieller Vermögenswert von der Kategorie erfolgswirksam zum beizulegenden Zeitwert bewertet in eine andere Kategorie umgegliedert wird. In diesen Fällen ist eine Neubeurteilung des eingebetteten Derivats vorzunehmen. Ob eine Änderung der vertraglichen Cashflows wesentlich ist, bestimmt sich anhand eines Vergleichs der Cashflows des strukturierten Finanzinstruments vor und nach der vertraglichen Änderung (IFRIC 9.7). Kann ein abzuspaltendes eingebettetes Derivat nicht separat bewertet werden, so ist das strukturierte Finanzinstrument insgesamt der Kategorie erfolgswirksam zum beizulegenden Zeitwert bewertet zuzuordnen. Dies gilt sowohl im Zeitpunkt des erstmaligen Ansatzes oder einer etwaigen Umgliederung als auch an nachfolgenden Bilanzierungsstichtagen (IAS 39.12).

42   **b) Art und Weise der Abtrennung vom Basisvertrag.** Liegt die Voraussetzung einer Abtrennung eines eingebetteten Derivats von seinem Basisvertrag vor, so ist die Abtrennung in Abhängigkeit des Typs des eingebetteten Derivats sowie dessen Anzahl vorzunehmen. Dabei ist zu beachten, dass die Art und Weise der Abtrennung nicht zu einem eingebetteten Derivat mit solchen Eigenschaften führt, die nicht bereits deutlich im strukturierten Finanzinstrument vorhanden sind (IAS 39 IG C.1). So darf z.B. insbesondere bei einem strukturierten Finanzinstrument mit dem Charakter eines festverzinslichen Instruments die Aufspaltung nicht zu einem Basisvertrag mit dem Charakter eines variabel verzinslichen Instruments führen (und umgekehrt).

43   Bei eingebetteten Derivaten *ohne Optionscharakter* erfolgt die Abtrennung vom Basisvertrag auf der Grundlage der explizit vertraglich festgelegten oder der implizit im Vertrag enthaltenen Konditionen. Dabei ist das eingebettete Derivat so zu kalibrieren, dass es im Zeitpunkt seiner Abtrennung einen beizulegenden Zeitwert von Null hat (IAS 39.AG28). Ein Beispiel ist ein Schuldinstrument dessen Zins- und Tilgungszahlungen und den Wert von Rohöl indexiert sind.[50] Das eingebettete Derivat ist in diesem Fall ein sogenannter „Basisswap", der variable Zins- und Tilgungszahlungen in variable Rohöl-indexierte Zins- und Tilgungszahlungen umwandelt. Damit verbleibt ein Basisvertrag mit variabler Verzinsung (z.B. in Abhängigkeit von LIBOR, wenn das der übliche Referenzzinssatz für variabel verzinsliche Schuldinstrumente ist) und der eingebettete Basisswap (Rohöl versus LIBOR) ist so zu kalibrieren, dass er einen beizulegenden Zeitwert von Null im Zeitpunkt der Abtrennung hat. Wenn dagegen die Rohöl-Indexie-

---

49   Siehe Rn 33(c).
50   Siehe Rn 38.

rung nur die Tilgungszahlung betrifft und die Zinszahlungen Festbeträge sind, so ist der Basisvertrag ein festverzinsliches Instrument und das eingebettete Derivat ist ein Rohöl-Termingeschäft mit demselben Fälligkeitsdatum wie das strukturierte Finanzinstrument und einem Nominalbetrag, der dem für die Indexierung im Vertrag festgelegten Volumen entspricht. Der Terminpreis ist so zu bestimmen, dass der beizulegende Zeitwert des Termingeschäfts im Zeitpunkt der Abtrennung des eingebetteten Derivats null beträgt.

Bei eingebetteten Derivaten *mit Optionscharakter* erfolgt die Abtrennung vom Basisvertrag auf der Grundlage der explizit vertraglich bedungenen Konditionen, die das Optionsmerkmal ausmachen (IAS 39.AG28). Im Gegensatz zu eingebetteten Derivaten *ohne Optionscharakter* hat ein eingebettetes Derivat *mit Optionscharakter* im Zeitpunkt seiner Abtrennung daher regelmäßig einen von null abweichenden beizulegenden Zeitwert. Der Zeitwert ist größer null bei erworbenen Optionen (long) und von kleiner null bei geschriebenen Optionen (short). Lediglich bei eingebetteten Derivaten, die sogenannte „Zero Cost Collars" sind, ergibt sich ein beizulegender Zeitwert von null im Zeitpunkt der Abtrennung, da sich die beizulegenden Zeitwerte von erworbener und geschriebener Option ausgleichen.

Sind mehrere Derivate in einen Basisvertrag eingebettet, sogenannte „multiple eingebettete Derivate", so werden diese so behandelt, als wären sie ein einziges, zusammengesetztes eingebettetes Derivat, es sei denn:

- die eingebetteten Derivate umfassen sowohl solche, die Eigenkapitalinstrumente gemäß IAS 32 darstellen, als auch andere, die Vermögenswerte oder Schulden sind; in diesem Fall sind die Eigenkapital darstellenden eingebetteten Derivate getrennt von den anderen zu bilanzieren oder
- die eingebetteten Derivate beziehen sich auf verschiedene Risiken und sind ohne Weiteres trennbar und voneinander unabhängig, so dass sie getrennt voneinander bilanziert werden.

3. Zusammenfassung von Verträgen. Die Regelungen für eingebettete Derivate betreffen die Fragestellung, wann ein Vertrag für Bilanzierungszwecke als zwei (oder mehr) Bilanzierungseinheiten zu behandeln ist. In anderen Fällen stellt sich die umgekehrte Frage, wann zwei (oder mehr) Verträge als eine Bilanzierungseinheit zu behandeln sind. Es gilt der Grundsatz, dass Verträge, die unabhängig voneinander übertragen, abgetreten oder erfüllt werden können zur Bilanzierung als separate Finanzinstrumente führen. Dies gilt auch dann, wenn Verträge in engem Zusammenhang stehen. Werden z.B. ein variabel verzinsliches Darlehen und ein auf dieses abgestimmter Zins-Swap, der die variablen Zinszahlungen dieses Schuldinstruments in feste Zahlungsbeträge umwandelt, zeitgleich abgeschlossen, so sind beide Verträge separate Bilanzierungseinheiten. Obwohl das Darlehen und das Zinsderivat zusammen betrachtet als ein „synthetisches" Festzinsdarlehen angesehen werden können, ist eine Bilanzierung als Festzinsdarlehen unzulässig (IAS 39 IG C.6). Daher kann der Zusammenhang zwischen den beiden Verträgen nur mittels der Anwendung der Regeln zur Bilanzierung von Sicherungsgeschäften bilanziell berücksichtigt werden.

In bestimmten Fällen gebietet jedoch die wirtschaftliche Betrachtungsweise Abweichungen von diesem Grundsatz. Werden z.B. gleichzeitig ein fest- und ein variabel verzinslicher Darlehensvertrag mit demselben Darlehensbetrag und derselben Fälligkeit geschlossen, bei denen die beiden Vertragsparteien jeweils Darlehensgeber in einem und Darlehensnehmer im anderen Vertrag sind, so haben die beiden Verträge zusammen betrachtet die wirtschaftliche Wirkung eines Zinsswaps. Da sich die Zahlungen des Darlehensbetrags vollständig ausgleichen, verbleiben die Zinszahlungen, welche dazu führen, dass die eine Vertragspartei feste Zinszahlungen leistet und variable Zinszahlungen erhält und umgekehrt die andere Vertragspartei variable Zinszahlungen leistet und feste Zinszahlungen erhält. In diesem Fall sind beide Darlehensverträge für bilanzielle Zwecke zusammen zu betrachten und als Derivat zu behandeln (IAS 39 IG B.6). Verallgemeinert man dieses Szenario, so lassen sich folgende Anhaltspunkte für eine gemeinsame Betrachtung verschiedener Verträge als ein Finanzinstrument ableiten (IAS 39 IG B.6):

44

45

46

47

- zeitgleicher Abschluss der Verträge im Hinblick aufeinander;
- Identität der jeweiligen Vertragsparteien;
- die Verträge beziehen sich auf dasselbe Risiko;
- Fehlen eines offensichtlichen wirtschaftlichen Bedarfs oder substanziellen Geschäftszwecks für die Strukturierung als separate Verträge, denen eine Transaktionsstruktur mit einem einzigen Vertrag nicht Rechnung tragen kann.

Die Würdigung dieser Kriterien ist im Einzelfall vorzunehmen und wie alle Fälle wirtschaftlicher Betrachtungsweise entsprechend ermessensbehaftet.

48   **4. Zweifelsfragen zur Bilanzierungseinheit.** Neben den in IAS 39 und den zugehörigen Leitlinien zur Anwendung[51] behandelten Fragestellungen zur Bilanzierungseinheit haben sich in der Praxis weitere Fragestellungen ergeben, für die es keine konkreten Regelungen gibt. Dies betrifft insbesondere die Frage, ob Verträge für Bilanzierungszwecke auch dann in verschiedene Bilanzierungseinheiten aufgeteilt werden können, wenn letztere keine eingebetteten Derivate und Basisverträge sind.

49   Im Zusammenhang mit der **Eigenbedarfsausnahme**,[52] die den Anwendungsbereich des IAS 39 beeinflusst, hat das IFRS Interpretations Committee[53] die Frage behandelt, ob Verträge über die Lieferung nicht-finanzieller Posten (die jederzeit in Zahlungsmittel umgewandelt werden können) mit **flexiblem Volumen** als ein einziger oder zwei verschiedene Verträge zu behandeln sind.[54] Es geht um Verträge, bei denen ein Teil des Liefervolumens vertraglich als Festmenge festgelegt ist, die zu einem Festpreis geliefert wird, während der Käufer das Recht hat, eine bestimmte zusätzliche Menge zu einem vorab festgelegten Festpreis zu beziehen. Solche Verträge sind z.B. typisch für die Elektrizitätswirtschaft, aber auch in anderen Industrien üblich (i.d.R. Industrien mit hohem Rohstoffverbrauch). Die Bilanzierungspraxis ist derzeit uneinheitlich. Teilweise werden solche Verträge als eine Bilanzierungseinheit behandelt und teilweise als zwei verschiedene, wobei der Vertrag für Bilanzierungszwecke in getrennte Teile für die Festmenge und die variable (Zusatz-)Menge aufgeteilt wird. Teilweise werden diese beiden Alternativen auch im Wahlrecht hinsichtlich der Rechnungslegungsmethode gesehen.

50   Das IFRS Interpretations Committee hat trotz der uneinheitlichen Bilanzierungspraxis eine Stellungnahme unter Verweis auf das Projekt zur Ablösung von IAS 39 auf der aktiven Agenda des IASB abgelehnt. Insbesondere hat das IFRS Interpretations Committee in seiner Stellungnahme keine Andeutung gemacht, welche der in der Bilanzierungspraxis vorkommenden Alternativen IFRS-konform oder unzulässig ist. Daher ist davon auszugehen, dass die derzeitige uneinheitliche Bilanzierungspraxis bis zu einer Neuregelung durch das IASB fortbesteht.

51   **IV. Ansatz.** Der **erstmalige Ansatz** eines Finanzinstruments erfolgt grundsätzlich im Zeitpunkt des Vertragsschlusses (IAS 39.14). Dies betrifft z.B. Darlehensgewährungen oder Verträge, die Derivate sind. Soweit Kreditzusagen vom Anwendungsbereich des IAS 39 ausgenommen sind,[55] erfolgt der erstmalige Ansatz als Finanzinstrument im Zeitpunkt der Auszahlung des Darlehensbetrags statt bei Vertragsschluss. Bei Zahlungsmitteln (z.B. Bargeld, Sichteinlagen bei Kreditinstituten) ist ein Vertragsschluss aufgrund der Art des Gegenstands nicht zutreffend. Stattdessen ist hier der Zeitpunkt des Zahlungsmittelzugangs maßgeblich.

52   Von dem Grundsatz des erstmaligen Ansatzes im Zeitpunkt des Vertragsschlusses bestehen folgende Ausnahmen:

---

51 „Guidance on Implementing" (IG).
52 Siehe Rn 4.
53 Vormals „IFRIC".
54 IFRS Interpretations Committee Sitzungen im November 2009 sowie im Januar und März 2010.
55 Siehe Rn 13-15.

         Friedhoff / Berger

- Verträge über den Kauf oder Verkauf von Gütern und den Bezug oder das Erbringen von Dienstleistungen, die als **schwebende Geschäfte** behandelt werden. Die mit diesen Geschäften verbundenen Forderungen und Verbindlichkeiten aus Lieferungen und Leistungen werden erst dann angesetzt, wenn der Auftragnehmer seine Verpflichtung ganz oder mindestens teilweise erbracht hat (IAS 39.AG35(b)). Soweit es sich bei diesen Geschäften um Verträge über den Kauf oder Verkauf nicht-finanzieller Posten mit finanziellem Nettoausgleich handelt,[56] ist zu prüfen, ob sie aufgrund der Eigenbedarfsausnahme als schwebende Geschäfte zu behandeln sind.

- Im Rahmen der Vorschriften zur Ausbuchung finanzieller Vermögenswerte können bestimmte Derivate einer Ausbuchung übertragener finanzieller Vermögenswerte entgegenstehen (IAS 39.AG34). Diese Derivate sind von den Ansatzvorschriften ausgenommen, da die betreffenden finanziellen Vermögenswerte ungeachtet ihrer rechtlichen Übertragung weiterhin vom übertragenden Unternehmen angesetzt werden. Andernfalls würde sich eine Doppelerfassung des Sachverhalts ergeben. Umgekehrt werden rechtlich übertragene finanzielle Vermögenswerte, die beim übertragenden Unternehmen nicht zur Ausbuchung führen, vom empfangenden Unternehmen nicht als Vermögenswert angesetzt.

V. Ausbuchung. Unter Ausbuchung (**derecognition**) versteht man die Entfernung eines Vermögenswertes, Schuld bzw. Eigenkapital von der Bilanz. Für Zwecke von IAS 39 sind aufgrund der unterschiedlichen Ausbuchungskonzepte finanzielle Vermögenswerte und finanzielle Verbindlichkeiten zu unterscheiden. Die Ausbuchung von Eigenkapitalinstrumenten iSv. IAS 32 wird nachfolgend nicht weiter behandelt.   53

1. Ausbuchung von finanziellen Vermögenswerten. a) Grundlegendes. Das Ausbuchungsmodell für finanzielle Vermögenswerte in IAS 39 stellt eine Kombination aus Kontroll- und Risiken/Chancen-Test dar.[57] Ziel der Vorschriften ist es, eine vollständige Ausbuchung eines finanziellen Vermögenswertes nur dann zuzulassen, wenn das Unternehmen nach einer Übertragung den Risiken aus dem finanziellen Vermögenswert (bspw. dem Bonitätsrisiko) nicht mehr ausgesetzt ist. Dabei ist entscheidend, dass die Risiken-/Chancenüberprüfung eine Indikation von Kontrolle (im Sinne einer Kontrolle der Nutzenziehung aus einem finanziellen Vermögenswert) darstellen soll. Das IAS 39-Ausbuchungsmodell ist geprägt von einer sog. „Klebrigkeit" (**stickiness**) von finanziellen Vermögenswerten, d.h. es ist verhältnismäßig einfach, ein Finanzinstrument in der Bilanz zu aktivieren, aber ungleich schwieriger, es davon wieder zu entfernen. Während für eine Aktivierung idR. die Tatsache genügt, dass ein Unternehmen Vertragspartei eines Instruments wird, welches aus seiner Sicht einen finanziellen Vermögenswert darstellt (IAS 39.14), reicht zur Ausbuchung nicht nur die Übertragung des Anspruches aus rechtlicher Sicht. Vielmehr muss auch das wirtschaftliche Risiko übertragen worden sein – was bei bestimmten Transaktionen (z.B. bestimmte Verbriefungen) oftmals nicht der Fall ist. Aber auch bei üblichen Transaktionen wie Forderungsverkäufen (**factoring** bzw. Forfaitierung) stellen sich regelmäßig die Ausbuchungsvorschriften als komplex in der Anwendung dar, da oftmals Teile der Risiken, insbesondere das Ausfallrisiko, vom übertragenden Unternehmen zurückbehalten wird.   54

Grundsätzlich hat die Ausbuchung eines finanziellen Vermögenswerte zu erfolgen, falls (IAS 39.17):   55
- die vertraglichen Ansprüche auf die Zahlungen aus dem finanziellen Vermögenswert erlöschen oder
- das Berichtunternehmen den finanziellen Vermögenswert iSv. IAS 39 überträgt und diese Übertragung die Anforderungen an eine Ausbuchung in IAS 39 erfüllen.

Die Kombination aus Kontroll- und Risiken-/Chancentest (und die daraus resultierende Komplexität) wird durch den Entscheidungsbaum in IAS 39.AG36 deutlich: 56

---

56 Siehe Rn 4 und 16.
57 Siehe *Deloitte (Hrsg.)* iGAAP - Financial Instruments, 488.

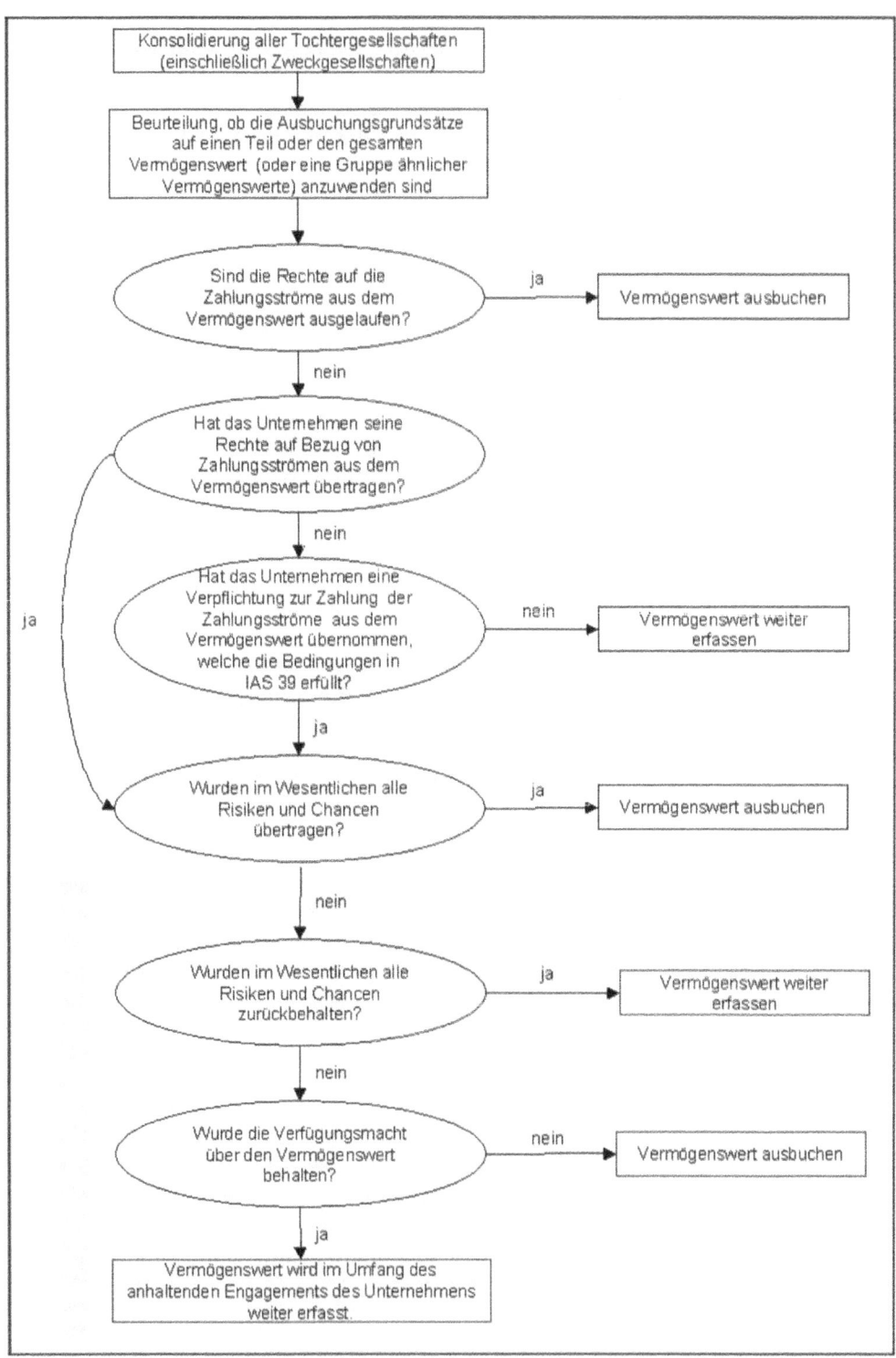

Im Folgenden sollen die jeweiligen Schritte des Prüfschemas darstellt werden.

b) Konsolidierung aller Tochtergesellschaften. Zuerst gilt es, die Beurteilungsebene für die Aus- 57
buchungsentscheidung festzulegen: Einzel- oder Konzernabschluss. Ist die Beurteilungsebene der
Konzern, dann muss zuerst eine Konsolidierung gemäß IAS 27 vorgenommen werden. Dies schließt
auch alle Zweckgesellschaften iSv. SIC-12 ein. Erst dann werden die Vorschriften in IAS 39.16-23 iVm.
AG34-AG52 angewendet (IAS 39.15). Dies stellt sicher, dass auch Übertragungen unter Nutzung von
Zweckgesellschaften von den Ausbuchungsregeln erfasst werden (IAS 39.BC64). Relevant ist diese Unterscheidung vor allem bei **Verbriefungstransaktionen**, die in der Regel solche Zweckgesellschaften
zwischenschalten.

c) Anwendung auf gesamten Vermögenswert oder Teile. Im nächsten Schritt ist zu ermitteln, was 58
das Beurteilungsobjekt für die Ausbuchungsprüfung ist (IAS 39.16). Grundsätzlich sind zu unterscheiden:

(a) Teile von finanziellen Vermögenswerten

(b) Einzelne Vermögenswerte

(c) Gruppen von ähnlichen Vermögenswerten

Startpunkt sollte dabei immer der einzelne Vermögenswert sein, somit erscheinen (a) und (c) Aus- 59
nahmen von diesem Grundsatz.[58] Die Ausbuchungsvorschriften finden jedoch analog auf jedes Beurteilungsobjekt Anwendung.

Als Beurteilungsobjekt ist ein Teil eines Vermögenswertes festzulegen, falls dieser folgendes darstellt: 60

(a) Gesondert abgegrenzte Zahlungen eines finanziellen Vermögenswertes, bspw. die Zinszahlungen
eines Schuldtitels wie bei einem Zinsstrip.

(b) Exakt proportionaler Teil der Zahlungen aus einem finanziellen Vermögenswert, bspw. 80% aller
Zahlungen aus einem Wertpapier.

(c) Exakt proportionaler Teil an gesondert abgegrenzten Zahlungen eines finanziellen Vermögenswertes, also eine Kombination aus (a) und (b) – bspw. 80% aus den Zinszahlungen eines Darlehens.

Als zweite Ausnahme kann die Bildung von **Gruppen finanzieller Vermögenswerte** für Zwecke 61
der Ausbuchungsbeurteilung angesehen werden. Dabei ist das entscheidende Kriterium die Ähnlichkeit
der zu gruppierenden Instrumente. Der Standard schweigt sich dazu aus, was als ähnlich betrachtet
werden kann. Es erscheint zielführend, die in Frage kommenden Instrumente hinsichtlich ihrer Ausstattungsmerkmale zu vergleichen, die deren Werttreiber darstellen (Zinsbedingungen, Kündigungsrech-
te, Währung, etc.). Unterschiede müssen per definitionem zulässig sein, ansonsten würde es sich um
identische Instrumente handeln.[59] Bestimmte Arten von Finanzinstrumenten können aufgrund ihrer
Wertindividualität nicht als ähnlich angesehen, insbesondere Eigenkapitalinstrumente. Daneben hat das
IFRIC in einer vorläufigen Agendaentscheidung aus dem November 2006 festgestellt, dass Derivate und
Kassainstrumente nicht ähnlich sind. Dies hat zur Konsequenz, dass bei Übertragungen, die beide In-
strumententypen enthalten, jeweils Derivate und Kassainstrumente gesondert auf eine Ausbuchung zu
prüfen sind.[60] Daneben wurde bei dieser vorläufigen Agendaentscheidung festgehalten, dass übertragene
Derivate, die während der Laufzeit sowohl Vermögenswerte (positiver beizulegender Zeitwert) als auch
Verbindlichkeiten (negativer beizulegender Zeitwert) sein können (z.B. Zinsswaps), sowohl die Ausbu-

---

58 Siehe *Berger/Kaczmarska* KoR 2008, 316f.
59 Siehe *Deloitte (Hrsg.)* iGAAP - Financial Instruments, 495.
60 Siehe IFRIC Update November 2006, 12.

chungskriterien für finanzielle Vermögenswerte als auch Verbindlichkeiten erfüllen müssen.[61] Letztendlich wurde jedoch diese Agendaentscheidung vor dem Hintergrund des laufenden IASB-Projekts zur Ausbuchung nicht finalisiert, kann jedoch einen möglichen Interpretationsansatz aufzeigen.

62   **d) Auslaufen der Ansprüche auf Zahlungsmittel.** Sobald die vertraglichen Rechte auf Zahlungsmittel aus einem finanziellen Vermögenswert auslaufen, ist dieser auszubuchen (IAS 39.17(a)) – dies ist regelmäßig bei Erfüllung der Fall. Laufen nur Teile dieser Rechte aus (z.B. bei einem Ratenkredit) dann ist nur dieser Teil auszubuchen. Solche Rechte können auch ohne den Erhalt von Zahlungsmittel verfallen, z.B. bei nicht ausgeübten gekauften Optionen.

63   **e) Übertragung der Rechte auf Zahlungsmittel.** Auch die Übertragung der Rechte auf Zahlungsmittel (oder andere finanzielle Vermögenswerte) können (oder können nicht) zu einer Ausbuchung eines finanziellen Vermögenswertes führen (IAS 39.17(b)). „**Übertragung**" (**transfer**) ist dabei ein in IAS 39 festgelegter Begriff. Eine Übertragung liegt danach nur dann vor, falls das Berichtsunternehmen (IAS 39.18):

(a) entweder die vertragliche Ansprüche auf die Zahlungen aus dem finanziellen Vermögenswert übertragen hat; oder

(b) die vertraglichen Ansprüche auf die Zahlungen aus dem finanziellen Vermögenswert zurückbehalten hat, jedoch eine vertragliche Verpflichtung eingegangen ist, diese Zahlungen an einen oder mehrere Empfänger im Rahmen einer Durchleitvereinbarung iSv. IAS 39.19 weiterzuleiten.

64   Dabei gilt zu beachten, dass die Übertragung iSv. (a) auch bei Insolvenz rechtlichen Bestand hat, egal ob dies durch ein Aus- oder Absonderungsrecht zu Gunsten des übernehmenden Unternehmens sichergestellt wird.[62] Daneben stellt sich die Frage, was unter einer **Durchleitvereinbarung** iSd. Standards zu verstehen ist. Ermittelt werden soll, ob das Berichtsunternehmen nach der Übertragung nur noch als Agent handelt. IAS 39.19 sieht das Berichtsunternehmen in der Rolle eines Agenten falls:

(a) Es nur dann zu Zahlungen an die Endempfänger verpflichtet ist, wenn es die entsprechenden Beträge aus dem ursprünglichen Vermögenswert vereinnahmt. Kurzfristige Vorauszahlungen, die das Unternehmen zum vollständigen Einzug des geliehenen Betrags zuzüglich aufgelaufener Zinsen zum Marktzinssatz berechtigen, verstoßen gegen diese Bedingung nicht.

(b) Es den ursprünglichen Vermögenswert laut Übertragungsvertrag weder verkaufen noch verpfänden darf, es sei denn, dies dient der Absicherung seiner Verpflichtung, den Endempfängern die Cashflows zu zahlen.

(c) Es verpflichtet ist, die für die Endempfänger eingenommenen Cashflows ohne wesentliche Verzögerung weiterzuleiten. Auch ist es nicht befugt, solche Cashflows während der kurzen Erfüllungsperiode vom Inkassotag bis zum geforderten Überweisungstermin an die Endempfänger zu reinvestieren, außer in Zahlungsmittel oder Zahlungsmitteläquivalente (im Sinne von IAS 7 *Statement of Cash Flows*), wobei die Zinsen aus solchen Finanzinvestitionen an die Endempfänger weiterzugeben sind.

65   Die Formulierung „ohne wesentliche Verzögerung" in (c) ist interpretationsbedürftig und vom Einzelfall abhängig. Es kann davon ausgegangen werden, dass weder eine sofortige Durchleitung zwingend noch eine längerer Zeitraum statthaft ist.[63] Daher ist eine Gesamtwürdigung der Transaktion nebst dem dazugehörigen Vertragswerk dahingehend vorzunehmen, was die Motivation einer etwaigen Verzögerung ist. Oftmals sind es rein administrative Gründe, die zu einer Verzögerung in der Durchleitung

---

61   Siehe IFRIC Update November 2006, 12.
62   Siehe IDW RS HFA 9.119.
63   Siehe *Deloitte (Hrsg.)* iGAAP 2010 - Financial Instruments, 498.

führen. Beispielsweise ist dies der Fall, wenn die Zahlungen über einen Monat hinweg an verschiedenen, nicht festgelegten Tagen eintreffen können, die Durchleitung aber zur Prozessoptimierung erst am Ende des Monats für den Gesamtsaldo erfolgt.

Die Durchleitungsprüfung in IAS 39.18(b) iVm. IAS 39.19 ist nur notwendig, wenn nicht alle Rechte   66
an den Zahlungsströmen übertragen werden. Dabei wurde dem IFRIC 2005 die Frage gestellt, ob dies in allen Situation gelte. Das IFRIC hat darauf in einer vorläufigen Entscheidung festgestellt, dass die Durchleitungsvereinbarungsvorschriften regelmäßig nur auf disproportionale Übertragungen anzuwenden sind – proportionale Übertragungen (z.B. 30% aller Zahlungen aus einem Portfolio von finanziellen Vermögenswerten) unterliegen diesen Vorschriften nicht, sondern sind gemäß IAS 39.18(a) zu bilanzieren.[64]

Das Bestehen der Durchleitungsprüfung legt jedoch nur fest, ob es sich um eine Übertragung im   67
Sinne des Standards handelt, obwohl die Rechte aus einem finanziellen Vermögenswert nicht übertragen wurden. Für eine Ausbuchung ist desweiteren die Übertragung der wesentlichen Chancen und Risiken notwendig.[65]

f) Übertragung aller wesentlichen Chancen und Risiken aus dem Vermögenswert. Die-   68
ser Schritt spiegelt die bereits oben angesprochene **Risikobetrachtung** im Ausbuchungsmodell nach IAS 39 wider. Dabei wird die Risikoposition des Berichtsunternehmens vor und nach der Übertragung ermittelt (Vorher-Nachher-Vergleich) ermittelt. Führt die Analyse zur Ausbuchung, erfolgt keine erneute Einbuchung des finanziellen Vermögenswertes für den Fall, dass sich die Bedingungen ändern (IAS 39.AG41) – dies darf nur bei einem erneuten Erwerb erfolgen. Es lassen sich im Wesentlichen drei mögliche Ergebnisse dieser Analyse unterscheiden:

- Das übertragende Berichtsunternehmen überträgt im Wesentlichen alle Chancen und Risiken aus dem Vermögenswert. In diesem Fall hat das Unternehmen den Vermögenswert auszubuchen. Ggf. sind weitere Vermögenswerte und Schulden zu bilanzieren.

- Das übertragende Berichtsunternehmen behält im Wesentlichen alle Chancen und Risiken aus dem Vermögenswert. In diesem Fall hat das Unternehmen den Vermögenswert weiterhin vollumfänglich zu bilanzieren. Aus der Übertragung erhaltene Leistungen sind als Verbindlichkeit zu erfassen (Abbildung analog einer besicherten Kreditaufnahme).

- Das übertragende Berichtsunternehmen behält weder die wesentlichen Chancen und Risiken aus dem Vermögenswert zurück noch überträgt es sie. In diesem Fall ist zu unterscheiden:

  - Die Verfügungsgewalt wird nicht vom Unternehmen zurückbehalten (das empfangende Unternehmen kann den Vermögenswert einseitig veräußern). In diesem Fall hat das Unternehmen den Vermögenswert auszubuchen. Ggf. sind weitere Vermögenswerte und Schulden zu bilanzieren.

  - Die Verfügungsgewalt wird vom Unternehmen zurückbehalten. Dann ist eine Vermögenswert/ Verbindlichkeit in Höhe des anhaltenden Engagements (continuing involvement) zu bilanzieren.

In der Praxis ist vor allem die Auslegung des Begriffs „im Wesentlichen alle" von Bedeutung bei   69
der **Risiken-/Chancenübertragung**. Dabei gibt der Standard keine unmittelbare Konkretisierung dieses Begriffs vor. Es wird vielmehr in das Ermessen des Bilanzierenden gelegt, wie er diese Grenze definiert. Jedoch finden sich in IAS 39 an anderen Stellen Hinweise, wie diese Grenze zu interpretieren ist. Insbesondere bei den Vorschriften zur Ausbuchung von finanziellen Verbindlichkeiten wird bei Vertragsneuverhandlung eine Barwertdifferenz von mindestens 10% als „substanziell unterschiedlich" (substantially different) konkretisiert (IAS 39.AG62). Dies kann, unter Beachtung der jeweiligen Besonderheiten der zu beurteilenden Transaktion, als Richtschnur Anwendung finden.

---

64   Siehe IFRIC Update November 2006, 12.
65   Siehe *PwC (Hrsg.)* Manual of Accounting – Financial instruments, 8020.

70   Obwohl bei vielen Vermögenswertübertragungen die Einwertung der Risiken-/Chancenübertragung ohne quantitative Analyse, d.h. ohne Berechnungen, möglich ist, ist dies in Grenzfällen oftmals unvermeidlich (IAS 39.22). Bei dieser Berechnung muss das Berichtsunternehmen seine Chancen-/Risikoposition vor und nach der Übertragung ermitteln. Dies geschieht gemäß IAS 39.21 durch den Vergleich der Variabilität des Betrags und des zeitlichen Anfalls der (Netto-)Zahlungsströme des übertragenen Vermögenswerts vor und nach Übertragung.

71   Bei der Berechnung sind angemessene Marktrenditen bei der Diskontierung heranzuziehen. Daneben sind alle vernüftigerweise möglichen Szenarien zu berücksichtigen und denjenigen Szenarien höheres Gewicht beizumessen, deren Eintrittswahrscheinlichkeit höher ist. Mithin handelt es sich hier also um eine Erwartungswertermittlung. Der Standard selbst gibt jedoch keine Methode für die Ermittlung vor, auch keine Beispiele.

72   Es bietet sich aufgrund der offensichtlichen Ausprägung des Modells als Erwartungswertansatz die Anwendung statistischer Verfahren zur Ermittlung der Variabilität an. In der Praxis häufig anzutreffen ist insbesondere die **Anwendung der Standardabweichung**, um zu ermitteln, wie viel Variabilität auf die Gegenpartei übertragen wurde. In die zu berücksichtigenden Szenarien sind je nach übertragenen Instrument typischerweise folgende Risiken zu berücksichtigen:[66]

- Ausfallrisiko,
- Zinsänderungsrisiko,
- Fremdwährungsrisiko,
- Risiko des verspäteten Zahlungseingangs (bei fehlender Kompensation durch Schuldner),
- Risiko des verfrühten Zahlungseingangs,
- Risiko der rechtlichen Existenz eines Zahlungsanspruches.

73   Bei der Risiken-/Chancenanalyse ist stets eine Einzelwürdigung der Transaktion vorzunehmen. Dies ist insbesondere bei **hochstrukturierten Transaktionen**, wie sie zum Beispiel bei Verbriefungstransaktionen anzutreffen sind, zu beachten. So können z.B. Derivate und Garantien das Chancen-/Risikenprofil in erheblichem Maße abändern, so dass diese zwingend in die Analyse einzubeziehen sind. Daneben gilt es zu beachten, dass sich die Chancen-/Risikenanalyse auf den übertragenen Vermögenswert bezieht, andere Chancen und Risiken aus der Transaktion, die nicht unmittelbar aus dem Vermögenswert entstehen sind insoweit unbeachtlich.[67] Dies trifft zum Beispiel auf das Liquiditätsrisiko bei Verbriefungsvehikeln zu (also das Risiko, die emittierten Anleihen nicht bedienen zu können, weil nicht genug Zahlungsmittel zur Verfügung stehen), da dieses Risiko aus dem Vehikel selbst entsteht, nicht aus den ihm übertragenen Vermögenswerten.

74   Bei Übertragung eines festverzinslichen Schuldtitels ist eine Ausbuchung nicht ausgeschlossen, wenn gleichzeitig die beiden Vertragsparteien einen Zinsswap vereinbaren, der aus Sicht des übertragenden Unternehmens feste in variable Zinszahlungen über den gleichen Nominalwert führt. Dies gilt jedoch nur, falls die Zahlungen aus dem Zinsswap nicht abhängig von Zahlungen des übertragenen Schuldtitels sind (IAS 39.AG51(p)).

75   Beispiele, in dem ein Berichtsunternehmen im Wesentlichen alle Chancen und Risiken übertragen hat sind (IAS 39.AG39):

- Unbedingter Verkauf eines finanziellen Vermögenswerts;
- Verkauf eines finanziellen Vermögenswerts in Kombination mit einer Option, den finanziellen Vermögenswert zu dessen beizulegendem Zeitwert zum Zeitpunkt des Rückkaufs zurückzukaufen; und

---

66   Siehe IDW RS HFA 9.130.
67   Siehe *Deloitte (Hrsg.)* iGAAP 2010 - Financial Instruments, 512f.

- Verkauf eines finanziellen Vermögenswerts in Kombination mit einer Verkaufs- oder Kaufoption, die weit aus dem Geld ist (d. h. einer Option, die so weit aus dem Geld ist, dass es äußerst unwahrscheinlich ist, dass sie vor Fälligkeit im Geld sein wird).

g) Rückbehalt der wesentlichen Chancen und Risiken. Ergibt der Chancen-/Risikotest, dass das **76** Berichtsunternehmen die wesentlichen Chancen und Risiken aus dem Vermögenswert trotz Übertragung zurückbehalten hat, ist der Vermögenswert in Gänze weiterhin beim Unternehmen zu bilanzieren (IAS 39.20(b)). Dabei finden sich in IAS 39.AG40 Beispiele für Transaktionen, bei denen eine Ausbuchung nicht statthaft ist:

- ein Verkauf, kombiniert mit einem Rückkauf (**repurchase agreement**), bei dem der Rückkaufpreis festgelegt ist oder dem Verkaufspreis zuzüglich einer Verzinsung entspricht; es handelt sich hier im wesentlichen um eine Darlehensvereinbarung – hier bleibt das übertragende Unternehmen unmittelbar dem Preisrisiko des übertragenen Instruments ausgesetzt, behält also die wesentlichen Chancen und Risiken aus dem Papier zurück.
- eine **Wertpapierleihe** – auch hier bleibt das übertragende Unternehmen den Preisrisiken des Wertpapiers ausgesetzt und hat somit das Wertpapier nach IAS 39 weiterhin zu bilanzieren.
- ein Verkauf eines finanziellen Vermögenswerts, gekoppelt mit einem **Total Return Swap**, bei dem das Marktrisiko auf das Unternehmen zurückübertragen wird – hier wird das Preisrisiko durch den Total Return Swap wieder unmittelbar auf das übertragende Unternehmen zurückgegeben, es zahlt im wesentlichen einen Darlehenszins. Das übertragende Unternehmen hat daher weiterhin das Instrument zu bilanzieren.
- ein Verkauf eines finanziellen Vermögenswerts in Kombination mit einer **Verkaufs- oder Kaufoption, die weit im Geld ist** (d. h. einer Option, die so weit im Geld ist, dass es äußerst unwahrscheinlich ist, dass sie vor Fälligkeit aus dem Geld sein wird) – da bei solchen Transaktionen die Ausübung der Optionen sehr wahrscheinlich ist, verbleiben die Chancen und Risiken aus dem übertragenen Finanzinstrument im wesentlichen beim Unternehmen, daher hat es das Finanzinstrument weiterhin zu bilanzieren.
- ein Verkauf kurzfristiger Forderungen, bei dem das Unternehmen eine **Garantie** auf Entschädigung des Empfängers für wahrscheinlich eintretende Kreditausfälle übernimmt – hier ist die Kurzfristigkeit entscheidend, denn somit spielt das Zinsänderungsrisiko kaum eine Rolle und das Ausfallrisiko ist der primäre Risikotreiber. Dieses verbleibt durch die Garantie beim Unternehmen und somit auch die wesentlichen Chancen und Risiken. Als Konsequenz hat das übertragende Unternehmen die Forderung weiterhin zu bilanzieren.

Bei Rückkaufvereinbarungen, sog. **Repos**, handelt es sich um typische Transaktionen zur kurzfristi- **77** gen Liquiditätsbeschaffung, **Wertpapierleihen** hingegen werden typischerweise eingesetzt, um Leerverkäufe von Wertpapieren zu decken.

Für den Fall, dass bei der Übertragung die Verfügungsgewalt nicht übergeht, hat das Unternehmen **78** weiterhin den Vermögenswert zu bilanzieren (es erfolgt also keine Ausbuchung) und erfasst zusätzlich eine Verbindlichkeit für das erhaltene Entgelt (Darstellung in Bruttoform bzw als besicherte Kreditaufnahme). Es ergibt sich für den übertragenen Vermögenswert keine Änderung in der Klassifizierung, im Wertmaßstab und in der Erfolgsrealisation.[68] Daneben dürfen weder der Vermögenswert und die entstandene Verbindlichkeit noch aus diesen entstehende Erträge und Aufwendungen miteinander verrechnet werden (IAS 39.36), obwohl dies oftmals unter den Aufrechnungsvorschriften in IAS 32 zulässig wäre. Hier überschreibt IAS 39.36 jedoch als Spezialvorschrift die allgemeine Vorschrift in IAS 32.42ff. Ist ein Derivat Bestandteil der Vermögensübertragung wird es zur Vermeidung einer Doppelzählung nicht gesondert bilanziert (IAS 39.AG49).

---

68 Siehe *Deloitte (Hrsg.)* iGAAP 2010 - Financial Instruments, 523.

79   **h) Keine Übertragung bzw. kein Rückbehalt der wesentlichen Chancen und Risiken.** Für den Fall, dass das übertragende Unternehmen weder alle Chancen und Risiken aus dem übertragenen finanziellen Vermögenswert überträgt noch zurückbehält, ist in einem weiteren Schritt der Rückbehalt der Verfügungsgewalt (control) über den übertragenen Vermögenswert zu prüfen.

80   Dabei sind folgende Fallkonstellationen zu unterscheiden (IAS 39.20(c)):

- **Das übertragende Unternehmen hat nach der Übertrgung keine Verfügungsgewalt mehr über den Vermögenswert.** In diesem Falle ist der finanzielle Vermögenswert auszubuchen. Gleichzeitig sind bei der Transaktion entstehende bzw. zurückbehaltene finanzielle Vermögenswerte bzw. Verbindlichkeiten (z.B. Garantien) zu aktivieren resp. zu passivieren. Deren Ansatz erfolgt zum beizulegenden Zeitwert (IAS 39.25). Für Abwicklungs- bzw. Verwaltungsvereinbarungen, die für das übertragende Unternehmen nachteilig sind, ist eine entsprechende Verbindlichkeit einzubuchen (IAS 39.24). Ergibt sich aus einer solchen Vereinbarung ein positiver Wertbeitrag, so ist entsprechend ein Vermögenswert zu aktivieren.

- **Das übertragende Unternehmen hat nach der Übertragung weiterhin die Verfügungsgewalt über den Vermögenswert.** In diesem Falle hat das Unternehmen den übertragenen finanziellen Vermögenswert weiterhin in Höhe seines anhaltenden Engagements zu bilanzieren.

81   Hieraus ergibt sich unmittelbar die Frage, wann das Unternehmen die Verfügungsgewalt zurückbehält. Das ist dann der Fall, wenn das Unternehmen in der Lage ist, den Vermögenswert zu veräußern. Hat das empfangende Unternehmen jedoch die **praktische Möglichkeit** (practical ability), den Vermögenswert in seiner Gesamtheit an eine nichtverbundene Vertragspartei zu veräußern und ist diese Fähigkeit einseitig und ohne für die Übertragung weitere Einschränkungen zu verhängen (z.B. eine Kaufoption, um den Vermögenswert wieder „zurückholen" zu können), ausübbar, dann hat das übertragende Unternehmen die Verfügungsgewalt verloren (IAS 39.23). In allen anderen Fällen hat es die Verfügungsgewalt zurückbehalten. Für in einem aktiven Markt gehandelte Instrumente ist von einer Veräußerungsfähigkeit durch das empfangende Unternehmen auszugehen, da es im Zweifel den Vermögenswert in diesem Markt bei einer verpflichtenden oder optionalen Rückgabe erwerben kann (IAS 39.AG42). Der Empfänger verfügt gemäß IAS 39.AG43 nur dann über die tatsächliche Fähigkeit zur Veräußerung des übertragenen Vermögenswerts, wenn er ihn als Ganzes veräußern und von dieser Fähigkeit einseitig Gebrauch machen kann, ohne dass die Übertragung zusätzlichen Beschränkungen unterliegt. Die entscheidende Frage lautet, welche Möglichkeiten der Empfänger tatsächlich hat und nicht, welche vertraglichen Verfügungsmöglichkeiten oder -verbote ihm in Bezug auf den übertragenen Vermögenswert zustehen bzw. auferlegt sind. Gemäß IAS 39.AG43 gilt insbesondere:

- ein vertraglich eingeräumtes Recht auf Veräußerung eines übertragenen Vermögenswerts hat kaum eine tatsächliche Auswirkung, wenn für den übertragenen Vermögenswert kein Markt vorhanden ist; und

- die Fähigkeit, einen übertragenen Vermögenswert zu veräußern, hat kaum eine tatsächliche Auswirkung, wenn von ihr nicht frei Gebrauch gemacht werden kann. Aus diesem Grund gilt:

  - die Fähigkeit des Empfängers, einen übertragenen Vermögenswert zu veräußern, muss von den Handlungen Dritter unabhängig sein (d. h. es muss sich um eine einseitige Fähigkeit handeln) und

  - der Empfänger muss in der Lage sein, den übertragenen Vermögenswert ohne einschränkende Bedingungen oder Auflagen für die Übertragung zu veräußern (z. B. Bedingungen bezüglich der Bedienung eines Kredits oder eine Option, die den Empfänger zum Rückkauf des Vermögenswerts berechtigt).

Dabei ist die fehlende Wahrscheinlichkeit einer Weiterveräußerung für sich genommen kein Indiz der Verfügungsmacht des übertragenden Unternehmens (IAS 39.AG44).

Bei **vollständiger Ausbuchung** eines **gesamten** finanziellen Vermögenswertes ist in der Gewinn- und Verlustrechnung folgende Differenz zu erfassen:

- Buchwert
- der Summe aus:

  - dem erhaltenen Entgelt (einschließlich jedes neu erhaltenen Vermögenswerts abzüglich jeder neu übernommenen Verbindlichkeit)
  - aller kumulierten Gewinne oder Verluste, die gemäß IAS 39.55(b) im sonstigen Ergebnis erfasst wurden (bei als zur Veräußerung verfügbaren klassifizierten Vermögenswerten).

82

Bei **vollständiger Ausbuchung eines Teils** eines finanziellen Vermögenswerts (zum Beispiel bei Veräußerung nur der Zinszahlungen) hat eine Aufteilung auf Basis der relativen beizulegenden Zeitwerte zu erfolgen. Danach ist in der Gewinn- und Verlustrechnung folgende Differenz zu erfassen:

- Buchwert, der dem ausgebuchten Teil zugeordnet wurde
- der Summe aus:

  - dem für den ausgebuchten Teil erhaltenen Entgelt (einschließlich jedes neu erhaltenen Vermögenswerts abzüglich jeder neu übernommenen Verbindlichkeit)
  - aller kumulierten ihm zugeordneten Gewinne oder Verluste, die gemäß IAS 39.55(b) im sonstigen Ergebnis erfasst wurden (bei als zur Veräußerung verfügbaren klassifizierten Vermögenswerten).

83

Dabei hat die Aufteilung des im sonstigen Ergebnis erfassten Betrags ebenfalls auf Basis der relativen beizulegenden Zeitwerte zu erfolgen.

Die Ermittlung der relativen beizulegenden Zeitwerte für die entsprechenden Teile hat zuerst auf Basis von Preisen bei vergangenen ähnlichen Transaktionen (vom Unternehmen selbst oder anderen Marktteilnehmern) zu erfolgen. Gibt es für den Teil, der weiter erfasst wird, keine Preisnotierungen oder aktuelle Markttransaktionen zur Belegung des beizulegenden Zeitwerts, so besteht die bestmögliche Schätzung in der Differenz zwischen dem beizulegenden Zeitwert des größeren finanziellen Vermögenswerts als Ganzem und dem vom Empfänger für den ausgebuchten Teil vereinnahmten Entgelt (IAS 39.28). Daneben finden bei der Ermittlung des weiterhin bilanzierten Teils die Vorschriften zur Ermittlung von beizulegenden Zeitwerten in IAS 39.48-49 sowie IAS 39.AG69-AG82 Anwendung (IAS 39.AG46).

84

Für den Fall, dass das Unternehmen bei der Übertragung weder alle wesentlichen Chancen und Risiken aus dem Vermögenswert zurückbehält noch überträgt und gleichzeitig die Verfügungsgewalt über den Vermögenswert hat, ist eine Bilanzierung des **anhaltenden Engagement** (continuing involvement) angezeigt (IAS 39.30). Die Idee hinter der Bilanzierung des anhaltenden Engagements ist die bilanzielle Abbildung der verbleibenden Risikoexposition des Unternehmens nach der Übertragung. Beispiele für die aus diesem Prinzip resultierenden Wertansätze sind (IAS 39.30):

85

- Wenn das anhaltende Engagement eines Unternehmens der Form nach den übertragenen Vermögenswert garantiert, ist der Umfang dieses anhaltenden Engagements entweder der Betrag des Vermögenswerts oder der Höchstbetrag des erhaltenen Entgelts, den das Unternehmen eventuell zurückzahlen müsste (der garantierte Betrag), je nachdem, welcher von beiden der Niedrigere ist.
- Wenn das anhaltende Engagement des Unternehmens der Form nach eine geschriebene oder eine erworbene Option (oder beides) auf den übertragenen Vermögenswert ist, so ist der Umfang des anhaltenden Engagements des Unternehmens der Betrag des übertragenen Vermögenswerts, den das Unternehmen zurückkaufen kann. Im Fall einer geschriebenen Verkaufsoption auf einen Ver-

mögenswert, der zum beizulegenden Zeitwert bewertet wird, ist der Umfang des anhaltenden Engagements des Unternehmens allerdings auf den beizulegenden Zeitwert des übertragenen Vermögenswerts oder den Ausübungspreis der Option – je nachdem, welcher von beiden der Niedrigere ist – begrenzt.

- Wenn das anhaltende Engagement des Unternehmens der Form nach eine Option ist, die durch Barausgleich oder vergleichbare Art auf den übertragenen Vermögenswert erfüllt wird, wird der Umfang des anhaltenden Engagements des Unternehmens in der gleichen Weise wie bei Optionen, die nicht durch Barausgleich erfüllt werden, ermittelt.

86   Es wird darüber hinaus auch eine Verbindlichkeit passiviert. Dabei ist die Bewertung von Vermögenswert und Verbindlichkeit abhängig davon, ob der Vermögenswert zu fortgeführten Anschaffungskosten oder zum beizulegenden Zeitwert bewertet wird (IAS 39.31):

- Wird der Vermögenswert zu fortgeführten Anschaffungskosten bewertet, so muss der Nettobuchwert aus Vermögenswert und Verbindlichkeit den fortgeführten Anschaffungskosten der zurückbehaltenen Rechte und Pflichten entsprechen.

- Wird der Vermögenswert zum beizulegenden Zeitwert bewertet, so muss der Nettobuchwert aus Vermögenswert und Verbindlichkeit dem beizulegenden Zeitwert der zurückbehaltenen Rechte und Pflichten entsprechen.

87   Für alle Übertragungen gilt daneben, dass bei geschriebenen **Ausfallgarantien,** die eine vollständige Ausbuchung verhindert haben, der verbleibende Vermögenswert mit dem niedrigeren Betrag aus dem Buchwert und dem Höchstbetrag des erhaltenen Entgelts, den das Unternehmen eventuell zurückzahlen müsste, bewertet wird (IAS 39.AG48).

88   Auch hier gilt das oben bereits erwähnte **Aufrechnungsverbot** von Vermögenswert/ Verbindlichkeit bzw. Erträgen/Aufwendungen (IAS 39.32 i.V.m. IAS 39.33). Daneben ist für die passivierte Verbindlichkeit die Fair-Value-Option nicht verfügbar, um eine mit dem Vermögenswert konsistente Bewertung sicherzustellen (IAS 39.35).

89   Bei Teilübertragungen ist wiederum eine Allokation des Ursprungsbuchwerts auf Basis der relativen beizulegenden Zeitwerte vorzunehmen (IAS 39.34). Die Rechenschritte sind mit den oben dargestellten identisch. Ein Beispiel aus IAS 39.AG52 soll die Rechenlogik verdeutlichen.

Beispiel

Es wird angenommen, dass ein Unternehmen ein Portfolio vorzeitig rückzahlbarer Kredite mit einem Kupon- und Effektivzinssatz von 10 Prozent und einem Kapitalbetrag und fortgeführten Anschaffungskosten in Höhe von € 10.000 besitzt. Das Unternehmen schließt eine Transaktion ab, mit der der Empfänger gegen eine Zahlung von € 9.115 ein Recht auf die Tilgungsbeträge in Höhe von € 9.000 zuzüglich eines Zinssatzes von 9,5 Prozent auf diese Beträge erwirbt. Das Unternehmen behält die Rechte an € 1.000 der Tilgungsbeträge zuzüglich eines Zinssatzes von 10 Prozent auf diesen Betrag zuzüglich der Überschussspanne von 0,5 Prozent auf den verbleibenden Kapitalbetrag in Höhe von € 9.000. Die Zahlungseingänge aus vorzeitigen Rückzahlungen werden zwischen dem Unternehmen und dem Empfänger im Verhältnis von 1:9 aufgeteilt; alle Ausfälle werden jedoch vom Anteil des Unternehmens in Höhe von € 1.000 abgezogen, bis dieser Anteil erschöpft ist. Der beizulegende Zeitwert der Kredite zum Zeitpunkt der Transaktion beträgt € 10.100 und der geschätzte beizulegende Zeitwert der Überschussspanne von 0,5 Prozent beträgt € 40.

Das Unternehmen stellt fest, dass es einige mit dem Eigentum verbundene wesentliche Risiken und Chancen (beispielsweise ein wesentliches Vorauszahlungsrisiko) übertragen, jedoch auch einige mit dem Eigentum verbundene wesentliche Risiken und Chancen (aufgrund seines nachrangigen zurückbehaltenen Anteils) behalten hat und außerdem weiterhin die Verfügungsgewalt ausübt. Es wendet daher das Konzept des anhaltenden Engagements an.

Bei der Anwendung dieses Standards analysiert das Unternehmen die Transaktion als (a) Beibehaltung eines zurückbehaltenen Anteils von € 1.000 sowie (b) Nachordnung dieses zurückbehaltenen Anteils, um dem Empfänger eine Kreditsicherheit für Kreditausfälle zu gewähren.

Das Unternehmen berechnet, dass € 9.090 (90 % × € 10.100) des erhaltenen Entgelts in Höhe von € 9.115 der Gegenleistung für einen Anteil von 90 Prozent entsprechen. Der Rest des erhaltenen Entgelts (€ 25) entspricht der Gegenleistung, die das Unternehmen für die Nachordnung seines zurückbehaltenen Anteils erhalten hat, um dem Empfänger eine Kreditsicherheit für Kreditausfälle zu gewähren. Die Überschussspanne von 0,5 Prozent stellt ebenfalls eine für die Kreditsicherheit erhaltene Gegenleistung dar. Dementsprechend beträgt die für die Kreditsicherheit erhaltene Gegenleistung insgesamt € 65 (€ 25 + € 40).

Das Unternehmen berechnet den Gewinn oder Verlust aus der Veräußerung auf Grundlage des 90-prozentigen Anteils an den Cashflows. Unter der Annahme, dass zum Zeitpunkt der Übertragung keine gesonderten beizulegenden Zeitwerte für den übertragenen Anteil von 10 Prozent und den zurückbehaltenen Anteil von 90 Prozent verfügbar sind, teilt das Unternehmen den Buchwert des Vermögenswerts gemäß Paragraph 28 wie folgt auf:

	Geschätzter beizulegender Zeitwert	Prozentsatz	Zugewiesener Buchwert
Übertragener Anteil	9.090	90 %	9.000
Zurückbehaltener Anteil	_1.010_	_10 %_	_1.000_
Summe	**_10.100_**		**_10.000_**

Zur Berechnung des Gewinns oder Verlusts aus dem Verkauf des 90-prozentigen Anteils an den Cashflows zieht das Unternehmen den zugewiesenen Buchwert des übertragenen Anteils von der erhaltenen Gegenleistung ab. Daraus ergibt sich ein Wert von € 90 (€ 9090 – € 9.000). Der Buchwert des vom Unternehmen zurückbehaltenen Anteils beträgt € 1.000.

Außerdem erfasst das Unternehmen das anhaltende Engagement, das durch Nachordnung seines zurückbehaltenen Anteils für Kreditverluste entsteht. Folglich setzt es einen Vermögenswert in Höhe von € 1.000 (den Höchstbetrag an Cashflows, den es aufgrund der Nachordnung nicht erhalten würde) und eine zugehörige Verbindlichkeit in Höhe von € 1.065 an (den Höchstbetrag an Cashflows, den es aufgrund der Nachordnung nicht erhalten würde, d. h. € 1.000 zuzüglich des beizulegenden Zeitwerts der Nachordnung in Höhe von € 65).

Unter Einbeziehung aller vorstehenden Informationen wird die Transaktion wie folgt gebucht:

	Soll		Haben
Ursprünglicher Vermögenswert	–		9.000
Angesetzter Vermögenswert bezüglich Nachordnung des Residualanspruchs	1.000		–
Vermögenswert für das in Form einer Überschussspanne erhaltene Entgelt	40		–
Gewinn oder Verlust (Gewinn bei der Übertragung)	–		90
Schuld	–		1.065
Erhaltene Zahlung	9.115		–
Summe	**10.155**		**10.155**

Unmittelbar nach der Transaktion beträgt der Buchwert des Vermögenswerts € 2.040, bestehend aus € 1.000 (den Kosten, die dem den zurückbehaltenen Anteil zugewiesen sind) und € 1.040 (dem zusätzlichen anhaltenden Engagement des Unternehmens aufgrund der Nachordnung seines zurückbehaltenen Anteils für Kreditverluste, wobei in diesem Betrag auch die Überschussspanne von € 40 enthalten ist).

In den Folgeperioden erfasst das Unternehmen zeitproportional das für die Kreditsicherheit erhaltene Entgelt (€ 65), grenzt die Zinsen auf den erfassten Vermögenswert unter Anwendung der Effektivzinsmethode ab und erfasst etwaige Kreditwertminderungen auf die angesetzten Vermögenswerte. Als Beispiel für Letzteres soll angenommen werden, dass im darauffolgenden Jahr ein Kreditwertminderungsaufwand für die zugrunde liegenden Kredite in Höhe von € 300 anfällt. Das Unternehmen schreibt den angesetzten Vermögenswert um € 600 ab (€ 300 für seinen zurückbehaltenen Anteil und € 300 für das zusätzliche anhaltende Engagement, das durch Nachordnung des zurückbehaltenen Anteils für Kreditverluste entsteht) und verringert die erfasste Verbindlichkeit um € 300. Netto wird der Gewinn oder Verlust also mit einer Kreditwertminderung von € 300 belastet.

90   **2. Ausbuchung von finanziellen Verbindlichkeiten. a) Allgemeine Vorschriften.** Die Vorschriften zur Ausbuchung von finanziellen Verbindlichkeiten in IAS 39 gestalten sich ungleich einfacher als für Finanzaktiva. IAS 39.39 legt fest, dass eine finanzielle Verbindlichkeit (bzw. ein Teil davon) nur dann ausgebucht werden darf, wenn diese getilgt ist – d. h. die im Vertrag genannten Verpflichtungen erfüllt oder aufgehoben sind oder auslaufen. Die Aufhebung einer Verpflichtung kann von Rechts wegen erfolgen oder durch Verhandlung mit dem Gläubiger (IAS 39.AG57). Der Rückerwerb von Schuldtiteln gilt als Tilgung, auch wenn das Unternehmen ein Eigenhändler ist oder kurzfristig eine erneute Platzierung des Instruments anstrebt (IAS 39.AG58).

91   Für den Fall, dass ein Unternehmen einen Dritten dafür bezahlt, eine bestehende Schuld zu tilgen (**in substance defeasance**), gilt die finanzielle Verbindlichkeit nicht als getilgt, bis auch das Berichtsunternehmen rechtlich keine Verpflichtung mehr hat (IAS 39.AG59). Übernimmt das Berichtsunternehmen eine neue Verpflichtung im Gegenzug für den Verzicht des Gläubigers auf seinen Anspruch ist zwar die bestehende finanzielle Verbindlichkeit auszubuchen, gleichzeitig aber eine neue finanzielle Verbindlichkeit zu passivieren (IAS 39.AG60). Zum Beispiel ist dies der Fall, wenn das Berichtsunternehmen seine Verpflichtung auf einen Dritten überträgt, gleichzeitig aber die Zahlungen durch den Dritten garantiert, d.h. bei Ausfall dieses Dritten die Zahlungen übernimmt. Hier wäre zwar die ursprüngliche finanzielle Verbindlichkeit auszubuchen, gleichzeitig aber die Garantie einzubuchen.

Des Weiteren ist bei einem **Austausch von Schuldinstrumenten zu wesentlich verschiedenen Be-** 92
dingungen eine Ausbuchung angezeigt genauso wie bei einer Neuverhandlung der Konditionen, wenn sich die neuen Bedingungen wesentlich von den ursprünglichen Konditionen unterscheiden (IAS 39.40) – dabei spielt es keine Rolle, ob es zu dieser Neuverhandlung aufgrund von finanziellen Schwierigkeiten des Schuldners gekommen ist. Wie bereits oben dargestellt, wird davon ausgegangen, dass bei einem (Netto-) Barwertunterschied von 10% zwischen den verbleibenden Zahlungen gemäß dem Ursprungs-vertrag und den Zahlungen aus dem ausgetauschten bzw. neuverhandelten Vertrag (einschließlich er-haltener bzw. gezahlter Gebühren) sich die Vertragsbedingungen wesentlich unterscheiden (IAS 39. AG62). Dabei ist für die Diskontierung der ursprüngliche Effektivzins der finanziellen Verbindlichkeit gemäß IAS 39.9 anzuwenden. Effekte aus Anwendung der Vorschriften zur bilanziellen Abbildung von Sicherungsbeziehungen (hedge accounting) sind auszublenden. Es gilt auch zu beachten, dass selbst bei Bilanzierung der finanziellen Verbindlichkeit als erfolgswirksam zum beizulegenden Zeitwert bewertet für die Beurteilung der Effektivzins bei erstmaligem Ansatz heranzuziehen ist. Im Einzelfall kann diese Ermittlung, insbesondere nachträglich, schwierig sein.

Eine ggf. entstehende Differenz zwischen Buchwert und geleistetem Entgelt, welches sowohl zah- 93
lungswirksame als auch zahlungsunwirksame Komponenten sowie übernommene Verpflichtungen mit-einschließt, ist in der Gewinn- und Verlustrechnung zu erfassen (IAS 39.41).

Anfallende Gebühren oder sonstige Aufwendungen sind bei einem **Schuldinstrumenttausch** bzw. 94
einer -modifikation als Teil des Abgangerfolgs zu erfassen, sofern sich die neuen Vertragsbedingungen wesentlich vom ursprünglichen Instrument unterscheiden (also eine Ausbuchung iSv. IAS 39 angezeigt ist). Falls es zu keiner Ausbuchung kommt, sind solche Aufwendungen als Anpassung des Buchwerts der ursprünglichen finanziellen Verbindlichkeit zu behandeln und dementsprechend über die Restlaufzeit des Instruments gemäß der Effektivzinsmethode zu amortisieren (IAS 39.AG62).

Für den Fall, dass nur ein **Teil einer bestehenden finanziellen Verbindlichkeit** auszubuchen ist 95
(bspw. bei einem teilweisen Rückerwerb einer Anleihe), erfolgt die Buchwertminderung im relativen Verhältnis der beizulegenden Zeitwerte im Zeitpunkt der Teilausbuchung.

b) Tilgung finanzieller Verbindlichkeiten durch Eigenkapitalinstrumente. Im Rahmen der Fi- 96
nanzmarktkrise erfreuten sich sog. **debt for equity swaps** wachsender Beliebtheit. Diese sind ein Mittel für einen Schuldner, der sich in finanziellen Schwierigkeiten befindet, seine Schulden durch Übertra-gung von eigenen Eigenkapitalinstrumenten zu tilgen. Die mit solchen Transaktionen verbundenen Bilanzierungsfragen veranlassten das IFRIC im November 2009 eine Interpretation, IFRIC 19 *Extin-guishing Financial Liabilities with Equity Instruments*, zu veröffentlichen. IFRIC 19 ist für Geschäftsjahre anzuwenden, die am oder nach dem 1. Juli 2010 beginnen, wobei eine vorzeitige Anwendung statthaft ist, sofern dies im Anhang offengelegt wird (IFRS 19.12). Die Interpretation ist gemäß IAS 8 *Accounting Policies, Changes in Accounting Estimates and Errors* als Änderung einer Bilanzierungsmethode retro-spektiv anzuwenden (IFRIC 19.13).

Der Anwendungsbereich dieser Interpretation erstreckt sich nur auf die Bilanzierung beim Schuld- 97
ner und darf nicht auf folgende Situationen angewendet werden (IFRIC 19.3):
- der Gläubiger ist gleichzeitig direkter oder indirekter Anteilseigner und in seiner Eigenschaft als gegenwärtiger, direkter oder indirekter Anteilseigner handelt.
- der Gläubiger und das Unternehmen werden vor und nach der Transaktion von derselben Partei/ denselben Parteien beherrscht und der wirtschaftliche Gehalt der Transaktion eine Kapitalausschüt-tung des Unternehmens oder eine Kapitaleinlage in das Unternehmen einschließt.
- die ursprünglichen Vertragsbedingungen der finanziellen Verbindlichkeit sehen die Möglichkeit einer Tilgung durch die Ausgabe von Eigenkapitalinstrumenten vor.

98   Die Interpretation stellt klar, dass die emittierten Eigenkapitalinstrumente des Schuldners einen Teil des Entgelts iSv. IAS 39.41 darstellen. Dies ist in den Augen des IFRIC damit zu begründen, dass die Transaktion wirtschaftlich identisch auch in zwei Transaktionen aufgespalten werden könnte:

- Emission von Eigenkapitalinstrumenten gegen Barmittel.
- Verwendung der Barmittel zur Tilgung der Schuld.

99   Mithin wird bei diesen **debt for equity swaps** nur die Barmittelseite dieser Transaktionen miteinander aufgerechnet. Beide Durchführungswege sollten aufgrund der wirtschaftlichen gleichen Substanz auch bilanziell gleich abgebildet werden.

100   Die emittierten Eigenkapitalinstrumente sind mit ihrem beizulegenden Zeitwert im Zeitpunkt der Tilgung der finanziellen Verbindlichkeit zu bewerten. Eine Ausnahme gilt, wenn der beizulegende Zeitwert der Eigenkapitalinstrumente nicht zuverlässig ermittelt werden kann. Dann sind die Eigenkapitalinstrumente mit dem beizulegenden Zeitwert der getilgten finanziellen Verbindlichkeit zu bewerten. Mit Ausnahme einer (unwahrscheinlichen) Wertidentität wird sich aus solchen Transaktionen also regelmäßig eine Erfolgswirkung iSv. IAS 39.41 ergeben. Dieser Gewinn oder Verlust ist daneben gesondert in der Gewinn- oder Verlustrechnung darzustellen, alternativ im Anhang offenzulegen (IFRIC 19.11).

101   Bei **nur teilweiser Tilgung** einer finanziellen Verbindlichkeit im Rahmen einer solchen Transaktion hat das Berichtsunternehmen zu beurteilen, ob das gezahlte Entgelt auch eine Teilmodifikation der verbleibenden finanziellen Verbindlichkeit darstellt (IFRIC 19.8). Wenn dies der Fall ist, ist die Gegenleistung auf den getilgten und den modifizierten Teil der finanziellen Verbindlichkeit aufzuteilen. Dieser Betrag ist auch bei der sich anschließenden Beurteilung der Modifikation hinsichtlich eines Ausbuchungstatbestandes iSv. IAS 39.40 einzubeziehen.

102   **VI. Kategorisierung**. Die IFRS teilen Finanzinstrumente zum Zweck ihrer Bewertung in verschiedene Kategorien ein. Die beiden derzeit für die Bewertung von Finanzinstrumenten gültigen IFRS (d.h. IAS 39 und IFRS 9)[69] unterscheiden sich hierbei sowohl hinsichtich ihrer Struktur als auch in der Art und Anzahl der Kategorien. Im Folgenden wird zuerst auf IAS 39 und dann auf IFRS 9 eingegangen.

103   **1. Kategorisierung nach IAS 39.** Die Kategorisierung von Finanzinstrumenten nach IAS 39 erfolgt auf der Basis der *Definitionen* der einzelnen **Kategorien von Finanzinstrumenten**. IAS 39 hat folgende (Haupt-)[70]Kategorien für finanzielle Vermögenswerte:

- Erfolgswirksam zum beizulegenden Zeitwert bewertet,
- Bis zur Endfälligkeit zu haltende Finanzinvestitionen,
- Kredite und Forderungen,
- Zur Veräußerung verfügbare finanzielle Vermögenswerte.

104   Die Hauptkategorien für finanzielle Verbindlichkeiten in IAS 39 sind:

- Erfolgswirksam zum beizulegenden Zeitwert bewertet,
- Alle übrigen finanziellen Verbindlichkeiten (d.h. solche, die weder zum erfolgswirksam zum beizulegenden Zeitwert bewertet werden noch einer anderen besonderen Folgebewertung unterliegen). Dies ist keine in IAS 39 definierte Kategorie sondern ergibt sich aus den Vorschriften zur Folgebewertung finanzieller Verbindlichkeiten und wird daher im entsprechenden Abschnitt behandelt.[71]

105   Die nachfolgenden Rn. erläutern die einzelnen Kategorien näher. Dabei wird die Kategorie „erfolgswirksam zum beizulegenden Zeitwert bewertet" für finanzielle Vermögenswerte und finanzielle Verbindlichkeiten zusammengefasst behandelt.

---

69 Siehe Rn 1f.
70 Als Hauptkategorien werden hier diejenigen bezeichnet, die explizit als eine eigene Kategorie definiert sind (sowie die daraus folgende Residualkategorie derjenigen Verbindlichkeiten, die nicht der Kategorie „erfolgswirksam zum beizulegenden Zeitwert bewertet" angehören).
71 Siehe Rn 140.

Die Kategorie **erfolgswirksam zum beizulegenden Zeitwert bewertet** umfasst zwei Unterkategorien (IAS 39.9):

- Zu Handelszwecken gehalten,
- Fair Value Option.

106

Die Kategorisierung von Finanzinstrumenten als „**zu Handelszwecken gehalten**" (held for trading) ergibt sich als *verbindliche* Zuordnung aufgrund eines von drei Merkmalen. Erstens, Finanzinstrumente, die hauptsächlich zwecks Verkaufs oder Wiedererwerbs in naher Zukunft erworben oder abgeschlossen wurden. Folglich sind die Umstände im Zeitpunkt des erstmaligen Ansatzes des Finanzinstruments maßgeblich. Diese Absicht spiegelt sich regelmäßig in einem häufigen Umschlag der Finanzinstrumente wider, mittels dessen kurzfristige Preisschwankungen ausgenutzt oder Händlermargen erzielt werden (IAS 39.AG14). Bei finanziellen Verbindlichkeiten liegt dies z.B. bei **Leerverkäufen** (dem sog. short selling) oder dem **Eigenhandel** des Emittenten in Verbindlichkeiten vor (IAS 39.AG15(b)-(c)). Davon zu unterscheiden ist, ob eine Verbindlichkeit der Finanzierung von Handelsaktivitäten dient. Dieser Umstand ist nicht gleichbedeutend mit einer Handelsabsicht und führt folglich für sich genommen nicht zur Kategorisierung als zu Handelszwecken gehalten (IAS 39.AG15).

107

Zweitens umfasst die Kategorie zu Handelszwecken gehalten diejenigen Finanzinstrumente, bei denen sich die kurzfristige Gewinnerzielungsabsicht aus der Zugehörigkeit zu einem Portfolio mit empirischem Beleg kurzfristiger Gewinnmitnahmen in jüngerer Vergangenheit ergibt. Im Vergleich zum ersten Kriterium stellt dieses Kriterium auf die Portfolioebene ab, d.h. ein Finanzinstrument ist auch dann zu Handelszwecken gehalten, wenn die Handelsabsicht nicht für das einzelne Finanzinstrument vorliegt, aber sich aus dem Portfoliokontext ergibt. Für die Beurteilung ist auf die Umstände (d.h. Portfoliozugehörigkeit) im Zeitpunkt des erstmaligen Ansatzes des Finanzinstruments abzustellen.

108

Drittens fallen alle Derivate zwingend in die Kategorie zu Handelszwecken gehalten, es sei denn, das Derivat[72] ist eine *finanzielle Garantie*[73] oder ein Sicherungsinstrument, auf das die Vorschriften über die Bilanzierung von Sicherungsgeschäften Anwendung finden. Dieses Kriterium hat in der Praxis große Bedeutung, weil in vielen Fällen Unternehmen Derivate im Rahmen des Risikomanagements zur wirtschaftlichen Absicherung gegen Risiken verwenden, aber nicht die Regelungen zur Bilanzierung von Sicherungsgeschäften anwenden (sei es, weil dies gar nicht erst versucht wird oder aber die strengen Voraussetzungen nicht erfüllt werden können). Obwohl die Kategorisierung dieser Derivate eindeutig ist, führt unter diesen Umständen die Bezeichnung als zu Handelszwecken gehalten oft zu Missverständnissen in der Interpreation der Abschlüsse.

109

Die zweite Unterkategorie der Finanzinstrumente, die erfolgswirksam zum beizulegenden Zeitwert bewertet werden, ist die sogenannte „**Fair Value Option**". Im Gegensatz zur Unterkategorie „zu Handelszwecken gehalten" handelt es sich hierbei *nicht* um eine *verbindliche* Zuordnung, *sondern* um das *Wahlrecht*, ein Finanzinstrument als erfolgswirksam zum beizulegenden Zeitwert bewertet einzustufen. Das Wahlrecht kann nur im Zeitpunkt des erstmaligen Ansatzes des Finanzinstruments ausgeübt werden und die Entscheidung ist unwiderruflich. Die Fair Value Option hat drei alternative Voraussetzungen, von denen (mindestens) eine erfüllt sein muss, damit das Wahlrecht zur Einstufung als erfolgswirksam zum beizulegenden Zeitwert bewertet besteht:

110

(a) Die Einstufung als erfolgswirksam zum beizulegenden Zeitwert bewertet dient der Vermeidung der Aufspaltung eines strukturierten Finanzinstruments in seinen Basisvertrag und ein oder mehrere eingebettete Derivate;

---

72 Siehe Rn 28ff.
73 Siehe Rn 141.

(b) Die Einstufung als als erfolgswirksam zum beizulegenden Zeitwert bewertet kann eine Rechnungslegungsanomalie vermeiden oder mindestens erheblich verringern und führt somit zu relevanteren Informationen;

(c) Das Management und die Beurteilung der Wertentwicklung einer Gruppe von Finanzinstrumenten erfolgt auf Basis des beizulegenden Zeitwerts, so dass die Einstufung als erfolgswirksam zum beizulegenden Zeitwert bewertet zu relevanteren Informationen führt.

Auf die einzelnen Voraussetzungen wird in den nachfolgenden Rn. kurz eingegangen.

111   Hinsichtlich der **Vermeidung der Aufspaltung strukturierter Finanzinstrumente** mittels Ausübung der Fair Value Option wird auf die Ausführungen zu eingebetteten Derivaten verwiesen.[74]

112   Eine **Rechnungslegungsanomalie** (accounting mismatch) im Sinne der zweiten Voraussetzung liegt vor, wenn die Ansatz- oder Bewertungsvorschriften dazu führen, dass Vermögenswerte und Verbindlichkeiten verschieden bewertet werden oder die Wertänderungen verschieden erfasst werden (z.B. erfolgswirksam als Teil von Gewinn oder Verlust im Gegensatz zu einer Erfassung im sonstigen Ergebnis) (IAS 39.AG4D). So kann z.B. ein Unternehmen finanzielle Vermögenswerte oder Derivate haben, die erfolgswirksam zum beizulegenden Zeitwert bewertet werden, während mit diesen in Zusammenhang stehende finanzielle Verbindlichkeiten (z.B. die finanziellen Vermögenswerte finanzierende oder durch die Derivate abgesicherte Verbindlichkeiten) zu fortgeführten Anschaffungskosten bewertet werden (IAS 39.AG4E(c)). In diesen Fällen kann eine Einstufung dieser finanziellen Verbindlichkeiten als erfolgswirksam zum beizulegenden Zeitwert bewertet eine Verzerrung des Ergebnisses in der Gewinn- und Verlustrechnung vermeiden.[75] Die zweite Voraussetzung der Fair Value Option bzgl. der Vermeidung von Rechnungslegungsanomalien wird in der Praxis oft als Alternative zur Bilanzierung als Sicherungsgeschäft angesehen. Der Vorteil ist, dass die oft aufwendigen und schwer zu erfüllenden Voraussetzungen für die Bilanzierung als Sicherungsgeschäft – insbesondere die Anforderungen an die Wirksamkeit der Sicherungsbeziehung – vermieden werden können. Der Nachteil ist, dass die Ausübung der Fair Value Option nur beim erstmaligen Ansatz des Finanzinstruments erfolgen kann und unwiderruflich ist. Die Fair Value Option ist daher wesentlich weniger flexibel als eine Bilanzierung als Sicherungsgeschäft. Im Rahmen der globalen Finanzkrise mit den einhergehenden extremen Schwankungen der Risikoaufschläge[76] hat die Ausübung der Fair Value Option allerdings bei vielen Unternehmen zu einer unvorhergesehenen Verzerrung der Gewinn- und Verlustrechnung geführt. Das lag daran, dass die Schwankung des beizulegenden Zeitwerts finanzieller Verbindlichkeiten aufgrund der Veränderung der eigenen Bonität des jeweiligen Unternehmens nicht oder nur in geringem Umfang durch gegenläufige Wertschwankungen bei finanziellen Vermögenswerten oder Derivaten kompensiert wurde. Aufgrund dieser Erfahrung ist in der Praxis künftig mit einer erheblich vorsichtigeren Ausübung der Fair Value Option zur Vermeidung von Rechnungslegungsanomalien zu rechnen.

113   Bei der Ausübung der Fair Value Option zur Vermeidung von Rechnungslegungsanomalien ist auch zu beachten, dass diese nicht willkürlich erfolgen darf, sondern mindestens eine erhebliche Verringerung der Rechnungslegungsanomalie bewirken muss. Dies hat Auswirkungen auf den Umfang, in dem die Ausübung zu erfolgen hat. So ist z.B. die Ausübung für ein einzelnes Finanzinstrument aus einer Gruppe unzulässig, wenn dadurch nur eine minimale Verringerung der Rechnungslegungsanomalie erfolgt, während durch die Einstufung der gesamten Gruppe als erfolgswirksam zum beizulegenden Zeitwert bewertet eine erhebliche Verringerung bewirkt werden könnte (IAS 39.AG4G).

---

74   Siehe Rn 40.
75   IAS 39.AG4E enthält weitere Beispiele.
76   Der Risikoaufschlag (sogenannter „credit spread") ist die Differenz zwischen der Verzinsung eines Instruments und dem risikofreien ZinssaRn. In der Praxis wird der Risikoaufschlag auch oft als Differenz zu einem üblichen Referenzzinsatz (z.B. LIBOR) ausgedrückt.

Management und Beurteilung der Wertentwicklung einer Gruppe von Finanzinstrumenten auf Basis des beizulegenden Zeitwerts im Sinne der dritten Voraussetzung erfordert, dass dies auf Basis einer dokumentierten Risikomanagement- oder Anlagestrategie erfolgt und dass die interne Berichterstattung an die Personen in Schlüsselpositionen auf dieser Bewertungsbasis erfolgt (IAS 39.9). Dabei ist keine umfangreiche Dokumentation erforderlich, um den Nachweis zu erbringen, dass die Voraussetzung erfüllt ist (IAS 39.AG4K). In der Praxis werden die Anforderungen an die Dokumentation im Risikomanagement und das interne Berichtswesen häufig bereits dazu führen, dass die Dokumentation gleichzeitig auch die Anforderungen aus Rechnungslegungssicht erfüllt. Die einzige Zusatzanforderung für die Ausübung der Fair Value Option ist dann lediglich, dass diese Ausübung im Zeitpunkt des erstmaligen Ansatzes der betreffenden Finanzinstrumente eindeutig dokumentiert ist. Ein Beispiel einer Steuerung auf Basis des beizulegenden Zeitwerts ist z.B. die Steuerung eines Portfolios auf Gesamtrendite-Basis, d.h. unter Berücksichtigung von Ertrag aus Zinsen und Dividenden sowie von Änderungen des beizulegenden Zeitwerts (IAS 39.AG4I(a)).   114

Ähnlich zur zweiten Voraussetzung der Ausübung der Fair Value Option[77] ist auch hier zu beachten, dass die Ausübung nicht willkürlich erfolgen darf. Entsprechend dem Zweck der dritten Voraussetzung ist die Fair Value Option für *alle* diese Voraussetzung erfüllenden Finanzinstrumente, die einer gemeinsamen Steuerung und Beurteilung ihrer Wertentwicklung unterliegen, auszuüben (vorbehaltlich, dass dies bei deren erstmaligem Ansatz erfolgen muss) (IAS 39.AG4J).   115

Die Kategorie „**bis zur Endfälligkeit zu haltende Finanzinvestitionen**" dient dazu, einem Unternehmen für von ihm gehaltene börsennotierte Schuldinstrumente die Bewertung zu fortgeführten Anschaffungskosten zu ermöglichen. Die wesentliche Voraussetzung dafür ist, dass das Unternehmen diese finanziellen Vermögenswerte grundsätzlich[78] bis zu deren Endfälligkeit hält. Diese Bedingung beruht darauf, dass nicht aus dem Bonitätsrisiko resultierende Schwankungen des beizulegenden Zeitwerts, wie z.B. aufgrund von Änderungen des Marktzinsniveaus oder eines Liquiditätsabschlags, sich bis zur Endfälligkeit wieder umkehren.[79] Für Unternehmen, die Schuldtitel bis zur Endfälligkeit halten, haben diese Wertschwankungen daher nur Interimscharakter, da sie nicht realisiert werden.   116

Konkret ergeben sich aus der Definition (IAS 39.9) der Kategorie „bis zur Endfälligkeit zu haltende Finanzinvestitionen" folgende kumulative Voraussetzungen für eine Einbeziehung von Finanzinstrumenten in diese Kategorie: 117

- der finanzielle Vermögenswert hat feste oder bestimmbare Zahlungen und ist kein derivatives Finanzinstrument,
- der finanzielle Vermögenswert hat eine feste Laufzeit und
- das Unternehmen hat sowohl die Absicht als auch die Fähigkeit, den finanziellen Vermögenswert bis zur Endfälligkeit zu halten.

Wertpapiere im Bestand der **Liquiditätsreserve** eines Unternehmens erfüllen die Voraussetzungen häufig nicht, da es an der Halteabsicht des einzelnen Instruments bis zur Endfälligkeit mangelt (IAS 39.AG16(b)). Finanzinstrumente, die dem Inhaber eine **Vorfälligkeitsoption** gewähren, erfüllen die Voraussetzung aus demselben Grund ebenfalls nicht (IAS 39.AG19). Ferner enthält IAS 39 eine Bestimmung, die einem Unternehmen jegliche Nutzung der Kategorie bis zur Endfälligkeit zu haltende Finanzinvestitionen untersagt, wenn es im laufenden oder den beiden vorangehenden Geschäftsjahren einen mehr als unwesentlichen Teil dieser finanziellen Vermögenswerte verkauft oder in eine andere Kategorie umgegliedert hat (**Tainting**), vgl. IAS 39.9. Als nicht schädlich im Sinne dieser Bestimmung gelten Verkäufe und Umgliederungen, die so kurz vor Endfälligkeit erfolgen, dass Marktzinsänderungen den bei-   118

---

77 Siehe Rn 113.
78 Zu den Ausnahmen siehe Rn 118.
79 Im Englischen wird dies als „pull to par" Effekt bezeichnet.

zulegenden Zeitwert nicht mehr wesentlich beeinflussen, oder erst erfolgen, nachdem der Kapitalbetrag im wesentlichen bereits durch planmäßige oder vorzeitige Zahlungen getilgt war. Ferner sind Verkäufe und Umgliederungen aufgrund einmaliger, vom Unternehmen weder vorhersehbarer noch kontrollierbarer Umstände unschädlich für die Beurteilung der Halteabsicht für andere finanzielle Vermögenswerte (z.B. eine wesentlich Bonitätsverschlechterung beim Emittenten oder ein wesentlicher Strukturwandel des Unternehmens im Rahmen eines Unternehmenszusammenschlusses oder –veräußerung) (IAS 39. AG22). Aufgrund dieser restriktiven Voraussetzungen hat die Kategorie „bis zur Endfälligkeit zu haltende Finanzinvestitionen" in der Praxis nur eine geringe Bedeutung.

119   Außerdem darf der finanzielle Vermögenswert nicht in eine andere Kategorie fallen. Daher sind folgende finanziellen Vermögenswerte unabhängig von ihren Eigenschaften und der Halteabsicht des Unternehmens bis zur Endfälligkeit *nicht* Teil der Kategorie bis zur Endfälligkeit zu haltende Finanzinvestitionen:

- finanzielle Vermögenswerte, die das Unternehmen durch Ausübung der Fair Value Option als erfolgswirksam zum beizulegenden Zeitwert bewertet eingestuft hat,[80]
- finanzielle Vermögenswerte, die das Unternehmen in Ausübung seines Wahlrechts als zur Veräußerung verfügbare finanzielle Vermögenswerte eingestuft hat[81] oder
- finanzielle Vermögenswerte, die die Definition der Kategorie Kredite und Forderungen erfüllen.

120   Die Kategorie **„Kredite und Forderungen" (IAS 39.9)** umfasst diejenigen finanziellen Vermögenswerte, die feste oder bestimmbare Zahlungen haben und keine derivativen Finanzinstrumente sind. Ferner darf der finanzielle Vermögenswert keine Notierung in einem aktiven Markt haben, andernfalls ist eine Kategorisierung als bis zur Endfälligkeit zu haltende Finanzinvestitionen zu prüfen,[82] wenn eine Bewertung zu fortgeführten Anschaffungskosten angestrebt wird. Ein Anteil an einer Gruppe von finanziellen Vermögenswerten erfüllt nur dann die Definition von Krediten und Forderungen, wenn die Gruppe ausschließlich finanzielle Vermögenswerte umfasst, die selbst die Definition von Krediten und Forderungen erfüllen. Bei der Kategorisierung von Anteilen an Gruppen von finanziellen Vermögenswerten ist daher eine Analyse der Finanzinstrumente, die die Gruppe ausmachen, erforderlich.

121   Beispiele für Kredite und Forderungen sind **Forderungen aus Lieferungen und Leistungen**, Darlehen, Schuldverschreibungen (sofern diese nicht in einem aktiven Markt notiert sind) und Bankeinlagen (IAS 39.AG26). Bei **Verbriefung** solcher finanzieller Vermögenswerte erfüllt das daraus resultierende Finanzinstrument häufig nicht mehr die Definition von Krediten und Forderungen, weil entweder ein in einem aktiven Markt notiertes Finanzinstrument entsteht oder ein Anteil an einer Gruppe, die auch Finanzinstrumente umfasst, die nicht die Definition von Krediten und Forderungen erfüllen (z.B. Zinsswaps).

122   Außerdem darf der finanzielle Vermögenswert nicht in eine andere Kategorie fallen. Daher sind folgende finanziellen Vermögenswerte unabhängig von ihren Eigenschaften *nicht* Teil der Kategorie „Kredite und Forderungen":

- finanzielle Vermögenswerte, die in die Kategorie „erfolgswirksam zum beizulegenden Zeitwert bewertet" fallen, weil entweder die Absicht zur Veräußerung unmittelbar oder in naher Zukunft nach dem erstmaligen Ansatz besteht oder die Fair Value Option[83] ausgeübt wurde,
- finanzielle Vermögenswerte, die das Unternehmen in Ausübung seines Wahlrechts als „zur Veräußerung verfügbare finanzielle Vermögenswerte" eingestuft hat[84] oder

---

80   Siehe Rn 110.
81   Siehe Rn 123-124.
82   Siehe Rn 116-119.
83   Siehe Rn 110.
84   Siehe Rn 123-124.

- finanzielle Vermögenswerte, bei denen der Inhaber aufgrund anderer Ursachen als des Kreditriskos potenziell nicht im Wesentlichen seine ursprüngliche Investition wiedererlangt (was zur Kategorisierung als zur Veräußerung verfügbare finanzielle Vermögenswerte führt). Hierbei ist zu beachten, dass Wechselkursverluste *nicht* als Ursache eines potenziellen Verlusts der ursprünglichen Investition anzusehen sind. Dies liegt daran, dass das Wechselkursrisiko kein Vertragsmerkmal im engeren Sinne ist, sondern aus der funktionalen Währung des Inhabers resultiert und entsprechend durch die Vorschriften zur Währungsumrechnung des IAS 21 berücksichtigt wird. Ein Beispiel für einen finanziellen Vermögenswert mit potenziellem Verlust der ursprünglichen Investition ist ein sogenannter „**Interest-only Strip**"[85], der aus dem **Bondstripping** einer Schuldverschreibung mit vorzeitiger Rückzahlbarkeit entstanden ist (IAS 39.BC29). Im Fall der vorzeitigen Rückzahlung entfallen weitere Zinszahlungen, was beim Inhaber des Interest-only Strips wirtschaftlich einem (mindestens teilweisen) Ausfall eines Annuitätendarlehens entspricht.

Die Kategorie **zur Veräußerung verfügbare finanzielle Vermögenswerte (IAS 39.9)** umfasst diejenigen finanziellen Vermögenswerte, die entweder ein Unternehmen in Ausübung seines Wahlrechts als solche eingestuft hat oder die in keine der drei anderen Kategorien finanzieller Vermögenswerte fallen. Insoweit stellt diese Kategorie die Residualkategorie für die Aktivseite dar.   123

Das Wahlrecht zur Einstufung eines finanziellen Vermögenswerts als zur Veräußerung verfügbar besteht im Zeitpunkt des erstmaligen Ansatzes bei finanziellen Vermögenswerten, die ansonsten die Definition der Kategorie bis zur Endfälligkeit zu haltende Finanzinvestitionen oder Kredite und Forderungen erfüllen würden.   124

2. Kategorisierung nach IFRS 9. Der neue Standard zur Bilanzierung von Finanzinstrumenten – IFRS 9 – betrifft **vorerst nur die Aktivseite**.[86] Im Gegensatz zu IAS 39 erfolgt die Kategorisierung von Finanzinstrumenten nach IFRS 9 nicht auf der Basis von *Definitionen* einzelner Kategorien von Finanzinstrumenten, sondern mittels zweier kumulativer Kriterien, die für die Folgebewertung zwischen den beiden Bewertungsmethoden beizulegender Zeitwert und fortgeführte Anschaffungskosten entscheiden. Ferner besteht nach IFRS 9 die **Fair Value Option**, wenn dadurch eine Rechnungslegungsanomalie vermieden oder mindestens erheblich verringert werden kann (d.h. wie unter der zweiten Voraussetzung der Fair Value Option nach IAS 39).[87]   125

Die beiden kumulativen Kriterien, mittels derer IFRS den Wertmaßstab für die Folgebewertung für finanzielle Vermögenswerte bestimmt, betreffen (IFRS 9.4.1):   126
- das **Geschäftsmodell** des Unternehmens; und
- die **Cashflow-bezogenen Vertragsmerkmale** des Finanzinstruments.

Aufgrund der Stellungnahmen zum Standardentwurf änderte das IASB die **Reihenfolge der beiden Kriterien**, so dass IFRS 9 zuerst das Geschäftsmodell-bezogene Kriterium behandelt (IFRS 9.BC21). Allerdings hat dies *keine* inhaltliche Auswirkung auf das Ergebnis, d.h. die Bestimmung der Bewertungskategorie. Es liegt in der Logik eines kumulativen Kriteriums, dass alle Voraussetzungen (ausnahmslos) erfüllt sein müssen. Daher ist die Reihenfolge der Beurteilung der einzelnen Kriterien ausschließlich eine Frage der Effizienz der Implementierung von IFRS 9 in den betrieblichen Prozessen. Bei Banken wird es i.d.R. effizienter sein, zuerst das Geschäftsmodell-bezogene Kriterium zu beurteilen, da sich z.B. für das **Handelsbuch** die Beurteilung des Vertragsmerkmal-bezogenen Kriteriums erübrigt. Umgekehrt kann es für viele Industrieunternehmen effizienter sein, zuerst das Vertragsmerkmal-bezogene Kriterium zu beurteilen, weil das Geschäftsmodell (ggf. unter Ausklammerung des Treasurybereichs) oftmals offenkundig die Voraussetzung für die Bewertung zu fortgeführten Anschaffungskosten erfüllt. Entgegen dem

---

85 Teilweise auch als „isoliert gehandelter Zins" bezeichnet.
86 Siehe Rn 1f. und IFRS 9.2.1.
87 Siehe Rn 110 (Unterparagraph ii.) und 112f.

Wortlaut in der Grundlage für die Schlussfolgerungen bzgl. IFRS 9 (IFRS 9.BC21) sind Unternehmen in der Praxis *nicht* durch die im Standard gewählte Reihenfolge der Kriterien in der Umsetzung der Beurteilung dieser Kriterien in seinen Rechnungslegungsprozessen gebunden, sondern jedes Unternehmen kann die jeweils in seinen Umständen effizienteste Reihenfolge wählen (z.B. auch unterschiedlich je nach Unternehmensbereich).

127   Ein finanzieller Vermögenswert ist – vorbehaltlich der Ausübung der Fair Value Option[88] – für die Folgebewertung zu fortgeführten Anschaffungskosten zu bewerten, wenn beide folgenden Bedingungen (d.h. kumulativ) erfüllt sind (IFRS 9.4.2):

- **Geschäftsmodell**: der finanzielle Vermögenswert unterliegt einem Geschäftsmodell, welches zum Ziel hat, Vermögenswerte zur Vereinnahmung der vertraglichen Zahlungen (Cashflows) zu halten.
- **Cashflow-bezogene Vertragsmerkmale**: die Vertragsbedingungen des finanziellen Vermögenswerts führen an festgelegten Zeitpunkten zu Zahlungen (Cashflows), die *ausschließlich* Tilgungs- und Zinszahlungen auf den ausstehenden Kapitalbetrag darstellen. Zinsen im Sinne dieses Kriteriums sind Zahlungen als Entgelt für den Zeitwert des Geldes und das mit dem jeweils ausstehenden Kapitalbetrag verbundene Kreditrisiko (IFRS 9.4.3). Dabei ist der Begriff der Zinsen jedoch nicht zu eng auszulegen. Wirtschaftliche Transaktionen enthalten regelmäßig einen Gewinnanteil (einschließlich eines Beitrags zur Deckung von durch die Transaktion entstandenen oder noch entstehenden Kosten). Daher steht in der praktischen Anwendung eine Gewinnmarge der Beurteilung vertraglicher Zahlungen als Zinsen nicht entgegen.

128   Alle finanziellen Vermögenswerte, die diese Bedingungen nicht erfüllen, sind zum beizulegenden Zeitwert zu bewerten. Dies gilt für alle Eigenkapitalinstrumente aus Sicht des Investors,[89] weil diese nicht das Kriterium bzgl. der Cashflow-bezogenen Vertragsmerkmale erfüllen. So sind z.B. typischerweise die „Zinszahlungen" auf **Hybridkapitalinstrumente** (z.B. sogenannte **Trust Preferred Securities**) mindestens teilweise im Ermessen des Emittenten und stellen daher keine Zinszahlungen im Sinn von IFRS 9 dar.

129   **3. Umgliederung nach IAS 39.** Umgliederungen sind Änderungen der Kategorie eines Finanzinstruments nach dessen erstmaligem Ansatz. IAS 39 beschränkt Umgliederungen in Abhängigkeit einzelner Kategorien wie folgt:

(a) **in die Kategorie erfolgswirksam zum beizulegenden Zeitwert bewertet**: ein Wechsel in diese Kategorie ist unzulässig (IAS 39.50). Derivate, die zuvor als Sicherungsinstrument in einer Sicherungsbeziehung zur Absicherung von Zahlungsströmen oder Nettoinvestitionen behandelt wurden, sind jedoch erfolgswirksam zum beizulegenden Zeitwert zu bewerten, sobald die Voraussetzungen für die Bilanzierung als Sicherungsinstrument entfallen (IAS 39.50A(a)). Außerdem ist ein Derivat, das sich auf ein nicht auf einem aktiven Markt notiertes Eigenkapitalinstrument bezieht und durch Übertragung dieser Instrumente zu erfüllen ist, in diese Kategorie umzugliedern, wenn der beizulegende Zeitwert dieses Eigenkapitalinstruments verlässlich ermittelbar wird. Die Differenz zwischen beizulegendem Zeitwert und dem vorherigen Buchwert ist erfolgswirksam in der Gewinn- und Verlustrechnung zu erfassen (IAS 39.53 i.V.m. 55(a)).

(b) **aus der Kategorie erfolgswirksam zum beizulegenden Zeitwert bewertet**: ein Wechsel aus dieser Kategorie ist unzulässig für Finanzinstrumente, für die die Fair Value Option[90] ausgeübt wurde, sowie für Derivate (IAS 39.50(a)-(b)) und generell für finanzielle Verbindlichkeiten. Derivate, die als Sicherungsinstrument Teil einer Sicherungsbeziehung zur Absicherung von Zahlungsströmen oder Nettoinvestitionen behandelt werden, sind jedoch aus der Kategorie erfolgswirksam zum bei-

---

88   Siehe Rn 125.
89   Aus Sicht des Emittenten findet IAS 32 auf die Bilanzierung von Eigenkapitalinstrumenten Anwendung.
90   Siehe Rn 110ff.

zulegenden Zeitwert bewertet herauszunehmen, sobald die Voraussetzungen für die Bilanzierung als Sicherungsinstrument erfüllt sind (IAS 39.50A(b)). Ein Unternehmen darf nicht-derivative finanzielle Vermögenswerte, für die es *nicht* die Fair Value Option ausgeübt hat und die die Definition der Kategorie Kredite und Forderungen erfüllen würden, wenn sie nicht ursprünglich als zu Handelszwecken gehalten hätten bilanziert werden müssen, in die Kategorie Kredite und Forderungen umgliedern. Entgegen einer strengen Auslegung des Wortlauts stellt die Praxis für die Erfüllung der Definition der Kategorie Kredite und Forderungen auf den Zeitpunkt der Umgliederung statt vorhergehende Zeitpunkte ab, d.h. die Definition ist auch dann erfüllt, wenn es zwar im Zeitpunkt des erstmaligen Ansatzes einen **aktiven Markt** für den finanziellen Vermögenswert gab, dieser aber im Zeitpunkt der Umgliederung nicht mehr aktiv ist. Diese Auslegung entspricht dem Zweck der im Oktober 2008 vorgenommenen Änderung aus Anlass der Finanzkrise und ist daher nicht zu beanstanden. Voraussetzung einer solchen Umgliederung ist, dass das Unternehmen die Fähigkeit und Absicht hat, diese finanziellen Vermögenswerte mindestens für die absehbare Zukunft zu halten. In diesem Fall entsprechen die fortgeführten Anschaffungskosten im Zeitpunkt der Umgliederung dem beizulegenden Zeitwert zu diesem Zeitpunkt (IAS 39.50(c) i.V.m. 50D). Alle anderen als die in diesem Absatz zuvor genannten finanziellen Vermögenswerte[91] dürfen nur dann aus der der Kategorie erfolgswirksam zum beizulegenden Zeitwert bewertet umgegliedert werden, wenn das Unternehmen für diese keine kurzfristige Veräußerungsabsicht mehr hat. Ferner ist dies nur in *seltenen* Umständen zulässig (IAS 39.50(c) i.V.m. 50B-C). IAS 39 führt nicht näher aus, was seltene Umstände ausmacht.[92] Jedoch hat das IASB diese Umgliederungsmöglichkeit im Oktober 2008 aus Anlass der **Finanzkrise** geschaffen, woraus sich der Kontext für die Auslegung von „seltenen Umständen" ergibt. Andere seltene Umstände können ggf. dann vorliegen, wenn sich außerhalb einer Finanzkrise das Geschäftsmodell eines Unternehmens fundamental ändert, z.B. durch Aufgabe des Geschäftsmodells eines ganzen Segments wie Investmentbanking. Reine Portfolioverschiebungen zwischen Segmenten erfüllen dieses Kriterium dagegen nicht. Im Fall einer Umgliederung entsprechen die Anschaffungskosten oder die fortgeführten Anschaffungskosten im Zeitpunkt der Umgliederung dem beizulegenden Zeitwert in diesem Zeitpunkt. Außerdem ist ein nicht auf einem aktiven Markt notiertes Eigenkapitalinstrument aus der Kategorie erfolgswirksam zum beizulegenden Zeitwert bewertet umzugliedern, wenn der beizulegende Zeitwert dieses Eigenkapitalinstruments nicht mehr verlässlich ermittelbar ist. Dasselbe gibt für Derivate, die sich auf solche Eigenkapitalinstrumente beziehen und durch Übertragung dieser Instrumente zu erfüllen sind. In diesen Fällen stellt der beizulegende Zeitwert im Zeitpunkt der Umgliederung die Anschaffungskosten dar (IAS 39.54).

(c) **in die Kategorie „bis zur Endfälligkeit zu haltende Finanzinvestitionen":** Umgliederungen in diese Kategorie können sich als Folge in der Fähigkeit oder Absicht des Unternehmens, ein Schuldinstrument der Kategorie zur Veräußerung verfügbare finanzielle Vermögenswerte nunmehr bis zur Endfälligkeit zu halten, ergeben (IAS 39.54). Ferner kann eine Umgliederung aus der Kategorie erfolgswirksam zum beizulegenden Zeitwert bewertet unter den zuvor genannten seltenen Umständen (siehe Unterabschnitt (b) in dieser Rn.) zu einer Umgliederung in die Kategorie bis zur Endfälligkeit zu haltende Finanzinvestitionen führen. Außerdem kann sich eine Umgliederung in die Kategorie bis zur Endfälligkeit zu haltende Finanzinvestitionen aus dem Ablauf der Sperrfrist für die Nutzung dieser Kategorie nach einem sog. **Tainting**[93] ergeben.

---

91 Einschließlich derer, die die Oberbegriffe Finanzinstrument oder Derivat mit umfassen.
92 In der Grundlage für die Schlussfolgerungen wird auf einmalige, ungewöhnliche Umstände, deren Wiederholung in naher Zukunft unwahrscheinlich ist, Bezug genommen (siehe IAS 39.BC104D).
93 Siehe Rn 118.

(d) **aus der Kategorie „bis zur Endfälligkeit zu haltende Finanzinvestitionen"**: Umgliederungen aus dieser Kategorie können sich ergeben, wenn das Unternehmen nicht länger die Fähigkeit oder Absicht hat, ein Schuldinstrument bis zur Endfälligkeit zu halten (IAS 39.51). Umgliederungen ergeben sich auch als Folge des sog. Tainting[94], das jegliche Nutzung dieser Kategorie während einer Sperrfrist untersagt, so dass alle in der Kategorie „bis zur Endfälligkeit zu haltende Finanzinvestitionen" befindlichen finanziellen Vermögenswerte umzugliedern sind. In beiden Fällen erfolgt die Umgliederung in die Kategorie „zur Veräußerung verfügbare finanzielle Vermögenswerte". Die Differenz zwischen Buchwert vor Umgliederung und dem beizulegenden Zeitwert in diesem Zeitpunkt ist im sonstigen Ergebnis zu erfassen.

(e) **in die Kategorie Kredite und Forderungen**: Umgliederungen in diese Kategorie können sich aus der Umgliederung von finanziellen Vermögenswerten der Kategorien erfolgswirksam zum beizulegenden Zeitwert bewertet und zur Veräußerung verfügbare finanzielle Vermögenswerte ergeben, wenn ein Unternehmen nunmehr die Fähigkeit und Absicht hat, diese finanziellen Vermögenswerte mindestens für die absehbare Zukunft zu halten und die finanziellen Vermögenswerte die Definition der Kategorie „Kredite und Forderungen" erfüllen (IAS 39.50D-E). Der beizulegende Zeitwert im Zeitpunkt der Umgliederung stellt die fortgeführten Anschaffungskosten in diesem Zeitpunkt dar. Bei einer Umgliederung aus der Kategorie „zur Veräußerung verfügbare finanzielle Vermögenswerte" sind sowohl zuvor im sonstigen Ergebnis erfasste Gewinne und Verluste als auch der Unterschiedsbetrag zwischen den fortgeführten Anschaffungskosten im Zeitpunkt der Umgliederung und dem Rückzahlungsbetrag bei Endfälligkeit gemäß der **Effektivzinsmethode** über die Restlaufzeit erfolgswirksam zu erfassen. Im Falle einer Wertminderung ist der Gesamtbetrag etwaiger zuvor im sonstigen Ergebnis erfasster Gewinne und Verluste sofort erfolgswirksam zu erfassen.

(f) **aus der „Kategorie Kredite und Forderungen"**: IAS 39 erlaubt keine Umgliederungen aus dieser Kategorie.

(g) **in die Kategorie „zur Veräußerung verfügbare finanzielle Vermögenswerte"**: Umgliederungen in diese Kategorie können sich aus Umgliederungen aus der Kategorie „bis zur Endfälligkeit zu haltende Finanzinvestitionen" ergeben (siehe Unterabschnitt (d) in dieser Rn.) Ferner können Umgliederungen aus der Kategorie „erfolgswirksam zum beizulegenden Zeitwert" bewertet unter den zuvor genannten seltenen Umständen (siehe Unterabschnitt (b) in dieser Rn.) zu einer Umgliederung in die Kategorie „zur Veräußerung verfügbare finanzielle Vermögenswerte" führen. Außerdem ist ein nicht auf einem aktiven Markt notiertes Eigenkapitalinstrument in die Kategorie zur Veräußerung verfügbare finanzielle Vermögenswerte umzugliedern, wenn der beizulegende Zeitwert dieses Eigenkapitalinstruments verlässlich ermittelbar wird. In diesen Fällen ist die Differenz zwischen vorherigem Buchwert und dem beizulegenden Zeitwert im Zeitpunkt der Umgliederung bis zu einer späteren Veräußerung oder Wertminderung im sonstigen Ergebnis zu erfassen (IAS 39.53 i.V.m. IAS 39.55).

(h) **aus der Kategorie „zur Veräußerung verfügbare finanzielle Vermögenswerte"**: Umgliederungen aus dieser Kategorie können sich aus Umgliederungen in die Kategorie „bis zur Endfälligkeit zu haltende Finanzinvestitionen" ergeben (siehe Unterabschnitt (c) in dieser Rn.) Ferner können sich Umgliederungen aus der Kategorie „zur Veräußerung verfügbare finanzielle Vermögenswerte" in die Kategorie „Kredite und Forderungen" aus einer Änderung der Fähigkeit und Absicht eines Unternehmens, diese finanziellen Vermögenswerte nunmehr mindestens für die absehbare Zukunft zu halten, ergeben (siehe Unterabschnitt (e) in dieser Rn.) Außerdem ist ein nicht auf einem aktiven Markt notiertes Eigenkapitalinstrument aus der Kategorie zur Veräußerung verfügbare finanzielle Vermögenswerte umzugliedern und zu Anschaffungskosten zu bewerten, wenn der beizulegende

---

94 Siehe Rn 118.

Zeitwert dieses Eigenkapitalinstruments nicht mehr verlässlich ermittelbar ist. In diesen Fällen stellt der beizulegende Zeitwert im Zeitpunkt der Umgliederung die Anschaffungskosten dar. Zuvor im sonstigen Ergebnis erfasste Gewinne und Verluste werden erst bei einer späteren Veräußerung oder Wertminderung erfolgswirksam in der Gewinn- und Verlustrechnung erfasst (IAS 39.54(b)).

4. Umgliederungen nach IFRS 9. Umgliederungen nach IFRS 9 ergeben sich ausschließlich bei einer **Änderung des Geschäftsmodells (IFRS 9.4.9)**.[95] IFRS 9 stellt klar, dass solche Umstände sehr selten sind, z.B. im Zusammenhang mit einem fundamentalen Strukturwandel im Zusammenhang mit einem Unternehmenszusammenschluss oder der Einstellung eines Geschäftsbereichs (IFRS 9.B5.9). Insbesondere sind reine Absichtsänderungen bzgl. individueller finanzieller Vermögenswerte, vorübergehende Änderungen von Marktgegebenheiten wie **Liquiditätsschwankungen** (für sich genommen – ohne dass dies einen fundamentalen, permanenten Strukturwandel auslöst) oder die Übertragung finanzieller Vermögenswerte zwischen Unternehmensbereichen mit verschiedenen Geschäftsmodellen keine Änderung des Geschäftsmodells i.S.v. IFRS 9 (IFRS 9.B5.11). 130

Eine Änderung des Geschäftsmodells wird erst prospektiv zum Beginn der auf diese Änderung folgenden Berichtsperiode (Umgliederungszeitpunkt) wirksam (IFRS 9.5.3.1). Bei einem Wechsel von einer Folgebewertung zu fortgeführten Anschaffungskosten zu einer zum beizulegenden Zeitwert ist der Unterschied zwischen diesen Beträgen (ermittelt zum Umgliederungszeitpunkt) erfolgswirksam in der Gewinn- und Verlustrechnung zu erfassen (IFRS 9.5.3.2). Umgekehrt stellt bei einem Wechsel von einer Folgebewertung zum beizulegenden Zeitwert zu einer zu fortgeführten Anschaffungskosten der beizulegende Zeitwert (ermittelt zum Umgliederungszeitpunkt) den neuen Buchwert im Umgliederungszeitpunkt dar (IFRS 9.5.3.3). 131

VII. Zugangsbewertung. Die Vorschriften zur Zugangsbewertung von Finanzinstrumenten nach IAS 39 und IFRS 9 sind gleich. Die nachfolgenden Ausführungen beziehen sich daher soweit sie finanzielle Vermögenswerte betreffen gleichermaßen auf diese beiden Standards. 132

Die Bewertung von Finanzinstrumenten bei Zugang, die erfolgswirksam zum beizulegenden Zeitwert bewertet werden, erfolgt zum beizulegenden Zeitwert. Für alle anderen finanziellen Vermögenswerte werden dem beizulegenden Zeitwert **Transaktionskosten** hinzugerechnet und bei finanziellen Verbindlichkeiten entsprechend abgezogen (IAS 39.43; IFRS 9.5.1.1)). Transaktionskosten sind definiert (IAS 39.9) als zusätzliche Kosten, die ohne die Transaktion, die zum erstmaligen Ansatz des Finanzinstruments führt, nicht entstanden wären und der Transaktion unmittelbar zurechenbar sind. Beispiele sind Provisionen, Gebühren, Abgaben und Steuern. Dabei ist es unerheblich, ob diese an externe Parteien (z.B. Berater, Makler, Börsen, Finanzintermediäre oder Behörden) oder Mitarbeiter des Unternehmens (z.B. interne Provisionen) gezahlt werden. Daher sind interne und externe Gemeinkosten keine Transaktionskosten, d.h. solche Kosten dürfen nicht einzelnen Transaktionen zugeschlüsselt werden. Folglich sind z.B. Finanzierungskosten und interne Verwaltungskosten nicht in die erstmalige Bewertung einzubeziehen (IAS 39.AG13). 133

Die Verwendung des beizulegenden Zeitwerts zum Zweck der Zugangsbewertung hat in zwei Umständen praktische Bedeutung: 134

- **Abweichung des beizulegenden Zeitwerts vom Transaktionspreis:** weicht der beizulegende Zeitwert vom Transaktionspreis (ausschließlich etwaiger Transaktionskosten) ab, so ist die Art der Ermittlung des beizulegenden Zeitwerts entscheidend für die Bilanzierung. Ist der beizulegende Zeitwert entweder ein direkt (d.h. für das gleiche Finanzinstrument) beobachtbarer Marktpreis oder das Ergebnis eines Bewertungsverfahrens, das ausschließlich an Märkten beobachtbare Parameter verwendet, so ist die Differenz zwischen Transaktionspreis und beizulegendem Zeitwert sofort erfolgs-

---

95   Zum Geschäftsmodell siehe Rn 127.

wirksam als Gewinn oder Verlust zu erfassen (**day one gain/loss**). Wird der beizulegende Zeitwert dagegen auf eine andere Art ermittelt (d.h. unter Verwendung wesentlicher nicht an einem Markt beobachtbarer Variablen), so ist eine Differenz zwischen Transaktionspreis und beizulegendem Zeitwert nur nach der erstmaligen Bewertung und nur insoweit zu erfassen, wie er auf Änderungen eines Faktors beruht, den Marktteilnehmer bei der Preisbildung berücksichtigen würden. Solche Faktoren umfassen auch den Zeitablauf (IAS 39.AG76-76A). Allerdings lassen die Vorschriften offen, welche Verteilungsmethoden für die Differenz konkret in Betracht kommen. Im Hinblick auf die Frage, ob eine lineare Verteilung über die Laufzeit des Finanzinstruments zulässig sei, lehnte das IASB eine Klarstellung ab und gab lediglich den Hinweis, dass eine solche Verteilung in einigen Fällen angemessen sein könne, in anderen dagegen nicht (IAS 39.BC222(v)(ii)). Dazu ist anzumerken, dass eine lineare Verteilung nur in Ausnahmefällen die Preisbildung durch Marktteilnehmer widerspiegelt. Dies liegt daran, dass Zinsberechnungen (und damit die Einbeziehung des **Zeitwerts des Geldes**) mit Ausnahme vereinfachter unterjähriger Verzinsung auf Exponentialrechnung statt linearer Mathematik beruhen. Insbesondere der Faktor Zeit kann daher regelmäßig *nicht* als Grundlage einer linearen Verteilung angeführt werden, sondern erfordert im Gegenteil eine nicht-lineare Verteilung. In der Praxis finden als angemessene Verteilungsmethoden z.B. die folgende Vorgehensweisen Anwendung: eine Erfassung der Differenz in dem Zeitpunkt, in dem erstmals alle verwendeten Variablen an einem Markt beobachtbar sind (z.B. wenn in die Berechnung einfließende Terminpreise erstmals in den Zeitraum der Terminkurve fallen, der an einem aktiven Markt beobachtbar ist). Eine andere Methode ist die Kalibrierung der Ermittlung des beizulegenden Zeitwerts auf den Transaktionspreis, indem eine nicht an einem aktiven Markt beobachtbare Variable angepasst wird. Diese Variable wird dann an den folgenden Bewertungsstichtagen in gleicher Weise wie zum Zeitpunkt der erstmaligen Bewertung angepasst. Bei Finanzinstrumenten mit periodischen Zahlungen wie z.B. Swaps mit monatlichen oder quartalsweisen Nettozahlungen ergibt sich implizit eine Erfassung der ursprünglichen Differenz über die Laufzeit (jedoch auf einer nicht-linearen Basis).

- **Abweichung zwischen Transaktion und Finanzinstrument**: Wenn das zwischen den Parteien gezahlte Entgelt sich nicht ausschließlich auf das Finanzinstrument bezieht, sondern auch andere Aspekte betrifft, umfasst die Transaktion mehr als nur das Finanzinstrument. Das Entgelt stellt unter diesen Umständen daher nicht den Transaktionspreis des Finanzinstruments (allein) dar. Daher ist der Transaktionspreis auf den beizulegenden Zeitwert des Finanzinstruments einerseits und seine übrigen Bestandteile andererseits aufzuteilen. Diese übrigen Bestandteile sind separat unter Heranziehung der IFRS insgesamt hinsichtlich ihrer Bilanzierung zu würdigen (IAS 39.AG64). Gewährt z.B. ein Mutterunternehmen einem Tochterunternehmen ein **unverzinsliches Darlehen** zum Nominalwert, so beträgt der beizulegende Zeitwert des Darlehens für den Zweck dessen erstmaliger Bewertung den Barwert des Tilgungsbetrags diskontiert mit dem Zinssatz, der vom Tochterunternehmen für ein nach Höhe, Fälligkeit und Besicherung (Kreditrisiko) sowie etwaiger anderer Ausstattungsmerkmale (u.a. Nullkupon) vergleichbares Darlehen als marktgerechter Zins zu entrichten wäre. Der Unterschiedsbetrag zwischen dem gezahlten Nominalwert und dem niedrigeren beizulegenden Zeitwert stellt eine Kapitaleinlage des Mutterunternehmens beim Tochterunternehmen dar und ist als solche zu bilanzieren. Ein anderes Beispiel sind sogenannte **Lockangebote** (oder **loss leader**), bei denen ein Unternehmen Finanzprodukte unter Marktwert anbietet, um Marktanteile zu gewinnen. Wenn z.B. eine Bank ein Darlehen mit einer unterverzinslichen Anfangsperiode (die nicht durch nachfolgende überverzinsliche Perioden insgesamt auf Marktniveau ausgeglichen wird) ausreicht, um Neukunden zu gewinnen, so erfolgt die erstmalige Bewertung durch die Bank zum beizulegenden Zeitwert und die Differenz zum höheren Auszahlungsbetrag des Darlehens stellt Vertriebsaufwand dar, der sofort in vollem Umfang erfolgswirksam zu erfassen ist.

Die Zugangsbewertung von **Forderungen aus Lieferungen und Leistungen** ist ein Sachverhalt, bei   **135**
dem die IFRS-Vorschriften einerseits und die Praxis andererseits in einem problematischen Verhältnis
stehen. IAS 39 erfordert die erstmalige Bewertung aller Finanzinstrumente zum beizulegenden Zeitwert
(ggf. mit Anpassung für Transaktionskosten). In der Praxis werden kurzfristige Forderungen aus Lieferungen und Leistungen bei ihrem erstmaligen Ansatz regelmäßig zum **Nominalwert** bewertet. Dies wird
oft damit gerechtfertigt, dass IAS 39 explizit im Hinblick auf die Bewertung zum beizulegenden Zeitwert
ausführt, dass kurzfristige Forderungen und Verbindlichkeiten ohne festgelegten Zinssatz mit dem ursprünglichen **Rechnungsbetrag** bewertet werden können, sofern der Abzinsungseffekt unwesentlich ist
(IAS 39.AG79). Dabei ist jedoch zu beachten, dass IAS 39 diese Vereinfachung davon abhängig macht,
dass ihr Effekt nicht wesentlich ist, und dass diese Wesentlichkeitsbeurteilung auch den Effekt des Kreditrisikos einbeziehen muss. Dies liegt daran, dass der relevante Diskontierungszinssatz das mit der jeweiligen Forderung verbundene Kreditrisiko widerspiegeln muss (IAS 39.AG79 und AG82(b)).[96] Eine
Wesentlichkeitsbeurteilung, die auf der Laufzeit der Forderung und dem riskofreien Zinsniveau oder
dem den Swapsätzen zu Grunde liegenden Kreditrisiko (z.B. LIBOR Zinsniveau) beruht, ist daher nicht
im Einklang mit IAS 39. Auch ein Verweis auf IAS 18 *Revenue* führt zum selben Ergebnis, da Umsatzerlöse zum *beizulegenden Zeitwert* des zu beanspruchenden Entgelts (d.h. des Zahlungsversprechens) statt
zum Nominalwert zu bewerten sind (IAS 18.9). In der Praxis wird dagegen erst bei mittel- und langfristigen Forderungen eine Abzinsung und damit auch eine Bewertung des Kreditrisikos vorgenommen.

VIII. Folgebewertung. 1. Folgebewertung nach IAS 39. a) Finanzielle Vermögenswerte. Die Fol-   **136**
gebewertung nach IAS 39 folgt weitgehend den Kategorien[97], die der Standard für Finanzinstrumente
definiert (IAS 39.45). Grundsätzlich erfolgt die Folgebewertung zum beizulegenden Zeitwert oder zu
fortgeführten Anschaffungskosten mit einigen Sonderregelungen für bestimmte Finanzinstrumente, die
speziellen Bewertungsmethoden unterliegen. Für nicht zum beizulegenden Zeitwert bewertete Finanzinstrumente kann sich ferner aufgrund der Vorschriften zur Bilanzierung für Sicherungsgeschäfte eine
Abweichung von der normalen Folgebewertung ergeben (siehe dazu den Abschnitt „Bilanzierung von
Sicherungsgeschäften").

Für finanzielle Vermögenswerte ergibt sich die Folgebewertung in Abhängigkeit ihrer Kategorisie-   **137**
rung wie folgt:
- **Erfolgswirksam zum beizulegenden Zeitwert bewertet**: beizulegender Zeitwert.
- **Bis zur Endfälligkeit zu haltende Finanzinvestitionen**: fortgeführte Anschaffungskosten.
- **Kredite und Forderungen**: fortgeführte Anschaffungskosten.
- **Zur Veräußerung verfügbare finanzielle Vermögenswerte**: beizulegender Zeitwert.

Für Finanzinvestitionen in Eigenkapitalinstrumente besteht eine Ausnahme von der Bewertung   **138**
zum beizulegenden Zeitwert, wenn diese Instrument nicht auf einem **aktiven Markt** notiert sind und
auch mittels Bewertungsverfahren der beizulegende Zeitwert nicht verlässlich ermittelbar ist. Dies gilt
auch für derivative Finanzinstrumente, die sich auf solche Eigenkapitalinstrumente beziehen und durch
Übertragung dieser Instrumente (d.h. physisch) zu erfüllen sind. Die Bewertung dieser Eigenkapitalinstrumente und derivativen Finanzinstrumente erfolgt zu deren Anschaffungskosten ggf. abzüglich
Wertminderung (IAS 39.46(c)).

In der Praxis ist diese Ausnahme teilweise sehr weitgehend angewandt worden, so dass für Anteile   **139**
an nicht notierten Unternehmen die Bewertung zu Anschaffungskosten eher die Regel als die Ausnahme
darstellt. Dies ist im Hinblick auf die Anwendungsleitlinien zu dieser Ausnahme problematisch. Diese
stellen klar, dass die Schätzung des beizulegenden Zeitwerts für von Dritten erworbene finanzielle Ver-

---

96   IAS 18.11(a) enthält eine entsprechende Regelung im Zusammenhang mit Forderungen aus Lieferungen und Leistungen.
97   Siehe Rn 103f.

mögenswerte in der Regel *möglich* ist (IAS 39.AG81). Daher ist die weit verbreitete Praxis, nicht notierte Eigenkapitalinstrumente wie z.B. **GmbH-Anteile** allein mangels Notierung an einer Börse zu Anschaffungskosten zu bewerten, fragwürdig.

140   **b) Finanzielle Verbindlichkeiten.** Für finanzielle Verbindlichkeiten ergibt sich die Folgebewertung in Abhängigkeit ihrer Kategorisierung wie folgt:

- **Erfolgswirksam zum beizulegenden Zeitwert bewertet**: beizulegender Zeitwert.
- **Alle übrigen finanziellen Verbindlichkeiten** (dies sind finanzielle Verbindlichkeiten, die weder zum erfolgswirksam zum beizulegenden Zeitwert bewertet werden noch einer der im Folgenden beschriebenen besonderen Folgebewertungen unterliegen): fortgeführte Anschaffungskosten.

141   Daneben bestehen folgende besondere Folgebewertungen für finanzielle Verbindlichkeiten:

- **Derivate auf nicht notierte Eigenkapitalinstrumente**: im Einklang mit der Ausnahme bzgl. finanzieller Vermögenswerte[98] besteht auch für derivative Finanzinstrumente die Verbindlichkeiten sind eine Ausnahme von der Bewertung zum beizulegenden Zeitwert. Dies betrifft derivative Verbindlichkeiten, die sich auf Eigenkapitalinstrumente ohne Notierung auf einem aktiven Markt beziehen, deren beizulegender Zeitwert nicht verlässlich ermittelbar ist, wenn das Derivat durch Übertragung solcher Eigenkapitalinstrumente zu erfüllen ist. Die Bewertung dieser Derivate erfolgt zu Anschaffungskosten (IAS 39.47(a)).
- **Finanzielle Verbindlichkeiten als Folge der Übertragung finanzieller Vermögenswerte**: in bestimmten Fällen ergibt sich als Folge der Bilanzierung von Übertragungen finanzieller Vermögenswerte, die nicht zu deren vollständiger Ausbuchung führen, eine Verbindlichkeit *sui generis*. Solche Verbindlichkeiten unterliegen einer besonderen Folgebewertung, die im Zusammenhang mit den Vorschriften zur Ausbuchung finanzieller Vermögenswerte geregelt ist (IAS 39.47(b)).
- **Finanzielle Garantien**: eine finanzielle Garantie ist definiert als Vertrag zwischen Garantiegeber und Garantienehmer, der bestimmte Entschädigungszahlungen im Fall eines Verlusts des Garantienehmers aufgrund nicht fristgemäßer Zahlung eines bestimmten Schuldners unter den Bedingungen eines Schuldinstruments erfordert. Die Folgebewertung einer finanziellen Garantie erfolgt zum höheren Betrag aus (i) demjenigen, der sich gemäß IAS 37 (für eine Rückstellung) ergeben würde, und (ii) dem Betrag bei erstmaliger Bewertung abzüglich der kumulierten als Ertrag gemäß IAS 18 erfassten Beträge (IAS 39.47(c)).
- **Kreditzusagen zu Zinskonditionen unterhalb des Marktzinssatzes**: obwohl solche Kreditzusagen derivative Finanzinstrumente sind (IAS 39.BC15), erfolgt die Folgebewertung nicht zum beizulegenden Zeitwert, sondern wie die für finanzielle Garantien.[99]

142   **2. Folgebewertung nach IFRS 9.** Für die Folgebewertung nach IFRS 9 wird auf die Ausführungen zur Kategorisierung verwiesen (siehe Abschnitt „**Kategorisierung nach IFRS 9**").

143   **3. Bewertungsmethoden zur Folgebewertung. a) Beizulegender Zeitwert.** Der **beizulegende Zeitwert** ist in IAS 39[100] (und durch Bezugnahme darauf in gleicher Weise in IFRS 9[101]) definiert als derjenige Betrag, der dem Tausch eines finanziellen Vermögenswerts oder der Begleichung einer finanziellen Verbindlichkeit in einer Transaktion zwischen sachverständigen, vertragswilligen voneinander unabhängigen Parteien zugrunde liegen würde. Aus dieser Definition folgt, dass der beizulegende Zeitwert unter Annahme der **Unternehmensfortführung** bestimmt wird, so dass Werte, die Transaktionen oder eine Liquidation unter Zwang oder Notverkäufe widerspiegeln, außer Acht bleiben (IAS 39.AG69).

---

98   Siehe Rn 138.
99   Siehe den zweiten Unterpunkt in dieser Rn.
100   Siehe IAS 39.9.
101   Siehe IFRS 9, Anhang A.

Die Bestimmung des beizulegenden Zeitwerts nach IAS 39 (und damit auch IFRS 9) erfolgt auf der Basis der folgenden Hierarchie: 144

- **Preisnotierungen auf einem aktiven Markt**: liegen solche Preisnotierungen vor, so sind diese als beizulegender Zeitwert zu verwenden, da sie den besten objektiven Hinweis auf den beizulegenden Zeitwert darstellen (IAS 39.AG71).
- **Bewertungsverfahren**: die Bestimmung des beizulegenden Zeitwerts von Finanzinstrumenten, die nicht auf einem aktiven Markt notiert sind, erfolgt mittels Bewertungsverfahren. Generell muss ein Bewertungsverfahren alle Faktoren einbeziehen, die von Marktteilnehmern berücksichtigt werden würden, und im Einklang mit anerkannten wirtschaftlichen Methoden zur Preisfindung für Finanzinstrumente stehen (IAS 39.AG76). Wenn es ein unter Marktteilnehmern weit verbreitetes Bewertungsverfahren gibt, das sich als gute Näherung für tatsächliche Transaktionspreise erwiesen hat, so ist dieses Verfahren zu wählen. Generell hat ein Bewertungsverfahren so weit wie möglich Marktdaten statt unternehmensspezifischer Daten zu verwenden. Die Art der verwendeten Daten hat Auswirkungen auf die Bilanzierung einer etwaigen Abweichung des beizulegenden Zeitwerts vom Transaktionspreis (siehe die Ausführungen zur erstmaligen Bewertung in Rn. 134). **Bewertungsmethoden** umfassen z.B. die Verwendung von Informationen aus Markttransaktionen in jüngerer Vergangenheit oder aktuellen beizulegenden Zeitwerten ähnlicher Finanzinstrumente, Barwertverfahren und Optionspreismodelle (IAS 39.48A).

In der Praxis hat die Bestimmung beizulegender Zeitwerte zu zahlreichen Problemen geführt. Dies   145 betrifft insbesondere die Einbeziehung des **Kreditrisikos** in den beizulegenden Zeitwert. So sehen z.B. viele Standardprogramme zur Ermittlung beizulegender Zeitwerte keine expliziten Eingabeparameter für das Kreditrisiko vor. Bei Derivaten, die wechselseitige Zahlungen der Vertragsparteien auf Brutto- oder Nettobasis vorsehen (z.B. Zinsswaps), ist zudem das Kreditrisiko aller Parteien (d.h. auch das des bilanzierenden Unternehmens) zu berücksichtigen. Dies wird zusätzlich dadurch erschwert, dass das Kreditrisiko des jeweils zu bewertenden Finanzinstruments maßgeblich ist, was aufgrund von Kreditsicherheiten, der Rangfolge im Insolvenzfall etc. von der Bonität der Vertragspartei abweichen kann. Die Art und Verfahren der Einbeziehung des Kreditrisikos in die Bestimmung beizulegender Zeitwerte befindet sich für komplexe Produkte derzeit noch in der Entwicklung.

b) Fortgeführte Anschaffungskosten. Die Bewertungsmethode „fortgeführte Anschaffungskosten"   146 ist für IAS 39 und IFRS 9 identisch (IAS 39.9; IFRS 9, Appendix A). Die Beschreibung dieser Bewertungsmethode erfolgt weitgehend mittels der beiden Definitionen von „fortgeführte Anschaffungskosten eines finanziellen Vermögenswerts oder einer finanziellen Verbindlichkeit" und „Effektivzinsmethode", die gegenseitig auf einander Bezug nehmen. Die beiden Definitionen beschreiben die Bewertungsmethode aus zwei verschiedenen Perspektiven, was das Verständnis der Bewertungsmethode in der Praxis erschwert hat.

Die Definition „fortgeführte Anschaffungskosten eines finanziellen Vermögenswerts oder einer finanziellen Verbindlichkeit" beschreibt die Bewertung als denjenigen Betrag, der sich aus der Anpassung des Betrags bei erstmaligem Ansatz für die (kumulierte) Amortisation eines Unterschiedsbetrags zwischen diesem Betrag und dem Fälligkeitsbetrag, Tilgungen und Wertminderungen ergibt. Diese Beschreibung spiegelt die traditionelle Sichtweise eines anschaffungskostenbasierten Betrags wider, der dann für Abgrenzungsbuchungen etc. angepasst wird. Allerdings ist zu beachten, dass für die Bestimmung der kumulierten Amortisation die **Effektivzinsmethode** anzuwenden ist. Das präzisere und umfassendere Verständnis der Bewertungskategorie ergibt sich daher – insbesondere für kompliziertere Fälle – aus der Definition der Effektivzinsmethode.   147

148   Die Definition der „Effektivzinsmethode" beschreibt die Bewertung – indirekt – als den **mittels des Effektivzinssatzes ermittelten Barwert der geschätzten künftigen Cashflows** des Finanzinstruments. Dabei sind die Cashflows auf Basis der Vertragskonditionen wie z.B. bzgl. vorzeitiger Rückzahlungen zu schätzen. Nur wenn eine solche Schätzung nicht verlässlich möglich ist, kann stattdessen die maximale Vertragslaufzeit herangezogen werden. Für Gruppen von Finanzinstrumenten besteht die widerlegbare Vermutung, dass eine verlässliche Schätzung möglich ist. Für die Bestimmung des Effektivzinssatzes sind alle zwischen den Vertragsparteien gezahlten Gebühren, die gem. IAS 18 integraler Bestandteil der Effektivverzinsung sind, **Transaktionskosten** sowie **Agien** und **Disagien** einzubeziehen. Im Gegensatz dazu sind künftige Kreditausfälle von der Schätzung der Cashflows auszunehmen. Bei finanziellen Vermögenswerten, die mit einem hohen Abschlag erworben werden, der bereits objektive Hinweise auf Kreditausfälle widerspiegelt, sind diese Kreditausfälle jedoch bei der Schätzung der Cashflows zum Zweck der Effektivzinssatzermittlung einzubeziehen (IAS 39.AG5). Die Ermittlung der fortgeführten Anschaffungskosten als Barwert führt auch dazu, dass sich auch nach Erfassung einer Wertminderung auf einen finanziellen Vermögenswert weiterhin ein Zinsertrag ergibt (IAS 39.AG93). Dies ist auf den Effekt des Anstiegs des Barwerts aufgrund des Zeitfortschritts, d.h. der sich verkürzenden Abzinsungsperiode (sog. „**unwinding**" Effekt) zurückzuführen. Daher ergibt sich nach IFRS immer ein Zinsertrag, es sei denn, ein finanzieller Vermögenswert ist vollständig wertberichtigt (d.h. hat einen Buchwert von Null).

149   Der Effektivzinssatz ist derjenige Zinssatz, der die geschätzten künftigen Cashflows des Finanzinstruments auf dessen Buchwert abzinst (IAS 39.9). Es handelt sich somit um einen **internen Zinsfuß**, der mittels Iteration zu bestimmen ist. In der Praxis sind iterative Berechnungen nur schwierig in IT-Systeme zu integrieren, insbesondere da die relevanten Cashflows oft über die vertraglich bedungenen hinausgehen (z.B. Transaktionskosten) oder Schätzungen im Rahmen vertraglich vereinbarter Bandbreiten erfordern (z.B. Annahmen bzgl. vorzeitiger Rückzahlung). Für größere Gruppen oder Portfolien ist die Erfassung der erforderlichen Rohdaten für geschätzte Cashflows und die nachfolgende Ermittlung eines internen Zinsfußes mittels **Iteration** ebenfalls schwierig. Für geschlossene Portfolien kann die Berechnung zwar wie für ein einzelnes Finanzinstrument vorgenommen werden, aber für die in der Praxis vorherrschenden offenen Portfolien werden in der Regel Näherungslösungen verwendet. Dabei handelt es sich z.B. um eine Erfassung der Transaktionskosten auf Portfolioebene, für die ein Amortisationsprofil ermittelt wird, das als Anpassung des Zinsertrags (oder –aufwands) dem Ergebnis einer Effektivzinsberechnung nahe kommt. Die Ermittlung des Amortisationsprofils ist in Abhängigkeit der konkreten Umstände mehr oder minder kompliziert (z.B. linear oder nicht-linear).

150   Für **festverzinsliche** Finanzinstrumente wird der Effektivzinssatz im Zeitpunkt des erstmaligen Ansatzes bestimmt und dann für die gesamte Laufzeit konstant gehalten (der sog. ursprüngliche Effektivzinssatz) (IAS 39.AG8). Dies gilt auch, wenn im Rahmen der Folgebewertung eine Wertminderung zu bilanzieren ist (IAS 39.AG84). Aufgrund der Verwendung eines konstanten Effektivzinssatzes führt jede Änderung in der Schätzung der künftigen Cashflows zu einer Abweichung des Barwerts dieser Cashflows von dem Buchwert, der sich ohne Schätzungsänderung ergeben hätte. Diese Differenz ist sofort (d.h. in der Periode, in der die Schätzung revidiert wurde) erfolgswirksam in der Gewinn- und Verlustrechnung zu erfassen (IAS 39.AG8). Solche Schätzungsänderungen betreffen z.B. Annahmen bzgl. der vorzeitigen Rückzahlung eines Finanzinstruments.

151   Für **variabel verzinsliche** Finanzinstrumente ist die Anwendung der Effektivzinsmethode komplizierter als bei festverzinslichen Finanzinstrumenten. Ursache ist, dass der Effektivzinssatz nicht wie bei festverzinslichen Finanzinstrumenten für die gesamte Laufzeit konstant gehalten wird, sondern sich mit jeder Änderung des Markzinsniveaus ändert (IAS 39.AG7). Dies liegt daran, dass jede Änderung der **Zinsstrukturkurve** des Referenzzinssatzes die Terminzinssätze und damit die darauf beruhende Schätzung der künftigen variablen Zins-Cashflows ändert. Sofern der Buchwert des variabel verzinslichen

Finanzinstruments dem Nominalwert entspricht, hat die Änderung der Zinsstrukturkurve keinen Effekt im Vergleich zu einer Nominalwertbilanzierung mit Zinsabgrenzung auf Basis des jeweils festgelegten Zinskoupons (d.h. bgzl. der jeweils laufenden Zinsperiode). In solchen Fällen heben sich die Auswirkungen der Änderung Schätzung der künftigen variablen Zins-Cashflows einerseits und der Änderung der Diskontierungszinssätze andererseits auf. Daher entspricht bei zu pari emittierten oder erworbenen variabel verzinslichen Darlehen oder Anleihen der Zinsertrag oder -aufwand oft dem anteiligen Koupon (oder anteiligen Koupons) der für die jeweilige(n) Periode(n) entsprechend dem bedungenen Referenzzinssatz festgelegt wurde.

Weicht jedoch der Buchwert mehr als nur unwesentlich vom Nominalwert ab, so kann die Änderung der Zinsstrukturkurve Auswirkungen auf den Buchwert des Finanzinstruments haben. Dies ist z.B. bei signifikanten Transaktionskosten, Agien oder Disagien, oder nach der Erfassung einer Wertminderung der Fall. Die Anwendung der Effektivzinsmethode in diesen Fällen ist in der Praxis uneinheitlich und umstritten. Im Mai und Juli 2008 hat das IFRIC die Anwendung der Effektivzinsmethode im Zusammenhang mit inflationsindexierten Produkten und anderen vertraglich vereinbarten Änderungen von Zinszahlungen diskutiert (z.B. im Hinblick auf Anpassungen von Zinszahlungen aufgrund der Änderung der Bonität des Schuldners im Hinblick auf vertraglich festgelegte Kennzahlen oder Ratings).[102] Das IFRIC verwies die Frage an das IASB zwecks Klarstellung der Regelungen in IAS 39. Das IASB diskutierte die Anwendung der Effektivzinsmethode im Oktober 2008 und kam zum vorläufigen Ergebnis, dass ein variabel verzinsliches Finanzinstrument eine Variabilität der vertraglichen Cashflows in Abhängigkeit von Änderungen von Markt-Variablen aufweist, und dass *diese Art* der Cashflow-Variabilität bei Ermittlung des Effektivzinssatzes nicht berücksichtigt wird.[103] Diese Änderungen sollten im Rahmen des „Annual Improvement Process" umgesetzt werden, sind aber im Hinblick auf das aktive Projekt zur Ablösung von IAS 39 nicht vollendet worden. Der im November 2009 vom IASB veröffentlichte Standardentwurf *Financial Instruments: Amortised Cost and Impairment* sieht eine Anwendung der Effektivzinsmethode vor, die für variabel verzinsliche Finanzinstrumente eine Verwendung von Cashflow Schätzungen auf Basis von Terminzinssätzen erfordert. Bis zur Vollendung dieses Projektabschnitts bzgl. der Bewertungsmethode „fortgeführte Anschaffungskosten" ist daher eine weiterhin uneinheitliche Praxis bzgl. der zuvor genannten Fragestellungen zu erwarten. Je nach Auslegung der Regelungen können sich daher auch[104] bei variabel verzinslichen Finanzinstrumenten Gewinne und Verluste aus Schätzungsänderungen der künftigen Cashflows ergeben.

Bei variabel verzinslichen Finanzinstrumenten ist die Behandlung von Transaktionskosten, Agien und Disagien davon abhängig, auf welchen Zeitraum sie sich jeweils beziehen. Ein Agio oder Disagio, das die Änderung des beizulegenden Zeitwerts eines Instruments während der aktuellen Zinsperiode aufgrund der bereits zu Periodenbeginn erfolgten Zinsfestlegung widerspiegelt, ist über die verbleibende Laufzeit dieser Zinsperiode zu verteilen. Dagegen sind Transaktionskosten, die die Gesamt- oder verbleibende Restlaufzeit betreffen, sowie bonitätsbedingte Agien oder Disagien über die jeweils verbleibende Restlaufzeit des Finanzinstruments zu verteilen (IAS 39.AG6).

4. Erfassung von Gewinnen und Verlusten. Die Erfassung von Gewinnen und Verlusten, die sich im Rahmen der Folgebewertung[105] ergeben, erfolg in Abhängigkeit der Bewertungskategorien.

Die Gewinne und Verluste aus Änderungen des beizulegenden Zeitwerts für Finanzinstrumente der Kategorie **„erfolgswirksam zum beizulegenden Zeitwert bewertet"** werden in der jeweiligen Periode, in der sie entstehen, in der Gewinn- und Verlustrechnung erfasst.

152

153

154

155

---

102 Siehe IFRIC Update vom Juli 2008, 3.
103 Siehe IASB Update vom Oktober 2008, 2.
104 Siehe Rn 150 bzgl. festverzinslicher Finanzinstrumente.
105 Zu Gewinnen und Verlusten, die im Rahmen der erstmaligen Bewertung auftreten können, siehe Rn 134.

156   Für **zur Veräußerung verfügbare finanzielle Vermögenswerte** sind Gewinne und Verluste aus Änderungen des beizulegenden Zeitwerts wie folgt zu unterscheiden (IAS 39.55(b) und AG83):

- Die Änderungen des beizulegenden Zeitwerts im Hinblick auf Wertminderungen, den nach der Effektivzinsmethode ermittelten Zinsertrag (für Investitionen in Schuldinstrumente), den Dividendertrag gem. IAS 18 (für Investitionen in Eigenkapitalinstrumente) sowie für Investitionen in *Schuldinstrumente* in einer Fremdwährung den Wechselkursgewinn oder -verlust werden erfolgswirksam in der Gewinn- und Verlustrechnung erfasst.

- Alle übrigen Änderungen des beizulegenden Zeitwerts sind im sonstigen Ergebnis zu erfassen, bis der jeweilige Vermögensert ausgebucht wird. Im Zeitpunkt der Ausbuchung wird der kumulative im sonstigen Ergebnis erfasste Gewinn- oder Verlust in den Abgangserfolg einbezogen und damit erfolgswirksam.

157   Für Investitionen in Schuldinstrumente in einer Fremdwährung wird der erfolgswirksam zu erfassende Wechselkursgewinn oder -verlust unter Anwendung von IAS 21 auf Basis der fortgeführten Anschaffungskosten in der Fremdwährung erfasst. Der erfolgsneutral im sonstigen Ergebnis zu erfassende Gewinn oder Verlust ergibt sich als der Änderung der Differenz zwischen fortgeführten Anschaffungskosten und beizulegendem Zeitwert in der funktionalen Währung des bilanzierenden Unternehmens (IAS 39 IG E.3.2).

158   Eine von den zuvor genannten Regelungen abweichende Erfassung in der Gewinn- und Verlustrechnung oder im sonstigen Ergebenis kann sich aufgrund der Vorschriften zur Bilanzierung für Sicherungsgeschäfte ergeben.[106]

159   Für zu **fortgeführten Anschaffungskosten** bewertete Finanzinstrumente (d.h. die Kategorien „bis zur Endfälligkeit zu haltende Finanzinvestitionen", „Kredite und Forderungen" sowie zu fortgeführten Anschaffungskosten bewertete finanzielle Verbindlichkeiten) werden Gewinne und Verluste im Zeitpunkt der Ausbuchung in den Abgangserfolg einbezogen und damit erfolgswirksam. Auf Wertminderungen beruhende Verluste sowie Gewinne aus Wertaufholungen werden dagegen sofort erfolgswirksam in der Gewinn- und Verlustrechnung erfasst (IAS 39.56). Außerdem können sich Gewinne und Verluste im Zusammenhang mit Schätzungsänderungen bzgl. künftiger Cashflows ergeben, die im Rahmen der Effektivzinsmethode sofort ergebniswirksam erfasst werden.[107]

160   Eine von den zuvor genannten Regelungen abweichende Erfassung in der Gewinn- und Verlustrechnung oder im sonstigen Ergebenis kann sich aufgrund der Vorschriften zur Bilanzierung für Sicherungsgeschäfte ergeben.[108]

161   **5. Die Wertminderungen.** Die Bilanzierung von Wertminderungen nach IAS 39 beruht auf dem sog. „**incurred loss**" Modell. Demzufolge liegt eine Wertminderung ausschließlich dann vor, wenn sich aufgrund eines Ereignisses nach dem Zeitpunkt des erstmaligen Ansatzes objektive Hinweise auf eine Wertminderung ergeben (IAS 39.58-59). IAS 39 führt Beispiele von objektiven Hinweisen auf eine Wertminderung an, die teilweise nach Art des finanziellen Vermögenswerts differenzieren. Liegen solche Hinweise vor, ist ein ggf. bestehender Wertminderungsbedarf zu ermitteln und sofort in der Gewinn- und Verlustrechnung zu erfassen. Die Bemessung des Wertminderungsaufwands erfolgt in Abhängigkeit der Bewertungskategorien.

162   **a) Objektive Hinweise auf eine Wertminderung.** Objektive Hinweise auf eine Wertminderung umfassen u.a. die folgenden Beispiele (IAS 39.59):

---

106   Siehe Rn 202ff.
107   Siehe Rn 150 und 152.
108   Siehe Rn 202ff.

- Der Emittent oder Schuldner befindet sich in erheblichen finanziellen Schwierigkeiten. Die Herabstufung eines Bonitätsratings für sich genommen ist kein ausreichender Anhaltspunkt für eine Wertminderung. Allerdings kann eine solche Herabstufung in Verbindung mit anderen Informationen ein objektiver Hinweis sein. In ähnlicher Weise ist eine Verringerung des beizulegenden Zeitwerts bzgl. der Ursachen zu analysieren, um z.B. die Auswirkung eines Anstiegs des riskofreien Zinssatzes zu eliminieren (IAS 39.60).
- Nichterfüllung des Vertrags, z.B. Zahlungsausfall oder -verzug.
- Der Kreditgeber macht dem Kreditnehmer im Hinblick auf finanzielle Schwierigkeiten Zugeständnisse, die ansonsten nicht gewährt werden würden.
- Eine Insolvenz oder ein sonstiges Sanierungsverfahren des Kreditnehmers wird wahrscheinlich.
- Der aktive Markt für einen finanziellen Vermögenswert verschwindet aufgrund finanzieller Schwierigkeiten. Die Einstellung der Notierung eines börsennotierten Wertpapiers für sich genommen ist kein ausreichender Anhaltspunkt für eine Wertminderung, sondern ist auf eine Verbindung zu finanziellen Schwierigkeiten des Emittenten zu untersuchen (IAS 39.60).
- Wenn für eine Gruppe von finanziellen Vermögenswerten eine messbare Verringerung der erwarteten künftigen Cashflows seit deren erstmaligem Ansatz besteht, die auf beobachtbaren Daten beruht (selbst wenn die Verringerung noch nicht auf einzelne finanzielle Vermögenswerte in der Gruppe zurückgeführt werden kann). Dies betrifft z.B. nachteilige Veränderungen im Zahlungsstatus von Kreditnehmern in der Gruppe wie Minimumzahlungen oder Limiterreichung bei Kreditkarteninhabern. Ein anderes Beispiel sind Daten bzgl. der Korrelation von volkswirtschaftlichen oder regionalen wirtschaftlichen Rahmenbedingungen mit Kreditausfällen in der Gruppe wie bei einem Anstieg der Arbeitslosenquote oder einem Verfall der Immobilienpreise in den relevanten Gebieten des Wohnsitzes des Kreditnehmers oder Standorts der als Sicherheit dienenden Immobilie. Ferner kann z.B. auf Branchenebene ein Rückgang des Ölpreises für Unternehmenskredite in dieser Branche eine nachteilige Veränderung bei Kreditausfällen signalisieren. Diese Art von Hinweisen beruht auf dem sog. „incurred but not reported (**IBNR**)" Konzept (IAS 39.AG90). In der Praxis hat insbesondere die Auslegung der Frage, welche Informationen unter einem IBNR Ansatz einen objektiven Hinweis auf eine Wertminderung darstellen, für erhebliche Unterschiede beim Zeitpunkt der Erfassung von Wertminderungen geführt. Dies ist einer der Gründe, warum das IASB derzeit die Bilanzierung von Wertminderungen bei Finanzinstrumenten reformiert.[109]

Für Investitionen in Eigenkapitalinstrumente umfassen objektive Hinweise auf eine Wertminderung 163 u.A. die folgenden Beispiele (IAS 39.61):
- Informationen bzgl. wesentlicher für den Emittenten nachteiliger Änderungen in dessen technologischen, marktbezogenen, wirtschaftlichen oder rechtlichen Umfeld.
- Ein wesentlicher oder länger anhaltender Rückgang des beizulegenden Zeitwerts unter die Anschaffungskosten des Eigenkapitalinstruments. Dieses Kriterium war in der globalen **Finanzkrise** erheblichem Druck ausgesetzt und hat zu Unterschieden in seiner Auslegung geführt. Das IFRIC hat verschiedene Fragestellungen zu diesem Kriterium im Mai und Juli 2009 diskutiert und im Rahmen einer Agendaentscheidung folgende Auffassung vertreten:[110]
  - das Kriterium ist nicht kumultativ, d.h. ein Rückgang des beizulegenden Zeitwerts der *entweder* wesentlich *oder* länger anhaltend ist, stellt bereits einen objektiven Hinweis auf eine Wertminderung dar (das Kriterium kann daher nicht auf einen wesentlichen und länger anhaltenden Rückgang beschränkt werden);

---

109 Siehe Rn 1.
110 Siehe IFRIC Update vom Juli 2009, 5.

- wenn ein wesentlicher oder länger anhaltender Rückgang des beizulegenden Zeitwerts vorliegt, stellt dies einen objektiven Hinweis auf eine Wertminderung dar, so dass eine erfolgswirksame Wertberichtigung vorgenommen werden *muss*;

- die Tatsache, dass der Rückgang des beizulegenden Zeitwerts im Einklang mit der allgemeinen Entwicklung des relevanten Markts steht, rechtfertigt nicht die Schlussfolgerung, dass das Eigenkapitalinstrument nicht wertgemindert ist;

- das Vorliegen eines wesentlichen oder länger anhaltenden Rückgangs des beizulegenden Zeitwerts kann nicht durch Prognose einer erwarteten Erholung der Marktwerte kompensiert werden (solche Prognosen sind für die Beurteilung des Kriteriums irrelevant); und

- für Eigenkapitalinstrumente in Fremdwährung ist die Beurteilung, ob ein wesentlicher oder länger anhaltender Rückgang des beizulegenden Zeitwerts unter die Anschaffungskosten des Eigenkapitalinstruments vorliegt, auf Basis der Werte in der funktionalen Währung des Investors vorzunehmen (d.h. ein objektiver Hinweis auf eine Wertminderung kann sich auch allein aufgrund von Wechselkursänderungen ergeben).

164   Für zu fortgeführten Anschaffungskosten bewertete finanzielle Vermögenswerte enthält IAS 39 darüber hinaus auch Vorschriften bzgl. der Gruppierung für die Beurteilung, ob objektive Hinweise für eine Wertminderung vorliegen. Es ergibt sich folgende Vorgehensweise (IAS 39.64):

- Für individuell bedeutsame finanzielle Vermögenswerte ist zuerst eine Beurteilung auf individueller Basis vorzunehmen.
- Für nicht individuell bedeutsame finanzielle Vermögenswerte kann eine Beurteilung auf individueller Basis erfolgen. Andernfalls ist eine Beurteilung auf kollektiver Basis erforderlich.
- Alle auf individueller Basis beurteilten finanziellen Vermögenswerte, für die sich auf dieser Basis keine objektiven Hinweise auf eine Wertminderung ergeben haben, sind in Gruppen mit ähnlichen Kreditrisikomerkmalen zusammenzufassen und zusätzlich auf dieser Basis zu beurteilen. Wenn ein Unternehmen keine ähnlichen finanziellen Vermögenswerte hat, die eine solche Gruppierung ermöglichen, unterbleibt die zusätzliche Beurteilung (IAS 39.AG87).
- Sobald ein finanzieller Vermögenswert in einer Gruppe einzeln als wertgemindert identifiziert werden kann, ist er aus der Gruppe zu entfernen und einzeln zu beurteilen IAS 39.AG88). Einzeln als wertgemindert identifizierte finanzielle Vermögenswerte, für die eine Wertberichtigung erfasst ist, dürfen nicht in eine kollektive Beurteilung einbezogen werden.

165   **b) Bemessung einer Wertminderung und Wertaufholung.** Für zu **fortgeführten Anschaffungskosten** bewertete finanzielle Vermögenswerte (d.h. die Kategorien „bis zur Endfälligkeit zu haltende Finanzinvestitionen" und „Kredite und Forderungen") wird die Wertminderung als Differenz zwischen dem Buchwert und dem Barwert der geschätzten künftigen Cashflows ermittelt. Bei der Ermittlung des Barwerts sind diejenigen Kreditausfälle zu berücksichtigen, für die bereits objektive Hinweise aufgrund eines vergangenen Ereignisses vorliegen. Kreditausfälle, die ebenfalls bereits erwartet werden, für die aber noch keine objektiven Hinweise aufgrund vergangener Ereignisse vorliegen, sind dagegen nicht in die Barwertermittlung einzubeziehen (IAS 39.63). In der Praxis hat diese Unterscheidung des erwarteten Kreditausfalls in einen bereits objektiv eingetretenen und einen darüber hinaus erwarteten, aber noch nicht hinreichend konkretisierten Teil zu erheblichen Schwierigkeiten geführt. Insbesondere vor dem Hintergrund des sog. „incurred but not reported (**IBNR**)" Konzepts[111] ist diese Differenzierung von Kreditausfällen schwer fassbar, wenn überhaupt willkürfrei möglich.

166   Der relevante Diskontierungszinssatz bei der Barwertermittlung hängt von der Art des finanziellen Vermögenswerts ab:

---

111 Siehe Rn 162.

- Für **festverzinsliche** finanzielle Vermögenswerte ist der ursprüngliche Effektivzinssatz[112] maßgeblich (IAS 39.63).
- Für **variabel verzinsliche** finanzielle Vermögenswerte ist dagegen der aktuelle Effektivzinssatz heranzuziehen,[113] d.h. der Effektivzinssatz nach Anpassung für Änderungen des Markzinsniveaus (IAS 39.AG84).

Als Vereinfachung kann eine Wertminderung auf Basis des beizulegenden Zeitwerts des finanziellen Vermögenswerts statt des Barwerts der mit dem Effektivzinssatz diskontierten erwarteten künftigen Cashflows ermittelt werden. Voraussetzung ist, dass der beizulegende Zeitwert ein beobachtbarer Marktpreis ist (IAS 39.AG84). Ferner können **formel-basierte Ansätze** oder **statistischen Methoden** zur Bemessung von Wertminderungen bei Gruppen von finanziellen Vermögenswerten verwendet werden. Allerdings müssen solche Verfahren folgende Mindestanforderungen erfüllen (IAS 39.AG92): | 167

- Das Verfahren berücksichtigt den Effekt des Zeitwerts des Geldes (d.h. es dürfen keine undiskontierten Cashflows statt Barwerten verwendet werden).
- Die einbezogenen Cashflows (und damit die erwarteten Kreditausfälle) beziehen sich auf die gesamte Restlaufzeit des finanziellen Vermögenswerts (nicht nur z.B. das nächste Jahr).
- Das Verfahren berücksichtigt das Alter der finanziellen Vermögenswerte innerhalb des Portfolios.
- Es darf keine Wertminderung beim erstmaligen Ansatz des finanziellen Vermögenswerts (d.h. Auswirkung auf die Gewinn- und Verlustrechnung) geben. Somit sind **Pauschalwertberichtigungen** unzulässig, die – mindestens auch – Forderungen im Zeitpunkt ihres erstmaligen Ansatzes oder unmittelbar danach (ohne dass ein Ereignis eingetreten ist, das einen objektiven Hinweis auf eine Wertminderung darstellt) einbeziehen.[114]

Kreditsicherheiten sind bei der Ermittlung der geschätzten künftigen Cashflows zu berücksichtigen. Der relevante Cashflow ist der sich aus einer Zwangsvollstreckung ergebende nach Abzug der Kosten für Zwangsvollstreckung und Verwertung. Dies gilt unabhängig davon, ob eine Zwangsvollstreckung wahrscheinlich ist (IAS 39.AG84). Eine Kreditsicherheit wird erst dann nach den Vorschriften eines anderen Standards unmittelbar erfasst, wenn die Ansatzkriterien desjenigen Standards erfüllt sind (IAS 39.IG E.4.8) (z.B. IAS 16 *Property, Plant and Equipment* für Maschinen, die sicherungsübereignet waren). **Kreditgarantien**, die Garantieverträge sind, werden wie andere Kreditsicherheiten bei der Ermittlung der geschätzten künftigen Cashflows berücksichtigt. Jedoch ist zu beachten, dass viele Verträge über die Absicherung von Kreditrisiken Derivate statt Garantieverträge darstellen.[115] Derivate (z.B. Credit Default Swaps) dürfen nicht in die Bemessung der Wertminderung des zu fortgeführten Anschaffungskosten bewerteten finanziellen Vermögenswerts einbezogen werden, sondern sind als separates Finanzinstrument zu bilanzieren. In keinem Fall darf eine Doppelerfassung stattfinden. | 168

Eine **Wertaufholung** ist erfolgswirksam in der Gewinn- und Verlustrechnung zu erfassen, wenn sich die Höhe der Wertberichtigung verringert und diese Verringerung objektiv auf ein Ereignis nach Erfassung der Wertminderung zurückgeführt werden kann (IAS 39.65). Dabei können Umstände, die das Gegenteil von objektiven Hinweisen auf eine Wertminderung[116] darstellen, herangezogen werden. Die Wertaufholung darf nicht dazu führen, dass der Buchwert denjenigen übersteigt, der sich ohne vorherige Wertminderung ergeben hätte. D.h. für die Praxis die fortgeführten Anschaffungskosten schattenmäßig mitzuführen, um diese Organe zu ermitteln. | 169

---

112 Siehe Rn 150.
113 Siehe Rn 151ff.
114 Zu den Implikationen des im Zeitpunkt des erstmaligen Ansatzes bestehenden Kreditrisikos siehe Rn 135.
115 Siehe Rn 109.
116 Siehe Rn 162.

170   Für zu **Anschaffungskosten** bewertete finanzielle Vermögenswerte[117] wird die Wertminderung als Differenz zwischen dem Buchwert und dem Barwert der geschätzten künftigen Cashflows ermittelt. Der relevante Diskontierungszinssatz ist die aktuelle Marktrendite eines ähnlichen finanziellen Vermögenswerts. Für Wertminderungen dieser finanziellen Vermögenswerte besteht ein **Wertaufholungsverbot** (IAS 39.66).

171   Für **zur Veräußerung verfügbare finanzielle Vermögenswerte** entspricht die Wertminderung dem kumulierten im sonstigen Ergebnis erfassten Verlust. Dieser ist bei vorliegen eines objektiven Hinweises auf eine Wertminderung vom kumulierten sonstigen Ergebnis in die Gewinn- und Verlustrechnung umzugliedern, d.h. in voller Höhe erfolgswirksam zu erfassen (IAS 39.67). Dies gilt auch dann, wenn sich z.B. für ein Schuldinstrument eine geringe Wertminderung auf Basis des Wertminderungstests für zu fortgeführten Anschaffungskosten bewertete finanzielle Vermögenswerte ergeben würde. Mit anderen Worten, wenn eine Wertminderung vorliegt, erfolgt der Wertminderungstest immer auf Basis des beizulegenden Zeitwerts, ungeachtet der Tatsache, dass der beizulegende Zeitwert auch nicht kreditrisikobezogene Wertänderungen umfasst (z.B. aufgrund von Änderungen des **risikofreien Zinssatzes**).

172   Für **Wertaufholungen** ist nach der Art des finanziellen Vermögenswerts zu unterscheiden:
- Für Eigenkapitalinstrumente gilt ein Wertaufholungsverbot, d.h. ein späterer Anstieg des beizulegenden Zeitwerts darf nicht erfolgswirksam in der Gewinn- und Verlustrechnung erfasst werden, sondern stattdessen im sonstigen Ergebnis (IAS 39.69).
- Für Schuldinstrumente ist ein späterer Anstieg des beizulegenden Zeitwerts erfolgswirksam in der Gewinn- und Verlustrechnung als Wertaufholung zu erfassen, wenn er sich objektiv auf ein Ereignis nach der Erfassung der Wertminderung zurückführen lässt.

173   **IX. Sicherungsgeschäfte (hedging).** Die Bilanzierung von Sicherungsgeschäften (**hedge accounting**) gehört zu den kompliziertesten Fragestellungen der IFRS. Ein allgemeiner IFRS Kommentar kann dieses Spezialgebiet nicht umfassend behandeln, so dass im Folgenden ausschließlich die Grundzüge behandelt werden. Daher wird hier nicht auf die Bilanzierung von Sicherungsgeschäften bzgl. der Absicherung des beizulegenden Zeitwerts gegen Zinsänderungen auf Portfolioebene, die besonderen Vorschriften unterliegt (IAS 39.81A, 89A und AG114-AG132), eingegangen. Die Bilanzierung der Absicherung einer Nettoinvestition in einen ausländischen Geschäftsbetrieb wird im Kapitel zur Fremdwährungsumrechnung behandelt.

174   **1. Hintergrund.** Die Bilanzierung von Sicherungsgeschäften in IAS 39 wurde im Zusammenhang mit der Bilanzierung von derivativen Finanzinstrumenten entwickelt. Im Hinblick auf die grundsätzlich erfolgswirksame Bilanzierung von Derivaten zum beizulegenden Zeitwert dienen die besonderen Regelungen bzgl. Sicherungsgeschäften dazu, die Auswirkung dieser Bilanzierung in der Gewinn- und Verlustrechnung zu begrenzen. Dies geschieht auf der Grundlage der Kompensation (offset) von Änderungen des beizulegenden Zeitwerts oder der Cashflows, die auf Seiten des Sicherungsinstruments und des gesicherten Grundgeschäfts auftreten.

175   Die Bestimmung von Sicherungsinstrument und des zugehörigen gesicherten Grundgeschäfts ist daher die zentrale Fragestellung der Bilanzierung von Sicherungsgeschäften. Sie wirkt sich auf die Wirksamkeit der Sicherungsbeziehung aus und damit auch darauf, ob die Voraussetzungen für die Bilanzierung als Sicherungsgeschäft erfüllt sind, sowie auf den in der Gewinn- und Verlustrechnung für den unwirksamen (d.h. nicht gegenseitig kompensierenden) Teil der Änderungen des beizulegenden Zeitwerts oder der Cashflows zu erfassenden Betrag.

---

117 Siehe Rn 138.

Vor diesem Hintergrund wird auch deutlich, dass die Bilanzierung von Sicherungsgeschäften in IAS 39 nicht primär dazu dient, Informationen über die Risikomanagementstratgie eines Unternehmens, soweit sie auf Derivaten oder anderen Finanzinstrumenten beruht, zu vermitteln. Stattdessen ist der Zweck primär darauf beschränkt, Inkongruenzen oder Rechnungslegungsanomalien in Folge der Bilanzierung von Derivaten abzumildern. Dies hat in der Praxis zu einer erheblichen Divergenz zwischen der IFRS Bilanzierung und dem **Risikomanagement** von Unternehmen geführt. Mit anderen Worten, die Bilanzierung von Sicherungsgeschäften hat sich in vielen Fällen zu einem rein bilanziellen „Kunstgebilde" entwickelt (daher auch das aktive Projekt des IASB zur Reform der Bilanzierung von Sicherungsgeschäften[118]).

176

Eine Sicherungsbeziehung besteht zwischen Sicherungsinstrumenten einerseits und gesicherten Grundgeschäften andererseits. IAS 39 enthält Regelungen zur Bestimmung dieser beiden Bestandteile jeder Sicherungsbeziehung und regelt dann die Voraussetzungen, unter denen sich eine Sicherungsbeziehung für die besonderen Regelungen zur Bilanzierung von Sicherungsgeschäften qualifiziert. Diese besonderen Regelungen werden für drei verschiedene Arten von Sicherungsbeziehungen differenziert.[119]

177

2. Sicherungsinstrumente. Sicherungsinstrumente sind grundsätzlich auf derivative Finanzinstrumente beschränkt (IAS 39.72). Dabei kann es sich sowohl um freistehende Derivate als auch um diejenigen eingebetteten Derivate handeln, die von ihrem Basisvertrag abgespalten wurden (IAS 39.11 und IG F.1.2). **Geschriebene Optionen** (written options) können ungeachtet ihres Charakters als Derivat nicht als Sicherungsinstrument bestimmt werden, es sei denn, sie dienen der Absicherung einer erworbenen Option. Dabei kann die erworbene Option freistehend oder in ein anderes Finanzinstrument eingebettet sein (IAS 39.AG94). Im Falle einer freistehenden erworbenen Option stellt sich allerdings die Frage, was die Bilanzierung als Sicherungsbeziehung bewirken soll, da bereits die Bilanzierung als Derivat zur erfolgswirksamen Erfassung der Änderung des beizulegenden Zeitwerts in der Gewinn- und Verlustrechnung führt.

178

Ob eine erworbene Option vorliegt, ist auf Basis des jeweiligen Vertrags zu beurteilen. Bei Finanzinstrumenten, die sowohl geschriebene als auch erworbene Optionscharakteristika enthalten (z.B. **Zins-Collars**, also einer Kombination aus einem Zins-Cap und einem Zins-Floor) kommt es darauf an, ob bei einer Gesamtbetrachtung auf *Nettobasis* eine geschriebene Option vorliegt. Folgende (kumulative) Faktoren indizieren, dass – bei Nettobetrachtung – keine geschriebene Option vorliegt (IAS 39 IG F.1.3):

179

- die Vertragspartei erhält keine Optionsprämie, weder bei Vertragsschluss noch über die Laufzeit, während derer die verschiedenen Optionskomponenten kombiniert sind; und
- bis auf die Ausübungspreise oder -kurse (sog. strikes) sind alle anderen Vertragsmerkmale der geschriebenen und erworbenen Optionskomponenten identisch (z.B. Referenzinsatz, Währung, Laufzeit, etc.) Dabei darf die Bezugsgröße (z.B. der Nominalbetrag) der geschriebenen Optionskomponente diejenige der erworbenen Optionskomponente nicht übersteigen. Wird z.B. ein Collar für den Verkauf von Rohöl abgeschlossen, darf die Referenzmenge für den Rohöl-Cap (Preisobergrenze) nicht größer sein als die Referenzmenge für den Rohöl-Floor (Preisuntergrenze). Bei Absicherung des Rohöl-Einkaufs gilt dies entsprechend umgekehrt.

Sogenannte **Zero-Cost-Collar**, bei denen keine Prämie zwischen den Parteien gezahlt wird, qualifizieren sich demnach als Sicherungsinstrumente (aus Sicht beider Parteien). Da die Beurteilung auf Basis des jeweiligen Vertrags erfolgt (IAS 39.77), kann die Kombination zweier separater Optionsverträge, die in Kombination einen Collar darstellen (sog. **synthetischer Collar**), nicht als Sicherungsinstrument bestimmt werden. Obwohl die wirtschaftliche Wirkung der eines Collars entspricht, ist nur die erworbene Option zur Bestimmung als Sicherungsinstrument verfügbar.

---

118 Siehe Rn 1.
119 Siehe Rn 202.

180   Als Ausnahme können *nicht-derivative* finanzielle Vermögenswerte oder Verbindlichkeiten als Sicherungsinstrument (ausschließlich) für die Absicherung des Währungsrisikos bestimmt werden (IAS 39.72). Alle anderen nicht-derivativen Finanzinstrumente sind dagegen nicht für die Bestimmung als Sicherungsinstrument verfügbar. Dies hat insbesondere Auswirkungen auf hybride Finanzinstrumente,[120] bei denen das eingebettete Derivat nicht abgespalten wird. In diesen Fällen ist das eingebettete Derivat integraler Bestandteil des hybriden Finanzinstruments und somit (im Gegensatz zu abgespaltenen eingebetteten Derivaten[121]) ein nicht-derivatives Finanzinstrument und daher grundsätzlich nicht für eine Bestimmung als Sicherungsinstrument verfügbar.

181   Alle Sicherungsinstrumente müssen aus Sicht des bilanzierenden Unternehmens Verträge mit externen Parteien darstellen (IAS 39.73). Daher sind Verträge zwischen Konzerngesellschaften auf Ebene des Konzernabschlusses nicht für eine Bestimmung als Sicherungsinstrument verfügbar. Dagegen können auf Ebene des Einzelabschlusses einer Konzerngesellschaft Verträge mit anderen Konzerngesellschaften als Sicherungsinstrument bestimmt werden. Hintergrund dieser Beschränkung ist, dass konzerninterne Transaktionen im Rahmen der Konsolidierung eliminiert werden und ein konzerninternes Sicherungsgeschäft nicht zur Abwälzung von Risiken außerhalb des Konzerns sondern lediglich zu deren konzerninternen Umverteilung führt (IAS 39.BC170).

182   Sicherungsinstrumente können entweder in ihrer Gesamtheit oder in den folgenden Komponenten als Bestandteil einer Sicherungsbeziehung bestimmt werden:
- **Optionen** können in ihren Zeitwert und ihren inneren Wert aufgespalten werden. Der innere Wert kann als Sicherungsinstrument bestimmt werden mit der Folge, dass der Zeitwert wie ein freistehendes Derivat behandelt wird (IAS 39.74(a)).
- **Termingeschäfte** können in ihre Zinskomponente und ihren Kassakurs aufgespalten werden. Die mit dem Kassakurs verbundenen Wertänderungen des Termingeschäfts können als Sicherungsinstrument bestimmt werden mit der Folge, dass die mit der Zinskomponente verbundenen Wertänderungen des Termingeschäfts wie ein freistehendes Derivat behandelt werden (IAS 39.74(b)). Der Begriff des Termingeschäfts in IFRS ist demnach enger als nach dem Wertpapierhandelsgesetz (§2 Abs. 2 Nr. 1 WpHG) und umfasst nur Festgeschäfte. Der als „Zinskomponente" bezeichnete Bestandteil des Termingeschäfts ist dabei weit auszulegen. Eine Zinskomponente im engeren Sinn ergibt sich insbesondere bei Devisentermingeschäften sowie bei Zinstermingeschäften. Bei Warentermingeschäften dagegen ist der nach Abspaltung der Kassakurskomponente verbleibende Bestandteil keine reine Zinskomponente sondern umfasst Haltekosten im weiteren Sinne (cost of carry). Dies sind z.B. Kosten für die Lagerung von Rohstoffen. Daher ist für die Auslegung von IAS 39 die Zinskomponente als genereller Terminauf- oder -abschlag auszulegen (statt eines rein zinsbezogenen Auf- oder Abschlags).
- Ein **Teilbetrag** des Nominalvolumens eines Sicherungsinstruments kann als Bestandteil einer Sicherungsbeziehung bestimmt werden mit der Folge, dass der verbleibenden Teilbetrag wie ein freistehendes Derivat behandelt wird. Eine Aufteilung der Laufzeit des Sicherungsinstruments in Teilabschnitte zum Zweck der Bestimmung als Bestandteil einer Sicherungsbeziehung ist dagegen unzulässig (IAS 39.75). Daher ist ein Sicherungsinstrument stets für seine gesamte (Rest-) Laufzeit im Zeitpunkt der Bestimmung als Bestandteil einer Sicherungsbeziehung in diese einzubeziehen. Dies ist jedoch nicht damit zu verwechseln, dass die Laufzeit des Sicherungsinstruments nicht die des gesicherten Grundgeschäfts überschreiten dürfe. Wenn z.B. ein Zinsswap zwei Tage nach Laufzeitende des gesicherten Darlehens ausläuft hat dies Auswirkungen auf die Wirksamkeit der Sicherungsbeziehung aber verhindert nicht generell die Bestimmung des Zinsswaps als Sicherungsinstrument.

---

120 Siehe Rn 32.
121 Siehe Rn 178.

Friedhoff / Berger

Ein einzelnes Sicherungsinstrument kann darüber hinaus auch zur Absicherung verschiedener Risiken verwendet werden. Die Risiken können sich dabei auf verschiedene gesicherte Grundgeschäfte beziehen (z.B. Fremdwährungsverbindlichkeiten und -forderungen) und verschiedene Arten von Sicherungsbeziehungen darstellen (z.B. Absicherung von beizulegenden Zeitwerten und Zahlungsströmen) (IAS 39.776 und IG F.1.12). Solche Situationen treten z.B. im Zusammenhang mit der gleichzeitigen Absicherung verschiedener Währungen oder von Währungs- und Zinsrisiken mittels eines Sicherungsinstruments (z.B. Zins- und Währungsswap, sog. „**Cross Currency Interest Rate Swap**") auf. Für eine Bestimmung als Sicherungsinstrument zur Absicherung verschiedener Risiken bestehen folgende kumulative Voraussetzungen (IAS 39.76):

183

- die abgesicherten Risiken können eindeutig identifiziert werden;
- die Wirksamkeit des Sicherungsgeschäfts kann belegt werden; und
- die eindeutige Zuordnung des Sicherungsinstruments zu den jeweiligen Risikopositionen kann sichergestellt werden.

Aus diesen Beschränkungen folgt auch, dass *alle* risikobezogenen Bestandteile des Sicherungsinstruments Teil einer Sicherungsbeziehung sein müssen. Wenn ein risikobezogener Bestandteile nicht Teil einer Sicherungsbeziehung wäre, würde dies die Beschränkungen bzgl. der Aufteilung von Sicherungsinstrumente in Komponenten[122] unterlaufen.

Ferner können mehrere verschiedene Sicherungsgeschäfte zusammengefasst und gemeinsam als Sicherungsinstrument in einer einzigen Sicherungsbeziehung bestimmt werden. Dabei können derivative und nicht-derivative Sicherungsinstrumente kombiniert werden, selbst dann, wenn sich einzelne Risiken zwischen den Sicherungsinstrumenten (statt im Hinblick auf das gesicherte Grundgeschäft) kompensieren. Hierbei ist jedoch zu beachten, dass diese Kompensation von Risiken zwischen den Sicherungsinstrumenten nicht die Beschränkungen bzgl. der Bestimmung einer **geschriebenen Option** als Sicherungsinstrument[123] erweitert, sondern nachrangig ist. Daher kann eine geschriebene Option (oder Vertragsmerkmale eines Finanzinstruments, die eine solche darstellen) nicht in Kombination mit einer erworbenen Option gemeinsam als Sicherungsinstrument bestimmt werden (IAS 39.77).

184

3. Gesicherte Grundgeschäfte. IAS 39 enthält eine Vielzahl von Regelungen bzgl. der Art von Vermögenswerten, Schulden und Transaktionen, die als gesicherte Grundgeschäfte bestimmt werden können. Die Regelungen differenzieren nach verschiedenen Dimensionen der Art des Gegenstands oder der Transaktion (existierend oder künftiges Ereignis, Kategorisierung finanzieller Vermögenswerte, konzernintern oder -extern, finanziell oder nicht-finanziell) sowie ob es sich um eine Bestimmung auf Einzel- oder auf Gruppenbasis handelt.

185

Gesicherte Grundgeschäfte nach IAS 39 umfassen (IAS 39.78):

186

- in der Bilanz angesetzte Vermögenswerte und Schulden. Ausgenommen sind Derivate (freistehende und abgespaltene eingebettete Derivate), es sei denn, es handelt sich um eine erworbene Option, die das gesicherte Grundgeschäft in der Absicherung des beizulegenden Zeitwerts durch eine geschriebene Option ist (IAS 39 IG F.2.1). Außerdem dürfen als „bis zur Endfälligkeit zu haltende Finanzinvestitionen" kategorisierte finanzielle Vermögenswerte nicht als gesicherte Grundgeschäfte bzgl. des Zinsänderungsrisikos (sowohl bzgl. der Absicherung des beizulegenden Zeitwerts als auch von Zahlungsströmen) oder des Risikos vorzeitiger Rückzahlung bestimmt werden (IAS 39.79 und IG F.2.9).
- nicht in der Bilanz angesetzte feste Verpflichtungen (z.B. schwebende Beschaffungs- oder Absatzgeschäfte);

---

122 Siehe Rn 182.
123 Siehe Rn 178.

- hoch wahrscheinliche, erwartete Transaktionen (highly probable **forecast transactions**), z.B. bugetierte Beschaffungs- oder Absatzgeschäfte, für die noch keine vertraglichen Verpflichtungen bestehen; und

- Nettoinvestitionen in ausländische Geschäftsbetriebe[124].

187   Die gesicherten Grundgeschäfte können einer Sicherungsbeziehung sowohl auf Einzelbasis als auch als Gruppe zugeordnet werden, sofern die Bestandteile der Gruppe ein vergleichbares Risikoprofil aufweisen (IAS 39.78). Ein vergleichbares Risikoprofil liegt vor, wenn die jeweiligen Posten gleichartig sind und demselben Risikofaktor unterliegen, der mit der Sicherungsbeziehung abgesichert wird. Darüber hinaus muss die Erwartung bestehen, dass bzgl. des abgesicherten Risikos die Änderung des beizulegenden Zeitwerts jedes einzelnen Postens der Gruppe annähernd proportional zur Änderung des beizulegenden Zeitwerts der Gruppe insgesamt ist (IAS 39.83). Obwohl IAS 39 keine weitere Erläuterung enthält, wie „annähernd proportional" auszulegen ist, hat sich in der Praxis teilweise in Anlehnung an U.S. GAAP[125] eine 10%-Regel gebildet. Eine solche Interpretation ist jedoch keineswegs zwingend, da IAS 8 die Regelungen anderer Standardsetzer als unterste Ebene in der Hierarchie von Quellen nennt und deren Berücksichtigung nicht verbindlich ist (IAS 8.13). Generell ist jeglicher Rückgriff auf U.S. GAAP für die Auslegung von IFRS Regelungen zur Bilanzierung von Sicherungsgeschäften fragwürdig, weil die Regelungen der beiden Rechnungslegungssysteme in dieser Hinsicht erheblich divergieren. Gruppen mit Bestandteilen, deren Änderung des beizulegenden Zeitwerts sich *gegensätzlich* zu derjenigen der Gruppe verhalten kann, erfüllen das Kriterium einer annähernd proportionalen Wertänderung dagegen nicht.

188   Eine Bestimmung von gesicherten Grundgeschäften als **Nettoposition** aus Vermögenswerten und Verbindlichkeiten oder positiven und negativen Cashflows aus verschiedenen Transaktionen ist unzulässig (IAS 39.84). Allerdings kann ein Unternehmen einen Teil einer solchen Nettoposition auf Bruttobasis als Sicherungsgeschäft bestimmen (IAS 39.AG101). So kann z.B. ein Unternehmen mit EUR als funktionaler Währung bei einer Nettoposition eines Zahlungsmittelabflusses in Fremdwährung von 100 USD, die aus 500 USD Zahlungsmittelzuflüssen und 600 USD Zahlungsmittelabflüssen besteht, 100 USD der 600 USD als gesichertes Grundgeschäft bestimmen. Im Hinblick auf die Auswirkung auf den Periodengewinn stehen sich beide Alternativen gleich. Unterschiede gibt es jedoch im Hinblick auf die einzelnen Posten in der Gewinn- und Verlustrechnung, d.h. welche Posten im Hinblick auf den Gewinn oder Verlust aus dem Sicherungsgeschäft angepasst werden, sowie ggf. im Falle der Änderung von Schätzungen von Betrag und Zeitpunkt des Zahlungsmittelabflusses, die sich nach IAS 39 nur auf die als gesichertes Grundgeschäft bestimmten 100 USD beziehen.

189   Ähnlich zu den Regelungen für Sicherungsinstrumente[126] müssen gesicherte Grundgeschäfte aus Sicht des bilanzierenden Unternehmens grundsätzlich Verträge oder Transaktionen mit externen Parteien darstellen. Daher können Verträge und Transaktionen zwischen Konzerngesellschaften grundsätzlich nur auf Ebene des Einzelabschlusses einer Konzerngesellschaft als gesicherte Grundgeschäfte bestimmt werden. Hiervon bestehen zwei Ausnahmen (IAS 39.80):

- konzerninterne monetäre Posten, die zwischen zwei Geschäftsbetrieben mit unterschiedlichen funktionalen Währungen bestehen, so dass in der Konzern-Gewinn- und -verlustrechnung ein Wechselkursgewinn oder -verlust verbleibt. Solche Posten können bzgl. ihres *Währungsrisikos* als gesichertes Grundgeschäft bestimmt werden.

- hoch wahrscheinliche erwartete Transaktionen zwischen Geschäftsbetrieben mit unterschiedlichen funktionalen Währungen, die aus Sicht eines der beteiligen Geschäftsbetriebe ein Fremdwährungsgeschäft darstellen, und deren Währungsrisiko die Konzern-Gewinn- und -verlustrechnung beein-

---

124 Diese werden in diesem Kapitel nicht weiter behandelt (siehe Rn 173).
125 Siehe ASC 815-20-55-14 (vormals SFAS 133.21).
126 Siehe Rn 181.

flussen wird. Solche erwarteten Transaktionen können bzgl. ihres *Währungsrisikos* als gesichertes Grundgeschäft bestimmt werden. Beispiele für künftige Transaktionen, die *nicht* die Konzern-Gewinn- und -verlustrechnung beeinflussen werden, sind konzerninterne Belastungen für Zinsen, **Lizenzgebühren** oder **Verwaltungspauschalen** ohne Anknüpfung an konzernexterne Transaktionen. Solche erwarteten Transaktionen können auf Konzernebene nicht als gesicherte Grundgeschäfte bestimmt werden. Im Gegensatz dazu werden z.B. künftige konzerninterne Lieferungen von Vorräten für den konzernexternen Weiterverkauf durch das empfangende Konzernunternehmen die Konzern-Gewinn- und -verlustrechnung beeinflussen. Daher können solche erwarteten Transaktionen auf Konzernebene als gesicherte Grundgeschäfte bestimmt werden (IAS 39.AG99A). Lizenzentgelte, die von einem Konzernunternehmen einem anderen belastet werden, das die Lizenz an *konzernexterne* Unternehmen gewährt und von diesen Lizenzentgelte erhält, beeinflussen die Konzern-Gewinn- und -verlustrechnung ähnlich wie die zuvor genannte Lieferung von Vorräten und können ebenfalls auf Konzernebene als gesicherte Grundgeschäfte bestimmt werden. Ähnlich verhält es sich mit künftigen konzerninternen Lieferungen von Sachanlagen, die über den Abschreibungsaufwand in der funktionalen Währung des empfangenden Konzernunternehmens die Konzern-Gewinn- und -verlustrechnung beeinflussen werden (IAS 39.AG99A).

Diese beiden Ausnahmen für konzerninterne Fremdwährungsposten und -transaktionen beziehen sich auf bestehende konzerninterne Forderungen und Verbindlichkeiten sowie erwartete Transaktionen, umfassen jedoch nicht konzerninterne *feste Verpflichtungen*, deren Währungsrisiko die Konzern-Gewinn- und -verlustrechnung beeinflussen wird. Im Hinblick auf die Beweggründe für die beiden gewährten Ausnahmen ist es nicht nachvollziehbar, warum feste Verpflichtungen unter ansonsten gleichen Voraussetzungen nicht als gesicherte Grundgeschäfte bestimmt werden können. Die Auswirkungen sind denen von erwarteten Transaktionen vergleichbar, nur dass die Unsicherheit bzgl. der Durchführung der Transaktion aufgrund des Bestehens einer rechtlich verbindlichen Vereinbarung höher als bei erwarteten Transaktionen ist. Daher kann logisch abgeleitet werden, dass feste Verpflichtungen ceteris paribus mindestens die Bilanzierung rechtfertigen, die für erwartete Transaktionen zulässig ist. Somit ist es als zulässig zu erachten, konzerninterne feste Verpflichtungen ebenso wie erwartete Transaktionen auf Konzernebene als gesicherte Grundgeschäfte bzgl. des Währungsrisikos zu bestimmen, wenn die für erwartete Transaktionen geltenden Voraussetzungen entsprechend erfüllt sind.[127]

190

IAS 39 enthält Beschränkungen bzgl. der Möglichkeit, nur Komponenten eines gesicherten Grundgeschäfts statt des Grundgeschäfts in seiner Gesamtheit als Bestandteil einer Sicherungsbeziehung zu bestimmen. Diese Beschränkungen unterscheiden sich danach, ob das gesicherte Grundgeschäft ein finanzieller oder ein nicht-finanzieller Posten ist.

191

a) Finanzielle Posten als gesichertes Grundgeschäft. Finanzielle Posten können in Komponenten zerlegt und auf dieser Basis als gesichertes Grundgeschäft bestimmt werden, sofern die Wirksamkeit des Sicherungsgeschäfts messbar ist. Das bedeutet, Komponenten müssen identifizierbar sein und als solche verlässlich bewertet werden können (IAS 39.81). Damit ergeben sich folgende Möglichkeiten einer Aufteilung in Komponenten:

192

(a) proportional zum Nominalwert (z.B. 70% des Nennwerts eines Darlehens);

(b) nach vertraglich spezifizierten Cashflows (z.B. die auf die ersten beiden Zinszahlungen folgenden acht Zinszahlungen einer variabel verzinslichen Anleihe mit 20 Zinszahlungen, d.h. die Coupons drei bis 10);

---

127 Ähnlich *Ernst & Young (Hrsg.)* International GAAP, 2540.

(c) zeitproportional (z.B. das den beizulegenden Zeitwert betreffende Zinsänderungsrisiko, das sich auf die ersten fünf Jahre der insgesamt 10-jährigen Gesamtlaufzeit einer festverzinslichen endfälligen Anleihe bezieht, d.h. die Zinszahlungen während der ersten fünf Jahre sowie den auf die ersten fünf Jahre der Laufzeit entfallenden Teil der Änderung des beizulegenden Zeitwerts des Tilgungszahlung bei Endfälligkeit) (IAS 39 IG F.2.17);

(d) nach Art des Risikos.

193   Die Aufteilung finanzieller Posten in Komponenten nach **Art des Risikos (Risikokomponenten)** gehört zu den schwierigsten Fragestellungen der Bilanzierung von Sicherungsgeschäften. Eine geläufige Risikokomponente ist der Teil des **Zinsänderungsrisikos**, der sich auf einen Benchmark-Zinssatz bezieht (z.B. **Euribor** oder **LIBOR**). Alternativ kann auch das auf den risikofreien Zinssatz bezogene Zinsänderungsrisiko als Risikokomponente verwendet werden. Aufgrund der Entwicklung der Staatsverschuldung im Zuge der globalen Finanzkrise ist jedoch der **risikofreie Zinssatz** mittlerweile zu einem weitgehend hypothetischen Konstrukt geworden, so dass davon auszugehen ist, das seine Verwendung an Bedeutung verliert (oder zumindest einen Benchmark-Zinssatz statt eines risikofreien darstellt). Bei der Bestimmung von Zins-Risikokomponenten als gesichertes Grundgeschäft ist zu beachten, dass die Risikokomponente nicht auf Cashflows beruhen darf, die die Gesamt-Cashflows des Finanzinstruments übersteigen. Dies betrifft z.B. Unternehmen oder Finanzinstrumente mit höchster Bonität, die eine geringere Verzinsung als zum Benchmark-Zinssatz aufweisen. Wenn z.B. eine Anleihe mit LIBOR *minus* 30 Basispunkten verzinst wird, darf keine LIBOR Benchmark-Zinskomponente als gesichertes Grundgeschäft bestimmt werden (mit einer „negativen Residualkomponente" in Höhe des Kapitalwerts von 30 Basispunkten über die Restlaufzeit). In diesen Fällen muss stattdessen das gesicherte Grundgeschäft auf der Basis aller Cashflows bestimmt werden (d.h. Nennwert verzinst zu LIBOR *minus* 30 Basispunkte). Allerdings kann zur Verbesserung der Wirksamkeit des Sicherungsgeschäfts die Relation zwischen gesichertem Grundgeschäft und Sicherungsinstrument variiert werden (d.h. von 1:1 abweichend bestimmt werden) (IAS 39.AG99C). Wenn jedoch umgekehrt der Benchmark-Zinssatz über dem vertraglichen Zinssatz eines festverzinslichen Instruments liegt, kann dennoch die Benchmark-Zinskomponente als gesichertes Grundgeschäft bestimmt werden, wenn die *Effektivverzinsung* des festverzinslichen Instruments den Benchmark-Zinssatz übersteigt. Dies kann z.B. auftreten, wenn das Zinsniveau seit Ausgabe des festverzinslichen Instruments gestiegen und damit dessen Kurs entsprechend gefallen ist (IAS 39. AG99D).

194   Eine andere Risikokomponente, die als gesichertes Grundgeschäft bestimmt werden kann, ist das **Währungsrisiko** von auf Fremdwährung lautenden Finanzinstrumenten. Bei nicht-monetären Finanzinstrumenten wie z.B. Aktien ist allerdings zu beachten, dass das Währungsrisiko deutlich identifizierbar sein muss. Dies ist nur dann der Fall, wenn die Aktie nicht in einem Markt gehandelt wird, dessen Quotierungen in derselben Währung wie die funktionale Währung des bilanzierenden Unternehmens erfolgen und die Dividenzahlungen ebenfalls nicht in dieser funktionalen Währung erfolgen (IAS 39 IG F.2.19). Bei der Absicherung des Währungsrisikos von monetären Finanzinstrumenten wie Forderungen oder Anleihen ist zu erwägen, ob die Regelungen zur Bilanzierung von Sicherungsgeschäften überhaupt eine nennenswerte Auswirkung haben. Wird z.B. das Währungsrisiko mittels eines nicht-derivativen Sicherungsinstruments[128] abgesichert, so hat die Anwendung der Regelungen zur Bilanzierung von Sicherungsgeschäften keine Auswirkung, da die Umrechnung von monetären Fremdwährungsposten nach IAS 21 bereits zur erfolgswirksamen Erfassung der Wechselkursgewinne und -verluste für beide Finanzinstrumente führt (IAS 39 IG F.1.1). Bei Absicherung des Währungsrisikos mittels Derivaten ergibt sich aufgrund der (sofortigen) erfolgswirksamen Umrechnung des gesicherten Grundgeschäfts gemäß IAS 21 regelmäßig kein wesentlicher Effekt. Dies gilt auch bei Bilanzierung als Absicherung von

---

128 Siehe Rn 180.

Zahlungsströmen, da die zunächst im sonstigen Ergebnis erfassten Gewinne und Verluste aus der Änderung des beizulegenden Zeitwerts des Derivats in der Periode in die Gewinn- und Verlustrechnung umzugliedern sind, in der die auf das gesicherte Grundgeschäft entfallenden Wechselkursgewinne und -verluste die Gewinn- und Verlustrechnung beeinflussen. Aufgrund der (sofortigen) erfolgswirksamen Umrechnung des gesicherten Grundgeschäfts gemäß IAS 21 erfolgt somit die Umgliederung der Beträge in derselben Periode in der sie im sonstigen Ergebnis erfasst werden, so dass sich keine kumulierten Beträge im Eigenkapital aufbauen (IAS 39 IG F.3.3 und F.3.4). Die Anwendung der Regelungen zur Bilanzierung von Sicherungsgeschäften auf das Währungsrisiko von monetären Finanzinstrumenten ist in der Praxis in der Regel nur bei langfristigen Sicherungsbeziehungen oder komplexeren Sicherungsbeziehungen, die Währungs- und Zinsrisiko kombinieren, von Bedeutung. Wenn z.B. ein langfristiger Fremdwährungsposten mittels eines Derivats abgesichert wird, kann die Abweichung zwischen Kassa- und Terminkursen einen nennenswerte Auswirkung bekommen. Ein anderes Beispiel ist die Absicherung eines festverzinslicher Fremdwährungsposten mittels eines kombinierten Zins- und Währungsswaps (**Cross Currency Interest Rate Swap**), bei der sich aufgrund der im Derivat enthaltenen sog. „Basis" ein nennenswerter Effekt ergeben kann.

Die Absicherung des Ausfall- oder **Kreditrisikos** als separate Risikokomponente ist in der Praxis bisher auf erhebliche Schwierigkeiten gestoßen. Das Kreditrisiko eines Finanzinstruments lässt sich nur schwer isolieren, weil es keinen Markt gibt, der das Kreditrisiko separat in der Form handelt, in der es in einem nicht-derivativen Finanzinstrument wie einem Darlehen oder einer Anleihe enthalten ist. Das typische Derivat zur Absicherung des Kreditrisikos ist ein **Credit Default Swap (CDS)**. Hierbei handelt es sich um ein Derivat, bei dem eine Partei ein bestimmtes Kreditrisiko für eine bestimmte Adresse (Schuldner oder Schuldinstrument) oder bezogen auf einen Index für eine bestimmte Laufzeit gegen Zahlung einer Prämie von einer anderen Partei übernimmt. Die Prämie kann eine Einmalzahlung, über die Laufzeit verteilte periodische Zahlungen oder eine Kombination davon sein. Aufgrund der Unterschiede zwischen derivativen und nicht-derivativen Finanzinstrumenten ist die Arbitrage zwischen CDS und den entsprechenden Anleihen nicht perfekt. Außerdem weichen CDS und entsprechende Anleihen in Ausstattungsmerkmalen voneinander ab (z.B. die sog. „cheapest to deliver" Option in CDS, die Default-Kriterien oder die Fälligkeit). Dazu kommen Verwerfungen aufgrund von Unterschieden in Angebot und Nachfrage in den jeweiligen Märkten. Aufgrund dieser Unterschiede kann der Marktpreis oder die Marktrendite von CDS nicht direkt als Anhaltspunkt für eine Kreditrisiko-Komponente einer Anleihe oder eines Darlehens herangezogen werden. In der Praxis ist daher der Versuch, für CDS eine Bilanzierung als Sicherungsgeschäft auf Basis der Bestimmung des Kreditrisikos einer Anleihe oder eines Darlehens (Risikokomponente) als gesichertes Grundgeschäft zu erzielen, bislang häufig erfolglos geblieben.

Die Möglichkeit, das mit einem finanziellen Posten verbundene **Inflationsrisiko** als separate Risikokomponente zu betrachten und als gesichertes Grundgeschäft zu bestimmen, war in der Praxis lange umstritten. Mittels einer Änderung von IAS 39 hat das IASB klar gestellt, dass das Inflationsrisiko zwecks Bestimmung als gesichertes Grundgeschäft nur dann als separate Risikokomponente identifiziert werden kann, wenn es sich um im Vertrag explizit bestimmte Teile der Cashflows einer in der Bilanz angesetzten inflationsindexierten Anleihe handelt und diese nicht die anderen (restlichen) Cashflows des Instruments beeinflussen (IAS 39.AG99F).

b) Nicht-finanzielle Posten als gesichertes Grundgeschäft. Im Gegensatz zu finanziellen Posten können **nicht-finanzielle Posten** grundsätzlich nicht in Komponenten nach der Art des Risikos zerlegt werden. Die einzige Ausnahme ist ein mit dem nicht-finanziellen Posten verbundenes Währungsrisiko, das separat als gesichertes Grundgeschäft bestimmt werden kann. Daher kann ein Unternehmen z.B. den Verkauf von Vorräten in Höhe eines (Mindest-)Volumens von 1 Mio. USD gegen das Risiko

195

196

197

von Wechselkursänderungen gegenüber dem Euro absichern und nur bzgl. dieses Risikos als gesichertes Grundgeschäft bestimmen, d.h. ohne andere Risiken wie z.B. das Risiko einer Änderung des Verkaufspreises einzubeziehen. Ansonsten ist ein nicht-finanzieller Posten bzgl. der Gesamtheit seiner Risiken als gesichertes Grundgeschäft zu bestimmen.

198   Diese strikte Beschränkung bzgl. der Bestimmung von Komponenten nach der Art des Risikos hat in der Praxis zu erheblichen Schwierigkeiten bei der Absicherung von Transaktionen gegen Rohstoff-Preisrisiken und Inflationsrisiken geführt. Verträge über die Lieferung von **Erdgas** enthalten z.B. oft **Preisformeln**, die den Preis von Erdgas in Abhängigkeit verschiedener bestimmer Treibstoffsorten (wie z.B. Sorten von leichtem Heizöl), einer Inflationsindexierung und einem variablen Transportkosten-Bestandteil bestimmen. In diesen Fällen kann das aus einer Heizöl-Indexierung resultierende Risiko von Preisschwankungen nicht separat als gesichertes Grundgeschäft bestimmt werden. Ähnliche Probleme bestehen bei **Stromlieferverträgen**, deren Preis oft an Brennstoffe (z.B. Gas, Rohöl oder Kohle) und Produktionskosten des Energieerzeugers (z.B. mittels einer Indexierung an Investitionsgüter, Löhne oder Erzeugerpreise) ist.

199   Die Beschränkung bzgl. der Bestimmung von Komponenten nach der Art des Risikos bereitet auch Probleme bei Transaktionen von Rohstoffen oder rohstoffnahen Produkten, die bzgl. des sog. „Benchmark" (oder Standard) Preisrisikos abgesichert werden. Das **Benchmark Preisrisiko** bezieht sich auf das Risiko von Preisänderungen des Rohstoffs im Hinblick auf seine Preisnotierung in einem standardisierten Handel, wie z.B. an Rohstoffbörsen. Ein Unternehmen, das **Kaffee** einer bestimmten Sorte aus einem bestimmten Herkunftsland bezieht und sich gegen das Kaffeepreisrisiko mittels eines börsengehandelten Terminkontrakts absichert, kann z.B. nicht dieses Benchmark-Preisrisiko auf Basis von Qualität, Herkunftsland und Erfüllungsort laut Terminkontrakt als gesichertes Grundgeschäft bestimmen. Stattdessen ist das gesicherte Grundgeschäft auf Basis von Qualität, Herkunftsland und Erfüllungsort der Kaffeeeinkäufe des Unternehmens zu bestimmen. Ein ähnliches Beispiel ist die die Absicherung des künftigen Verbrauchs von **Kerosin** in der Luftfahrtindustrie. Aufgrund der hohen Marktliquidität für Rohöl-bezogene Derivate insbesondere im mittel- und langfristigen Bereich werden von den Luftfahrtgesellschaften regelmäßig Rohöl-Termingeschäfte oder -optionen verwendet. In diesen Fällen kann das auf Rohöl-preisänderungen entfallende Preisrisiko künftiger Kerosinkäufe nicht separat als gesichertes Grundgeschäft bestimmt werden. Allerdings kann ein Unternehmen das Verhältnis von Sicherungsgeschäften zu gesicherten Grundgeschäften (**hedge ratio**) variieren, um die Wirksamkeit der Wirksamkeit des Sicherungsgeschäfts zu verbessern. Dies bedeutet, die Relation zwischen gesichertem Grundgeschäft und Sicherungsinstrument kann abweichend von 1:1 bestimmt werden (IAS 39.AG100). Die optimale Relation wird mittels **Regressionsanalyse** ermittelt.

200   Nicht-finanzielle Posten können allerdings proportional zum Nominalwert oder-betrag aufgeteilt und die daraus resultierenden Komponenten separat als gesichertes Grundgeschäft bestimmt werden. So kann z.B. 70% einer festen Verplichtung zum Erwerb von 100.000 Barrel Rohöl als gesichertes Grundgeschäft bestimmt werden. Von großer praktischer Relevanz ist die Möglichkeit, ein bestimmtes Nominalvolumen einer Gruppe von erwarteten Transaktionen als gesichertes Grundgeschäft zu bestimmen. Ein Unternehmen mit Verkäufen in Fremdwährung kann z.B. die ersten 3 Mio. USD an Verkäufen in einem bestimmten Monat als gesichertes Grundgeschäft zu bestimmen. Hierbei ist zu beachten, dass die Bestimmung eindeutig sein muss. Daher kann z.B. nicht 50% des Umsatzes in USD in einem Monat als gesichertes Grundgeschäft bestimmt werden, weil erst am Monatsende feststehen würde, was das gesicherte Grundgeschäft gewesen ist (IAS 39 IG F.3.10).

Außerdem ist das **Zeitfenster** bei erwarteten Transaktionen als gesicherten Grundgeschäften hinreichend genau und innerhalb einer grundsätzlich engen Bandbreite ab dem wahrscheinlichsten Transaktionsdatum zu bestimmen (IAS 39, IG F.3.11). Generell ist eine Bandbreite von drei Monaten[129] als Obergrenze dessen anzusehen, was noch als enge Bandbreite interpretiert werden kann.

4. Die Bilanzierung von Sicherungsgeschäften. a) Die verschiedenen Arten von Sicherungsgeschäften. IAS 39 unterteilt die Sicherungsgeschäfte in drei verschiedene Arten (IAS 39.86):

- die Absicherung des beizulegenden Zeitwerts;
- die Absicherung von Zahlungsströmen; und
- die Absicherung einer Nettoinvestition in einen ausländischen Geschäftsbetrieb (diese Art von Sicherungsgeschäft wird im Kapitel zur Fremdwährungsumrechnung behandelt).

Die Absicherung des beizulegenden Zeitwerts (**fair value hedge**) bezieht sich auf das Risiko, dass sich der beizulegende Zeitwert von in der Bilanz angesetzten Vermögenswerten oder Schulden oder von nicht in der Bilanz angesetzten festen Verpflichtungen ändert. Das Risiko kann sich dabei auf den Posten insgesamt oder eine separat als gesichertes Grundgeschäft bestimmbare Komponente des Postens[130] beziehen. Ferner muss es sich bei dem abgesicherten Risiko um ein Risiko handeln, das Auswirkungen auf das Periodenergebnis haben *kann*. Dies bedeutet, dass es ausreicht, wenn sich *potenziell* Auswirkungen auf den Periodenerfolg ergeben. Daher können z.B. als „Kredite und Forderungen" kategorisierte finanzielle Vermögenswerte, die gegen zinsinduzierte Schwankungen des beizulegenden Zeitwerts abgesichert werden, als gesichertes Grundgeschäft bestimmt werden. Obwohl Zinsschwankungen nicht die Bewertung festverzinslicher finanzieller Vermögenswerte zu fortgeführten Anschaffungskosten beeinflussen, würde sich bei einem Verkauf des Vermögenswerts vor seiner Fälligkeit die zinsinduzierte Änderung des beizulegenden Zeitwerts als Teil des Veräußerungsgewinns oder -verlusts im Periodenergebnis niederschlagen (IAS 39 IG F.2.13).

Die Absicherung von Zahlungsströmen (**cash flow hedge**) bezieht sich auf das Risiko der Schwankung von Zahlungsströmen aufgrund eines bestimmten Risikos in Verbindung mit (IAS 39.86(b)):

- in der Bilanz angesetzten Vermögenswerten oder Schulden *oder*
- hoch wahrscheinlichen erwarteten Transaktionen.

Auch wenn nicht ausdrücklich in IAS 39 genannt, können auch in der Bilanz nicht angesetzte feste Verpflichtungen die Ursache des abgesicherten Risikos sein.[131] Genauso wie bei einer Absicherung des beizulegenden Zeitwerts muss es sich bei dem abgesicherten Risiko um ein Risiko handeln, das Auswirkungen auf das Periodenergebnis haben *kann*. Dabei kann diese Auswirkung auch indirekt sein. So kann z.B. die beabsichtigte künftige Aufnahme eines festverzinslichen Darlehens gegen das Zinsänderungsrisiko abgesichert und als gesichertes Grundgeschäft im Rahmen einer Absicherung von Zahlungsströmen bestimmt werden. Obwohl die Darlehensaufnahme an sich keine Auswirkungen auf das Periodenergebnis hat, beeinflusst die Änderung des Zinsniveaus bis zur Aufnahme des Darlehens die darauf zu zahlenden Zinsen und damit künftige Periodenergebnisse (IAS 39 IG F.2.2).

Für die Absicherung des Währungsrisikos *fester Verpflichtungen* (**firm commitments**) besteht ein Wahlrecht, diese entweder als eine Absicherung des beizulegenden Zeitwerts oder als eine Absicherung von Zahlungsströmen zu behandeln (IAS 39.87). Dieses Wahlrecht spiegelt wider, dass das Währungsrisiko sowohl die Zahlungsströme als auch den beizulegenden Zeitwert des gesicherten Grundgeschäfts beeinflusst (IAS 39.BC154). Die praktische Bedeutung dieses Wahlrechts ist, dass ein gesichertes Grundgeschäft, das als (hoch wahrscheinliche) erwartete Transaktion beginnt und später zu einer festen Ver-

201

202

203

204

205

---

129 Eines der Beispiele der Implementation Guidance zu IAS 39 erwähnt eine drei-monatige Periode (siehe IG F.3.10).
130 Siehe Rn 185-201.
131 Dies ergibt sich daraus, dass die Absicherung des Währungsrisikos fester Verpflichtungen als eine Absicherung von Zahlungsströmen behandelt werden kann (siehe IAS 39.87).

pflichtung wird, die Sicherungsbeziehung für alle Phasen als Absicherung von Zahlungsströmen bilanziert werden kann. Da die Art des Sicherungsgeschäfts in diesem Fall beibehalten wird, ist im Zeitpunkt des Entstehens der festen Verpflichtung keine erneute Bestimmung als gesichertes Grundgeschäft im Rahmen der Absicherung des beizulegenden Zeitwerts erforderlich. Auch eine etwaige im Anschluss an die feste Verpflichtung entstehende Fremdwährungsforderung oder -verbindlichkeit kann bzgl. des Währungsrisikos als Absicherung von Zahlungsströmen behandelt werden.[132] Daher kann auch eine Sicherungsbeziehung mit drei Phasen (d.h. ein gesichertes Grundgeschäft in Form einer erwarteten Transaktion, einer festen Verpflichtung und einer Fremdwährungsforderung oder -verbindlichkeit) einheitlich als Absicherung von Zahlungsströmen behandelt werden.

206

b) Die Voraussetzungen für die Bilanzierung von Sicherungsgeschäften

Die Bilanzierung von Sicherungsgeschäften nach IFRS ist ein Wahlrecht, das nur bei Erfüllung einer Reihe restriktiver Voraussetzungen besteht. Das Wahlrecht kann einzeln für jede Sicherungsbeziehung ausgeübt werden, d.h. es besteht kein Stetigkeitsgebot. Um sich für die Bilanzierung von Sicherungsgeschäften zu qualifizieren, sind folgende Voraussetzungen *kumulativ* zu erfüllen:

- **Dokumentation**: die Sicherungsbeziehung und die mit ihr verfolgte Zielsetzung müssen spätestens im Zeitpunkt des Beginns der Sicherungsbeziehung dokumentiert sein.
- **Eintrittswahrscheinlichkeit erwarteter Transaktionen**: handelt es sich bei dem gesicherten Grundgeschäft um eine erwartete künftige Transaktion, so muss diese eine hohe Eintrittswahrscheinlichkeit haben.
- **Mindestgrad der Wirksamkeit**: es besteht die Erwartung, dass das Sicherungsgeschäft in „hohem Maße" wirksam ist.
- **Messbarkeit der Wirksamkeit**: die Wirksamkeit des Sicherungsgeschäfts muss verlässlich bestimmbar sein.
- **Tatsächliche Wirksamkeit**: das Sicherungsgeschäft muss für alle Rechnungslegungsperioden, die die Laufzeit der Sicherungsbeziehung umfasst, tatsächlich in hohem Maße wirksam gewesen sein.

207

Die **Dokumentation** der Sicherungsbeziehung hat folgende Aspekte zu umfassen:

- die mit der Absicherung verfolgten Risikomanagementzielsetzungen und -strategien;
- die genauen Bestandteile der Sicherungsbeziehung, d.h. das Sicherungsinstrument, das gesicherte Grundgeschäft sowie die Art des abgesicherten Risikos;
- wie die Wirksamkeit des Sicherungsgeschäfts bestimmt wird; dies erfordert eine Beschreibung der dazu verwendeten Methoden einschließlich der Art ihrer Auswertung (siehe auch die Ausführungen zu den Voraussetzungen bzgl. der Wirksamkeit des Sicherungsgeschäfts in diesem Abschnitt).

Die gesamte Dokumentation muss spätestens in dem Zeitpunkt, ab dem das Sicherungsinstrument als Sicherungsgeschäft bestimmt ist, vorliegen (d.h. zu Beginn der Laufzeit der Sicherungsbeziehung). Eine nachträgliche Dokumentation oder Nachdatierung ist nicht zulässig (IAS 39 IG F.3.8), d.h. die Bilanzierung als Sicherungsgeschäft kann nicht beginnen, bevor die Dokumentation komplett vorliegt.

208

In der Praxis haben sich verschiedene Ansätze entwickelt, die Dokumentationserfordernisse effizient zu erfüllen. So sind Softwarelösungen verfügbar, die Teile der Dokumentation automatisieren. Dies betrifft z.B. die Bestimmung von Derivaten als Sicherungsinstrument und die Erfassung und Zuordnung der durch sie gesicherten Grundgeschäfte. Die Effizienz der Dokumentation kann auch durch die **Verwendung von Querverweisen** erhöht werden. Wenn ein Unternehmen bestimmte Arten von Sicherungsgeschäften häufig abschließt, kann z.B. die Dokumentation von Risikomanagementzielsetzungen und -strategien, die Art des abgesicherten Risikos, die Art von Sicherungsgeschäft (d.h. Absicherung des beizulegenden Zeitwerts oder Absicherung von Zahlungsströmen) und die Beschreibung, wie

---

132 Siehe Rn 194.

die Wirksamkeit des Sicherungsgeschäfts bestimmt wird, in einem zentralen Dokument (**master document**) wie z.B. einem Bilanzierungshandbuch erfolgen. Dies kann für verschiedene Arten von Strategien oder Absicherungen getrennt erfolgen, so dass eine Bezugnahme auf die jeweils einschlägige Art von Strategie oder Absicherung möglich ist (z.B. mittels Nummerierung als Strategie 1 etc.) Die Dokumentation des jeweiligen Sicherungsgeschäfts kann dann auf die entsprechende Dokumentation dieser Aspekte im zentralen Dokument Bezug nehmen.

Für die Dokumentation, wie die Wirksamkeit des Sicherungsgeschäfts bestimmt wird, ist es empfehlenswert, nicht nur eine rein verbale Beschreibung vorzunehmen, sondern eine eine konkrete Beispielrechnung hinzuzufügen. Ein konkretes **Berechnungsbeispiel** hat einen höheren Bestimmtheitsgrad als rein verbale Beschreibungen und auch den Vorteil, dass das bilanzierende Unternehmen sicherstellt, die beschriebene Berechnung auch tatsächlich durchführen zu können.

Hinsichtlich der **Eintrittswahrscheinlichkeit erwarteter Transaktionen** ist zu beachten, dass sich dieses Kriterium *ausschließlich* auf gesicherte Grundgeschäfte bezieht, die *erwartete künftige Transaktionen* sind. In der Praxis wird dieses Kriterium teilweise auf alle gesicherten Grundgeschäfte, die eine Absicherungen von Zahlungsströmen darstellen, angewendet. Diese Auslegung von IAS 39 ist jedoch nicht sachgerecht. Aus der Definition der Absicherungen von Zahlungsströmen (IAS 39.86(b)) folgt, dass erwartete Transaktionen eine Untergruppe dieser Art von Sicherungsbeziehung sind.[133] Daher ist z.B. bei der Absicherung von in der Bilanz angesetzten variabel verzinslichen Finanzinstrumenten gegen Schwankungen der Zinszahlungen *keine* gesonderte Würdigung im Hinblick auf eine hohe Eintrittswahrscheinlichkeit der künftigen Zinszahlungen erforderlich (d.h. dieses Kriterium ist in diesen Fällen nicht einschlägig).

Die erforderliche *hohe* **Eintrittswahrscheinlichkeit** stellt einen erheblich höheren Schwellenwert dar, als eine lediglich überwiegende Wahrscheinlichkeit (d.h. mehr als 50%). Die Beurteilung der Eintrittswahrscheinlichkeit erwarteter Transaktionen erfordert Ermessen. Eine bloße Absicht des Unternehmens ist nicht hinreichend, um dieses Kriterium zu erfüllen. Indizien und Nachweise, die eine *hohe* Eintrittswahrscheinlichkeit hinreichend untermauern sind z.B.:

- das Volumen und die Häufigkeit ähnlicher Transaktionen in der Vergangenheit,
- die finanzielle und operative Kapazität des Unternehmens, die Transaktion durchzuführen,
- die Bindung wesentlicher Resourcen im Hinblick auf die Transaktion (z.B. der Betrieb einer Fertigungslinie, die diejenigen Rohstoffe verbraucht, deren künftiger Bezug die erwartete Transaktion ausmacht),
- das Ausmaß von Verlusten oder Betriebsunterbrechungen, die auftreten können, wenn die erwartete Transaktion nicht erfolgt,
- die Wahrscheinlichkeit der Verwendung alternativer Arten von Transaktionen, um das mit der erwarteten Transaktion verfolgte Ziel zu erreichen oder
- das Budget oder der Geschäftsplan.

Außerdem ist bei der Beurteilung der Höhe der Eintrittswahrscheinlichkeit zu beachten, wie weit die erwarteten Transaktionen in der Zukunft liegen und wie deren Volumen sich zu historischen Erfahrungswerten verhält (IAS 39 IG F.3.7).

Bei der Bestimmung von erwarteten Transaktionen empfiehlt es sich, einen angemessen Spielraum zwischen dem erwarteten Transaktionsvolumen und dem als gesichertes Grundgeschäft bestimmten Volumen zu belassen. Wenn die Schätzung des erwarteten Transaktionsvolumens revidiert werden muss und das als gesichertes Grundgeschäft bestimmte Volumen unterschreitet, führt dies zu sofort erfolgswirksam zu erfassender Unwirksamkeit in der Sicherungsbeziehung und kann auch dazu führen, dass

209

210

211

212

---

133 Siehe Rn 204.

die Bilanzierung als Sicherungsgeschäft zu beenden ist. In der Praxis wird dieses Problem häufig dadurch zu vermeiden versucht, dass das nominale Transaktionsvolumen in **Bänder** aufgeteilt wird,[134] die jeweils separat als Sicherungsbeziehung bestimmt werden. So kann z.B. ein nominales Bezugsvolumen im Wert von 100.000 USD in zehn Bänder von jeweils 10.000 USD zerlegt und als zehn separate Sicherungsbeziehungen bestimmt werden. Hierbei ist allerdings zu beachten, dass bei dieser Vorgehensweise das Risiko eines Rückgangs des Transaktionsvolumens unter das als gesichertes Grundgeschäft bestimmte Volumen durch das Risiko des Nichteintritts der erwarteten Transaktion ersetzt wird. Wenn das tatsächliche Volumen z.B. auf 90.000 USD sinkt, so ergibt sich statt einer Abweichung von 10% zwischen Sicherungs-instrument und gesichertem Grundgeschäft ein kompletter Ausfall einer erwarteten Transaktion (d.h. des Bands von 90.001 bis 100.000 USD). Hierbei ist zu beachten, dass eine Vorgeschichte von erwarteten Transaktionen, die zunächst als gesichertes Grundgeschäft bestimmt wurden, aber dann nicht einge-treten sind, die Fähigkeit des Unternehmens zu hinreichend verlässlichen Schätzungen der Eintritts-wahrscheinlichkeit erwarteter Transaktionen und damit generell die Bestimmung solcher erwarteten Transaktionen als gesicherte Grundgeschäfte in Frage stellt (IAS 39 IG F.3.7). Diese Konsequenz sollte bei der Entscheidung über die Strategie, wieviel Spielraum belassen wird und inwieweit eine Aufteilung von Transaktionsvolumina in Bandbreiten erfolgt, die als separate Sicherungsbeziehungen behandelt werden, beachtet werden.

213   Die Voraussetzungen in IAS 39 bzgl. der Eintrittswahrscheinlichkeit erwarteter Transaktionen neh-men auch darauf Bezug, dass das Risiko der Schwankung von Zahlungsströmen letztlich das Perioden-ergebnis beeinflussen können muss. Dies ist jedoch bereits in der Definition der Absicherung von Zah-lungsströmen[135] verankert und daher keine zusätzliche Anforderung.

214   Die Vorraussetzungen hinsichtlich der **Wirksamkeit bzw. Effektivität** von Sicherungsgeschäften umfassen verschiedene Anforderungen und werden zusammen auch als „**Wirkamkeitstest oder Effek-tivitätstest**" bezeichnet. Dieser Wirksamkeitstest umfasst zwei Elemente (IAS 39.88(b) und (e), AG105):

- den *prospektiven Test*, der sich auf die Erwartung bezieht, dass das Sicherungsgeschäft für die jeweils verbleibende Restlaufzeit der Sicherungsbeziehung in hohem Maße wirksam sein wird (wobei der erste prospektive Test auf den Beginn der Sicherungsbeziehung entällt);

- den *retrospektiven Test*, der sich darauf bezieht, ob die Wirksamkeit des Sicherungsgeschäfts in der Vergangenheit (d.h. während der bereits verstrichenen Laufzeit der Sicherungsbeziehung) tatsäch-lich ein hohes Maß erreicht hat.

215   Grundvoraussetzung jedes Wirksamkeitstests ist, dass sowohl der beizulegende Zeitwert des Siche-rungsinstruments als auch der beizulegende Zeitwert oder die Cashflows des Grundgeschäfts (ggf. sepa-rat bestimmt als Komponente)[136] verlässlich ermittelt werden können (IAS 39.88(d)).

216   Die Wirksamkeit des Sicherungsgeschäfts wird anhand der Kompensation gemessen, die das Siche-rungsinstrument bzgl. der Änderungen des beizulegenden Zeitwerts oder der Cashflows, die dem abgesi-cherten Risiko zuzuordnen sind, erzielt. Diese Beurteilung muss in Einklang mit der ursprünglich doku-mentierten Risikomanagementstrategie stehen (IAS 39.88(b)). Die Beurteilung der Kompensation kann auf verschiedene Weise erfolgen, z.B. mittels Vergleich der bisherigen Änderungen des beizulegenden Zeitwerts oder der Cashflows des Sicherungsinstruments mit den bisherigen Änderungen des beizule-genden Zeitwerts oder der Cashflows des gesicherten Grundgeschäfts (auf Basis der Dokumentation der Sicherungsbeziehung, d.h. es kann sich dabei um einen Posten insgesamt oder eine separat als gesicher-tes Grundgeschäft bestimmbare Komponente des Postens[137] handeln). Dies ist die sog. „**Dollar Offset**"

---

134 Siehe Rn 192 und 200.
135 Siehe Rn 204.
136 Siehe Rn 193ff.
137 Siehe Rn 193ff.

Friedhoff / Berger

Methode. Alternativ kann die Kompensation auch anhand einer Analyse der statistischen Korrelation zwischen dem beizulegenden Zeitwert oder den Cashflows des gesicherten Grundgeschäfts und denen des Sicherungsinstruments beurteilt werden (d.h. mittels **Regressionsanalyse**) (IAS 39.AG105(a)).

In der Praxis hat teilweise die Verwendung sog. „**hypothetischer Derivate**" zur Beurteilung der **217** Wirksamkeit von Sicherungsgeschäften für Verwirrung gesorgt. Ein hypothetisches Derivat ist ein Derivat, dessen Änderung des beizulegenden Zeitwerts diejenige des abgesicherten Risikos vollständig (d.h. zu 100%) kompensieren würde. Es handelt sich *nicht* um eine eigene Methode zur Messung der Wirksamkeit sondern vielmehr um eine mögliche Weise, die Änderung des beizulegenden Zeitwerts des gesicherten Grundgeschäfts, soweit sie auf das abgesicherte Risiko entfällt, zu ermitteln. Die so ermittelte Änderung des beizulegenden Zeitwerts bzgl. des Grundgeschäfts kann dann z.B. im Rahmen der Dollar Offset mit der Änderung des beizulegenden Zeitwerts des Sicherungsinstruments verglichen oder aber als Eingangsdaten im Rahmen einer Regressionsanalyse verwendet werden. Wichtig ist, dass die Verwendung eines hypothetischen Derivats zu keinem anderen Ergebnis führen darf, als es sich aus einer „direkten" Ermittlung der Änderung des beizulegenden Zeitwerts bzgl. des Grundgeschäfts ergeben würde.

Im Hinblick auf den retrospektiven Wirksamkeitstest konkretisiert IAS 39 das mindestens erfor- **218** derliche „hohe Maß" an Wirksamkeit als eine **Bandbreite zwischen 80% und 125%**. Die Obergrenze von 125% ist dadurch bedingt, dass durch diese Definition die Entscheidung, welcher Wert als Zähler oder Nenner verwendet wird, keine Auswirkung auf die Beurteilung hat, ob das Sicherungsgeschäft eine Wirksamkeit innerhalb der Bandbreite aufweist (IAS 39.AG105(b)). Obwohl IAS 39 diese quantitive Bandbreite nur für den retrospektiven Test festlegt, ist für den prospektiven Test dieselbe Bandbreite heranzuziehen. Dies ergibt sich daraus, dass die Mindestanforderung sowohl für den prospektiven als auch den retrospektiven Test als in „hohem Maße" wirksam beschrieben wird (IAS 39.88(b) und (e)), als auch aus der Zwecksetzung der beiden Tests. Der prospektive Test soll sicherstellen, dass die Sicherungsbeziehung tatsächlich zu einem hohen Kompensationsgrad führt und der retrospektive Test soll dies im Nachgang überprüfen.

Die Beurteilung der Wirksamkeit hat nach IFRS hinsichtlich des **retrospektiven Tests** *immer* quan- **219** titativ zu erfolgen (IAS 39.88(e), IG F.4.7). Im Gegensatz zu U.S. GAAP kann daher auch bei Übereinstimmung aller relevanten Parameter oder Vertragsmerkmale zwischen Sicherungsinstrument und gesichertem Grundgeschäft keine vollständige Wirksamkeit (d.h. 100%) angenommen werden (d.h. die sog. „**short cut**" Methode ist nach IFRS nicht erlaubt). Insbesondere erfüllt bei Sicherungsinstrumenten in Form von Swaps der lediglige Vergleich der variablen Zahlungen mit denen des gesicherten Grundgeschäfts (die sog. „**change in variable cash flows**" Methode) nicht die Anforderungen von IAS 39 (IAS 39 IG F.5.5).

Für den **prospektiven Test** dagegen enthält IAS 39 kein explizites Erfordernis für einen quantitativen **220** Test. Zwar sind alle als Beispiele genannten Beurteilungsweisen (**Dollar Offset** und **Regressionsanalyse**)[138] quantitative Verfahren, jedoch ist die Dollar Offset Methode im Zeitpunkt des ersten prospektiven Tests zu Beginn der Sicherungsbeziehung nicht anwendbar, da sich noch keine *Änderungen* des beizulegenden Zeitwerts oder der Cashflows von Sicherungsinstrument und gesichertem Grundgeschäft (innerhalb der Laufzeit der Sicherungsbeziehung) ergeben haben können. Daher hat sich in der Praxis in den Fällen, in denen die Dollar Offset Methode für die Beurteilung der Wirksamkeit gewählt wird, ein Vorgehen entwickelt, bei dem (zumindest) der *erste* prospektive Test zu Beginn der Sicherungsbeziehung auf qualitativer Basis erfolgt (z.B. durch Analyse aller relevanten Parameter oder Vertragsmerkmale). In einfachen Szenarien, wenn alle relevanten Parameter oder Vertragsmerkmale vollständig übereinstimmen, wird ein prospektiver Test auf einer qualitativen Basis auch generell, d.h. während der gesamten Laufzeit der

---

138 Siehe Rn 215.

Sicherungsbeziehung, als zulässig erachtet.[139] Wenn ein Unternehmen eine quantitative Methode für den Wirksamkeitstest wählt, *kann* diese Methode sowohl für den prospektiven als auch den retrospektiven Test gleichzeitig verwendet werden.[140] Bei der Wahl eines qualitativen prospektiven Tests ist dies dagegen nicht möglich, da der retrospektive Test quantitativ sein muss.

221   Der Wirksamkeitstest hat ferner den **Effekt des Zeitwert des Geldes** zu berücksichtigen, d.h. er muss auf diskontierter Basis erfolgen (IAS 39.AG112). Dies gilt auch für die Absicherung von Zahlungsströmen, ungeachtet der (unglücklichen) Bezugnahme in IAS 39 auf die „Änderungen bei beizulegendem Zeitwert *oder Cashflows*" (z.B. IAS 39.88(b)). Daher kann bei Absicherungen von Zahlungsströmen die Beurteilung der Wirksamkeit *nicht* auf undiskontierter Basis erfolgen. Das IFRIC hat diese Fragestellung zu diesem Kriterium im Januar und März 2007 diskutiert und im Rahmen einer Agendaentscheidung ebenfalls diese Auffassung vertreten.[141]

222   Die Auswirkung des **Kreditrisikos** auf den beizulegenden Zeitwert des Sicherungsinstruments ist ebenfalls in die Beurteilung der Wirksamkeit einzubeziehen (IAS 39.AG109 und IG F.4.3). Eine Verschlechterung der Bonität der anderen Vertragspartei des Sicherungsinstruments hat verschiedenene Auswirkungen in Abhängigkeit der Art der Sicherungsbeziehung (IAS 39 IG F.4.3):

(a) *Absicherung des beizulegenden Zeitwerts*: die Verschlechterung der Bonität beeinflusst den beizulegenden Zeitwert des Sicherungsinstruments ohne dass es einen entsprechenden (kompensierenden) Effekt beim gesicherten Grundgeschäft gibt. Dies verschlechtert die Wirksamkeit des Sicherungsgeschäfts, was dazu führen kann, dass die Anforderungen des Wirksamkeitstests nicht mehr erfüllt werden.

(b) *Absicherung von Zahlungsströmen*: wenn die Verschlechterung der Bonität einen Ausfall der anderen Vertragspartei wahrscheinlich werden lässt, kann das Unternehmen nicht länger davon ausgehen, dass die Sicherungsbeziehung mit hoher Wahrscheinlichkeit eine Kompensation der Änderungen bei Cashflows des Sicherungsgeschäfts und des gesicherten Grundgeschäfts erreicht. Damit werden die Anforderungen des Wirksamkeitstests nicht mehr erfüllt. Selbst wenn der Ausfall der anderen Vertragspartei noch nicht wahrscheinlich ist, beeinflusst die Verschlechterung der Bonität beeinflusst den beizulegenden Zeitwert des Sicherungsinstruments und verschlechtert damit die Wirksamkeit des Sicherungsgeschäfts[142] (siehe Unterabschnitt (a) in dieser Rn.)

Änderungen in der Bonität der anderen Vertragspartei des Sicherungsinstruments haben allerdings nicht nur im Falle einer Verschlechterung Auswirkungen auf die Wirksamkeit des Sicherungsgeschäfts, sondern auch bei Verbesserungen, da letztere ebenfalls den beizulegenden Zeitwert des Sicherungsinstruments beeinflussen. Bei Vertragsparteien unterschiedlicher Bonität kann zudem eine Änderung der Kreditrisiko-Spannen (**credit spreads**) die Wirksamkeit des Sicherungsgeschäfts beeinflussen.

223   Obwohl IAS 39 die Diskussion der Auswirkung des Kreditrisikos auf die Wirksamkeit von Sicherungsgeschäften auf Änderungen in der Bonität der anderen Vertragspartei des Sicherungsinstruments beschränkt, kann auch die Bonität des bilanzierenden Unternehmens selbst relevant sein.[143] Dies ist von der Art des jeweiligen Sicherungsinstruments abhängig. Bei Sicherungsinstrumenten, die – mindestens potenziell – Zahlungen beider Vertragsparteien vorsehen, wird der beizulegende Zeitwert des Sicherungsinstruments von Änderungen in der Bonität *beider* Vertragsparteien beeinflusst. Solche Sicherungsinstrumente sind z.B. Zinsswaps, bei denen sich in Abhängigkeit des Zinsniveaus Zahlungen an das oder von dem bilanzierenden Unternehmen ergeben können. Daher beeinflusst eine Änderung in

---

139   Vgl. *PwC (Hrsg.)* IFRS Manual – Financial instruments, Rn 10.147 und 10.160.
140   So auch *PwC (Hrsg.)* IFRS Manual – Financial instruments, Rn 10.150.
141   Siehe IFRIC Update vom März 2007, S. 5.
142   Vgl. *PwC (Hrsg.)*, IFRS Manual of accounting – Financial instruments 2010, Rn 10.156.
143   Vgl. *Deloitte (Hrsg.)* iGAAP - Financial Instruments, 650.

der Bonität des bilanzierenden Unternehmens – sowohl eine Verbesserung wie eine Verschlechterung – auch die Wirksamkeit des Sicherungsgeschäfts. Für die Beurteilung ist allerdings das jeweilige Sicherungsinstrument an sich maßgeblich. Die Verwendung von **Sicherheiten** kann z.B. dazu führen, dass das die Kreditqualität des Sicherungsinstruments selbst weitgehend oder vollkommen unabhängig von der Bonität einer oder beider Vertragsparteien ist. Bei börsengehandelten Derivaten, die einem **Clearing** unterliegen, ist z.B. das Kreditrisiko der Vertragsparteien unerheblich. Die zunehmende Verbreitung der Besicherung von sog. **OTC** (over the counter) Derivaten, d.h. bilateralen Verträgen ohne Clearing, führt ebenfalls dazu, dass die Bonität der Vertragsparteien einen geringen Einfluss auf den beizulegenden Zeitwert hat. Bei Sicherungsinstrumenten, die aus Sicht des bilanzierenden Unternehmens stets einen Vermögenswert darstellen, ergeben sich dagegen keine Auswirkungen einer Änderungen in der Bonität des bilanzierenden Unternehmens auf die Wirksamkeit des Sicherungsgeschäfts. Der beizulegende Zeitwert von erworbenen Optionen[144] oder Fremdwährungsforderungen ist z.B. unabhängig von der Bonität des Inhabers.

Bei der Verwendung von **Optionen** als Sicherungsinstrument gab es in der Vergangenheit in der Praxis widersprüchliche Ansichten, wie der Wirksamkeitstest anzuwenden ist. Das IASB hat mittels einer Änderung von IAS 39 (IAS 39.AG99BA) klar gestellt, dass zur Bestimmung der Wirksamkeit des Sicherungsgeschäfts in diesen Fällen eine Annahme, dass das gesicherte Grundgeschäft einen Zeitwert einer Option aufweist, unzulässig ist. Daher ist die Änderung des beizulegenden Zeitwerts oder der Cashflows des gesicherten Grundgeschäft auf derselben Basis wie der *innere* Wert einer Option zu ermitteln. Die Wertänderung ergibt sich daher auf der Grundlage des Vergleichs zwischen dem (erwarteten) Preis oder Cashflow des gesicherten Grundgeschäfts mit dem abgesicherten Niveau (das so gewählt werden kann, dass es dem Ausübungspreis der Option entspricht). Da die aus dem Zeitwert der Option resultierende Änderung des beizulegenden Zeitwerts des Sicherungsgeschäfts kein Pendant im gesicherten Grundgeschäft hat, ergibt sich bei Bestimmung der Option in ihrer Gesamtheit als Sicherungsgeschäft eine Beeinträchtigung der Wirksamkeit des Sicherungsgeschäfts. Das führt zu einem hohen Risiko, dass das Sicherungsgeschäft die Voraussetzungen bzgl. der Wirksamkeit nicht erfüllt. Seit der Änderung von IAS 39 ist es daher in der Praxis empfehlenswert, bei Optionen generell eine Aufspaltung in Zeitwert und inneren Wert vorzunehmen und nur den inneren Wert als Sicherungsinstrument zu bestimmen.[145] Da die Einbeziehung des Zeitwerts der Option in die Sicherungsbeziehung ohnehin nur zu sofort erfolgswirksam in der Gewinn- und Verlustrechnung zu erfassender Unwirksamkeit[146] führt, hat die Nichtaufspaltung keinerlei Vorteil (jedoch den Nachteil der Beeinträchtigung des Wirksamkeitstests).

224

Bei der Verwendung der **Dollar Offset** Methode[147] haben sich in der Praxis häufig Probleme ergeben, wenn die Änderung des beizulegenden Zeitwerts oder der Cash-flows des Sicherungsinstruments und des gesicherten Grundgeschäfts geringfügig sind. Bei Sicherungsgeschäften, die nicht vollständig wirksam sind (d.h. 100%), können kleine Unterschiede in absoluten Beträgen zu großen prozentualen Abweichungen führen. Wenn sich z.B. der beizulegenden Zeitwert eines € 100m Zinsswaps um € 1.000 ändert während sich der beizulegenden Zeitwert des gesicherten Grundgeschäfts (z.B. das Benchmark-Zinsrisiko eines Darlehens) um 1.500 EUR ändert, so beträgt die Wirksamkeit nur 66,7% (oder alternativ 150%)[148] und liegt damit außerhalb der erforderlichen Bandbreite zwischen 80% und 125%.

225

---

144 Dies gilt nur im engen Sinn auf Bruttobasis, d.h. bei Optionen, die keine geschriebenen Optionselemente umfassen (wie z.B. Collars, die erworbene und geschriebene Optionselemente kombinieren).
145 Siehe Rn 182.
146 Siehe Rn 234.
147 Siehe Rn 215.
148 Siehe Rn 218.

226   Teilweise wird in der Praxis versucht, dieses Problem durch die Anwendung der Dollar Offset Methode auf kumulativer statt periodischer Basis zu lösen.[149] Die **kumulative Dollar Offset Methode** vergleicht die Änderung des beizulegenden Zeitwerts oder der Cashflows in Bezug auf den Zeitraum seit Beginn der Sicherungsbeziehung bis zum jeweiligen Bilanzstichtag. Die **periodische Dollar Offset Methode** dagegen vergleicht die Änderung des beizulegenden Zeitwerts oder der Cashflows in Bezug auf die aktuelle Berichtsperiode (d.h. den Zeitraum zwischen dem vorhergehenden Wirksamkeitstest und dem Bilanzstichtag). Ein Unternehmen kann für jede einzelne Sicherungsbeziehung zwischen diesen beiden Formen der Dollar Offset Methode wählen, wobei die gewählte Methode in die Dokumentation zu Beginn der Sicherungsbeziehung einzubeziehen ist (IAS 39 IG F.4.2).

227   Bei Wahl der **kumulativen Dollar Offset Methode** ist jedoch zu beachten, dass bei Sicherungsbeziehungen, in denen das Sicherungsinstrument ein Swap ist, der zu Beginn der Sicherungsbeziehung bereits im Geld oder aus dem Geld ist, spätestens beim letzten retrospektiven Test die Bandbreite zwischen 80% und 125% verfehlt wird. Dies liegt daran, dass sich die Änderung des beizulegenden Zeitwerts oder der Cashflows bzgl. des gesicherten Grundgeschäfts über die *Gesamtlaufzeit* der Sicherungsbeziehung auf Null ausgleichen (d.h. eine kumulative Änderung von Null haben), während sich beim Sicherungsinstrument eine kumulative Änderung von größer oder kleiner Null ergibt (aufgrund der auf den beizulegenden Zeitwert im Zeitpunkt des Beginns der Sicherungsbeziehung entfallenden Änderung des beizulegenden Zeitwerts). Daher ergibt sich eine Wirksamkeit von Null (oder alternativ von unendlich),[150] so dass in der letzten Periode der Sicherungsbeziehung die Voraussetzungen für die Bilanzierung als Sicherungsgeschäft nicht mehr vorliegen.[151]

228   IAS 39 enthält keine konkreten Vorgaben, wie die Mindestanforderung der Bandbreite zwischen 80% und 125% an die Wirksamkeit von Sicherungsgeschäften auf **statistische Verfahren** anzuwenden ist. Unternehmen, die für den Wirksamkeitstest z.B. eine **Regressionsanalyse** verwenden, haben daher angemessene *konkrete* Schwellenwerte für die Auswertung der Regressionsanalyse als Mindestanforderung an die Wirksamkeit des Sicherungsgeschäfts zu bestimmen und in die Dokumentation zu Beginn der Sicherungsbeziehung einzubeziehen (IAS 39.IG F.4.4). In der Praxis sind folgende Schwellenwerte bzgl. der Auswertung einer (linearen) Regressionsanalyse üblich:[152]

(a) Die Steigung der Regressionsgeraden liegt zwischen -0,8 und -1,25. Dabei ist diejenige Steigung relevant, die sich ggf. *nach* Anpassung der Relation zwischen gesichertem Grundgeschäft und Sicherungsinstrument ergibt.[153]

(b) Das Bestimmtheitsmaß (R^2 oder auch Determinationskoeffizient) beträgt mindestens 80%.

(c) Die Ergebnisse sind statistisch signifikant, nachgewiesen mittels Teststatistik (F-Test) auf Basis eines 95% Konfidenzniveaus.

229   Die **Frequenz des Wirksamkeitstests** muss mindestens so hoch sein, dass die Wirksamkeit eines Sicherungsgeschäfts zu jedem Berichtsstichtag ermittelt wird. Dies gilt sowohl für Jahresabschlüsse als auch für Zwischenabschlüsse (IAS 39.AG106). In der Praxis bedeutet dies, dass bei einem periodischen[154] Wirksamkeitstest die Wirksamkeit für den Zeitraum des jeweiligen Geschäftsjahres oder Zwischenberichtsperiode bestimmt wird. Bei einem kumulativen[155] Wirksamkeitstest wird die Wirksamkeit auf Basis des Zeitraums von Beginn der Sicherungsbeziehung bis zum jeweiligen Abschlussstichtag bestimmt.

---

149 Vgl. *PwC (Hrsg.)* IFRS Manual – Financial instruments, Rn 10. 165.
150 Siehe Rn 218.
151 Zu den Auswirkungen siehe Rn 237 und 248.
152 Siehe z.B. *Deloitte (Hrsg.)* iGAAP - Financial Instruments, 726ff; *PwC (Hrsg.)* IFRS Manual – Financial instruments, Rn 10.175 und *Ernst & Young (Hrsg.)* International GAAP, 2589.
153 Siehe Rn 193 und 199.
154 Siehe Rn 226.
155 Siehe Rn 226.

c) Die Bilanzierung einer Absicherung des beizulegenden Zeitwerts. Die Bilanzierung der Absicherung des beizulegenden Zeitwerts (**fair value hedge**) verändert grundsätzlich nicht die Bilanzierung des Sicherungsinstruments sondern nur die des gesicherten Grundgeschäfts.

230

Die Bilanzierung des **Sicherungsinstruments** im Rahmen der Absicherung des beizulegenden Zeitwerts bleibt für die folgenden Arten von Sicherungsinstrumenten unverändert:

231

- *Derivative* Finanzinstrumente. Die Gewinne und Verluste aus Änderungen des beizulegenden Zeitwerts werden ohnehin erfolgswirksam in der Gewinn- und Verlustrechnung erfasst.[156]
- *Nicht-derivative* finanzielle Vermögenswerte oder Verbindlichkeiten,[157] bei denen es sich um *monetäre* finanzielle Posten handelt (d.h. Fremdwährungsforderungen und -verbindlichkeiten). Die Wechselkursgewinne und -verluste dieser Finanzinstrumente werden bereits nach IAS 21 sofort erfolgswirksam in der Gewinn- und Verlustrechnung erfasst (IAS 21.28). Dies gilt auch bei monetären finanziellen Vermögenswerten, die als zur Veräußerung verfügbare finanzielle Vermögenswerte kategorisiert sind (IAS 39.AG95).
- *Nicht-derivative* finanzielle Vermögenswerte, bei denen es sich um *nicht-monetäre* finanzielle Posten handelt und deren Wechselkursgewinne und -verluste in der Gewinn- und Verlustrechnung erfasst werden (z.B. Investitionen in Eigenkapitalinstrumente der Kategorie „erfolgswirksam zum beizulegenden Zeitwert bewertet").[158]

Dagegen ändert sich die Bilanzierung des Sicherungsinstruments im Rahmen der Absicherung des beizulegenden Zeitwerts, wenn es sich beim Sicherungsinstrument um einen *nicht-derivativen* finanziellen Vermögenswert handelt, der ein *nicht-monetärer* Posten ist und dessen Wechselkursgewinne und -verluste im sonstigen Ergebnis erfasst werden (d.h. Investitionen in Eigenkapitalinstrumente der Kategorie „zur Veräußerung verfügbare finanzielle Vermögenswerte"[159]). Für diese Sicherungsinstrumente sind die Wechselkursgewinne und -verluste während der Laufzeit der Sicherungsbeziehung statt im sonstigen Ergebnis in der Gewinn- und Verlustrechnung zu erfassen (IAS 39.89(a)). Dagegen können Investitionen in Eigenkapitalinstrumente, die mangels verlässlicher Bestimmbarkeit ihres beizulegenden Zeitwerts zu Anschaffungskosten bewertet werden,[160] nicht als Sicherungsinstrument dienen (IAS 39. AG96).

232

Für das **gesicherte Grundgeschäft** ändert sich die Bilanzierung wie folgt:

233

(a) Erfolgt die Bewertung des gesicherten Grundgeschäfts nicht bereits zum beizulegenden Zeitwert, so ist dessen Buchwert um die auf das abgesicherte Risiko entfallende Änderung des beizulegenden Zeitwerts des Grundgeschäftes anzupassen. Diese Anpassung ist sofort als Gewinn oder Verlust ergebniswirksam in der Gewinn- und Verlustrechnung zu erfassen (IAS 39.89(b)). Dies betrifft gesicherte Grundgeschäfte, die zu fortgeführten Anschaffungskosten (z.B. festverzinsliche Darlehen) oder Anschaffungskosten (z.B. Rohstoffvorräte) bewertet werden.

(b) Handelt es sich beim gesicherten Grundgeschäft um eine *feste Verpflichtung*, so wird die kumulierte Änderung des beizulegenden Zeitwerts, die auf das gesicherte Risiko entfällt, als Vermögenswert oder Verbindlichkeit in der Bilanz angesetzt (IAS 39.93). Die Bilanzierung als Sicherungsgeschäft geht daher den normalen Ansatzkriterien für schwebende Geschäfte[161] vor. Die Änderung dieses Bilanzpostens ist sofort als Gewinn oder Verlust ergebniswirksam in der Gewinn- und Verlustrechnung zu erfassen. Im Zeitpunkt des Erfüllungsgeschäfts wird der Buchwert entsprechend in die Bewertung der Transaktion einbezogen (IAS 39.94). Bei der Absicherung des Einkaufs von Sachanlagen

---

156 Siehe Rn 155.
157 Siehe Rn 180.
158 Siehe Rn 155.
159 Siehe Rn 156.
160 Siehe Rn 138 und 170.
161 Siehe Rn 52.

im Rahmen einer festen Verpflichtung gegen Währungsrisiken werden z.B. die Anschaffungskosten dieser Sachanlagen um den Buchwert der festen Verpflichtung angepasst. Werden Verkaufserlöse aus einer festen Verpflichtung gegen Währungsrisiken abgesichert, werden z.B. die Umsatzerlöse aus der Transaktion um den Buchwert der festen Verpflichtung angepasst.

(c) Ist das gesicherte Grundgeschäft ein zur Veräußerung verfügbarer finanzieller Vermögenswert, so erfolgt die Bewertung bereits zum beizulegenden Zeitwert. Daher ist nur die Erfassung des Gewinns oder Verlusts aus der Änderung des beizulegenden Zeitwerts dahingehend zu ändern, dass der auf das abgesicherte Risiko entfallende Gewinn oder Verlust sofort erfolgswirksam in der Gewinn- und Verlustrechnung statt im sonstigen Ergebnis erfasst wird (IAS 39.89(b)).

Wenn nur bestimmte Risiken statt des gesamten Grundgeschäfts abgesichert werden, so bleibt die Bilanzierung von Änderungen des beizulegenden Zeitwerts des Grundgeschäfts im Hinblick auf diese nicht abgesicherten Risiken unverändert (IAS 39.90).

234   Aufgrund der Erfassung der Änderung des beizulegenden Zeitwerts sowohl des Sicherungsinstruments als auch des gesicherten Grundgeschäfts (soweit auf das abgesicherte Risiko entfallend) in der Gewinn- und Verlustrechnung ist bei der Absicherung des beizulegenden Zeitwerts automatisch sichergestellt, dass ein ggf. nicht kompensierter Teil der Änderung des beizulegenden Zeitwerts auf Seiten des Sicherungsinstruments oder des gesicherten Grundgeschäfts automatisch sofort erfolgswirksam erfasst wird. Ein solcher nicht kompensierter Teil der Änderung des beizulegenden Zeitwerts tritt auf, wenn das Sicherungsgeschäft nicht vollständig (d.h. 100%) wirksam ist und wird auch als „**Unwirksamkeit bzw. Ineffektivität**" (**hedge ineffectiveness**) bezeichnet.

235   In folgenden Fällen ist die Bilanzierung als Sicherungsgeschäft (prospektiv) zu beenden (IAS 39.91):
- Die Voraussetzungen für die Bilanzierung als Sicherungsgeschäft sind nicht mehr erfüllt.[162]
- Das Sicherungsinstrument entfällt. Dies ist der Fall, wenn das Sicherungsinstrument nicht mehr besteht, weil es ausgelaufen ist (d.h. seine Fälligkeit erreicht hat) oder veräußert, beendet oder ausgeübt wurde. Wenn ein Unternehmen im Rahmen seiner Sicherungsstrategie ein Sicherungsinstrument verlängert (**rollover**) oder durch ein anderes ersetzt ist dies nicht als Auslaufen oder Beendigung des Sicherungsinstruments zu werten. Allerdings ist diese Strategie explizit in die Dokumentation zu Beginn der Sicherungsbeziehung einzubeziehen.
- Das Unternehmen hebt die Bestimmung als Sicherungsgeschäft auf. Dies steht nach IAS 39 jederzeit im freien Ermessen des Unternehmens.

236   Die Folge der prospektiven Beendigung der Bilanzierung als Sicherungsgeschäft ist, dass die besondere Bilanzierung des gesicherten Grundgeschäfts[163] und ggf. des Sicherungsgeschäfts[164] endet. Soweit der Buchwert des gesicherten Grundgeschäfts angepasst wurde,[165] ergibt sich die Folgebilanzierung nach Beendigung der Bilanzierung als Sicherungsgeschäft wie folgt:
- Für zu Anschaffungskosten bewertete gesicherte Grundgeschäfte stellt der angepasste Buchwert die neuen Anschaffungskosten dar. Wurden z.B. Rohstoffvorräte bzgl. der Änderung[166] des beizulegenden Zeitwerts abgesichert, so werden diese mit ihrem diesbzgl. angepassten Buchwert in die Material- oder Umsatzkosten im Zeitpunkt ihres Verkaufs oder im Zeitpunkt ihres Verbrauchs in die Herstellungskosten anderer Vermögenswerte einbezogen.

---

162 Siehe Rn 206.
163 Siehe Rn 233.
164 Siehe Rn 232.
165 Siehe Rn 233(a)
166 Siehe Rn 233(b)

- Handelt es sich beim gesicherten Grundgeschäft um eine feste Verpflichtung, so bleibt deren Buchwert, der als Vermögenswert oder Verbindlichkeit erfasst wurde, bis zum Zeitpunkt des Erfüllungsgeschäfts unverändert.[167] Im Zeitpunkt des Erfüllungsgeschäfts wird der Buchwert entsprechend in die Bewertung der Transaktion einbezogen.

- Für zu fortgeführten Anschaffungskosten bewertete Finanzinstrumente ist der Anpassungsbetrag im Rahmen der **Effektivzinsmethode**[168] zu amortisieren. Die Amortisation kann beginnen, sobald ein Anpassungsbetrag besteht und muss spätestens ab Beendigung der Bilanzierung als Sicherungsgeschäft erfolgen. Der Effektivzinssatz ist im Zeitpunkt des Beginns der Amortisation des Anpassungsbetrags (neu) zu ermitteln (IAS 39.92).

Wenn das Nichterfüllen des **Wirksamkeitstests** zur Beendigung der Bilanzierung als Sicherungsgeschäft führt, so ist diese Bilanzierung ab dem Zeitpunkt zu beenden, in dem der Wirksamkeitstest das letzte Mal erfüllt wurde. Dies ist regelmäßig das Ende der vorhergehenden Berichtsperiode. Wenn ein Unternehmen jedoch das Nichterfüllen des Wirksamkeitstests auf ein bestimmtes Ereignis oder eine Änderung von Umständen zurückführen kann und die Wirksamkeit des Sicherungsgeschäfts für den vorhergehenden Zeitraum nachweisen kann, so wird die Bilanzierung als Sicherungsgeschäft erst ab dem Zeitpunkt des Eintritts dieses Ereignisses oder dieser Änderung der Umstände beendet (IAS 39. AG113). Wenn der Wirksamkeitstest z.B. aufgrund des mit dem Sicherungsinstrument verbundenen Kreditrisikos scheitert, lässt sich dies in der Praxis oft auf einen bestimmten Zeitpunkt nach dem Ende der vorhergehenden Berichtsperiode zurückführen (z.B. eine Ratingherabstufung oder ein starker Ausschlag im sog. „credit spread" für ein Unternehmen). — 237

d) Die Bilanzierung einer Absicherung von Zahlungsströmen. Die Bilanzierung der Absicherung von Zahlungsströmen (**cash flow hedge**) verändert sowohl die Bilanzierung des Sicherungsinstruments als auch die des gesicherten Grundgeschäfts. — 238

Die Bilanzierung des Sicherungsinstruments im Rahmen der Absicherung von Zahlungsströmen ändert sich dahingehend, dass derjenige Teil des Gewinns oder Verlusts, der die auf das abgesicherte Risiko entfallende Änderung der Cashflows des gesicherten Grundgeschäfts (bewertet zum beizulegenden Zeitwert)[169] kompensiert, im sonstigen Ergebnis statt erfolgswirksam in der Gewinn- und Verlustrechnung erfasst wird. Ein etwaiger verbleibender Teil des Gewinns oder Verlusts aus dem Sicherungsinstrument stellt keine wirksame Absicherung des gesicherten Risikos dar (sog. **Unwirksamkeit**)[170] und verbleibt entsprechend in der Gewinn- und Verlustrechnung (IAS 39.95). Der Gewinn oder Verlust aus dem Sicherungsinstrument ist die Änderung des beizulegenden Zeitwerts bei Derivaten bzw. der Wechselkursgewinn oder -verlust bei nicht-derivativen Sicherungsinstrumenten. — 239

Die genaue Ermittlung der im sonstigen Ergebnis und in der Gewinn- und Verlustrechnung zu erfassenden Teile des Gewinns oder Verlusts aus dem Sicherungsinstrument[171] basiert auf dem für das jeweilige Sicherungsgeschäft im *kumulierten* sonstigen Ergebnis (d.h. im Eigenkapital – die sog. **cash flow hedge reserve**) erfassten Betrag. Dieser Betrag ergibt sich als der geringere der beiden folgenden Beträge auf der Basis absoluter[172] Größen (IAS 39.96(a)): — 240

- dem kumulativen Gewinn oder Verlust aus dem Sicherungsinstrument vom Beginn der Sicherungsbeziehung bis zum Bilanzstichtag und

---

167 Ausgenommen Fälle, in denen ein Vermögenswert wertgemindert ist.
168 Siehe Rn 146-153.
169 Die Änderung der Cashflows bei der Absicherung von Zahlungsströmen kann nicht auf undiskontierter Basis erfolgen. Dies gilt sowohl für Zwecke des Wirksamkeitstests (siehe Rn 221) als auch die Ermittlung des wirksamen und des unwirksamen Teils des Gewinns oder Verlusts aus dem Sicherungsgeschäft (siehe IAS 39.96(a)(ii) mit explizitem Verweis auf den beizulegenden Zeitwert).
170 Siehe Rn 234.
171 Ggf. kann ein über den Gewinn oder Verlust aus dem Sicherungsinstrument hinausgehender Betrag zusätzlich erfolgswirksam in der Gewinn- und Verlustrechnung zu erfassen sein (siehe Rn 243).
172 Dies bedeutet negative Beträge werden als positive Beträge behandelt (d.h. mit -1 multipliziert).

- dem beizulegenden Zeitwert der kumulativen Änderung der erwarteten Cashflows aus dem gesicherten Grundgeschäft (soweit sie auf das abgesicherte Risiko entfallen) vom Beginn der Sicherungsbeziehung bis zum Bilanzstichtag. Die Bewertung der Änderung der erwarteten Cashflows zum beizulegenden Zeitwert bedeutet, dass eine Betrachtung zum *Barwert* zu erfolgen hat (d.h. eine Betrachtung undiskontierter Cashflows ist nicht zulässig).

241   Wenn nach Anpassung des kumulierten sonstigen Ergebnisses (d.h. des Eigenkapitals) an den so bestimmten Betrag noch ein Teil des Gewinns oder Verlusts aus dem Sicherungsinstrument verbleibt, ist dieser verbleibende Teil erfolgswirksam in der Gewinn- und Verlustrechnung zu erfassen (IAS 39.96(b)).

242   Die Auswirkung der Absicherung von Zahlungsströmen auf einzelne Perioden ist aufgrund der Ermittlung des Eigenkapitalpostens als geringerer aus zwei Beträgen (der sog. **„lower of" Test**) komplex. Eine Folge ist z.B., dass im Fall einer sog. „Untersicherung" (oft als **„underhedge"** bezeichnet) der gesamte kumulative Gewinn oder Verlust des Sicherungsinstruments (seit Beginn der Sicherungsbeziehung) erfolgsneutral im kumulierten sonstigen Ergebnis erfasst wird. Eine Untersicherung liegt vor, wenn der kumulative Gewinn oder Verlust aus dem Sicherungsinstrument geringer ist als die Änderung bzgl. des abgesicherten Risikos, so dass letzteres nicht vollständig kompensiert wird. Bei einer Untersicherung ergibt sich somit (*kumulativ* betrachtet) keine Auswirkung auf die Gewinn- und Verlustrechnung, obwohl das Sicherungsgeschäft nicht vollständig (d.h. 100%) wirksam war.

243   Allerdings kann sich in einer Periode, an deren Ende eine Untersicherung vorliegt, dennoch eine Auswirkung auf die Gewinn- und Verlustrechnung ergeben.

Beispiel

Periode:	P_0	P_1	P_2
Sicherungsgeschäft	0	10	20
Gesichertes Grundgeschäft	0	– 8	– 21
Kumuliertes sonstiges Ergebnis	0	– 8	– 20
Gewinn/Verlust	0	2	– 2

In Periode 2 beträgt Änderung des Betrags im kumulierten sonstigen Ergebnis 12 (Haben). Diese Änderung ist erforderlich, um den Saldo von 8 (Haben) zu Periodenbeginn auf den zum Periodenende ermittelten Wert von 20 (Haben) zu erhöhen. Der Gewinn aus dem Sicherungsgeschäft beträgt in Periode 2 jedoch nur 10 (Soll). Daher ist in Periode 2 ein Betrag von 2 (Soll) erfolgswirksam als Verlust gegen die Gewinn- und Verlustrechnung zu erfassen. In diesem Szenario ergibt sich somit eine Auswirkung auf die Gewinn- und Verlustrechnung obwohl am Periodenende eine Untersicherung vorliegt. Auf kumulativer Basis ist die Auswirkung auf die Gewinn- und Verlustrechnung dagegen Null, da der Verlust in Periode 2 die Umkehr des in Periode 1 als Folge einer Übersicherung erfassten Gewinns darstellt. Das Beispiel zeigt außerdem, dass sich eine Auswirkung auf die Gewinn- und Verlustrechnung ergeben kann, die nicht Teil des Gewinns oder Verlusts aus dem Sicherungsgeschäft ist (sondern über diesen hinaus geht).

244   Wenn ein Sicherungsinstrument statt in seiner Gesamtheit nur bzgl. einer seiner Komponenten als Bestandteil einer Sicherungsbeziehung bestimmt wird, so bleibt die Bilanzierung des nicht in die Sicherungsbeziehung einbezogenen Teils des Sicherungsinstruments unverändert (IAS 39.96(c)).[173]

245   Aufgrund der Bilanzierung als Absicherung von Zahlungsströmen verändert sich die **Bilanzierung des gesicherten Grundgeschäfts** in Abhängigkeit seiner jeweiligen Art wie folgt:

---

173 Siehe Rn 182.

- *Künftige finanzielle Vermögenswerte oder Verbindlichkeiten*: wenn die erwartete Transaktion zum Ansatz eines finanziellen Vermögenswerts oder einer finanziellen Verbindlichkeit führt, so ist der zuvor im kumulierten sonstigen Ergebnis erfasste Betrag in denselben Perioden vom Eigenkapital in die Gewinn- und Verlustrechnung umzugliedern, in denen das gesicherte Grundgeschäft im Hinblick auf das abgesicherte Risiko erfolgswirksam wird (IAS 39.97). Wenn z.B. der erwartete Erwerb einer Anleihe mittels eines Forward-Zinsswaps gegen das Zinsänderungsrisiko abgesichert wird, so wird der zwischen Beginn der Sicherungsbeziehung und dem Zeitpunkt des Erwerbs der Anleihe im kumulierten sonstigen Ergebnis erfasste Betrag über die Laufzeit der Anleihe als Anpassung des Zinsertrags in die Gewinn- und Verlustrechnung umgegliedert (so dass sich der Zinsertrag auf Basis des abgesicherten effektiven Zinssatzes ergibt). Dabei ist zu beachten, dass ein im kumulierten sonstigen Ergebnis erfasster Verlust sofort erfolgswirksam in die Gewinn- und Verlustrechnung umzugliedern ist, sobald nicht mehr damit gerechnet wird, dass er in künftigen Perioden ausgeglichen wird (IAS 39.97). Wenn sich z.B. im Fall der Absicherung des erwarteten Erwerbs einer Anleihe nach deren Erwerb eine Wertminderung ergibt, so ist nicht nur der Buchwert der Anleihe in die Betrachtung einzubeziehen, sondern auch der im Hinblick auf diese Anleihe noch im kumulierten sonstigen Ergebnis erfasste Betrag aus der Absicherung von Zahlungsströmen.
- *Künftige nicht-finanzielle Vermögenswerte oder Verbindlichkeiten*: wenn die erwartete Transaktion zum Ansatz eines nicht-finanziellen Vermögenswerts oder einer nicht-finanziellen Verbindlichkeit führt, hat ein Unternehmen ein *Methodenwahlrecht*. Die erste Alternative ist, dieselbe Bilanzierung wie im Fall von künftigen *finanziellen* Vermögenswerten oder Verbindlichkeiten anzuwenden (IAS 39.98(a)) (siehe Unterabschnitt i in dieser Rn.) Die zweite Alternative ist, den im kumulierten sonstigen Ergebnis erfassten Betrag als integralen Bestandteil der erstmaligen Bewertung des nicht-finanziellen Vermögenswerts oder der nicht-finanziellen Verbindlichkeit zu behandeln. Dazu wird der gesamte Betrag in einem Schritt aus dem kumulierten sonstigen Ergebnis ausgebucht und in den Buchwert des gesicherten Grundgeschäfts einbezogen (**basis adjustment**) (IAS 39.98(b)). Bei dieser Alternative ist zu beachten, dass das Gesamtergebnis (d.h. die Summe aus Gewinn oder Verlust und dem sonstigen Ergebnis) verzerrt werden kann. Bei der Absicherung des Erwerbs einer Sachanlage gegen das Währungsrisiko beeinflusst z.B. die Umgliederung des Wechselkursgewinnes oder -verlusts aus dem Sicherungsgeschäft vom kumulierten sonstigen Ergebnis in die Anschaffungskosten der Sachanlage das Gesamtergebnis in Höhe des gesamten Betrags in der Periode der Anschaffung der Sachanlage (IAS 39 IG F.1.7). Im Vergleich dazu würde das Gesamtergebnis bei Wahl der ersten Alternative in Teilbeträgen über die Nutzungsdauer der Sachanlage in das Gesamtergebnis einbezogen. Da es sich um ein Methodenwahlrecht handelt, hat ein Unternehmen eine der beiden Alternativen zu wählen und dann stetig auf alle erwarteten Transaktion, die zum Ansatz eines nicht-finanziellen Vermögenswerts oder einer nicht-finanziellen Verbindlichkeit führen, anzuwenden (IAS 39.99).
- *Alle übrigen erwarteten Transaktionen*: wenn die erwartete Transaktion nicht zum Ansatz eines Vermögenswerts oder einer Verbindlichkeit führt, so ist der zuvor im kumulierten sonstigen Ergebnis erfasste Betrag in denselben Perioden vom Eigenkapital in die Gewinn- und Verlustrechnung umzugliedern, in denen das gesicherte Grundgeschäft im Hinblick auf das abgesicherte Risiko erfolgswirksam wird (IAS 39.100). Bei der Absicherung von erwarteten Instandhaltungsaufwendungen oder erwarteten Verkäufen wird z.B. der zwischen Beginn der Sicherungsbeziehung und dem Zeitpunkt der Transaktion im kumulierten sonstigen Ergebnis erfasste Betrag in der Periode, in der der Instandhaltungsaufwand bzw. die Umsatzerlöse anfallen, in die Gewinn- und Verlustrechnung umgegliedert.

246

In folgenden Fällen ist die Bilanzierung als Sicherungsgeschäft (prospektiv) zu beenden (IAS 39.101):
- Die Voraussetzungen für die Bilanzierung als Sicherungsgeschäft sind nicht mehr erfüllt.[174] Wenn dies auf das Unterschreiten der erforderlichen „hohen Eintrittswahrscheinlichkeit"[175] im Hinblick auf eine erwartete Transaktion zurückzuführen ist, so ergeben sich unterschiedliche Konsequenzen in Abhängigkeit davon, ob mit dem Eintreten der erwarteten Transaktion noch gerechnet wird. Diese Schwelle spiegelt eine niedrigere Eintrittswahrscheinlichkeit wider als die „hohe Eintrittswahrscheinlichkeit" (IAS 39.101(c)).
- Das Sicherungsinstrument entfällt. Dies ist der Fall, wenn das Sicherungsinstrument nicht mehr besteht, weil es ausgelaufen ist (d.h. seine Fälligkeit erreicht hat) oder veräußert, beendet oder ausgeübt wurde. Wenn ein Unternehmen im Rahmen seiner Sicherungsstrategie ein Sicherungsinstrument verlängert (**rollover**) oder durch ein anderes ersetzt ist dies nicht als Auslaufen oder Beendigung des Sicherungsinstruments zu werten. Allerdings ist diese Strategie explizit in die Dokumentation zu Beginn der Sicherungsbeziehung einzubeziehen.
- Das Unternehmen hebt die Bestimmung als Sicherungsgeschäft auf. Dies steht nach IAS 39 jederzeit im freien Ermessen des Unternehmens.

247 Die Folge der prospektiven Beendigung der Bilanzierung als Sicherungsgeschäft ist, dass die besondere Bilanzierung des des Sicherungsgeschäfts[176] endet. Für das gesicherte Grundgeschäft ergibt sich die Folgebilanzierung nach Beendigung der Bilanzierung als Sicherungsgeschäft wie folgt:
- Der zwischen Beginn der Sicherungsbeziehung und dem Zeitpunkt der Beendigung der Bilanzierung als Sicherungsgeschäft im kumulierten sonstigen Ergebnis erfasste Betrag wird grundsätzlich[177] bis zum Eintritt der erwarteten Transaktion unverändert gelassen. Bei Eintritt der erwarteten Transaktion erfolgt die Bilanzierung des gesicherten Grundgeschäfts in Abhängigkeit seiner jeweiligen Art wie bei Sicherungsbeziehungen, die nicht vorzeitig beendet wurden (siehe Rn. 245).
- Wenn nicht mehr mit dem Eintreten der erwarteten Transaktion gerechnet wird,[178] wird der zwischen Beginn der Sicherungsbeziehung und dem Zeitpunkt der Beendigung der Bilanzierung als Sicherungsgeschäft im kumulierten sonstigen Ergebnis erfasste Betrag sofort in voller Höhe erfolgswirksam in die in die Gewinn- und Verlustrechnung umgegliedert (IAS 39.101(c)).

248 Wenn das Nichterfüllen des Wirksamkeitstests zur Beendigung der Bilanzierung als Sicherungsgeschäft führt, so gelten für den relevanten Zeitpunkt dieselben Überlegungen wie bei der Absicherung des beizulegenden Zeitwerts (siehe Rn. 237).

249 **X. Inkrafttreten und Übergangsvorschriften. 1. IAS 39.** Die derzeit gültige Fassung von IAS 39 beruht auf der Version, die im Rahmen des „Improvement Projects" entwickelt wurde, um eine stabile Plattform für 2005 für die Erstanwendung von IFRS in der Europäischen Union, Australien und Neuseeland zu schaffen. Diese Fassung hat seitdem zahlreiche Änderungen erfahren. Zu den wichtigsten zählen:
- *Option der Bilanzierung zum beizulegenden Zeitwert (fair value option)*: im Juni 2005 veröffentlichte das IASB Änderungen, die die Ausübbarkeit der Option zur Bilanzierung zum beizulegenden Zeitwert vom Vorliegen mindestens einer von drei Voraussetzungen abhängig machte. Diese Änderungen unterlagen komplexen Übergangsvorschriften in Abhängigkeit davon, ob die Erstanwendung vor oder nach dem 1. Januar 2006 erfolgte.

---

174 Siehe Rn 206.
175 Siehe Rn 206
176 Siehe Rn 239-244.
177 Ausgenommen sind Fälle, in denen eine Wertminderung vorliegt (siehe Rn 245) sowie die im folgenden Unterabschnitt ii dieser Rn genannten Fälle.
178 Siehe Rn 246 ersten Unterpunkt.

- *Finanzielle Garantien (financial guarantee contracts)*: im August 2005 veröffentlichte das IASB Änderungen zur Bilanzierung von finanziellen Garantien sowie zur Anwendungskonkurrenz zwischen IFRS 4 *Insurance Contracts* und IAS 39. Die Übergangsvorschriften erlaubten bilanzierenden Unternehmen, die bereits zuvor IFRS 4 auf diese Art von Verträgen angewendet hatten, weiterhin IFRS 4 statt IAS 39 anzuwenden. Diese Änderungen traten für Geschäftsjahre beginnend am oder nach dem 1. Januar 2006 in Kraft.

- *Qualifizierende gesicherte Grundgeschäfte*: als Reaktion auf vom IFRIC[179] diskutierte Fragen, wie das Inflationsrisiko und der Zeitwert von Optionen in die Bestimmung von gesicherten Grundgeschäften einbezogen werden können, wurden im Juli 2008 diesbzgl. spezielle Regelungen zu IAS 39 hinzugefügt. Diese Änderungen traten für Geschäftsjahre beginnend am oder nach dem 1. Juli 2009 in Kraft. Der Übergang auf die neuen Vorschriften erfolgte rückwirkend.

- *Umgliederungen*: als Reaktion auf die globale Finanzkrise wurden Möglichkeiten zur Umgliederung von nicht-derivativen finanziellen Vermögenswerten aus Kategorien mit einer Bewertung zum beizulegenden Zeitwert in Kategorien mit einer Bewertung zu fortgeführten Anschaffungskosten geschaffen. Diese Änderungen wurden im Oktober 2008 veröffentlicht, gefolgt von einer Klarstellung bzgl. des Inkrafttretens und der Übergangsvorschriften im November 2008. Diese Änderungen traten mit Rückwirkung zum 1. Juli 2008 in Kraft.

2. IFRS 9. Die Anwendung von IFRS 9 ist für Geschäftsjahre ab dem 1. Januar 2013 verpflichtend 250
(IFRS 9.8.1.1). Eine vorzeitige Anwendung ist erlaubt, in der Europäischen Union mangels Umsetzung in EU-Recht (**Endorsement**) bisher aber noch nicht möglich. Hierbei ist zu beachten, dass sich aufgrund der noch verbleibenden Phasen des Projekts zur Ablösung von IAS 39 sowie des Projekts bzgl. „insurance contracts" eine Verschiebung des Inkrafttretens von IFRS 9 ergeben kann (IFRS 9.BC93).

Die Anwendung von IFRS 9 erfolgt grundsätzlich retrospektiv. Es bestehen folgende wesentliche 251
Ausnahmen von diesem Grundsatz:

- IFRS 9 ist nicht auf finanzielle Vermögenswerte anzuwenden, die bereits vor dem Datum der erstmaligen Anwendung ausgebucht worden sind, d.h. im Hinblick auf diese finanziellen Vermögenswerte sind weder Vorjahreszahlen noch Zahlen für das aktuelle Geschäftsjahr anzupassen. Dabei können Unternehmen als Datum der erstmaligen Anwendung jedes Datum zwischen dem 12. November 2009 und dem 31. Dezember 2010 wählen. Ab dem 1. Januar 2011 ist das Datum der erstmaligen Anwendung der Beginn der Berichtsperiode, in der IFRS 9 erstmalig angewendet wird (IFRS 9.8.2.1-8.2.2).

- Die Beurteilung des Geschäftsmodell-bezogenen Kriteriums[180] für die Kategorisierung finanzieller Vermögenswerte erfolgt auf der Grundlage der Verhältnisse im Zeitpunkt des Datums der erstmaligen Anwendung statt des Zeitpunkts des erstmaligen Ansatzes (IFRS 9.8.2.4).

- Ein Unternehmen kann die Option zur erfolgswirksamen Bilanzierung zum beizulegenden Zeitwert (**fair value option**) sowie die Option zum Ausweis der Änderung des beizulegenden Zeitwerts bestimmter Investitionen in Eigenkapitalinstrumente auf der Grundlage der Verhältnisse im Zeitpunkt des Datums der erstmaligen Anwendung ausüben. Diese Wahlrechtsausübung gilt dann retrospektiv (IFRS 9.8.2.7). In ähnlicher Weise kann ein Unternehmen eine vorherige Ausübung der fair value option widerrufen. Wenn die Voraussetzungen der fair value option im Zeitpunkt des Datums der erstmaligen Anwendung nicht mehr erfüllt ist, *muss* die Ausübung der fair value option widerrufen werden (IFRS 9.8.2.8).

---

179 Das IFRIC wurde 2010 in „IFRS Interpretations Committee" umbenannt.
180 Siehe Rn 127.

- Die Verhältnisse im Zeitpunkt des Datums der erstmaligen Anwendung sind ferner maßgeblich für die Ausübung oder den Widerruf einer zuvor ausgeübten fair value option bzgl. finanzieller Verbindlichkeiten. Dies gilt für die fair value option für finanzielle Verbindlichkeiten im Hinblick auf die Vermeidung oder erhebliche Verringerung einer Rechnungslegungsanomalie (IFRS 9.8.2.9).
- Wenn die Ermittlung der fortgeführten Anschaffungskosten für vergangene Perioden undurchführbar (IAS 8.5) ist, so ist der beizulegende Zeitwert im Zeitpunkt im Zeitpunkt des Datums der erstmaligen Anwendung als die neuen fortgeführten Anschaffungskosten heranzuziehen. Für die Vergleichszahlen ist ebenfalls der der jeweilige beizulegende Zeitwert als fortgeführte Anschaffungskosten zu verwenden (IFRS 9.8.2.10).
- Investitionen in Eigenkapitalinstrumente oder damit zusammenhängende Derivate, die gem. der Ausnahmeregelung in IAS 39 zu Anschaffungskosten bewertet wurden,[181] sind im Zeitpunkt der erstmaligen Anwendung zum beizulegenden Zeitwert zu bewerten. Der Unterschiedsbetrag zum vorherigen Buchwert ist direkt mit dem Eröffnungssaldo der Gewinnrücklagen (retained earnings) zu verrechnen (IFRS 9.8.2.11).
- Unternehmen, die IFRS 9 für Berichtsperioden vor dem 1. Januar 2012 anwenden, brauchen ihre Vergleichsperioden nicht anzupassen. In dem Fall sind etwaige Unterschiedsbeträge zwischen dem vorherigen und dem neuen Buchwert mit dem Eröffnungssaldo des Eigenkapitals zu Beginn der Berichtsperiode, die das Datum der erstmaligen Anwendung umfasst, zu verrechnen (IFRS 9.8.2.12).

252   **XI. IFRS für kleine und mittelgroße Unternehmen. 1. Überblick über die Struktur der Vorschriften.** Die Bilanzierung von Finanzinstrumenten ist aufgrund der damit verbundenen Komplexität eine besondere Herausforderung für kleine und mittelständische Unternehmen. Für den *IFRS for Small and Medium-sized Entities* (IFRS-SMEs) hat das IASB daher eine besondere Vorgehensweise gewählt. Die Bilanzierung von Finanzinstrumenten wird in **zwei verschiedene Kapitel** unterteilt. Abschnitt 11 behandelt einfache (basic) Finanzinstrumente und Abschnitt 12 behandelt die komplexeren Finanzinstrumente.

Ein Unternehmen hat ein **Wahlrecht** zwischen der Anwendung der Abschnitte 11 und 12 des **IFRS-SMEs** einerseits und der Ansatz- und Bewertungsvorschriften des **IAS 39** i.V.m. den Angabevorschriften der Abschnitte 11 und 12 des IFRS-SMEs. Dabei handelt es sich um ein Methodenwahlrecht, das dem Stetigkeitsgebot unterliegt (IFRS-SMEs Abschnitt 11.2).

253   Mit der Trennung der Vorschriften zur Bilanzierung von Finanzinstrumenten in zwei verschiedene Kapitel beabsichtigt das IASB, *innerhalb* des IFRS-SMEs eine Differenzierung vorzunehmen, die für Unternehmen mit ausschließlich einfachen Finanzinstrumenten eine zusätzliche Erleichterung schafft. Die Abschnitte 11 und 12 haben aufeinander abgestimmte Anwendungsbereiche, was Unternehmen mit ausschließlich einfachen Finanzinstrumenten ermöglicht, außerhalb des Anwendungsbereichs von Abschnitt 12 zu bleiben. In diesen Fällen braucht sich das Unternehmen gar nicht erst mit den Regelungen für die komplexeren Finanzinstrumente in Abschnitt 12 (z.B. Finanzderivate) zu befassen (IFRS-SMEs Abschnitt 11.1).

254   **Einfache Finanzinstrumente**, die in den Anwendungsbereich des Abschnitts 11 fallen, sind (IFRS-SMEs Abschnitt 11.5) z.B.:
- Bargeld;
- Sicht- und Termineinlagen bei Kreditinstituten;
- Geldmarktpapiere wie Commercial Paper oder Wechsel, die das Unternehmen als Aktiva hält;
- Forderungen und Verbindlichkeiten aus Lieferungen und Leistungen, einschließlich von Wechseln, sowie Darlehensforderungen und -verbindlichkeiten;
- Anleihen und ähnliche Schuldinstrumente;

---

181 Siehe Rn 138.

- Anlagen in nicht-wandelbare (non-convertible) und nicht-andienbare (non-puttable) Vorzugsaktien (preference shares)[182] sowie nicht-andienbare Stammaktien;
- Kreditzusagen *an*[183] das bilanzierende Unternehmen, für die kein Nettoausgleich in Zahlungmitteln möglich ist.

2. Einfache Finanzinstrumente. Die in Abschnitt 11 geregelten einfachen Finanzinstrumente werden grundsätzlich zu fortgeführten Anschaffungskosten bewertet. Ausnahmen gelten für: 255

- Kreditzusagen *an* das bilanzierende Unternehmen werden zu Anschaffungskosten abzüglich etwaiger Wertminderungen bewertet. Wenn das Unternehmen kein Entgelt für die erhaltene Kreditzusage entrichtet hat, erfolgt die Bewertung daher zu einem Buchwert von Null.
- Anlagen in nicht-wandelbare und nicht-andienbare Vorzugsaktien sowie nicht-andienbare Stammaktien werden erfolgswirksam zum beizulegenden Zeitwert bilanziert, sofern sie entweder öffentlich gehandelt (z.B. bei einer Börsennotierung) werden oder ihr beizulegender Zeitwert anderweitig verlässlich ermittelt werden kann. In allen anderen Fällen erfolgt die Bewertung zu Anschaffungkosten abzüglich etwaiger Wertminderungen.

3. Komplexe Finanzinstrumente. Die in Abschnitt 12 geregelten komplexen Finanzinstrumente werden grundsätzlich erfolgswirksam zum beizulegenden Zeitwert bilanziert. Eine Ausnahme gilt für vom bilanzierenden Unternehmen gehaltene Eigenkapitalinstrumente, die nicht öffentlich gehandelt werden und deren beizulegender Zeitwert auch nicht anderweitig verlässlich ermittelbar ist. Die Ausnahme umfasst auch Finanzinstrumente, die durch Übertragung solcher Eigenkapitalinstrumente zu erfüllen sind. Alle Finanzinstrumente, die dieser Ausnahmen unterliegen, werden zu Anschaffungkosten abzüglich etwaiger Wertminderungen bewertet (IFRS-SMEs Abschnitt 12.8).   256

Abschnitt 12 enthält auch Regelungen zur Bilanzierung von Sicherungsgeschäften (**hedge accounting**). Für Unternehmen, die nicht vom Wahlrecht der Anwendung von IAS 39 Gebrauch machen, ist die Bilanzierung von Sicherungsgeschäften nach Abschnitt 12 auf einen abschließenden Katalog von häufig auftretenden, relativ einfachen Kombinationen bestimmter Risiken und Sicherungsgeschäfte beschränkt.   257

Die in IFRS-SMEs Abschnitt 12.17 für die Bilanzierung von Sicherungsgeschäften **erlaubten Risiken** sind: 258

- das Zinsrisiko bzgl. eines zu fortgeführten Anschaffungskosten bewerteten Schuldinstruments,
- das mit einer festen Verpflichtung oder einer erwarteten Transaktion mit hoher Eintrittswahrscheinlichkeit verbundene Währungsrisiko oder das Zinsrisiko,
- das Preisrisiko von Rohstoffvorräten oder Rohstoffein- oder -verkäufen (in der Form einer festen Verpflichtung oder einer erwarteten Transaktion mit hoher Eintrittswahrscheinlichkeit) und
- das mit einer Nettoinvestition in einen ausländischen Geschäftsbetrieb verbundene Währungsrisiko.

Die in IFRS-SMEs Abschnitt 12.18 für die Bilanzierung von Sicherungsgeschäften **erlaubten Sicherungsinstrumente** müssen folgende kumulative Voraussetzungen erfüllen: 259

- es handelt sich um Zinsswaps, Währungsswaps, Devisentermingeschäfte oder Rohstofftermingeschäfte,
- der Vertrag besteht mit einer externen Vertragspartei,
- das Derivat hat eine Bezugsgröße (notional amount), die mit der des abgesicherten Grundgeschäfts (z.B. Darlehensbetrag oder Transaktionsvolumen in Fremdwährung oder Tonnen) übereinstimmt,
- das Derivat hat eine Fälligkeit vor derjenigen des gesicherten Grundgeschäfts und
- das Derivat hat keine Vorfälligkeits- oder Verlängerungsoptionen.

---

182 Die Verwendung des Begriffs „preference share" in der englischen Fassung ist unglücklich, da international sehr verschiedene Ausgestaltungen möglich sind. Im Vergleich dazu ist die Vorzugsaktie des deutschen Aktienrechts eher restriktiv reglementiert.
183 Kreditzusagen *durch* das bilanzierende Unternehmen an eine andere Partei sind dagegen im Regelfall als komplexes Instrument gem. Abschnitt 12 zu bilanzieren.

260   Unternehmen, für die dieser Katalog erlaubter Sicherungsbeziehungen zu restriktiv ist, bleibt daher nur die Ausübung des Methodenwahlrechts dahingehend, dass die Ansatz- und Bewertungsvorschriften von IAS 39 angewendet werden. Insbesondere die fehlende Verfügbarkeit von Optionen als Sicherungsinstrument wird sich für viele Unternehmen mit einem modernen Risikomanagement als nicht akzeptabel erweisen.

261   **XII. Ausblick.** Wie bereits zu Anfang dieses Kapitels[184] erwähnt, wird die Bilanzierung von Finanzinstrumenten derzeit vom IASB umfassend neu geregelt. Dabei stellen sich dem IASB mehrere Probleme:

- Das U.S. Financial Accounting Standards Board (FASB) verfolgt eine fundamental andere Richtung bzgl. der Bilanzierung von Finanzinstrumenten. Das FASB strebt ein weitgehend auf der Bewertung zum beizulegenden Zeitwert beruhendes Bilanzierungsmodell für Finanzinstrumente an, während sich das IASB mit IFRS 9 auf ein sog. „mixed measurement model" festgelegt hat, d.h. die Verwendung von zwei verschiedenen Bewertungskategorien (beizulegender Zeitwert und fortgeführte Anschaffungskosten). Im Vergleich zum Projekt des IASB zur Ablösung von IAS 39 hat das FASB auch erheblich weniger Interesse an der Bilanzierung von Sicherungsgeschäften und strebt lediglich begrenzte Verbesserungen statt einer umfassenden Reform an. Die angestrebte Annäherung zwischen IASB und FASB im Bereich der Bilanzierung von Finanzinstrumenten ist daher fraglich geworden.

- Die Ansichten bzgl. der Bilanzierung von Finanzinstrumenten sind sehr verschieden. Es wird für das IASB zunehmend schwierig, eine hinreichende Mehrheit zu finden, die neue Vorschläge unterstützt. Die wachsende Vielfalt von Ländern, die IFRS anwenden, trägt auch zu dieser Entwicklung bei.

- Im Hinblick auf die nächste Welle von Ländern, die IFRS als Bilanzierungsstandards übernehmen wollen, hat das IASB die Absicht, alle größeren Projekte auf der aktiven Agenda bis Ende Juni 2011 abzuschließen. Das hat Auswirkungen auf die für die jeweiligen Projekte verfügbare Zeit in Board-Sitzungen. Da das IASB den Projekten bzgl. „leasing", „revenue recognition", „insurance contracts" und der Ablösung von IAS 39 Priorität einräumt, wird es schwierig, andere Projekte wie z.B. bezüglich der Ausbuchung von Finanzinstrumenten (Derecognition) oder der Unterscheidung von Eigen- und Fremdkapitalinstrumenten bis 2011 abzuschließen.

262   Aufgrund der Priorität des Projekts zur Ablösung von IAS 39 ist davon auszugehen, dass das IASB die drei Hauptphasen bis Mitte 2011 abschließen wird. Die erste Phase bezüglich der Kategorisierung und Bewertung finanzieller Vermögenswerte ist bereits im November 2009 mit der Veröffentlichung von IFRS 9 *Financial Instruments* abgeschlossen worden. Die Kategorisierung und Bewertung finanzieller Verbindlichkeiten auf der Grundlage des im Mai 2010 veröffentlichten Standardentwurfs *Fair Value Option für finanzielle Verbindlichkeiten* erscheint ebenfalls realistisch. Die zweite Phase bzgl. der Bewertung zu fortgeführten Anschaffungskosten und der Bilanzierung von Wertminderungen finanzieller Vermögenswerte erscheint ebenfalls möglich (auch wenn dies ggf. wie bzgl. der finanziellen Verbindlichkeiten einen zweiten Standardentwurf, sog. „Re-exposure", einschließen könnte). Der Abschluss der dritten Phase zur Bilanzierung von Sicherungsgeschäften ist technisch die anspruchvollste Phase. Andererseits ist damit zu rechnen, dass diese Phase die größte Zustimmung findet, wenn man davon ausgeht, dass das IASB die Regelungen vereinfacht und mehr Szenarien als bisher einer Bilanzierung als Sicherungsgeschäft zugänglich macht. Vor diesem Hintergrund erscheint es möglich, dass das IASB auch die dritte Phase bis Mitte 2011 abschließt. Dies erfordete jedoch die Ausklammerung des Portfolio- oder Makrohedging. Dieser komplexe Teil soll zu einem späteren Zeitpunkt zur Diskussion gestellt werden.

263   In der **Europäischen Union** befindet sich IFRS 9 noch im Übernahmeprozess und ist daher noch nicht in EU-Recht umgesetzt worden. Es ist nicht ersichtlich, wie die EU zu einer einheitlichen Meinung oder mindestens einer politisch tragfähigen Mehrheit bzgl. der Entscheidung zur Übernahme von IFRS 9 in EU-Recht kommen will. Es bleibt abzuwarten, ob die noch verbleibenden Projektphasen zu

---

184 Siehe Rn 1.

Ergebnissen kommen, die die Verhältnisse in der EU ändern. Strategisch kann die EU kein Interesse daran haben, sich aus der Rechnungslegung nach IFRS zu verabschieden und stattdessen eine parallele EU-Rechnungslegung zu entwickeln. Dieser Versuch war mit den Richtlinien zuvor bereits eindrucksvoll gescheitert. Das Taktieren von Brüssel wird allerdings dazu führen, dass der europäische Einfluss auf die IFRS Entwicklung abnimmt und ggf. sogar dazu, dass europäische Unternehmen mit internationaler Ausrichtung freiwillig direkt IFRS anwenden und die Version nach EU-Recht zu einer reinen Pflichtübung wird.

XIII. Angaben gem. IFRS 7. 1. Normzweck und Anwendungsbereich. Während die Angabepflichten regelmäßig einen integralen Abschnitt desjenigen Standards bilden, auf den sie sich beziehen, besteht bzgl. der Angaben zu Finanzinstrumenten mit IFRS 7 ein gesonderter Standard. Dies liegt an der Entwicklung der Standards für die Bilanzierung von Finanzinstrumenten. Ursprünglich hatte das IASC mit einem Standard begonnen, der Angabepflichten speziell für Banken und ähnliche Finanzinstitutionen vorsah (der ehemalige IAS 30). Die späteren Standards IAS 32 und IAS 39 enthielten ursprünglich ihre eigenen Angabepflichten. Das IASB gelangte zur Auffassung, dass Informationen über die Risiken, denen Unternehmen ausgesetzt sind, und wie diese Risiken gesteuert werden, an Bedeutung gewinnen. Daher hat das IASB die Angabepflichten für Finanzinstrumente in einem Standard zusammengefasst und dabei insbesondere die Angaben zu Risikokonzentrationen, Ausfallrisiko, Liquiditätsrisiko und Marktrisiken reformiert.

Der Anwendungsbereich von IFRS 7 erstreckt sich auf alle Finanzinstrumente mit folgenden Ausnahmen für:

- Anteile an Tochterunternehmen, assoziierten Unternehmen und Gemeinschaftsunternehmen, auf die IAS 27 *Consolidated and Separate Financial Statements*, IAS 28 *Investments in Associates* oder IAS 31 *Interests in Joint Ventures* Anwendung finden(IFRS 7.3(a)).
- Rechte und Verpflichtungen eines Arbeitgebers aus Altersversorgungsplänen, die gem. IAS 19 *Employee Benefits* bilanziert werden(IFRS 7.3(b)).
- Versicherungsverträge gem. IFRS 4. Allerdings gelten die Angabepflichten von IFRS 7 für in Versicherungsverträge eingebettete Derivate, die gem. IAS 39 von separat bilanziert werden. Dasselbe gilt für diejenigen finanziellen Garantien, auf die IAS 39 angewendet[185] wird (IFRS 7.3(d)).
- Rechte und Verpflichtungen aus anteilsbasierten Vergütungen, die gem. IFRS 2 *Share-based Payment* bilanziert werden (IFRS 7.3(e)).

Dagegen sind folgende Sachverhalte im Anwendungsbereich von IFRS 7:

- Finanzierungsleasingverhältnisse sowie die aus einem Operating-Leasingverhältnis im Hinblick auf jeweils fälligen oder abgegrenzten Zahlungen angesetzten Forderungen oder Verbindlichkeiten, da diese Posten Finanzinstrumente sind (IAS 32.AG9).
- Verträge über den Kauf oder Verkauf nicht-finanzieller Posten, die gem. IAS 39[186] als Finanzinstrument bilanziert werden (IFRS 7.5).
- Bilanzunwirksame Finanzinstrumente wie z.B. Kreditzusagen, die vom Anwendungsbereich des IAS 39 ausgenommen sind[187] und daher nicht als Finanzinstrument in der Bilanz angesetzt werden (IFRS 7.4).

2. Struktur und Art der Angaben. Im folgenden wird nicht einzeln auf jede in IFRS 7 geforderte Angabe eingegangen. Stattdessen werden allgemein die Struktur und die Art der Angaben erklärt. Lediglich einige ausgewählte, besonders herausfordernde Angaben werden im Einzelnen erläutert.

---

185 Siehe Rn 249
186 Siehe Rn 4 und 16ff.
187 Siehe Rn 13ff.

268   Einige Angaben gem. IFRS 7 sind separat für jede **Klasse von Finanzinstrumenten** zu machen. Zu diesem Zweck hat ein Unternehmen die Finanzinstrumente so in Klassen zu gruppieren, dass der Art der anzugebenden Information und den Eigenschaften der Finanzinstrumente angemessen Rechnung getragen wird. Die Angaben sind so zu machen, dass sie sich auf die einzelnen Bilanzposten überleiten lassen (IFRS 7.6). Diese Klassen sind unternehmensspezifisch und daher nicht mit den Kategorien in IAS 39[188] oder IFRS 9[189] identisch (IFRS 7.B1). Allerdings müssen die vom Unternehmen bestimmten Klassen mindestens zwischen Finanzinstrumenten, die zu fortgeführten Anschaffungskosten und solchen, die zum beizulegenden Zeitwert bewertet werden, unterscheiden. Ferner müssen Finanzinstrumente außerhalb des Anwendungsbereichs von IFRS 7 als separate Klasse behandelt werden (IFRS 7.B2).

269   **a) Bilanzbezogene Angaben.** IFRS 7 verlangt zahlreiche Angaben, die der Erläuterung von Bilanzposten für Finanzinstrumente dienen. Diese Angaben betreffen:

- eine Aufgliederung nach den Kategorien gem. IAS 39 oder IFRS 9,
- besondere Angaben für diejenigen Kredite oder Forderungen sowie finanziellen Verbindlichkeiten, für die das Unternehmen die Fair Value Option[190] ausgeübt hat,
- Umgliederungen finanzieller Vermögenswerte,
- Ausbuchungen (Derecognition),
- Kreditsicherheiten,
- Wertberichtigungskonten,
- multiple Derivate mit voneinander abhängigen Werten, die in zusammengesetzte Finanzinstrumente (mit Eigen- und Fremdkapitalkomponenten) eingebettet sind und
- Verbindlichkeiten, deren Vertragskonditionen vom Unternehmen nicht eingehalten wurden (z.B. Zahlungsverzug).

270   Für Kredite oder Forderungen sowie finanzielle Verbindlichkeiten, für die das Unternehmen die Fair Value Option ausgeübt hat, ist der Teilbetrag der Änderung des beizulegenden Zeitwerts anzugeben, der auf eine Änderung des **Ausfallrisikos** (Credit Risk) zurückzuführen ist. Diese Angabe ist für die jeweilige Berichtsperiode sowie auf kumulierter Basis erforderlich (IFRS 7.9(c), 10(a)). Die Isolierung des Effekts einer Änderung des Ausfallrisikos auf den beizulegenden Zeitwert eines Finanzinstruments ist schwierig. IFRS 7 erlaubt die Ermittlung dieses Effekts auf *indirekte* Weise, indem von der gesamten Änderung des beizulegenden Zeitwerts diejenige Änderung subtrahiert wird, die auf Änderungen von Marktbedingungen bzgl. des Zinsrisikos, des Währungsrisikos oder anderer Preisrisiken (z.B. Rohstoffpreise) zurückzuführen ist. Allerdings steht es jedem Unternehmen offen, eine alternative Methode zu wählen, die zu einem genaueren Ergebnis führt.

271   In der Praxis wird weitgehend die im Anhang zu IFRS 7 (IFRS 7.B4) dargestellte vereinfachte Vorgehensweise herangezogen. Wenn ein Finanzinstrument lediglich dem Zinsrisiko als relevante Änderung von Marktbedingungen unterliegt, kann der auf die Änderung des Ausfallrisikos zurückzuführende Betrag der Änderung des beizulegenden Zeitwerts in drei Schritten ermittelt werden:

(a) Im ersten Schritt wird zu Periodenbeginn der interne Zinsfuß des Finanzinstruments auf Basis seines beizulegenden Zeitwerts und der noch ausstehenden vertraglichen Zahlungen ermittelt. Von diesem internen Zinsfuß wird der laufzeitkongruente Referenzzinssatz (z.B. LIBOR oder Euribor) abgezogen, um den individuellen Spread des Finanzinstruments zu Periodenbeginn zu ermitteln. Die Ermittlung des beizulegenden Zeitwerts in diesen Fällen ist oftmals schwierig. Während für Verbindlichkeiten teilweise ein beobachtbarer Marktpreis zur Verfügung steht, ist dies aufgrund der

---

188 Siehe Rn 103-124.
189 Siehe Rn 125-128.
190 Siehe Rn 110ff.

Definition der Kategorie „Kredite und Forderungen" für diese finanziellen Vermögenswerte nicht der Fall. In Fällen ohne beobachtbaren Marktpreis ist daher auf andere Bewertungsverfahren (z.B. Multiplikatormethoden) zurückzugreifen.

(b) Im zweiten Schritt wird am Periodenende der Barwert der noch ausstehenden vertraglichen Zahlungen ermittelt. Als Diskontierungszinssatz wird dafür der aktuelle laufzeitkongruente Referenzzinssatz zu Periodenende zuzüglich des zuvor zum Periodenbeginn ermittelten individuellen Spreads verwendet.

(c) Im dritten Schritt wird der so ermittelte Barwert mit dem beizulegenden Zeitwert des Finanzinstruments zum Periodenende verglichen. Die Differenz zwischen diesen beiden Werten kann für die Angabe des Effekts der Änderung des Ausfallrisikos auf den beizulegenden Zeitwert verwendet werden.

b) Auf die Gesamtergebnisrechnung bezogene Angaben. Im Hinblick auf die Gesamtergebnisrechnung verlangt IFRS 7 Angaben, die der Aufgliederung von Posten der Gewinn- und Verlustrechnung sowie des sonstigen Ergebnisses im Hinblick auf Erträge, Aufwendungen, Gewinne und Verluste im Zusammenhang mit Finanzinstrumenten dienen.   272

Bei der Angabe von gem. der Effektivzinsmethode ermitteltem Zinsertrag und Zinsaufwand ist zu beachten, dass diese Angabepflicht nur für diejenigen Finanzinstrumente gilt, die *nicht* erfolgswirksam zum beizulegenden Zeitwert bewertet werden (IFRS 7.20(b)). Da diese Angabe auf Zinsbeträge beschränkt ist, die mittels der Effektivzinsmethode ermittelt worden sind, dürfen keine anderen, nicht gem. der Effektivzinsmethode ermittelten Beträge, einbezogen werden. Die Praxis, auch anders ermittelte Zinsbeträge und andere finanzielle Erträge und Aufwendungen in den als „Zinsertrag" oder „Zinsaufwand" angegebenen Betrag einzubeziehen, ohne dass explizit eine separate und eindeutige Angabe der gem. der Effektivzinsmethode ermittelten Beträge erfolgt, ist daher nicht IFRS-konform und nur unter Wesentlichkeitsaspekten zu rechtfertigen.   273

Im Hinblick auf Finanzinstrumente der Kategorie erfolgswirksam zum beizulegenden Zeitwert bewertet ist inbesondere zu beachten, dass die aus ihnen resultierenden Gewinne und Verluste aus Änderungen des beizulegenden Zeitwerts keinen Zinsertrag oder Zinsaufwand im Sinne der Effektivzinsmethode darstellen. Aufgrund der erstmaligen Bewertung dieser Finanzinstrumente zum beizulegenden Zeitwert *ohne* Anpassung für Transaktionskosten (IAS 39.43; IFRS 9.5.1.1) ist die Effektivzinsmethode für diese Kategorie nicht anwendbar, da die Transaktionskosten nicht in den Effektivzinssatz einbezogen und über die Laufzeit des Finanzinstruments verteilt werden können. Die Angabe des Zinsertrags oder Zinsaufwands für Finanzinstrumente der Kategorie erfolgswirksam zum beizulegenden Zeitwert bewertet kann daher allenfalls als (freiwillige) pro-forma Angabe erfolgen. Daher darf ein Zinsertrag oder Zinsaufwand für Finanzinstrumente dieser Kategorie auf Basis des Zinskupons nicht so anzugeben werden, dass er mit der Pflichtangabe gem. IFRS 7 auf Basis der Effektivzinsmethode verwechselt werden kann.   274

c) Weitere Angaben. Neben den auf die Bilanz und die Gesamtergebnisrechnung bezogenen Angaben verlangt IFRS 7 weitere Angaben im Hinblick auf: 275
- die Bilanzierung von Sicherungsgeschäften und
- den beizulegenden Zeitwert.

Die Angaben bzgl. der **Bilanzierung von Sicherungsgeschäften** betreffen: 276
- die Art der Sicherungsbeziehung,
- die Sicherungsinstrumente und deren beizulegender Zeitwert,
- die Art der gesicherten Risiken,
- Erläuterungen von im Hinblick auf die Absicherung von beizulegenden Zeitwerten, Zahlungsströmen und Nettoinvestitionen in ausländische Geschäftsbetriebe in der Gewinn- und Verlustrechnung sowie im sonstigen Ergebnis erfasster Beträge und

- weitere Erläuterungen bzgl. der Absicherung von Zahlungsströmen im Hinblick auf die Perioden, in denen abgesicherte Grundgeschäfte voraussichtlich eintreten und erwartete Transaktionen, mit deren Eintritt nicht mehr gerechnet wird.

277 Die Angaben zum beizulegenden Zeitwert wurden im März 2009 durch das Projekt „Improving Disclosures about Financial Instruments" geändert. Die wesentliche Auswirkung dieser Änderung auf die Angaben zum beizulegenden Zeitwert war die Übernahme der Hierarchie beizulegender Zeitwerte (**Fair Value Hierarchy**) aus U.S. GAAP.

278 Die Angaben zum beizulegenden Zeitwert lassen sich wie folgt zusammenfassen:
- die Methoden und bei Verwendung von Bewertungsverfahren die Annahmen sowie etwaige Änderungen des Verfahrens einschließlich der Begründung der Änderungen;
- eine Aufgliederung der beizulegenden Zeitwerte je Klasse von Finanzinstrumenten nach der Ebene in der Hierarchie beizulegender Zeitwerte, in die sie jeweils fallen;
- wesentliche Umgliederungen zwischen den ersten beiden Ebenen der Hierarchie beizulegender Zeitwerte;
- eine Überleitung des Saldos beizulegender Zeitwerte in der dritten Ebene der Hierarchie beizulegender Zeitwerte vom Periodenbeginn zum Periodenende;
- der Teilbetrag der Gewinne und Verluste aus Änderungen des beizulegenden Zeitwerts in der dritten Ebene der Hierarchie, der auf am Periodenende noch in der Bilanz erfasste Finanzinstrumente entfällt;
- wenn sich der beizulegende Zeitwert in der dritten Ebene der Hierarchie wesentlich ändern würde, wenn andere durchaus mögliche Bewertungsannahmen verwendet würden, ist diese Tatsache anzugeben sowie der Effekt, der sich aus den alternativen Annahmne ergeben würde; und
- bei Abweichung des beizulegenden Zeitwerts vom Transaktionspreis in Fällen, in denen der beizulegende Zeitwert unter Verwendung auch nicht an einem Markt beobachtbarer Variablen ermittelt wird,[191] ist die noch in künftigen Perioden zu erfassende Differenz zwischen Transaktionspreis und beizulegendem Zeitwert anzugeben sowie die Bilanzierungsmethode bzgl. der Erfassung dieser Differenz.

279 Die Hierarchie beizulegender Zeitwerte ergibt sich auf der Basis desjenigen Eingangswerts (Input), der in die niedrigste Ebene der Bewertungshierarchie fällt und für den beizulegenden Zeitwert ingesamt signifikant ist. Die Bewertungshierarchie der Eingangswerte ist wie folgt (IFRS 7.27A):

(a) in einem aktiven Markt notierte Preise (ohne Anpassungen) für identische Vermögenswerte oder Verbindlichkeiten (erste Ebene, sog. **Level 1**);

(b) andere Eingangswerte als die in die erste Ebene einbezogenen notierten Preise, sofern sie entweder direkt (d.h. Preise) oder indirekt (d.h. aus Preisen abgeleitet) für den jeweiligen Vermögenswert oder die jeweilige Verbindlichkeit beobachtbar sind (zweite Ebene, sog. **Level 2**);

(c) Eingangswerte, die nicht auf beobachtbaren Marktdaten beruhen (dritte Ebene, sog. **Level 3**).

280 Die Bestimmung der Hierarchieebene, in die ein beizulegender Zeitwert fällt, ist in der Praxis mit zahlreichen Zweifelsfragen verbunden. Einige dieser Zweifelsfragen werden vermutlich erst durch das Projekt des IASB zu *Fair Value Measurement*, das voraussichtlich in der Herausgabe eines eigenen Standards für die Ermittlung von beizulegenden Zeitwerten führt, gelöst werden. Dieses Projekt wird die Beispiele und Klarstellungen in U.S. GAAP zu diesem Thema übernehmen. Andere Zweifelsfragen und Praxisprobleme werden auch danach bestehen, z.B. das Problem, die von professionellen Anbietern von

---

191 Siehe Rn 134.

Finanzdaten (wie z.B. Bloomberg, Reuters oder markit) in die Ebenen einzuordnen. Die dafür erforderlichen Hintergrundinformationen, wie die Daten beschafft wurden, sind teilweise nicht einfach zu erhalten.

d) Angaben zu Risiken aus Finanzinstrumenten. Im Hinblick auf Art und Ausmaß von Risiken aus Finanzinstrumenten verlangt IFRS 7 qualitative und quantitative Angaben.[192] Die qualitativen Angaben beziehen sich auf die Art der Risiken und ihre Ursachen, die Ziele, Leitlininen, und Prozesse des Unternehmens im Hinblick auf das Management dieser Risiken sowie die Methoden zur Risikomessung. Außerdem hat ein Unternehmnen Änderungen in diesen Aspekten anzugeben (IFRS 7.33).   281

Die quantitativen Angaben zu Risiken aus Finanzinstrumenten umfassen: 282
- allgemeine Angaben, die die am Bilanzstichtag bestehenden Risiken aus Finanzinstrumenten quantifizieren sowie Risikokonzentrationen aufzeigen;
- Angaben zu Ausfallrisiken;
- Angaben zum Liquiditätsrisiko; und
- Angaben zu Marktrisiken.

Die Angaben zu **Ausfallrisiken** umfassen: 283
- Angaben zum maximalen Ausfallrisiko, wobei diese Angabe nicht für diejenigen Finanzinstrumente erforderlich ist, deren Buchwert in der Bilanz das maximale Ausfallrisiko darstellt;
- eine Beschreibung von Kreditsicherheiten und anderen Verbesserungen der Kreditqualität sowie deren finanzieller Auswirkung auf das maximale Ausfallrisiko;
- für finanzielle Vermögenswerte, die weder in Verzug noch wertgemindert sind, Informationen zur Kreditqualität;
- für finanzielle Vermögenswerte, die entweder in Verzug oder wertgemindert sind, Analysen zum Alter von in Verzug befindlichen aber nicht wertgeminderten finanziellen Vermögenswerten sowie Analysen bzgl. einzeln als wertgemindert identifizierter finanzieller Vermögenswerte (einschließlich der dabei verwendeten Kriterien);
- Angaben zu finanziellen und nicht-finanziellen Vermögenswerten, die das Unternehmen als Folge der Vollstreckung von Kreditsicherheiten erhalten hat und die zum Bilanzstichtag in der Bilanz angesetzt sind.

Die Angaben zum **Liquiditätsrisiko** umfassen: 284
- eine Analyse der Fälligkeiten von nicht-derivativen finanziellen Verbindlichkeiten (einschließlich vom Unternehmen begebener finanzieller Garantien[193]) auf der Basis der vertraglichen Restlaufzeiten;
- eine Analyse der Fälligkeiten auf Basis der vertraglichen Restlaufzeiten für diejenigen derivativen finanziellen Verbindlichkeiten, für die vertragliche Laufzeiten wesentlich für ein Verständnis des Zeitpunkts ihrer Cashflows ist; und
- eine Beschreibung, wie das Unternehmen das Liquiditätrisiko im Hinblick auf diese finanziellen Verbindlichkeiten steuert.

IFRS 7 enthält zahlreiche Ausführungen, wie die Angaben zum Liquiditätsrisiko genau zu machen sind. So ist z.B. für die Angaben zum Liquiditätsrisiko ein eingebettetes Derivat nicht vom Basisvertrag abzuspalten, sondern das hybride Finanzinstrument als nicht-derivative finanzielle Verbindlichkeit zu behandeln (IFRS 7.B11A). Für derivative finanzielle Verbindlichkeiten wird näher erläutert, wann die Darstellung der vertraglichen Restlaufzeiten erforderlich ist. Bei Derivaten, die zu Sicherungszwecken verwendet werden, ist eine Angabe erforderlich, ebenso wie für alle Kreditzusagen (IFRS 7.B11B). Dabei   285

---

192 Die Angabepflichten wurden durch die „Annual Improvements" im Mai 2010 geändert. Die folgenden Ausführungen beziehen diese Änderungen bereits ein.
193 Siehe Rn 109.

kommt es nicht darauf an, ob die Voraussetzung für die Bilanzierung als Sicherungsgeschäft erfüllt werden. Die Auswirkung auf das Liquiditätsrisiko ergibt sich vielmehr aus der Tatsache, dass solche Derivate entsprechend dem Sicherungszweck gehalten werden, um über ihre Laufzeit die vertraglichen Cashflows zu vereinnahmen oder auszutauschen. Von der Angabepflicht der vertraglichen Restlaufzeit sind daher nur diejenigen derivativen Verbindlichkeiten ausgenommen, mit denen das Unternehmen handelt, d.h. die einem häufigen Umschlag unterliegen und daher vorwiegend zu Cashflows aus Veräußerung, Transfer oder Glattstellung statt Durchführung des Vertrags über seine Restlaufzeit führen.

286   Für die Beurteilung der Restlaufzeit ist bei Finanzinstrumenten, die der Gegenpartei ein Wahlrecht bzgl. des Zeitpunkts von Zahlungen einräumen, auf den frühesten Zeitpunkt abzustellen, zu dem eine Zahlung verlangt werden kann (z.B. bei amerikanischen[194] Optionen). Bei finanziellen Garantien ist der maßgebliche Zeitpunkt entsprechend der früheste Zeitpunkt, zu dem die Garantie in Anspruch genommen werden kann (IFRS 7.B11C).

287   Bei der Ermittlung der Beträge für die Cashflows ist zu beachten, dass die Angaben zum Liquiditätsrisiko gem. IFRS 7 auf der Basis von undiskontierten vertraglichen Cashflows zu machen sind. Daher sind z.B. für eine Darlehensverbindlichkeit alle periodischen Zinszahlungen in das jeweils einschlägige Zeitband einzubeziehen. Dies gilt entsprechend auch für die Rückzahlung des Kapitalbetrags, wenn diese gestaffelt erfolgt. Bei variablen Zinsen ist der Referenzzins zum Bilanzstichtag für die restliche Laufzeit zu Grunde zu legen (IFRS 7.B11D).

288   Obwohl die Analyse der Fälligkeiten grundsätzlich nur finanzielle Verbindlichkeiten betrifft, kann auch eine Fälligkeitsanalyse für bestimmte finanzielle Vermögenswerte erforderlich sein. Dies ist der Fall, wenn ein Unternehmen finanzielle Vermögenswerte zum Liquiditätsmanagement hält und Informationen über diese Vermögenswerte erforderlich ist, damit Abschlussadressaten Art und Umfang des Liquiditätsrisikos beurteilen können (IFRS 7.B11E).

289   Die Angaben zu **Marktrisiken** gehören zu den schwierigsten Angaben in IFRS 7. Marktrisiken umfassen (IFRS 7, Appendix A):
- Zinsänderungsrisiko;
- Währungsrisiko;
- andere Preisrisiken (z.B. im Hinblick auf Änderungen bei Rohstoffpreisen oder Aktienkursen).

290   Die erforderlichen Angaben umfassen (IFRS 7.40):
- eine Sensitivitätsanalyse für jedes Marktrisiko, das am Bilanzstichtag besteht;
- die dabei verwendeten Methoden und Annahmen;
- Änderungen bei den Methoden und Annahmen einschließlich einer Begründung.

Die **Sensitivitätsanalyse** hat die Auswirkung von Änderungen des jeweiligen Risikoparameters auf Gewinn oder Verlust sowie das Eigenkapital darzustellen. Dabei ist zu beachten, dass eine disaggregierte Darstellung erforderlich sein kann, wenn andernfalls zu unterschiedliche Unternehmensbereiche zusammengefasst würden (z.B. wenn ein Unternehmen geografische Beriche mit sehr hoher Inflation und niedriger Inflation hat, oder einen Geschäftsbereich, der mit Finanzinstrumenten handelt) (IFRS 7.B17).

291   Die Sensitivitätsanalyse gem. IFRS 7 ist jedoch keine „pro-forma" Ergebnisrechnung, d.h. ein Unternehmen gibt nicht an, wie der Gewinn oder Verlust des Geschäftsjahres ausgefallen wäre, wenn z.B. ein anderes Zinsniveau oder andere Wechselkurse bestanden hätten. Stattdessen wird die Auswirkung von Änderungen des jeweiligen Risikoparameters auf Basis der Risikopositionen am Abschlussstichtag ermittelt (IFRS 7.B18(a)). Allerdings wirkt sich die Kategorisierung von Finanzinstrumenten auf die Sensitivitätsanalyse aus. So sind die Preisschwankungen von als zur Veräußerung verfügbar kategorisierten finanziellen Vermögenswerten nur im Fall einer Wertminderung relevant für den Gewinn oder

---

194 Amerikanische Optionen sind jederzeit während ihrer Laufzeit ausübbar.

Verlust der Periode während sich alle Wertschwankungen mindestens über das sonstige Ergebnis auf das Eigenkapital auswirken (IFRS 7.B27). In der Praxis wird die Auswirkung auf Gewinn oder Verlust sowie das Eigenkapital häufig auf der Basis vor Ertragsteuern gemacht. Dies liegt daran, dass die Folgewirkungen der Marktrisikoänderungen auf die Ertragsteuern oft nicht verlässlich ermittelt werden können (z.B. bei bestehenden Verlustvorträgen, Ergebnisabführungsverträgen, unterschiedlichen Steuersätzen für verschiedene Arten von Gewinnen und Verlusten, etc.) Ungeachtet des Wortlauts in IFRS 7 ist daher eine Angabe auf der Basis vor Ertragsteuern nicht zu beanstanden. Dies ergibt sich auch daraus, dass IFRS 7 keine „pro-forma" Ergebnisrechnung verlangt (die in vielen Fällen aber zur Bestimmung des Effekts nach Ertragsteuern erforderlich wäre).

Der Prognosehorizont für die Sensitivitätsanalyse beträgt regelmäßig ein Jahr (IFRS 7.B19(b)). Daher hat ein Unternehmen diejenigen Änderungen des jeweiligen Risikoparameters zu berücksichtigen, die innerhalb eines Jahres für möglich gehalten werden (reasonably possible). Dies ist demnach kein Stresstest oder „Worst Case" Szenario (IFRS 7.B19(a)). Bei variabel verzinslichen Instrumenten ist z.B. der Effekt der Änderung des Referenzzinssatzes über ein Jahr auf den Zinsaufwand oder -ertrag eines Jahres anzugeben. Die Sensitivitätsanalyse kann auf Basis einer Bandbreite erfolgen, ohne den Effekt von Änderungen des jeweiligen Risikoparameters innerhalb der Bandbreite gesondert darzustellen (IFRS 7.B18(b)). Hält ein Unternehmen z.B. eine Zinsänderung des Leitzinses von plus oder minus 70 Basispunkten für möglich, so kann es die Auswirkung eines Zinsanstiegs und einer Zinssenkung um 70 Basispunkte auf den Gewinn oder Verlust sowie das Eigenkapital angeben. Allerdings ist zu beachten, dass die Angabe nicht irreführend sein darf. Wenn ein Unternehmen z.B. Finanzinstrumente hat, die zu asymmetrischen Auswirkungen führen (z.B. ein Zinscap), so ist ein Hinweis auf diesen asymmetrischen Effekt in die Angabe aufzunehmen.

292

IFRS 7 erlaubt einem Unternehmen eine **alternative Sensitivitätsanalyse** statt der zuvor genannten darzustellen (IFRS 7.41). Voraussetzung dafür ist, dass diese alternative Sensitivitätsanalyse:
- die wechselseitigen Abhängigkeiten zwischen Risikovariablen widerspiegelt und
- vom Unternehmen zur Steuerung der finanziellen Risiken verwendet wird.

293

Daher kann diese alternative Sensitivitätsanalyse (z.B. auf einer Value-at-Risk-Basis) nicht allein für Angabezwecke gem. IFRS 7 erstellt werden, um die in IFRS 7 als Standardangabe (IFRS 7.40) beschriebene Sensitivitätsanalyse zu vermeiden. Wenn ein Unternehmen eine alternative Sensitivitätsanalyse zur Angabe gem. IFRS 7 verwendet, sind zusätzliche Angaben erforderlich, wie das Unternehmen diese Sensitivitätsanalyse erstellt hat, welche wesentlichen Annahmen ihr zu Grunde liegen, welche Ziele mit ihr verfolgt werden und Erläuterungen falls die verwendete Methode nicht vollständig die beizulegenden Zeitwerte der Finanzinstrumente widerspiegelt (IFRS 7.41).

Für den Fall, dass die vom Unternehmen dargestellte Sensitivitätsanalyse nicht repräsentativ für das mit einem Finanzinstrument verbundene Risiko ist, hat das Unternehmen auf diese Tatsache hinzuweisen und zu begründen, warum es zu dieser Einschätzung gelangt ist. Diese Situation kann sich z.B. ergeben, wenn die der Risikopositionen am Abschlussstichtag untypisch für die unterjährigen Risikopositionen sind (IFRS 7.42). In diesen Fällen hat ein Unternehmen zusätzliche Angaben zu machen, die repräsentativ sind (IFRS 7.35 und BC48). Dies kann z.B. auf Basis der durchschnittlichen, maximalen und minimalen Risikoposition während des Geschäftsjahrs erfolgen (IFRS 7.IG20).

294

The manufacturer's authorised representative in the EU is Springer
Nature Customer Service Centre GmbH, Europaplatz 3, 69115 Heidelberg,
Germany. If you have any concerns regarding our products, please
contact ProductSafety@springernature.com

Printed and bound by CPI Group (UK) Ltd, Croydon, CR0 4YY

28/04/2026

02098485-0011